PSYCHOLOGY

Traditions and Perspectives

Daniel N. Robinson

Georgetown University

D. VAN NOSTRAND COMPANY
New York • Cincinnati • Toronto • London • Melbourne

D. Van Nostrand Company Regional Offices:
New York   Cincinnati   Millbrae

D. Van Nostrand Company International Offices:
London   Toronto   Melbourne

Published by D. Van Nostrand Company
450 West 33rd Street, New York, N.Y. 10001

10 9 8 7 6 5 4 3 2 1

To Francine

Nemo assecutus est tantam laudam in vita quantum honestas me per amorem et benevolentiam.

Preface

It is encouraging to find increased sympathy for more traditional approaches to introductory psychology. Every sign indicates that the "ritual of relevance," which animated so much of undergraduate instruction over the past decade, is steadily being replaced by topics and texts reflecting a renewed seriousness about academic and scientific matters.

For reasons that require little elaboration, psychology was particularly affected during the long season of doubt and indecision. Standard encyclopedic works were quickly expanded to include "instant issues," apparently to prove to the fledgling student that, indeed, psychology has something to say about these, also. So-called personal perspective texts began to multiply although candor warrants the observation that very little by way of expanded perception resulted. More typically, these works merely conveyed the growing reservations some scholars had about the work they and their colleagues had been doing.

Psychology: Traditions and Perspec-

tives is a significant revision of my earlier text, *Psychology: A Study of its Origins and Principles,* written in part to offset these trends and also out of an abiding desire to improve the quality of instruction in the first course in psychology. The present work has been written in such a way as to preserve the strengths of the earlier work while overcoming its deficiencies.

William James was not the first to observe that *any* subject takes on humanistic value by being presented in an historical context. Subjects deserving of our greatest interest are those that have excited, vexed, moved, and inspired our ancestors. What is entirely "new" is not, *ipso facto,* interesting and what is "old" is not, *ipso facto,* dated. For too long, students in the first course in psychology have been led to believe that the discipline burst forth from the brow of some nineteenth-century Zeus and is now on the threshold of answering questions which were perceived only darkly until *we* came along. In my own experience, I have seen the effect of such tuition and have been distressed. The able and broadly educated student, confronting such a perspective, simply decides that the discipline is not to be taken seriously. The more sheltered student develops a quick enthusiasm, an intense loyalty, only to be depressed when he learns—if he is fortunate enough to learn—that he has been "taken in" by rhetoric posing as science.

Of course, one of the chief causes of instruction of this sort is the manner in which, until quite recently, the introductory course has been perceived and conceived. That is, until recently, the tendency has been to structure the course as a "survey" of the fullest range of *everything* psychologists happen to do. Once we decide to offer such a course, we naturally look to those enormous handbooks assembled for use in general psychology. And is it not in the very nature of a handbook that even the most complex matters are rendered in black and white?

For years, I have watched freshmen trundling off to "Psych-1" with five or ten pounds of text and have known only too well how many ounces they would ever learn. I have made a habit of stopping them, late in the term, and asking them questions like the following:

"What is the most important lesson
you learned from that book?"

"How do your course and your text
relate to the balance of your studies?"

"What issues give psychology its distinctive character?"

"What would you say are the most significant problems faced by modern psychology?"

"What is the basis of psychology's concern for such problems?"

When we step back some distance from the diligent if frantic activity characterizing psychology, we find the persistence of a set of issues which have animated thought for 10,000 years and serious scholarship for 3,000. In the broadest terms, the issues relate to *knowledge* and to *conduct;* the former establishing the foundations of *epistemology* and the latter of *ethics.* These issues are not going to go away, which is another way of saying that psychology has not "settled" them. Epistemology will endure as long as it continues to make sense to ask, following Lord Bertrand Russell, whether there is anything which can be known so well that no reasonable man could doubt it. And ethics will be with us as long as aggregations of human beings aspire to achieve society.

No single discipline, let alone a single course, is able to embrace these two issues. No single discipline has established its claim to being able to address the issues in a way that surpasses all other approaches. Still, psychology has forged both a method and a perspective for dealing with these issues in a way not duplicated by older and even more developed disciplines. This is what makes the subject worth studying; this is what makes it worth knowing.

If this much is granted, it is then clear what William James had in mind when he insisted that a subject becomes "humanistic" by framing itself in history. And it is still clearer how a *textbook* must differ from a *handbook.* Where the latter lists issues, the former examines them; where the latter lists criticisms, the former must develop them; where the latter is matter-of-fact, the former is a matter of judgment.

The present textbook examines the issues of knowledge and conduct within the context of modern psychology. The traditional topics of perception, learning and memory, psychobiology, language, personality, heredity, human development, and so on, are examined in light of these historic issues so that the student might learn how *psychology* approaches the matter. Psychologists, after all, *have said* important things about moral development, about our knowledge of the external world, about the material basis of thought, about cognitive structures, about "situationism" and ethical perception. And psychologists have shown that, within limits, experimental modes of inquiry can deepen and enrich our understanding of issues that literature and philosophy and natural science have been concerned with for so many centuries. The orientation of this text is *historical*, then, not in the sense of dating the march of the mind but in the sense of recognizing the historical nature and significance of the basic issues in psychology. And the text is critical not in the sense of a rebuke but in the sense of establishing precisely why these are issues and why psychology has not settled them.

Except in the narrowest professional regard, a subject is known when the student can articulate its issues and methods, when the student can trace its evolution, and when the student discerns its assets and liabilities. The present text attempts to present the discipline in such a way as to allow the student to *know* psychology in these terms.

Daniel N. Robinson

Contents

Chapter 6 *Adaptation by Learning and Memory* 160

Chapter 7 *Language* 242

Part III The Psychology of the Individual 263

The Foundations of Psychology

CHAPTER

1

Defining Psychology

WHAT IS SCIENCE?

A student entering the first course in an academic discipline generally arrives with a set of expectations and goals. The student later judges the course in terms of whether or not these expectations were satisfied and whether or not the goals were reached. However, a course can still succeed even if it fails in these two respects. This can be achieved by transforming the student's initial expectations and goals, by demonstrating that they were unrealistic, and by substituting others that are more capable of being accomplished.

All academic subjects are faced with this challenge, but the problems confronted by the discipline of psychology are especially difficult. Unlike many courses offered at colleges or universities, psychology usually has not been studied at the high school level. Also, unlike mathematics and the physical sciences, psychology has not been an integral part of university study for 500 years. Accordingly, it lacks the precise and widely accepted boundaries within which those subjects are explored. Thus, when a student learns that physics is the science of radiation and matter, there is no reason for surprise or doubt or disappointment: no one ever suggested that physics was anything else. The same is true of courses with such titles as, "Twentieth-Century American Fiction," or "European History since 1848," or "International Monetary Systems." It is clear what these courses cover, and a student's expectations are therefore more defined. However, the title "Introduction to Psychology" is not as informative. The student knows that psychologists show a strange fascination for rats and pigeons; that psychologists find odd meanings in the statements and conduct of ordinary people; that they spend a large part of their time testing people; that, in a manner of speaking, they peer through a variety of keyholes. The student also knows that psychologists help to form and are part of a major section of social commentators who *have shown* many things. For example, they "have shown" through observation and study that affluent people tend to be politically conservative; that monkeys reared without mothers are sexually maladjusted; that most people are far more obedient to authority than they would claim to be; that people respond more quickly to a bright light than to a dim one; that children try to imitate adult "models."

Perhaps one of the strongest motives a student may have for studying psychology is to discover what all these observations have in common. Just what *is* psychology? What does it mean to "have shown"? What sort of explanations does psychology offer as it directs its methods and hypotheses at life? And behind the student's scholarly curiosity, we often find a deeply personal motive: "Can psychology help me understand myself better?" "Can psychology help me relate to other people in a more rewarding way?" "Can it make me a better citizen of the world?"

Is Psychology a Science?

When the contemporary student inquires into a definition of psychology—and asks whether psychology can answer the above questions—the inquiry will probably produce replies such as: "Psychology is the science of human behavior," or "Psychology is the study of the mind," or "Psychology is the study of human interactions." Of course, only the most naïve student would settle for definitions of this sort. However, a subject does not become a science merely by proclaiming it is one. What does it mean to say that *X is science* or *Y is not science?* First, what is meant by "psychology is the science of human behavior?" Does this mean it includes everything from writing a novel to wiggling one's big toe? Is thinking

---

Shakespeare's searching analyses of the mind and human motivation are very well known. There are no "covering laws" in his lines, no pretense of a scientific explanation. But there is an enlarged intuition, refined by observation. In act 2, scene 1 of *Macbeth*, the villainous hero, in anticipation of the murder he must soon commit, has a vision of a dagger:

> "Art thou not, fatal vision, sensible
> To feeling as to sight? or art thou but
> A dagger of the mind, a false creation,
> Proceedings from the heat-oppressed brain?"

In this scene, there is an awareness of how reflection makes us hesitate, how too much examination blocks our purpose:

> "Whiles I threat, he lives;
> Words to the heat of deeds too cold breath gives."

And in the next scene, Lady Macbeth, consoling her husband while ridiculing his fear of the corpse of the King he has murdered, tells him:

> ". . . the sleeping and the dead
> Are but as pictures; 'tis the eye of childhood
> That fears a painted devil."

Shakespeare and many other literary giants comprehend human nature in a way that rings true to those who have experienced life fully. Academic or scientific psychology is not to be interpreted as an improvement on these literary insights, but as a subject providing insights and understandings of a unique sort.

considered "behavior?" Are hoping and wanting and worrying all "behavior?" Considering the second definition above, one might ask, what academic discipline is *not* concerned with the study of the human mind? Surely the study of either history, literature, scientific theory, or mathematical principles is ultimately a study of the human mind. The third definition is no better. If psychology is the study of human interaction, how is it different from what Shakespeare and Tolstoi were setting forth, or even the major philosophers of the past 3,000 years?

Suppose we agreed that psychology is the science of behavior, just for the purpose of arriving at some conclusion. Suppose we further agreed that by behavior we mean only those actions of animals that are readily observable by mere visual inspection. That is, suppose we agreed not to quibble about behavior. We would still have to decide what is meant by science. The easiest way around this issue would simply be to declare that science is whatever scientists happen to be doing. However, this definition will not work because it is obvious that we have no way of knowing who the scientists are until we have determined what *science* is.

Two Definitions of Science

There is no one definition of science that will satisfy everyone. Philosophers of science have struggled for centuries to create acceptable and useful criteria for a definition, but there is still no universal agreement. In very broad terms, there are two different sets of criteria. One set appeals to what we might call "common sense" notions of science; the other takes on a rigorously logical character. Science, according to the common sense account, involves a catalog of publicly observed events arranged in a way that allows one to make accurate and reliable predictions. The arrangement is achieved through certain generalizations called *empirical laws*. These laws are no more than statistical summaries of what has happened in the past. In other words, these laws state that when Y has always followed X on every occasion during which X has been observed, we can expect that Y will appear when X occurs in the future.

Many consider this definition of science to be too general. Consider the following example. During each of the last ten summers, the manager of a large department store has observed that his store sells more bathing suits as the temperature and humidity rise. The empirical generalization resulting from these observations is: *The purchase of bathing suits is caused by the weather.* There is nothing wrong with this statement. It is reasonable in all respects. Yet, do we want to call the manager a scientist? Do we want to say that he has made a scientific contribution?

In order to avoid the looseness of this common sense definition, certain philosophers—particularly Carl Hempel, a twentieth-century philosopher who has explored the nature of theoretical science—have insisted on criteria of a more formal nature. These philosophers have argued that we cannot understand science in terms of the methods it employs or in terms of the subjects it investigates. Instead, we must understand it in terms of the logical form of the *explanations* it offers. That is, what sets science apart from other kinds of activity and inquiry is the type of explanation it provides. To summarize, an explanation is *scientific* when: (1) it refers to empirical—that is, publicly observable—events; (2) it is based upon a universal, or "covering," law; (3) the event to be explained can be deduced logically from the covering law; and (4) the covering law is true. We can make use of an example from the study of physics. We set a match to a piece of paper and observe that the paper turns to ashes. We wonder whether we have destroyed matter, but our friends in physics quickly assure us that we have not. When we ask for an explanation, a physicist will tell us that *matter is conserved,* a covering law. All we have done is to create a chemical reaction that redistributed the matter into another form and caused some energy to escape in the form of heat. It is important to understand that the scientific law, in this case the law pertaining to the conservation of matter, is *stipulated.* It is not merely a generalization based upon limited observation within a limited context. Rather, it is a *premise,* stipulated to cover all exchanges of energy and all transformations of matter. If it is a true premise, true conclusions will follow from it logically.

Note the marked difference between the common sense approach and this logical definition of science. On the common sense account, we somehow explain what happens to the paper by saying that on all previous occasions when paper was burned all the original "matter" could be recollected in the form of heat and ashes. Therefore, it is a "law" that you never end up with more or less than what you had when you started. On the other hand, on the formal account, there is a universal proposition regarding *all* matter, of which paper is but one instance. According to this proposition, matter does not just happen to be conserved; it *must* be conserved. That is, if the covering law is correct, then the outcome becomes logically necessary, not just empirically reliable.

If we adopt the formal criteria, then, it follows that *psychology is not a science*. It does not encompass covering laws that are known to be correct in all instances. Therefore, it cannot provide explanations that have the logical character of the scientific explanations already discussed. If the loose criteria are adopted, however, psychology *is* a science, because it possesses reliable findings that can be summarized in the form of empirical generalizations. However, if we apply these criteria, psychology is difficult to distinguish from many other studies that also provide us with empirical generalizations—the department store manager and his "law of the bathing suit" provides one example.

It is worth exploring the question of explanation further, because psychology is expected to give explanations, whether we call it a science or not. As will be discussed throughout, psychology offers many kinds of explanations, some very far from the formal requirements of science. As one basis for comparison, we will use Sir Isaac Newton's explanation of why the moon remains in orbit, an instance of scientific explanation. We will then look at some common forms of explanation that are quite different from Newton's.

METHODS OF "KNOWING"—DEMONSTRATION, LOGICAL NECESSITY, AND BELIEF

Did Newton explain why the moon remains in orbit? In everyday conversation an explanation is an answer to the question, "Why?" When we ask, "Why is the sky blue?" we are seeking an explanation, a statement of those factors that *cause* the sky to be blue. But the question, which seems so simple, actually calls for an elaborate explanation. Indeed, a *complete* explanation may be impossible.

Demonstration

One would begin by saying that the color of the sky comes from the sun's radiation as it enters the earth's atmosphere. This radiation consists of many different wavelengths of light. (Light waves travel through space in the same way that waves travel through water. The distance from the peak of one wave to the peak of the next is termed the *wavelength*.) Each wavelength is affected differently by the layers of atmosphere that surround the earth. Some wavelengths will pass through the layers with relative ease, while others will be absorbed by the atmosphere before reaching the earth. Still others will be reflected back into space. Using measuring instruments, it is possible to determine how much of each wavelength reaches the earth. It seems that we could now answer the question adequately: The sky is "blue" because most of the light that reaches the earth is of a wavelength that we perceive as "blue." But remember the question itself: "Why is the sky blue?" The key word is *blue*. Blue is not a *physical* property of light itself, but a *perceptual* one. To explain, it is essential to inquire into the factors that govern human perception. As we will see in Chapter 5, studying perception is far more complicated than measuring the sun's radiation. It seems that complete explanations of even the most trivial matters are very hard to reach. We may find that a complete explanation cannot be assembled. The reader might pause to wrestle with seemingly simple questions such as, "Why did Jack die?" or "Was he just?"

Logical Necessity

There is another type of question that leads to a very different form of explanation. For example, "Why are there 360 degrees in a square?" or "Why are 3 plus 5 equal to 8?" The answers we give to questions of this sort are distinct from those we use to answer, "Why did Jack die?" For example, a square is defined as a four-sided figure equal on all sides, which contains four right angles. In other words, a square contains 360 degrees *by definition*. That is, the answer is *logically necessary* as long as we honor the definition of the term. If the explanation were not logically necessary, there could be no square.

The preceding examples of the blue sky and the square differ in that the first deals with matters of *fact*, whereas the second is concerned with rules of *argument*. The explanations that we seek to account for facts are rooted in what is called *scientific demonstration*, whereas those we seek in argument are based upon *deductive logic*. The difference is that demonstration allows us to draw plausible inferences from the facts, whereas deduction presents *proofs*.

Belief

There is yet a third class of explanations, which we may label *belief*. It goes under other names as well—intuition, conviction, or opinion. Beliefs may be called "superstitious" when they appear to have no basis in fact or in logic; for example, the belief that something terrible will occur after a black cat has crossed one's path. We consider certain other beliefs to be warranted by facts, such as the belief that all that lives will one day die. Still other beliefs fall into a gray region: They are not *necessary* in the logical sense, and they do not have enough evidence supporting them to make them highly plausible. An example of this is the belief that all natural events will be explained sooner or later by the methods of science. Scientific research, in fact, has uncovered many of the causal connections between events in nature. However, it is not true out of logical necessity that (a) research will uncover all of the links, (b) the total number of relationships is limited, or *finite*, (c) human life will last long enough to complete the task, or (d) the causal connections that exist now, which may justify one kind of explanation, will continue to operate in the same way in the future.

In any attempt to know something, there is a constant interplay among the three ways of knowing—scientific demonstration, logical argument, and belief. If Newton set out to explain why the moon did not fall to earth, he first must have *believed* that an explanation was possible. He also had to be *logically consistent* in his use of terms and in his phrasing of the final explanation. Finally, he had to assemble an explanation that would allow him to demonstrate the effects of whatever factors he held responsible for that event. What then, distinguishes Newton's procedures from ordinary common sense? That is, what are the identifying characteristics of science? We have already noted one of them: Scientific explanations must be based upon true laws. Now, let us examine several other characteristics.

FACTS AND RULES OF EVIDENCE

Newton's contribution revolutionized scientific thought. His thinking and all of science are set off from common sense through certain **rules of evidence**. Scientists all agree that some things count as *facts* while others do not and that certain generalizations are warranted while others are not.

The basic facts of science come from the material world. The basic rule of evidence states that something cannot be accepted as a fact unless it is drawn from the world that is publicly perceived.

Consistency

In addition, scientific accounts, unlike common sense, have to be *consistent* with everything else that is known in the particular field of inquiry. For example, suppose Newton had argued that the moon does not fall because the winds of the earth blow it away from the earth's surface. Then his explanation would have required the rejection of something that every scientist had observed to be a fact—that apples and other objects do fall to the earth; they are not blown away from the earth by wind.

DEMONSTRATION, ARGUMENT, AND BELIEF

One of the most influential figures in the history of psychology is Ivan Pavlov, a Russian physiologist. He provided the first scientific theory of *conditioned reflexes*, which explains how an animal learns to respond to a stimulus, such as a ringing bell, that ordinarily would not evoke a response. Pavlov was a product of the nineteenth century, when the scientific community was struggling to rid itself of "metaphysical" and philosophical methods and language. Scientists were in general agreement that all of nature could be understood in physical terms and that man, too, would finally be explained by physical principles. Pavlov shared this vision, which was, in fact, no more than a *belief*. That is, no one had proved—either through the force of logic or the facts of observation—that man could be reduced to a set of physical principles.

In Pavlov's time, one of the most secure psychological principles was that of *associationism*, (see Chapter 2 for further discussion) which stated that all learning and memory resulted from repeated experiences. Many philosophers had speculated on the biological basis of "associations," but Pavlov was the first to test these reflections experimentally. His studies of the *conditioned reflex* showed, in a scientifically meaningful way, that the older philosophical arguments were valid. In terms of the *logical* feature of Pavlov's effort, note that *if* the brain forms associative bonds between events that occur together often, *then* conditioning should work. In other words, it follows logically that conditioning will succeed if the principle of association is valid.

Here, then, is an illustration of the interplay among demonstration, argument (logic), and belief. If Pavlov had only demonstrated experimentally that conditioning occurs, he would have been left with an isolated fact having no implication beyond that fact. And, with the belief alone, Pavlov could have asserted no more than an opinion. By forcing his experiments to proceed along the logical lines required by the older theory of "associations," Pavlov was able to organize his findings and interpret them in a way that went far beyond the mere fact of conditioning. In fact, in his lecture upon receiving the Nobel Prize, he was quick to point out that people had known for many centuries that the odor of food could make a hungry man salivate! That is, since prehistoric times, human beings must have been aware of the *fact* of *conditioned associations*. However, not until this fact was incorporated into the larger realm of philosophical materialism (that is, a *belief*) and presented as the (logical) outcome of a formal theory, did the fact become scientifically useful.

Therefore, Newton's explanation would have been dismissed. As we can see, a scientific explanation must never require one to reject a fact, but only to reject an alternative and somehow inferior explanation. A scientific statement must account for all elements of the class of phenomena that it claims to explain. The Law of Universal Gravitation, as Newton stated it, *is* consistent with what we know about all events in which bodies or particles of matter are attracted or repelled.

Accuracy

In putting forth a scientific explanation, Newton also had to be *accurate*. A theory that predicted the distance between earth and moon only to the nearest 50,000 miles would not have been taken seriously. The *accuracy* of a scientific explanation is determined by measurement and controlled observation (see Chapter 3). Unlike the explanations that come from common sense, a scientific explanation is required to make predictions that can be tested quantitatively, that is, in numerical terms.

Generality

Finally, Newton's explanation had to have a *general* application; one that could account, not only for the moon's staying aloft, but for other heavenly bodies as well. In short, his law had to "cover" all that exists in the heavens.

The *generality* of a scientific statement carries it beyond the particular conditions that inspired its authorship. The statement thereby leads to new knowledge. In this sense, scientific explanations not only transmit what is known but create additional knowledge as well.

Common Sense

Common sense is not, by definition, *wrong*, nor is it necessarily improved by the application of scientific methods. Great insights have emerged from literature, the arts, and philosophy. In many instances, the validity of such insights cannot be tested. Their acceptance must be based upon an appeal to intuition, emotion, or some combination of the two. Political philosophers throughout the ages have advanced different views of the "good life," of the functions of the state, and of the responsibilities of the individual. However, we cannot test their opinions in the laboratory. In such cases, we can only refer to accurate historical accounts of the consequences of adhering to such opinions. But history is not a perfect teacher. People and their cultures change. What was effective in classical times may well be disastrous when applied to altered circumstances. In this respect, history and science are similar. Both fields of study must forecast what the consequences of events will be under conditions that differ from the conditions under which the events originally occurred. The predictive powers of the two disciplines depend upon the existence of similarities between the observed and the yet to be observed conditions. In any scholarly pursuit, a point is reached where common sense—some notion of what is "reasonable"—is the only means of understanding, or certainly the best. However, science differs from other pursuits not only at the point when common sense is invoked, but also in terms of the confidence one has when invoking it. In science, that which *seems reasonable* is itself the topic of inquiry. In the larger society, that which seems reasonable usually becomes a justification for action. If the action proves successful, that which seemed reasonable at once becomes a higher truth.

In summary, while there are no absolutes in separating science from common sense, the scientific attitude does tend to be more skeptical, more resistant to simplistic explanations, more reluctant to accept untested assumptions, and more critical of its own conclusions. In contrast, the judgments and conclusions made through common sense contain a generous amount of finality and assurance. (Nonetheless, scientists are also people; they too can be quite unscientific when expressing their own opinions.)

THE LIMITATIONS OF SCIENCE AND COMMON SENSE

In the sixteenth century, Nicolaus Copernicus affirmed that the earth revolves around the sun. Before Copernicus, astronomers accounted for the astronomical events they observed by using a model of the universe set forth by Ptolemy of Alexandria in the second century A.D.

They simply assumed that the earth was a sphere in the center of a larger sphere to which all the heavenly bodies were attached. As the outer sphere moved, an observer on the fixed, inner sphere—the earth—could witness the heavenly motions. This older view was accepted as truth for thousands of years because it allowed success in practical affairs. It predicted the motion of the planets with acceptable accuracy. It allowed farmers to distinguish the seasons and navigators to find their way home. It challenged no basic religious belief. The view was rooted in careful observation and was tested by the rigorous standards of economic necessity. It incorporated many of the tools of science and satisfied the dictates of common sense. Unfortunately, it was wrong. Had its successes been fewer, the view could have been renounced earlier.

Science has learned an important lesson from the Ptolemaicists. A scientific account must not only be correct (that is, consistent, accurate, and general) in its practical applications, but all alternative ideas must be incorrect or inconsistent. It is no wonder that so very few scientific assertions are currently accepted as truths. Rather, nearly all the basic principles of science are open to relentless probing.

The Psychologist: Investigator and Object of Investigation

There are interesting parallels that can be drawn between psychology and the classical astronomy that we have just discussed. Both are based on observation. The task of the classical astronomers was to offer a reasonable explanation for events that were visible to all. Any theory, therefore, had to appeal to common experience; it had to appear reasonable to many people. The psychologist's task, too, is to offer sensible explanations for events that nearly anyone can witness. Psychology has been concerned with the sum of psychological man—with consciousness, feeling, motivation, perception, and behavior. However, unlike scholars in any other discipline, the scientist in psychology is both the investigator and the object of investigation. He has learned, and he has been motivated to study *learning* and *motivation*. He can be depressed or elated. He perceives and thinks. He pays attention and ignores. His scientific endeavors, sooner or later, must confront his own experiences. If he studies only his personal experiences, he takes certain risks: His observations may be completely subjective, and the generality of his findings may be questionable. He will, therefore, be accused of making statements that are true only of himself. If, on the other hand, he studies the experiences of a larger group, he may be able to offer findings having general validity. However, the generalizations may not agree with any given individual's self-assessment. For example, each time he reports that "90 percent of American males" behave or think in a certain way, the remaining "10 percent" will deny his claim. The more *general* the statements, the more likely it is that, within the framework of common experience, many exceptions will rise to challenge them. The more *specific* the statements, the more likely it is that the court of common experience will find them irrelevant. For example, Freudian psychologists may assume that certain instinctual drives exist in everyone and that these drives make sexual conflicts inevitable. In response to this hypothesis, some people will simply deny that they feel sexual conflicts at all. In contrast, when an experimental psychologist asserts that people react faster to bright lights than to dim ones, he will find few doubters. However, he will also be greeted with, "Who cares?" or "So what?"

Two aspects of common experience thus affect psychological investigation: the subjective experience of the psychologist and the experience of the larger population to which the psychologist addresses himself. The first aspect pervades all of our pursuits. No one can confront a problem or project in his own absence! Rather, the subtle and complex features of each individual participate in his every endeavor. To this extent, all science and all scholarship are subjective. The biologist, after all, *interprets* his data; the engineer *reads* his meters; the physicist decides when a certain hypothesis *seems* to be true. Such subjectivity is inescapable. It is tempered, however, by a demand for *intersubjective agreement*. All engineers must obtain nearly the same meter-reading; the vast majority of biologists must concur on the interpretation of data; most physicists must agree on the validity of certain hypotheses. Such agreement does not eliminate subjectivity, since any human judgment is subjective. Nevertheless, we can make such strict demands for intersubjective agreement that we can establish our knowledge as nearly certain within the inevitable limits of our ability to perceive and to judge. For example, physicists and engineers have developed instruments and procedures that guarantee intersubjective agreement about facts in the physical sciences. Many of these facts are unintelligible to the layman, but scientists agree among themselves. Their record in the pursuit of reliable prediction and control is so impressive that the layman often is content to accept their statements on faith.

At this point, "common experience" of the population at large influences psychology in a unique way. Many of the issues and facts of psychology are accessible to the layman, or, at least, he insists that they are. Psychology thus abounds in expertise. Everyone is a scholar in terms of his own psychological makeup. For psychology to be believed, it must tell people what they already "know" to be "true." Having told them, psychology is then condemned for discovering what everyone knew in the first place! To be sure, many of the basic principles of psychology are restatements of what is commonly perceived about human experience. In the same way, Newton's Law of Universal Gravitation merely told everyone that objects fall. However, physics and psychology attempt to go beyond this common experience and to arrive at a small number of general laws that embrace many isolated facts. That is, they strive to offer *explanations* that are consistent, accurate, and general.

ELUSIVE OBJECTIVITY

Psychologists are fond of recalling the sad fate of one D. Kinnebrook, assistant at the great Greenwich astronomical observatory in the 1790s. The director of the observatory, N. Maskelyne, became distressed because of discrepancies between his measurements of stellar transit-times (a measure of the motion of stars) and those taken by Kinnebrook. In those days, transit-times of stars were determined by an "eye-and-ear" method. The observer would locate the star in a telescope equipped with a grid of small squares across the field of view. The squares were created by mounting thin wires over the telescope's lens. As the observer followed the movement of a star toward one of the squares, he would listen to a beating metronome. He would note the position of the star, listen to the beats, and—just at the moment when the star touched one of the cross-hairs—the observer would begin counting to himself. Aided by the beating clock, the observer would determine, to the nearest fraction of a second, how long it took the star to enter a box completely, counting from the time when it had just touched the side of the box.

All we know about Kinnebrook's measures is that they were, on the average, about one half-second to one-second slower than Maskelyne's measures. It seems that the idea never dawned on the director that *his* estimates may have been off. Instead, he chose to treat his own as "objective" and Kinnebrook's as "wrong." It was only years later that psychologically oriented astronomers recognized the subjective nature of the entire procedure. Once this quality was recognized, astronomers adopted a different method for measuring stellar transits, one that relied on intersubjective agreement. Each member of a group of experienced observers first measured the transit-time of a star. The different measurements were then evaluated *statistically* in order to obtain from them the best possible estimate.

Distinctions Between Popular and Scientific Language

The physical sciences lie concealed from the public beneath the puzzles and complexities of mathematics. Medicine and biology, with their Latinized language and countless bones and joints, numb the layman into quiet acceptance. Though psychology is concerned with very complex processes, it is deceptively open to the layman, because it uses ordinary language to define its problems and to discuss its results. Psychology's use of popular language, coupled with the influence of "common experience," has created a sense among the public at large that they are competent in psychological matters. When people refer to a *forceful* speech or to being plagued by *inertia* or to confronting a problem of some *gravity*, they know they are not using these terms as physicists would use them. They see the distinction between popular and scientific usage. However, when they use words such as *intelligence, personality, learning, motivation,* and *insight,* they often do not realize that psychologists have very special meanings for these terms. The psychologist employs such words to represent *processes.* For example, the word *motivation* is used in the same way a physicist uses the word *force.* The concept of motivation is part of a much larger theoretical system, which involves physiological, behavioral, and social factors that interact continuously and in complex ways. The process of which we may not be aware at a conscious level of experience nevertheless takes part in the psychological life of each human being. An example taken from the study of perception might make this clearer. It is known that for color vision to be possible, chemical pigments in cells within the retina of the eye must be altered by light. Only after this event takes place do the optic nerves carry to the brain information regarding the color of objects. Each time an observer sees a color, many millions of separate, photochemical reactions occur within the receptor cells of the retina. Nevertheless, the observer is entirely unaware of these microscopic events. At the same time, a psychologist interested in the color vision of human beings (which is part of the conscious experience of every normal observer) may study the phenomenon at the level of receptor-photochemistry. In doing so, the psychologist is investigating a complex process essential to color vision, but one completely beyond any individual's capacity for experience.

To explain psychological events, the psychologist refers to processes that are often inaccessible to personal experience. However, he uses the same language that is common to any lay audience. As discussed earlier, a psychologist may speak of the role of *motivation* in human performance. As the reader will discover (see Chapters 4, 6, 10, and 11), this popular noun has produced great difficulties in both theoretical and experimental psychology. When the psychologist uses the word, he sees before him an array of environmental, biological, and conceptual factors that impel or inhibit action. When the layman uses the term, he has in mind some notion of whether or not an individual "feels like" doing something. Thus, in lay terms, the fact that someone is "unmotivated" *is* the explanation. To the psychologist, such a lack of motivation is rather the event to be explained. To make matters more complex, the psychologist himself may lapse into the use of popular meanings when formulating scientific arguments. These obstacles have hampered progress in psychology.

A common language and commonly held views of the causes of natural events existed long before the science of psychology. In one way or another, common sense explanations survived because they worked. They were satisfying and usually simple. They were not easily overturned and generally were part of a larger system of thought shared by many generations. Any new theory had to work better in practice than the older theory, or at least work as well, and it had to explain nature in a more satisfying way.

The Goals of Science and Common Sense

In the *Ethics,* Aristotle distinguishes between the man of action and the man of deliberation:

> . . . a carpenter and a geometer investigate the right angle in different ways; the former does so in so far as the right angle is useful for his work, while the latter inquires what it is or what sort of thing it is; for he is a spectator of the truth. (Bk. 1, Ch. 8)

The aim of science is to discover the principles that underlie natural events. Aristotle defined scientific wisdom as the "capacity for demonstration," in contrast with practical wisdom, which he viewed as the "capacity for action." As a "spectator of the truth," the scientist must never confuse what nature is with what he would like it to be. In view of this requirement, some have considered the scientist's attitude as value-free (that is, unconcerned with the human condition). The evidence to support this judgment includes the terrors of nuclear warfare, the pollution of cities, and the ravages technology has wrought upon nature. But warfare, pollution, and natural spoliation arise from greed, selfishness, ignorance, and, most important of all, from a consensus of opinion. Governments represent the interests of their constituents, few of whom are scientists. Scientific insights always contain the potential for abuse, because they expand our capacity for action. This potential can be denied only at the expense of liberty itself, for liberty springs from choice and choice entails knowledge. Ultimately, the goals of science and common sense meet. But "ultimately" is usually a long way off. On the way, the goals of these two approaches arise from different considerations. Science is impelled by a passion to know; common sense, by a need to act. But common sense can lead to an enhancement of life only when it is informed. In this major respect, the two goals are compatible and interdependent.

DEFINING PSYCHOLOGY

By now, the reader must realize how arbitrary any definition of psychology is bound to be. In the present work, psychology is first restricted to those undertakings that at least conform to one of the models of science presented earlier in this chapter. That is, psychology is presented both as a search for empirical generalizations and as a formal system of explanations addressed to the observable aspects of conduct and experience. Further, the present work treats psychology as a scientific or prescientific study of *individuals*. No attempt is made to summarize the methods and findings of sociology or of social psychology. Of course, the methods of psychology are often the same as those employed by sociologists and social psychologists. In limited contexts, there are even overlapping findings. However, the central problem in social psychology is the problem of interpersonal influence. In sociology, the chief problem is that of explaining the behavior of groups. Neither of these issues was central to psychology at its inception as a distinct discipline, and neither of these problems needs to be solved here in order for individual psychology to set its house in order. Moreover, social psychology has grown so swiftly and in such diverse ways that it is now a separate discipline. The same is true of sociology. In the present text, then, attention will be focused on the individual person or individual animal and on the methods that are used to study how the individual adapts psychologically to the demands of the physical environment. The adaptive processes normally associated with the terms *perception, learning, memory, emotion, motivation, language,* and *personality* will be our central concern. The methods covered here will be principally experimental and only occasionally observational. Of course, to adhere strictly to this principle, we would have to ignore such extraordinary observers (that is, nonexperimentalists) as Darwin and Freud. There is no reason to be restricted by such a rule. Rather, the overriding consideration in presenting the findings and ideas that animate psychology must be twofold. Are these ideas and findings drawn from the domain of scientific inquiry, and are they sufficiently empirical in character to be confirmed and extended experimentally? By and large, facts and opinions that do not satisfy the demands of these two basic questions will not be examined.

SUMMARY

   After this brief examination of some of the factors to be kept in mind in attempting to define psychology, we will proceed in the following chapter with a study of the historical and philosophical foundations of modern psychology. In the first chapter, some essential ideas have been discussed. First, psychology, as a scientific enterprise, must develop theories that cover the sorts of events normally judged to be "psychological." Second, psychology must also provide explanations of a particular kind if it is to be distinguishable from older philosophical and literary attempts to understand human nature. Finally, the necessary *scientific* explanations must incorporate accurate observations and must be rooted in procedures that are public and repeatable.
   In light of these three requirements, we will proceed to review the problems and issues that were inherited by the new experimental discipline of modern psychology. These concerns were based initially in philosophy, where they had remained until well into the nineteenth century.

SUGGESTED READINGS

HEMPEL, C. *Aspects of Scientific Explanation and Other Essays in the Philosophy of Science.* New York: Free Press, 1965.

This edition contains the major statement of Professor Hempel on the issue of scientific explanation.

KEMENY, J. G. *A Philosopher Looks at Science.* New York: D. Van Nostrand Co., 1959.

Professor Kemeny conveys the spirit of scientific discourse, the important relationship between mathematics and science, and an excellent sense of research strategies in this very readable and entertaining treatise. Chapters 14 (*Science and Values*) and 15 (*The Social Sciences*) are especially relevant to Chapters 1 and 3 in this text.

KNICKERBOCKER, W. S., ed. *Classics of Modern Science.* Boston: Beacon Press, 1962.

This well-edited and annotated collection of readings offers selected writings by science's greatest figures from Copernicus to Robert Koch. The distinctions and interdependence between science and common sense are especially well evidenced in Copernicus' Introduction (pp. 20–21) to his *De Orbium Caelestium Revolutionibus.*

CHAPTER

2

The Roots of Modern Psychology

WHY STUDY THE HISTORY OF PSYCHOLOGY?

Roots are necessary to secure a tree firmly, to nourish it, to keep it from drifting aimlessly in response to the first strong breeze. At the same time, the trunk, the branches, and the fruit of that tree may bear no physical resemblance at all to its roots.

So when we discuss the historical and philosophical "roots" of psychology, it is wise to adopt the literal meaning of this term, so as not to mislead the reader. The psychologist today is not committed to the questions that concerned the ancient philosophers. Even scholars of the nineteenth century would be surprised and confused by the endeavors that characterize contemporary psychology. To this extent, the modern fruits and branches of psychology are unlike the ancient roots in all outward appearances. Nonetheless, psychology has remained interested in certain core problems; it has resisted many of the attractions presented by shifting

23

fashions; and it has benefited from both the successes and failures of earlier undertakings. History and philosophy, therefore, may be said to be the roots, or foundations, of modern psychology. To this extent, we cannot fully appreciate the important advances made in the present century nor easily anticipate likely developments unless we have a sense of how current interests and methods are related to older ones.

The present chapter does not pretend to offer a complete account of the development of psychology through the ages. Neither is it suggested that contemporary problems have been mechanically adopted from the past. Psychologists today do not study perception because Aristotle said it was important. Nor do they find it interesting for the same reason that the French mathematician and philosopher René Descartes did. Nor do they employ methods borrowed from the Dutch philosopher, Benedict Spinoza. Thus, if today's psychologist says much the same sort of thing as some historic figure said, it is only because the human mind has not changed very much over the ages and because certain problems are equally as old as human life. Indeed, if there were no enduring features of the human mind and condition, nothing we do today would benefit those who come after us. Moreover, in discovering that two historical ages knew of the same fact, we cannot conclude hastily that this fact had the same meaning to both ages, or that it was understood at the same level, or that the two ages would draw the same conclusions from it.

We look to history, then, not to learn why we are interested in this subject or that, but rather to find out if our knowledge is progressing. We might well be interested even if scholars had never before considered the question. If we know what our ancestors believed, if we know that we are examining the same issues but with very different methods, and finally, if we discover that our position is the same as the older one, then we can consider several conclusions. Perhaps the new methods are not so new after all; perhaps the new methods cannot advance our understanding beyond the point reached using older, simpler ones; or perhaps the issue at hand cannot be settled by technological advances.

In surveying the history of a discipline or, for that matter, of an entire civilization, we must not think negatively of an earlier period as if it were a younger or childish form of our own. The ancient Athenians did not occupy themselves with their ideas because they were ignorant of our wisdom. Though scientific and technical developments tend to be progressive, there is no evidence to suggest that philosophical, aesthetic, or literary ideas grow in such a cumulative way. Socrates is not the infant version of Immanuel Kant (eighteenth-century German philosopher) nor can we judge Albert Einstein as a more mature Isaac Newton. Older theories and ideas draw our attention to things and events that we otherwise might not notice. With more careful and prolonged attention to these problems, each succeeding age discovers discrepancies or contradictions that went undetected before. On the basis of these discoveries, the more current age can fashion different and, often, more effective theories and ideas. Before any such improvement is possible, however, that age must possess fully the most mature and creative human faculties.

The balance of this chapter will survey some of the major propositions that philosophers have advanced in trying to discover the laws of the mind, the determinants of human conduct, and the sources of our feelings. Entire volumes have been devoted to each of the philosophers cited in this chapter; therefore, it would be futile to attempt more than a brief introduction to the more psychological aspects of their contributions. This chapter will be highly successful if it encourages you to look more deeply into the works of these philosophers.

The major objective here is to show the reader that certain issues have persisted throughout man's history of looking into himself. There have been many varied contributions to the task of understanding human nature, but in one sense, all of these efforts can be divided into a small number of categories. The categories used in the present chapter and throughout the rest of the book are the following: *empiricism,* the idea that takes experience as the source of all knowledge; *idealism,* the concept that the ultimate reality lies beyond phenomena and experience; *materialism,* the theory that physical matter is the only reality and that all things and processes can be explained in terms of physical matter; and *nativism,* which holds that man is born with certain knowledge and understanding and that, with the right mental climate or cultivation, a person will be able to express these inborn truths. In later chapters, the reader will note that much of modern psychology fits easily into one or more of these four categories. Of course, the labels themselves do not tell us very much, but they do give us a convenient way of organizing diverse perspectives on human nature.

A SKETCH OF PHILOSOPHICAL PSYCHOLOGY

Thales

Bertrand Russell has remarked:

> In every history of philosophy for students, the first thing mentioned is that philosophy began with Thales, who said that everything is made of water. This is discouraging to the beginner, who is struggling—perhaps not very hard—to feel that respect for philosophy which the curriculum seems to expect. (Russell, p. 24)

Very little is known of the teaching of the Greek philosopher Thales (624-546 B.C.). It is not possible to summarize his philosophy as one can that of Aristotle. M. T. McClure, in his book *The Early Philosophers of Greece*, has divided the wisdom of Thales into *gnomic, practical, scientific,* and *philosophical*—categories which we will meet again throughout this book. *Gnomic* wisdom is what in Chapter 1 was referred to as common sense. Thales expressed a number of statements that illustrate his impressions of the nature of man; for example, "It is hard to be good," and, "Pay your debts and tell the truth." These sayings are similar to the aphorisms of Confucius and other early Oriental thinkers. They are not so much a philosophy as a folk-ethic. By *practical* wisdom, McClure means advice on political and economic matters. Here, Thales moves from impressions to principles and to an appreciation of the existence of laws guiding the processes of government and commerce. Practical wisdom had prospered in Egypt long before the rise of Greece. The Egyptians, for example, had developed geometry, which they used to compute the acreage of land and to solve other problems important to their economy. Thales visited Egypt, studied there, and later introduced geometry to Greece. But his *scientific* wisdom went beyond the practical. Unlike the Egyptians, he saw a value in studying mathematics for its own sake, apart from its everyday uses. Similarly, he studied astronomy (through which he gained fame by predicting an eclipse), not for any practical or commercial advantage, but as a search for knowledge. Finally, in his *philosophical* wisdom, Thales stirred the controversy over the nature of the soul (the psyche), an issue that recurs in all later Greek philosophy.

Pythagoras

One of the most important figures to be influenced by Thales was Pythagoras of Samos (active from 525-500 B.C.), who is famous to high school students for the theorem that relates the sides and the hypotenuse of the right angle triangle. He founded the Order of Pythagoreans for the purpose of moral and religious purification. A class system, with financiers and the military at the top, had led to great affluence for some on the island of Samos and a life of degradation for others. As a result, commitment to spiritual and moral values was weakened. The Pythagoreans launched a crusade against vice and lawlessness. Within their group excess of any kind was taboo. They imposed long periods of silence on themselves in order to prepare for a life of contemplation, through which the soul could be purified. Mathematics was also chosen as a purifying exercise. It soon began to dominate the activities of the Order. Pythagoras himself became a numerologist, one who believes that nature's secrets are contained in numbers and in the relationships among them. To Pythagoras, the right angle theorem that we study in geometry classes revealed the essential *truth* of the triangle. All right triangles—all that would ever be or had ever been—satisfied the relationship: the sum of the squares of the legs (the two sides that form the right angle) is equal to the square of the hypotenuse (the third side). This truth was arrived at rationally and independently of experience. Pythagoras believed that it came from the soul itself. We should not ridicule Pythagoras for his numerology. One of the cornerstones of modern science is a set of numerical relationships that we call *laws*. Newton's $F = ma$, Einstein's $E = mc^2$, Ohm's $E = I/R$ are just a few examples of contemporary "numerology."

Thales and Pythagoras treated the "soul" as a part of the Universe, driven by the same forces that they assumed operated everywhere. They were *cosmologists*—those concerned with the heavens. They believed in universal order and looked for universal truths. Before the rise of philosophy, as early as 1000 B.C., the soul was conceived of as completely spiritual. The Homeric poets located this soul within the body; only death could separate the two. After death the body decays, and the soul begins its eternal journey through the shadows of Hades, the dwelling place of the dead. Even before the Homeric poems, the ancients relied on the concept of the soul to explain dreams, fits, and drug-induced states of ecstasy.

When the body was fast asleep and all normal activities were suspended, the soul seemed to detach itself from the body and to wander abroad. What was experienced in dreams was what the soul encountered when separated from the body. (McClure, pp. 15-16)

THE SOUL'S JOURNEY

In Homer's *Odyssey*, Odysseus visits the land of the dead and meets Anticleia, his deceased mother. Odysseus fears that his senses have been tricked and that his mother, in fact, is only a phantom. She assures him, however, that:

It is not Persephone who is beguiling you, but all people are like this when they are dead. The sinews no longer hold the flesh and bones together; these perish in the fierceness of consuming fire as soon as life has left the body, and the soul flies away as though it were a dream. (Book XI, 185-234)

The Homeric epics not only treat the soul as a wanderer, but they also allow it to be occupied by divine agents. At the beginning of Book II of the *Iliad*, for example, Zeus decides to help Achilles by deceiving Agamemnon. The god sends a "lying dream" to visit Agamemnon, intrude upon his sleep, and occupy his slumbering soul, creating visions, sounds, and prophecies.

Thales, and to a lesser extent Pythagoras, had a less supernatural concept of the soul. They viewed it as the motive force, or cause, for the actions of men and of the heavens. After them, Greek philosophy's special attention to the heavens gave way to a *psychological* philosophy, introduced by Socrates (469-399 B.C.).

The Socratic view of the soul preserved many of the older notions. Socrates, however, shifted the emphasis from relations between the soul and the Universe to those between the soul and the *self*. To "know thyself" in the Socratic system is to free the soul from the imperfections of the body. Socrates makes his position clear in *Phaedo*, one of the dialogues written by Plato that present Socrates' ideas. In the following, he instructs Simmias in the need for liberating the soul:

> "Then the clearest knowledge will surely be attained by one who approaches the object so far as possible by thought, and thought alone, not permitting sight or any other sense to intrude upon his thinking, not dragging in any sense as accompaniment to reason: one who sets himself to track down each constituent of reality purely and simply as it is by means of thought pure and simple: one who gets rid, so far as possible, of eyes and ears and, broadly speaking, of the body altogether, knowing that when the body is the soul's partner it confuses the soul and prevents it from coming to possess truth and intelligence. Is it not such a man, Simmias, that will grasp that which really is?" "What you say, Socrates," replied Simmias, "is profoundly true." "On all these grounds then, must not genuine philosophers . . . say . . . 'It would seem that we are guided as it were along a track to our goal by the fact that, so long as we have the body accompanying our reason in its inquiries, so long as our souls are befouled by this evil admixture, we shall assuredly never fully possess that which we desire, to wit truth . . .' While we are alive we shall, it would seem, come nearest to knowledge if we have as little as possible to do with the body, if we limit our association therewith to absolute necessities, keeping ourselves pure and free. . . ." (Plato, pp. 47-48)

In this passage, we find both the influence of Pythagoras and a departure from Pythagorean thought. The separation of body and soul is retained, as is the need for purification. Here, too, a knowledge of truth cannot be achieved through the senses and can only be perfect after death. But for Socrates, the goal is not merely purifying the soul; that is only a means. The final goal is an awareness of truth, an understanding of reality.

Socrates lives for us principally through Plato's *Dialogues*. To speak of one is to speak of them both. Through their philosophy, the Greek concept of soul merges with the modern notion of *mind*—that which allows reason and knowledge. The mind is the force, the mechanism, of human psychology.

Plato

While keeping a safe political distance from the Pythagoreans, Plato (427-347 B.C.) borrowed heavily from them. He proposed that to understand nature, one must appreciate the *true forms* of natural events, forms that cannot be discovered in the changing appearance of things. For example, the true form of the right triangle is not *seen* in the arrangement of the three lines. It is *known* by the equation relating these three sides. In the Platonic (Socratic) sense, knowledge is always an awareness of *relationship*.

Plato contended that the senses deceive, offering no sure route to truth. He further argued that the soul was at one with nature and that only by cultivating the mind could one understand oneself. All truths, he stated, reside within the mind, so that our task is to gain access to the insights that we already possess. He offers an illustration in the dialogue, *Meno*.

Meno, a rich young man from Thessaly, visits Athens on business. He is accompanied by his servant. He meets Socrates in the street, and the two begin a philosophical discussion. With the arrogance of one with little learning, Meno quickly challenges Socrates, who has argued that knowledge is really only recollecting: One always has knowledge but cannot always retrieve it. Meno's argument (which he has borrowed from the Sophists, a group of Athenian teachers and thinkers) begins with the question, "How is learning possible?" If one knows something, he need not inquire into it. If he does not know, he does not know enough to inquire.

Socrates replies by calling upon Meno's servant, a boy who has little education and none in mathematics. By sketching figures in the sand and by carefully phrasing his questions—but never giving answers—Socrates leads the boy to the brink of a mathematical deduction. With still more prodding, the boy discovers for himself the relationships described in the Pythagorean Theorem—he recognizes the principle without being told. This episode reflects the Platonic (or Socratic) notion of truth: It is a *latent* awareness possessed by all, although the knowledge may remain untapped.

The mind can be cultivated in order to liberate these truths, so that the individual becomes actively aware rather than latently aware. The truths themselves concern relationships, not mere appearances.

We call these Platonic principles *nativism* and *idealism*. Nativistic philosophers propose that knowledge and understanding are *natural* to man. They are inborn (*innate*) but must await the right mental climate before they can be expressed. *Idealism* is the belief that the *idea* is the ultimate truth. It makes a distinction between perception and knowledge. It states that the key to ideas is the perception of relationships. We may try to test our knowledge through direct observation, but any discovery we make will be a creation of the mind. In Plato's philosophic psychology, man learns of nature by reflecting upon it, not by perceiving it. The truths that have been planted in man (ideas) emerge in the minds of those who have been tutored in philosophy. Without this training, the ideas remain within a soul that has not been awakened.

Aristotle

Plato's philosophy was revolutionized by his student Aristotle (384-322 B.C.). Aristotle, the son of a physician, tried to describe the nature of human understanding in terms of processes that were more readily understood than Plato's "true forms." He stated that knowledge begins with *sensation*. Our factual knowledge comes from *experience*, which is nothing more than an activity of the senses. In the *Posterior Analytics*, he states:

> It is also clear that the loss of any one of the senses entails the loss of a corresponding portion of knowledge, and that, since we learn either by induction or by demonstration, this knowledge cannot be acquired. (Bk. 1, Ch. 18)

For Aristotle, experiences are the material, or substance, of knowledge. These experiences lead to ideas, which result from the combination of several sensations. That is, two or more sensations that are similar yet distinct occur together in time and place. The sensations thus become associated. The more alike these adjoining experiences are and the more they are repeated, the stronger the associations will be.

By stating that knowledge comes from experience, Aristotle became one of the founders of *empirical philosophy*. He is also credited with founding a variety of psychological *associationism* by advancing the theory that ideas result from *associated experiences*. He also advanced the first laws of learning, stating that the strength of associations depends upon similarity, contiguity, and repetition. This last hypothesis will be discussed further in Chapter 6. For now, we will examine Aristotle's treatment of this hypothesis.

In a short treatise, Aristotle addresses himself to *Memory and Reminiscence*. He argues that since perception is immediate, or present, and since memory always refers to the past, perception and memory must be different. He considers memory to be a trace of perception. The perceptions must be "stamped in" in order to form memory. If the stamp is to be clear and permanent, according to Aristotle, it must be made when the soul is tranquil. Thus, the very young child (who is suffering from the "flux" of growth), the aged person (who endures the "flux" of decay), or the overly passionate person (who is burdened by the "flux" of the moment), all have poor memories. However, under the right conditions, if A and B are regularly paired and presented to someone, the appearance of A will call forth the memory of B. As Aristotle states, ". . . whenever a subject experiences the former of two movements thus connected, it will (invariably) experience the latter . . ." (*De Memoria et Reminiscentia,* Chap. 2, 451b: 10, p. 612). He also tells us that when someone tries to recall the items in a series, ". . . attempts at recollection succeed soonest and best when they start from a beginning . . ." (Chap. 2, 451b: 30, p. 613). (We will examine this and related theories further in Chapter 6.)

Although he was a spokesman for ancient empiricism, Aristotle also knew the limitations of approaches that viewed knowledge as purely sensation. He insists that scientific wisdom, for example, cannot be gained by observation alone, since observation always looks for the *particular*, while scientific wisdom seeks the *universal*. One can attain such scientific wisdom through *intuition,* a term invented by Aristotle. This term is similar to what Plato meant by "true forms." But even in pointing to the limits of empirical knowledge, Aristotle still held that the senses played a major part in acquiring knowledge—not wisdom, but accurate knowledge.

Aristotle restored the senses to a respectable position by viewing them as the sources of factual knowledge. He thus offered an alternative to idealism. Without breaking completely with Plato's philosophy, he succeeded in tying science to direct observation. Most importantly, he stated his opinions about psychology in a form that allowed them to be investigated *experimentally*. His "laws" of memory would not be tested until 2,000 years had passed, when conditions would finally allow the growth of experimental science. But Aristotle could still be thanked for having provided a subject matter.

Perhaps as a result of his father's work in medicine, Aristotle was a biologically oriented philosopher. He was not specifically interested in medicine, but he conducted many biological studies. He tried to connect certain psychological processes to biological mechanisms. Some of his biology was quite innovative; for example, he founded embryology by examining chick eggs during successive stages of development. However, much of his biological study was oversimplified (for example, he located all life-giving influences in the heart). His methods were crude and his conceptions were often misguided, but he did promote a new way of thinking about psychological matters. In suggesting that psychological functions were affected by biological functions, Aristotle supported a *materialist* psychology. Like his associationism, this concept would wait many centuries before it would be explored experimentally.

With Aristotle's death, further development of natural philosophy in Greece slowly came to a halt. It has been said that he was the last man to know everything that was known in his day. He was the model genius— biologist, physicist, psychologist, philosopher. Since he said everything, he was often wrong. He noted that only human beings had lashes on both the upper and lower eyelids. (If nothing else, this proves his devotion to observation.) He praised the intelligence of elephants, who knew enough to kneel in the presence of kings! He advanced biology and founded psychology. One of his pupils, Alexander the Great, extended his scholarship to the boundaries of the civilized world. Arabs, Romans, Persians, Turks— scholars in many nations—were guided in some way by Aristotle's achievements. He died in 322 B.C. at the age of 62, ending the most productive and sustained period of thought in our history. Three centuries passed from the birth of Thales to the death of Aristotle. There has been no comparable period of philosophic achievement since.

THE WANING OF THE PHILOSOPHIC SPIRIT

The spirit of independence and competitiveness that brought Greece success ultimately contributed to its decline. Though wracked by never-ending wars, Athens was morally opposed to using her slaves to risk their lives in defense of rights they did not possess. Without leadership and perhaps without even the desire to fight, the city-state fell to Sparta in 404 B.C. It later became an appendage of the Macedonian kingdoms of Philip II and his son, Alexander the Great. After Alexander's death in 323 B.C., Greece found itself overextended militarily and again locked in internal contests for power. Alexander had opened up the East to the Greeks. Many people, especially the young, left crowded Greek cities to find their fortunes in these far-off lands. Colonized regions such as Sicily began outproducing Greece in wine and oil, thus making emigration even more attractive. Alexander's generals had divided his empire among themselves, with Macedonia and Greece forming one domain, Persia another, and Egypt the third. The unity achieved by Alexander soon dissolved, and the end of imperial Greece swiftly followed. In less than 60 years, (beginning in 200 B.C.), Roman armies gained control of most of the major Macedonian and Greek provinces. These once-powerful centers of culture and commerce were soon way stations for the legions of the Roman Empire.

The Nature of Roman Rule

The only place that ancient Rome can claim in the history of psychology was earned by that part of Roman scholarship inherited from the Greeks. Despite her accomplishments in warfare, architecture, law, and politics, Rome did little to change, and nothing to improve, the philosophical legacy left by Athens. The Romans took their gods more seriously than the Greeks did, and for them, the division between philosophy and religion was not as clean. The rapid expansion of the Roman empire and the resulting burden of administering the world worked against the philosophic attitude. Gnomic, practical, and scientific wisdom evolved, but philosophical wisdom was borrowed or ignored. To the aristrocracy—taught by Greek tutors—philosophy was more a subject that had to be learned than a way toward understanding. However, the Romans were great educators, and some of the world's most notable scholars (Cicero, Pliny, and Virgil) lived among them. In fact, as "political scientists," Romans were more successful than their "purer" predecessors in applying Greek wisdom to the demands of government. Roman law surpassed the rules of the Athenian lawgiver,

Solon, and Roman schools made a reality of the Greek ideal of personal cultivation. Before they became conquerors, the Romans had been strongly influenced by the Greeks. They easily brought to their empire many of the attitudes and practices first fashioned by their Greek subjects. Alexander had commanded 10,000 of his soldiers to marry Persian women in order to put the stamp of Greek culture on the East. In contrast, Rome wisely appointed local leaders to govern the provinces they conquered. The Greek passion to convert failed, as the Roman passion to control succeeded.

Roman supremacy lasted longer than that of Greece. However, soon after the high point of the empire, overextension challenged Rome's power, and many enemies courted her wealth. Crop failures, increasing difficulties in collecting taxes, intrigues within the highest councils, and, finally, a series of invasions by barbarians toppled the empire, the most massive kingdom in antiquity. By the second century A.D., the signs of collapse were apparent. The intermixing of peoples, customs, and cults gave rise to an unrestricted growth of a brute tribalism. The classical life was obviously in decline. William H. McNeill writes in *The Rise of the West: A History of the Human Community:*

> In an age when violence and disease were disrupting the social universe of the Roman world, and when religions of salvation were competing for the allegiance of the populace, the optimistic rationalism of the Greek philosophic tradition seemed utterly inadequate to account for events. How could a reasonable man accept the Stoic doctrine of the supremacy of natural law, for example, when whim and chance so obviously dominated Roman politics . . .? (pp. 415-416)

After the fall of Rome around 476 A.D., all that remained of the Greek influence was a neo-Platonic mysticism. This was embraced by a Christian movement in search of philosophic foundations.

The early church has been described by Sir William C. Dampier in his history of science as being "based on the fundamental assumption that the ultimate reality of the Universe is spirit" (p. 64). For centuries, truth was "revealed," not discovered by observation or thought. Debate gave way to contemplation of religious truths. In the face of the grim prospect of eternal damnation, the wonders of everyday living first faded and then were forgotten. As Saint Augustine, the voice of the Church, put it,

"In regard to nature it is not necessary for the Christian to know more than that the goodness of the Creator is the cause of all things."

As the Dark Ages that followed Rome's fall gradually merged with the Middle Ages, scholarship again began to surface. But it was a new scholarship in which philosophy served religion and the citizen served both. Popes and kings sought some historic base for their power. Intellectuals gained and lost favor as they supported either church or state. Ever so slowly, tiny sparks and then little flames of curiosity began to flicker in the dim corridors of righteousness.

THE REBIRTH OF PHILOSOPHICAL TENSIONS

The size of the intellectual world is measured by the ease with which ideas travel. By the year 1200, ideas moved more freely. European universities, chiefly the University of Paris, were rediscovering Aristotle. In Paris, Albertus Magnus taught Aristotelian science within the context of the new Christian theology and his student, Thomas Aquinas (1225-1274), "took over from Aristotle and from the Christian doctrine of the day the assumption that man is the center and object of creation, and that the world is to be described in terms of human sensation and human psychology." (Dampier, p. 87)

Thomas Aquinas

Thomas Aquinas was the seventh of eight children in a prominent Italian family. He grew up as a loner—quiet, moody, and shy—and was thought dull by some. After years of religious study, he decided to join the priestly order of beggars—the Dominicans—rather than pursue a path that would have brought him and his family power in the Church. This decision smacked of that same irony so often witnessed in the children of prosperity. His family kidnapped him and held him captive for a year, trying to change his mind. But it became apparent that he was beyond reform.

Perhaps to move him beyond his family's influence or perhaps by chance, the Dominican district superior ordered Thomas to leave for France to study under the famous teacher Albertus Magnus. Only the most promising young minds in Europe were drawn to the University of Paris. The quiet and physically bullish Thomas seemed obviously out of place in such company. His nickname, given to him by classmates whom history has ignored, was "the dumb ox"! On hearing of this later, Albertus Magnus is said to have proclaimed, "You call him a Dumb Ox; I tell you this Dumb Ox shall bellow so loud that his bellowings will fill the world."

In contrast to Saint Augustine's Platonic reliance upon sober reflection as a way to truth, Thomas pressed for reason informed by experience. His chief mission was to prove rationally that the principles of Christian theology were true and to oppose increasing skepticism. Thomas lacked the specific interests that are associated with scientific creativity. Perhaps more than any of his contemporaries, however, he hastened a revolution of thought that had to take place before the Renaissance could occur. He turned people's attention back to daily life; he allowed the Christian believer's attention to drift away from the burdens of sin and imperfection. More importantly, Aquinas made a reinterpretation of the scripture acceptable.

His most important work, *Summa Theologica*, raised and answered questions that had occupied the minds of churchmen for centuries. Many of the questions were still colored with the tint of the Middle Ages; for example, *Is God composed of "form" and "matter"? Does God exist in everything?; Is the name "God" peculiar to God or not?* But others formed a philosophical bridge from ancient times to the Renaissance. Aquinas asked, *Is Christian theology wisdom?* He concludes that Christian theology *is* wisdom, but he insists that the validity of the religious principles does not depend on any human science. *Is truth in things or only in the mind?* Thomas does not commit himself one way or the other. Primarily, he asserts that truth is in the intellect, not the senses. Truth is that property of things toward which the intellect moves. This is a modified form of idealism. *Is God's will the cause of all things?* Thomas answers that it is. But he also asserts that God wills that the human will judge and make choices for itself. God thus allows the human will, not just His own, to shape an individual's destiny.

The importance of the *Summa*, in part, came from its style. Thomas used the form of a dialogue between adversaries to present his points. In the dialogues, the case against religious doctrines was argued intelligently and judiciously. No doubt, Thomas wanted his readers to arrive at the same conclusions he reached: God is good, and man's life is meaningful

only so far as it is holy. But the text permitted one to choose other conclusions, which were voiced by both fictional and actual antagonists. By
citing many older authorities, the *Summa* not only made other perspectives
known, but also lent a value to argument itself.

Some have suggested that Thomas spoke for empiricism while subtly
introducing a healthy dose of Platonic idealism. We cannot call Thomas'
revival of empiricism a rebirth of science, because it does not offer even
the outlines of an experimental science. Rather, the Thomistic method
rests on reason, argument, and intuition. It does not rest on observation,
measurement, and empirical demonstration of modern science. As a result,
Thomas was always forced to fit the facts of experience into a spiritual
context. Less pious scholars whose belief in Christian doctrine was not as
firm as Thomas' grew more and more impatient with the endless hypotheses
that he set forth. They preferred a rational philosophy stripped of religious
implications.

The Astronomers

Other profound influences besides that of Thomas Aquinas were felt
throughout Europe. The first printing press, invented by Johannes Guten-
berg in the fifteenth century, created the potential for mass education
and for the rapid communication of great insights to people outside the
intellectual centers. The Byzantine empire, which had formed from the
eastern half of the Roman empire after Rome fell, finally collapsed during
the Middle Ages. Its classical scholars fled to the West, further stimulating
the intellectual revival. The effects of the new climate were felt most
immediately in the field of astronomy. With a book on the heavens published in 1543, Copernicus introduced the scientific revolution that bears
his name, a revolution that ushered in the Age of Astronomy. The book
addresses the Pope:

> I can well believe, most holy father, that certain people, when they
> hear of my attributing motion to the earth in these books of mine,
> will at once declare that such an opinion ought to be rejected. . . .

The Copernican theory was not revolutionary just because it asserted that the earth rotates. Its implications went much farther than that. If, in fact, our planet is merely another sphere guided through space by a star, then what of man himself?

Johannes Kepler, in the sixteenth and early seventeenth centuries, combined the Copernican theory with the astronomical data collected by his teacher Tycho Brahe, whose observations of the heavens were then the most accurate made. The mathematical synthesis, or model, developed by Kepler was expressed in three laws governing planetary motion. As a result of this great achievement, respect for the rational processes increased. In the same year that Kepler published the first two of his laws (1609), Galileo built a telescope and observed four moons of Jupiter. The discovery threw into doubt another Church dogma: the doctrine that God favored the number seven in ordering the universe. (Seven was originally selected as a special number by the Pythagoreans.) When Galileo declared that there were at least eleven heavenly bodies, not seven, scholars had to find a new "magic" number, or else reject that Church teaching. Prudent men chose to reject the dogma.

The Age of Astronomy reached its height with the genius of Sir Isaac Newton (1642-1727). Since Newton considered his theory to be a description of God's work, he could not bring himself to view man as just a cog in the machinery of the universe. In the less religious climate of France, however, Voltaire could express a different outlook on man. He remarked on Newton's theory:

> It would be very singular that all nature, all the planets, should obey eternal laws, and that there should be a little animal, five feet high, who, in contempt of these laws, could act as he pleased, solely according to his caprice. (Dampier, p. 197)

THE BIRTH OF MODERN PHILOSOPHY

Descartes and Materialism

The great achievements of the astronomers encouraged scholars everywhere. The implications of the works of Copernicus and Kepler had a strong effect on the philosophy of the French philosopher René Descartes

(1596-1650), who, among many other accomplishments, founded analytic geometry.

Descartes was inspired by the "perfect machinery" of Kepler's universe. He created a *mechanistic* philosophy, which when applied to biology, formed the basis for the nineteenth-century study of the physiology of reflexes. Descartes conceived of the body as a perfect machine housing a part-rational, part-automatic mind. But in the human machine, there was also a rational soul. It was this soul that made human beings different from animals, because it gave the automatic movements, or reflexes, a purpose. According to Descartes, "animal spirits" flow through "nervous tubes" to the muscles, and parts of the body move according to the laws of physics. The flow of these spirits is controlled by a valve in the brain. In locating this valve, Descartes worked in his characteristic geometric way. In the brain, the parts on the left side duplicate those on the right, with one exception. This exception, the pineal gland, is appropriately found in the center of the head. Descartes thus identified the pineal gland as the valve and said that the soul determined its action.

Descartes used Aristotelian methods but believed in the Platonic theory of inborn ideas. He held that we are innately aware of the self, of God, and of mathematical principles.

His strong religious beliefs prevented him from applying his philosophic materialism to the soul itself. To the end of his life, he insisted that the mind and the body are distinct from each other. However, he did set the stage for *physiological psychology,* which investigates the *biochemical* and *physiological* foundations of *psychological functions* (see Chapter 4). In *A History of Experimental Psychology,* Edwin G. Boring (1959) has written about Descartes' role in founding materialism and about the transformation of that concept by those who followed:

> Animals, he said, are automata like the moving statues in the royal gardens which appear or disappear when the visitor provides the stimulus by stepping on a concealed plate; but man is automatic only in his bodily constitution. His body interacts with his soul. . . . Descartes, profoundly religious, was set to protect the integrity of the soul; yet, his conception of the mechanics of animals was symptomatic of the new learning and in itself provided a basis for the movement away from spiritualism toward materialism. (pp. 211-212)

English Empiricism: Hobbes, Locke, and Hume

Thomas Hobbes

In England, Thomas Hobbes (1588-1679) rejected Descartes' notion of innate ideas. It was also not clear to him why mind and body had to be separated. In his book *Leviathan*, he wrote:

> Concerning the thoughts of man . . . they are . . . of some quality . . . of a body without us, which is commonly called an *object*. . . . The original of them is all that which we call *sense*, for there is no conception in man's mind which hath not at first, totally or by parts, been begotten upon the organs of sense. The rest are derived from that original.

Hobbes stated that thought begins with experience, and knowledge comes from the *association* and *memory* of multiple experiences. He discused the merging of one thought into the next in a flow, or direction, governed by "some desire and design." Hobbes thus anticipated theories about "stream of consciousness," as well as those concerning the interplay between what we feel and what we perceive: ". . . in all your actions, look often upon what you would have, as the thing that directs all your thoughts in the way you attain it." (Hobbes, *Leviathan*)

John Locke

A good part of Hobbes' psychology was endorsed by John Locke (1632-1704) whose *Essay Concerning Human Understanding* established empiricism as the "official" English philosophy.

Locke was greatly influenced by Descartes, but even more so by the scientific achievements of his time.

> The commonwealth of learning is not at this time without master-builders, . . . but everyone must not hope to be a Boyle or a Sydenham; and in an age that produces such masters as the great Huygens, and the incomparable Mr. Newton, . . . it is ambition enough to be employed as an under-laborer in clearing the ground

a little, and removing some of the rubbish that lies in the way to knowledge; . . .

Like Hobbes before him, Locke found his thinking confined by the "scholastic" philosophy of his day. Descartes had stimulated his interest in science. Travel in France and Holland had encouraged him to reject the conventions of English education. In his *Essay* he wrote:

> If by this inquiry into the nature of the understanding, I can dis-
> cover the powers thereof, how far they reach, and where they fail
> us, I suppose it may be of use to prevail with the busy mind of
> man to be more cautious in meddling with things exceeding its
> comprehension, to stop when it is at the utmost extent of its tether,
> and to sit down in a quiet ignorance of those things which, upon
> examination, are found to be beyond the reach of our capacities.

In this statement of the problem, Locke points out the need to assess our psychological capacities. He goes even further in respecting the importance of *quantitative* assessment of discovering "to what things they are in any degree proportionate." Following in the path cleared by Hobbes, he rejects the nativism of Descartes: "I know it is a received doctrine, that men have native ideas and original characters stamped upon their minds in their very first being." He rejects this and instead proposes: "Let us then suppose the mind to be, as we say, white paper, void of all characters, without any ideas; how comes it to be furnished? . . . To this I answer, in one word, from experience." Locke affirms that experience itself is the product of the senses. "This great source of most of the ideas we have, depending wholly upon our senses, and derived by them to the understanding, I call sensation." Understanding emerges from the raw facts of sensation. The process by which these sense-data combine is called *association*. When we have finally acquired this knowledge, it must be retained. On the subject of memory, Locke writes:

> The mind has a power, . . . to revive perceptions which it has once
> had, . . . Attention and repetition help much to the fixing any ideas
> in the memory; but those which naturally at first make the deepest
> and most lasting impression, are those which are accompanied with
> pleasure or pain.

In the above passages, many contemporary psychological issues are set forth: The role of repetition, motivation, and attention in learning and memory; the acquisition of information as a result of sensory stimulation; and, the need for sensory enrichment during a person's development (one of the most modern psychological problems):

> I think it will be granted easily, that if a child were kept in a place where he never saw any other but black and white till he were a man, he would have no . . . ideas of scarlet or green. . . .

As for the "soul" that Descartes believed in, Locke elected to leave that question a mystery "to be disputed by those of who have better thought of that matter."

David Hume

Following in the empirical movement, David Hume (1711-1776) developed associationism further than his predecessors. He outlined the specific characteristics of sensory stimuli that cause associations to form. These he named *resemblance, contiguity,* and *causation* and described them as "the only bonds that unite our thoughts together." Briefly defined, *resemblance* is the physical similarity between stimuli; *contiguity* is the distance between stimuli in space and time; *causation* is the distance in time between stimuli and the reliability with which they occur together, in the order in which we normally experience them. Each of these characteristics was later to become an important issue in the psychology of learning.

Hume also addressed himself to the nature of understanding in animals. His theories stood as an authority for later research in animal intelligence. He wrote:

> When the circulation of the blood . . . is clearly proved to have place in one creature . . . it forms a strong presumption, that the same principle has place in all. . . . Any theory . . . of the understanding, or the origin and connection of the passions in man, will acquire additional authority, if we find, that the same theory is requisite to explain the same phenomena in all other animals.

Hume also offered ideas on this topic that have a peculiarly modern ring:

Animals, as well as man, learn many things from experience. . . . This is still more evident from the effects of discipline and education on animals, who, by the proper application of rewards and punishments, may be taught any course of action, the most contrary to their natural instincts and propensities. Is it not experience, which renders a dog apprehensive of pain, when you menace him, or lift up the whip to beat him? . . . Animals, therefore, are not guided in these inferences by reasoning. Neither are children. Neither are the generality of mankind, in their ordinary actions and conclusions. Neither are philosophers themselves, who, in all the active parts of life, are, in the main, the same with the vulgar, and are governed by the same maxims. Nature must have provided some other principle, of more ready, and more general use and application. . . . It may be asked how it happens, that men so much surpass animals in reasoning, and one so much surpasses another? . . . Where there is a complication of causes to produce any effect, one mind may be much larger than another, and better able to comprehend the whole system of objects, and to infer justly their consequences.

Hobbes, Locke, and Hume progressively stripped away more and more of the soul, of nativism, and of those ancient Platonic "realities." English empiricism stressed the importance of experience and of sensory connection with the world. It rejected or at least neglected to acknowledge any fixed nature for the human mind. The mind was merely something upon which life's experiences were recorded. The quality of mind was only a reflection of the quality of experience.

Kant's Reply to Empiricism

In continental Europe, strong opposition to this radical empiricism soon developed. Philosophers with a more theological orientation attacked Hume's conception of a mechanical and soulless man. The major attempt to reconcile the ideas of Hume and those of his detractors was made by Immanuel Kant (1724-1804), whose philosophy came to dominate German thought throughout most of the nineteenth century.

Kant stated that Hume's writings awakened him from "dogmatic slumber." He was influenced mainly by Hume's *mentalism;* that is, by the idea that the role of the mind is to help fashion reality. Hume contended that knowledge is merely the ideas of men and that there is no way to distinguish reality itself from our perception of reality. In accepting the basic premise of empiricism—that knowledge is the product of experience —he reasoned that all knowledge is subject to the idiosyncracies of human perception. Therefore, our understanding of reality and any laws we invent to explain the world are valid only within the limits of our sensory processes. Hume saw the concept of *causation,* for example, as no more than a habit of the mind. We are conditioned to believe that event A causes event B because we perceive B occurring whenever A takes place. However, there is no *necessary* connection between A and B, and there is no *logical* way of proving that A causes B. One can only say that—on the basis of all previous (subjective) observations—each time A has occurred, B has been observed after it. The assumption that one natural event causes another is little more than an act of faith or a simple conviction. It is hardly a logical necessity. Since the basis of both religion and science is *determinism*—an unfailing acceptance of the view that all events in the universe occur in response to some prior event—Hume's skepticism constituted a challenge of the greatest importance.

It is important for us to realize that this skeptical position was based on logical analysis, not on some personal belief. Hume had confidence in the methods and findings of science. As a private individual, as opposed to a philosopher, he accepted the concept of causation. His essay, however, set out to demonstrate that the idea of causation is simply a human *notion,* not supported by logic.

In the *Critique of Pure Reason,* Kant challenged the major premise of empiricism. He argued that before there can be experience, there must be an understanding mind. As examples, Kant offered certain mathematical principles whose truth was neither based upon, nor could ever be denied by experience. Our concepts of space and time do not arise from the senses. Rather, they must exist before experience if experience is to be meaningful at all. Experience assumes an active mind that organizes and transforms experience, as well as being modified by it. To Kant, the ability to coordinate experience was the basic property and function of the mind. The mind *will* organize. *What* it organizes is the contents of experience. He states the following in regard to the perception of space:

> Space is not an empirical conception, which has been derived from external experiences. . . . No experience of the external relations of sensible things could yield the idea of space, because without the consciousness of space there would be no external experience whatever. . . . Accordingly, no geometrical proposition, as, for instance, that any two sides of a triangle are greater than the third side, can ever be derived from the general conceptions of line and triangle, but only from perception. From the perception, however, it can be derived *a priori*, and with demonstrative certainty.

By *a priori* perception, Kant means that "found in us before we actually observe an object, and hence it must be pure, not empirical perception."

Kant stated that there were three distinct sources of all experience: the senses, the imagination, and something he called *apperception*. By apperception he meant the mind's awareness of itself—that is, knowing that one knows. He viewed these three as attributes of mind and argued that Locke and Hume had restricted their attention to the senses. Kant praises Hume for realizing that the senses alone cannot account for all knowledge, but he condemns him for not recognizing the innate features that do account for knowledge. According to Kant, Hume "never thought that possibly the understanding might itself . . . be the author of that experience in which its objects are found." In other words, the understanding itself fashions experience. Only within the understanding is knowledge of the experience found. In Kant's terms, all sensory events gain representation within man because he thinks about them. Without thought, there could be no representation:

> It must be *possible* that the *I think* should accompany all my representations: for otherwise something would be represented within me that could not be thought. . . . That representation, however (that *I think*), is an act of spontaneity, that is, it cannot be considered as belonging to sensibility. I call it *pure appreciation*.

Kant, then, founded a different kind of idealism,* which was the most

---

*Kant would not identify his philosophy with idealism in the traditional Platonic sense. Still, his theory of perception requires "pure categories of the understanding," which must be something like Plato's *ideas*.

influential argument against radical empiricism. It revived Descartes' nativism in that it viewed the mind's tendency to organize as innate and as essential to experience.

SUMMARY

This chapter has reviewed several of the major philosophical developments that have influenced the course of modern psychology. From *empiricism*, psychology has inherited theories of sensation and perception, associative learning, and the concept that the mind is the product of experience. *Idealism* set the stage for psychological studies of consciousness and cognitive processes (those processes associated with perception, learning, and thinking) in general. The *nativistic* aspects of idealism have played a large part in the emergence of genetic and developmental psychology and in that division of animal psychology that is concerned with instincts. The influence of Darwin has combined with the older philosophical *materialism* to produce physiological and comparative psychology. As these overall philosophical perspectives were considered and changed in the nineteenth and early twentieth centuries, new fields and specializations were formed. The nativistic concept that there are "types" of people—an idea as old as Plato's belief in "men of brass, men of silver, men of iron" —has surfaced again as the psychology of personality. *Utilitarianism* and *associationism* would lead almost directly to early forms of *behaviorism*.

None of these developments could have occurred, however, if only a philosophical tradition had existed. There also had to be a scientific tradition, particularly an experimental one. Physics provided this experimental tradition through the genius of Newton and Galileo. By the middle of the nineteenth century, many "experimental philosophers" were convinced that the mind was a part of nature, just as inclined planes and falling apples were. The mind, they thought, could also be explained by science. According to this view, people only had to adopt experimental methods—as opposed to speculative ones—and to apply mathematics and physiology to psychological issues.

In the next chapter we will examine these experimental and statistical methods, which were applied to the age-old philosophical issues, thus producing the new discipline of experimental psychology.

SUGGESTED READINGS

DAMPIER, W. C. *A History of Science*. London: Cambridge University Press, 1966.

This is a paperback edition of the 40-year-old classic. Chapters 1, 3, 7, 9, and 12 are especially germane to this text. Dampier presents complex ideas in their historic context and thereby gives them a liveliness usually missing in scientific texts.

KELLER, F. S. *The Definition of Psychology*. New York: Appleton-Century-Crofts, 1937.

Old but not at all dated is this brief review of the emergence of "schools" of psychology. Professor Keller points to the origins of structuralism, functionalism and gestalt psychology, ending with a hint of the behaviorism to come.

ROBINSON, D. N. *An Intellectual History of Psychology*. New York: Macmillan Publishing Co., 1976.

This text explores the major philosophical systems that have been advanced to deal with the issues of mind, conduct, governance, and epistemology. The emphasis is upon the psychological implications of the various philosophical systems.

ROSS, W. D., ed. *Aristotle: Selections*. New York: Charles Scribner's Sons. 1955.

This paperback edition offers much of Aristotle's psychology. The reader is encouraged in particular to examine Selections 8, 9, 10, 16, 17, 50, 51, 52, 53, 55, 66, 67, 68, 82, 83. These amount to well under 100 pages and reveal the style and direction of Aristotle's scientific thought.

SAHAKIAN, W. S., ed. *History of Psychology: A Sourcebook in Systematic Psychology*, Itasca, Ill.: F. E. Peacock Publishers, 1968.

Professor Sahakian draws from the writing of 133 different contributors to psychology's birth and development. Especially recommended are the passages from Augustine, Aquinas, Descartes, Locke, Leibnitz, Kant, and Darwin.

CHAPTER

3

The Methods of Modern Psychology

INTRODUCTION

There exists evidence that a sixteenth-century tribe called the Circassians, who lived in the foothills of the Caucasus mountains, developed a medical procedure of considerable value. The Circassians had neither fertile soil in which to cultivate crops nor healthy livestock with which they could trade. They had mastered very few crafts and, all in all, were nearly excluded from any possibilities for commerce in the world around them. It is said, however, that they did have beautiful daughters, and that these girls were raised for sale to the rulers of the East. The greatest threat to this unusual resource was smallpox, a disease that usually attacks the young and can scar them for life.

Some time in the sixteenth or seventeenth century, a wise Circassian observed that those who once had a mild case of this sickness never caught it again, no matter how severe an epidemic of smallpox occurred. It seemed that something in the sickness itself must have protected the victim against future attacks. On the basis of this observation, the Circassians began to *immunize* their children! They would lance the blisters of someone who was suffering from smallpox, drain the poisonous fluids, and rub them into cuts they had made on the arms and legs of healthy children.

This remarkable practice was reported by Voltaire, the eighteenth-century philosopher and writer in his *Letters on the English People*. Voltaire said that the same practice was already hundreds of years old in Turkey and perhaps thousands of years old in China. Note that Voltaire's account was written years before Edward Jenner, the English physician, even began those studies that would ultimately culminate in the discovery of the smallpox vaccine.

It takes nothing away from the ingenuity and rough intelligence of the Circassians to describe their efforts as *craft* while honoring Jenner's efforts with the term, *science*. The Circassians stumbled on to something and through trial and error made it work for them. We will never know how many children died as a result of their primitive vaccinations; how many were tormented beyond need; how many failed to develop the immunity after treatment. We have no reason to believe that the Circassians knew how much of the poisonous agent was needed, how often it should be applied, at what stage of the disease the blisters should be lanced, or at what age the children should be treated. The Circassians simply combined an insight and an accidental discovery and thus found a workable solution without understanding why it worked, how it worked, when it would work, or what its working implied. Jenner, with the aid of experiment, was not limited in any of these respects.

WHAT IS AN EXPERIMENT?

We hear a god deal these days about "experimental living" and "experimenting with drugs." University officials will describe what they are doing as "experimenting" with the curriculum or "experimenting" with coeducation. This talk usually means that someone has decided to do something and wants to create the illusion that it is a reasonable step to take by calling it an *experiment*. There may be sound reasons, for example, for no longer requiring all students to study mathematics as undergraduates.

But how is such a decision an "experiment"? People may choose to live on communes with their friends and pets, but in what way is this preference an "experiment"? In what respect is a coeducational dormitory "experimental?" The single answer to all three questions is that the cases are *not* experiments.

Every experiment, in any field of study, must include:

1. At least one *independent variable* that the experimenter can control and that is suspected of being able to produce changes in things or events;
2. At least one *dependent variable* whose condition or value can be modified by changes in the independent variable;
3. Methods and scales of measurement that can be used to describe both the independent and the dependent variables *quantitatively;* and,
4. Statistical methods that determine whether the effects the independent variable has on the dependent variable are *reliable* and *significant.*

If any of these four elements is missing, the particular undertaking is *not* an experiment. The effort might, for example, be a careful series of observations, such as those that resulted in Kepler's laws of planetary motion or Darwin's theory of evolution discussed earlier. It might be an opinion poll or a medical diagnosis or an enriching experience or a lovely painting. But it is not an experiment unless the four vital factors set forth above are included in the procedure for collecting the data.

We use the term *variable* to describe any event or object that can take on different values or undergo measurable changes. The term *dependent variable* applies to those events or objects whose values *depend upon* some other variable—the *independent variable.* This latter term is used to show our ability to vary the value of an event or the characteristics of an object. In general, independent variables are *causes* and dependent variables the *effects* that they produce. The examples that appear on p. 52 may be helpful.

From these examples, it is clear that experiments are done in order to establish *relationships* between types of events that occur in nature. Moreover, these relationships are not of an arbitrary or accidental nature. At this point, we will proceed by reviewing several kinds of relationships, as well as the meaning of reliability.

Independent Variables (Causes)	Dependent Variables (Effects)
The number of hours since an animal's last feeding.	The speed with which the animal runs down runway to get the food.
The intensity of clicks delivered to the right ear.	The percent of the clicks reported by the listener.
The amount of ether inhaled by a patient.	The number of minutes the patient remains asleep.
The number of dollars paid per item produced.	The number of items produced.

RELATIONSHIPS AND RELIABILITY

Although the studies done by different psychologists often seem to have little in common, the methods they use are nearly identical. That is, the subjects of inquiry may vary, but the approach taken by each remains very similar.

The basic goal of psychology is to discover *reliable relationships* between two types of factors—those features of advanced forms of life that help them adapt psychologically, and the environmental and biological factors that are responsible for the failure or success in the organism's adaptation. The phrase *reliable relationships* is stressed because both of these words have different meanings in psychology from the ones they have in ordinary usage. *Reliability* in any experiment is a *statistical* concept. It is based on the *theory of probability,* and it expresses *quantitatively* the confidence one can reasonably have that a relationship which has been observed before will continue to hold true. As we saw in Chapter 1, science looks for explanations and predictions. Its explanations are logical and try to include laws that we described earlier as "covering laws," laws of relationship. We also noted in the first chapter that, according to the loose definition, science tries to provide correct generalizations based on publicly observable events. When we call these generalizations "correct," we mean, finally, that they show a high *reliability*. Thus, to say that mammals cannot live without oxygen is to *generalize* from the frequent observation that mammals die soon after oxygen is removed. There has never been an exception and, therefore, it is probable that there never will be one.

Most scientific studies—and *all* psychological ones—involve events that are less reliable than the example offered above. It has always been true that an animal deprived of oxygen has soon died, but it is not always true that the children of schizophrenic parents are schizophrenic; or that people with average measured intelligence produce only average records of achievement; or that poverty leads to a lower sense of individual self-esteem; or that light of a certain wavelength is always described as "red." Many schizophrenic parents produce children considered to be psychologically normal. Many people whose I.Q. scores fall between 90 and 110, the range of average intelligence, have become important contributors to society. Children from deeply impoverished backgrounds have grown up with feelings of strong confidence in themselves and in their basic worth as human beings. Lights usually described as "red" appear colorless to those we call "color-blind."

Many other examples can be given, all indicating that the relationships sought and found by experimental psychologists are never perfect. But to say that a relationship is not perfect is not to say that there is no relationship at all. On the other hand, the fact that one has found *some* relationship between two factors or events does not mean that the relationship is reliable.

In addition to the fact that relationships differ in their reliability, they also differ in type. Science is not interested equally in all the different kinds of relationships. We will now review the kinds of relationships that exist and point out the one that interests science most. We will also look at the statistical method of testing the reliability of relationships when they are found.

Types of Relationships and Scales

Let us begin with *identity* relationships. Two events may be different forms of the same thing. In this instance, they are said to stand in an *identity* relationship. For example, the person in the next room may be John Smith, and we can acknowledge this fact by stating—Person X = John Smith. Such an identity relationship involves what is called *nominal scaling:* the use of *names* (nominal) to distinguish between (to *scale*) one class of things and another. Nominal scales are used in science in order to *classify,* not to quantify. For example, when we say that dogs are members of the *animal* kingdom, that they are *mammals,* and that they are *canines,* we are using *names* to distinguish between all dogs on the one hand and all things that are not dogs on the other. We are *naming* a certain type of animal in much the same way that we print numbers on uniforms, houses, or license plates. Such numbers are simply a convenient way of classifying. They have no quantitative value at all; that is, it would make no sense to add the numbers on a football uniform to those on the house on the corner, divide this sum by 2 and arrive at the average of a football player and a house.

The limitations of such nominal scales were pointed out by the philosopher and mathematician John Kemeny:

> Moliere gives a delightful example of the name-giving explanation. In his play, "The Physician in Spite of Himself," his doctor gets a prize for explaining why morphine puts one to sleep. He points out that all soporifics put you to sleep and morphine is a soporific; hence morphine puts you to sleep. The first statement in the explanation is your general theory; the second is a known fact; and hence we claim that this is a scientific explanation. Of course, "soporific" is synonymous with "a drug that puts you to sleep," and thus we again have an empty theory and a circular explanation. But the doctor may rest assured that he was not the only one in the history of Science who became famous for thinking up a new name. (Kemeny, p. 161)

Though nominal scales do not allow us to make quantitative distinctions, they are still useful. However, they are not the kind of identity relationship that is most interesting scientifically. There is another, more profound type of relationship which expresses the identity between two things that on the surface seem to have little or nothing in common. When Einstein stated that $E = mc^2$, he told the world that there is no fundamental difference between matter (m) and energy (E). (The constant c is the velocity of light in the equation.) He stated that the two variables were but different expressions of each other.

At the highest degree of development, science discovers identity relationships of this kind. With them, we stand under a single roof of explanation, and we can pull together an enormous number of otherwise separate events. But before this is possible, we must have better tools than just *names*. We must have *scaling* methods that are more precise than nominal scales. That is, we must go beyond classification to *quantification*.

The most primitive form of quantification is one that ranks things in some sequence. For example, Jack placed fifth in his graduating class, while Bill placed seventh and Tim placed ninth. From these facts, can we conclude that Jack did as much better than Bill as Bill did than Tim? Not at all. Jack's average grade may have been 98, Bill's 88, and Tim's 87. In other words, if we know only rank, we have only a very rough indication of quantity. We know that one person or item or event has a greater quantity of something than one of lower rank, but not how much more. The use of ranks is known as *ordinal scaling*. Unlike nominal scales, ordinal scales do imply quantity, but they do not give actual values. For that, we must use *interval scaling*—some measuring procedure in which the quantitative separation between the items is known. One example is the Fahrenheit thermometer. We arbitrarily select materials, such as mercury in a glass tube, and mark the tube so that each increase in heat causes an increase in the height of the mercury in the tube.

Though interval scales do provide exact quantitative measurements, they are limited, because they do not always refer to *real* quantities. The thermometer is an example of the limitations. When the thermometer reads "zero," what is it that no longer exists? That is, there is a "zero" amount of what? The answer is, *nothing*. The zero point on this thermometer does not correspond to a zero amount of anything in the physical world. It is chosen arbitrarily. The Fahrenheit scale coincides, at a value of +32, with the point at which water freezes. So, for scientific purposes, the interval scale is severely limited because it may report "zero" when, in fact, something is there. In science, we want our zeros to *mean* "nothing."

We also want our scales to show meaningful relationships. But does it mean anything to say that 80° is to 160° as 40° is to 80°? We all know that an 80° day is on the warm side but that a 160° day would probably kill us. On the other hand, 40° is cool but in no way intolerable. So, in terms of the realities of climate, it would be senseless to suggest that 80/160 = 40/80. The equation is correct in terms of arithmetic, but it relates in no way to what we know about temperature.

The most useful scale in science, therefore, is one that (a) precisely distinguishes between things that differ in magnitude, (b) has a true zero point, and (c) allows us to determine quantitatively the degrees of relationships. Such a scale is called a *ratio scale*. The most common example of this is the ruler. At "zero" on a ruler we have *no length*. Moreover, 16 inches are to 8 inches as 8 inches are to 4 inches; that is, equal ratios are equal in a meaningful way.

The above analysis will give you a good idea of how much information a scientific statement contains just by knowing what kind of scale was used. Take, for example, the following statements:

> Research has shown that many Romans are pleasant.
>
> Research has shown that Germans are taller than Pygmies.
>
> Research has shown that the temperature in Hawaii is twice as great as that in Iceland.
>
> Research has shown that turtles live twice as long as whales.

Reading the first statement, we can only ask, "What's in a name?" The second statement makes us wonder, "How much?" The third does not tell us whether either place is livable or comfortable. The fourth statement is the most informative. With this assertion, we can begin to search for *causes*.

In looking for causes, let's return to the three kinds of relationships. The first type, as we have said, is *identity*. The second is called *correlation*, and the third is termed *causal*. We can illustrate these by using simple algebra: $X = Y$. This is an identity relationship which may involve no more than naming or nominal scaling (such as, *structure X is the optic nerve*). However, this relationship may indicate an identity that has *explanatory* significance (such as, *matter equals energy*).

$X = f(Y)$; $Y = f(X)$. This is a *correlational relationship*, which states that every change in one variable (Y) is followed by a predictable change in the other (X) and vice versa. For example, this is the kind of relationship that exists between height and weight.

$X \neq f(Y)$; $Y = f(X)$. This is a *causal relationship*. Each change in one variable (X) leads to a predictable change in the other (Y)—but not vice versa. That is, the effects move in one direction in time. In causal relationships, one of the variables depends upon the magnitude of the other, and this dependency is one-way. For this reason, the variables are referred to as *dependent* and *independent*. An example of this is the time it takes for an individual to respond to a shock. The more intense the shock, the faster the response will occur. That is, reaction time depends upon shock intensity. Reaction time, therefore, is the *dependent variable,* and shock intensity is the *independent variable.* Usually, a dependent variable is influenced by many independent variables; in other words, there is *multiple causation.* In the example given above, reaction time also depends upon the attention of the subject, the location of the shock on the body, the time of day, and the degree of fatigue of the person receiving the shock. In order to determine the relationship between reaction time and intensity alone, one must control the other variables, either by eliminating them, holding them constant at known magnitudes, or reducing them to the point of being insignificant. Otherwise, results of the experiment will be too uncertain to be repeated; that is, the relationships obtained are unreliable.

Causes and Correlations

Recent reports that a surprisingly large number of criminals have abnormalities in their chromosomes have caused a stir. Some people have concluded, because of the greater-than-chance frequency of such genetic irregularities among prisoners, that criminality may be inherited. In Chapter 9, we will discuss psychological "heritability." However, for the present, it is sufficient to examine the reasoning that seems to underlie the hypothesis about prisoners presented above. The same investigators report that men who have an extra "Y" chromosome—the genetic irregularity that was discovered—are also taller than average, often have severe skin problems during adolescence and may, on the average, be less intelligent than others. Given these other qualities associated with this chromosomal abnormality, it is hard to know which are the dependent and which are the independent variables. An abnormally large boy, chided by his peers or rejected by them because of his appearance, may well come to use the only behavior guaranteed to be effective—aggression. While his peers may have neither the need nor the ability to control by force, he has both. One can conclude nothing, therefore, from correlations stated in the form, "Thirty-one percent of the men in American prisons are found to contain an extra Y chromosome." What about the sixty-nine percent with a normal chromosomal makeup? What of those who have the additional chromosome but are not in prison? What about women in prison?

Establishing causal relationships in psychology is difficult and arbitrary. Even when A always occurs in the presence of B, causation is not established. In life and in the laboratory, the unexamined correlation is an enemy of reason. It is the fuel for faulty "common sense," as well as the foundation for scientific theories that later generations come to ridicule. Science tries to guard against mere correlations by using statistical techniques, which allow the scientist to measure the reliability of the relationships he observes.

Because perfect reliability is never reached, experimental information must be analyzed statistically. All statistical methods are based on certain assumptions about the way in which variables influence results. Since statistics play an important part in psychological research, we will examine some key concepts in the statistical analysis of data.

STATISTICS

Distributions of Variables

Statistical methods save the investigator from having to conduct excessive numbers of trials. Many of the methods used are based on certain implications of the theory of probability. The application of these methods requires the satisfaction of certain assumptions about the experimental data. If the influences affecting any event are purely random, then it may be assumed that on most occasions the magnitude of the influence will be neither zero nor very much greater than zero. That is, the distribution of the values of a random variable is *normal*. Figure 3-1 is a representation of the normal (bell-shaped) distribution. This figure shows that the most frequently occurring values are centered about an average (mean) value and that larger deviations from this mean will occur with diminishing frequency.

A rough estimate of the normal distribution can be obtained by plotting the number of ways that one can get a given sum when two dice are tossed. If the dice are not biased, each face has the same chance of landing

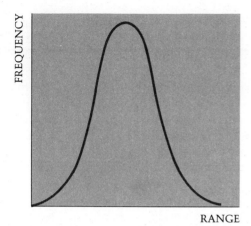

FREQUENCY

RANGE

Figure 3-1. A normal or bell-shaped distribution. Such distributions are found when the frequency of a large population with certain characteristics is graphed. For example, if the range of heights of Americans were placed along the baseline (abscissa), the overall distribution of heights would have this shape. The most frequently occurring height (the peak of the distribution) would occur at the average of the distribution; heights greater and less than this average would occur with diminishing frequency.

TABLE 1. The Number of Ways Sums of Dice Can Occur With Two Dice

Dice Tosses	Sum	Ways of Getting Sum
⚀ ⚀	2	1
⚀ ⚁ or ⚁ ⚀	3	2
⚀ ⚂ or ⚁ ⚀ or ⚂ ⚁	4	3
⚀ ⚃ or ⚃ ⚀ or ⚁ ⚂ or ⚂ ⚁	5	4
⚀ ⚄ or ⚄ ⚀ or ⚁ ⚃ or ⚃ ⚁ or ⚂ ⚂	6	5
⚀ ⚅ or ⚅ ⚀ or ⚁ ⚄ or ⚄ ⚁ or ⚂ ⚃ or ⚃ ⚂	7	6
⚁ ⚅ or ⚅ ⚁ or ⚃ ⚃ or ⚂ ⚄ or ⚄ ⚂	8	5
⚂ ⚅ or ⚅ ⚂ or ⚃ ⚄ or ⚄ ⚃	9	4
⚃ ⚅ or ⚅ ⚃ or ⚄ ⚄	10	3
⚄ ⚅ or ⚅ ⚄	11	2
⚅ ⚅	12	1

Total number of possible outcomes: 36

up as any other face. Thus, each die may show from 1 to 6 dots on any given toss. The sums that can be achieved tossing two dice range from 2 to 12. Table 1 will show you the number of ways that each of these possible sums can appear.

There are 36 possible outcomes in tossing the dice. The number of ways in which each of the possible sums can be reached is plotted in Figure 3-2. This distribution is "triangular," not nearly as smooth as that of the "normal" as shown in Figure 3-1. The normal curve, which is really a theoretical distribution, is the outcome of a *continuous variable,* that is, one that can change in infinitely small ways (for example, a change in length). With dice, the total number of changes (sums) is small and occurs one unit at a time. This is an example of a *discontinuous variable.* As the number of possible outcomes increases (for example, if three, four, five, or any number up to an infinite number of dice were tossed), a discontinuous variable will be distributed more and more like the normal distribution of Figure 3-1. An example of changes that occur with increases in the number of possible outcomes is shown in Figure 3-3. If the distribution of experi-

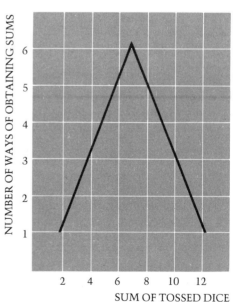

Figure 3-2. The distribution of sums obtained when two dice are tossed many times. The most likely or frequent sum is 7; the least likely, 2 and 12. Sums from 2 to 12 can occur in 36 different ways. Note that the distribution of all possible sums is triangular and not at all smooth as that shown in Fig. 3-1.

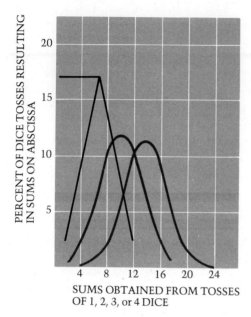

PERCENT OF DICE TOSSES RESULTING IN SUMS ON ABSCISSA

SUMS OBTAINED FROM TOSSES
OF 1, 2, 3, or 4 DICE

Figure 3-3. The distributions of sums obtained in tossing one die (sums fall from 1-6), two dice (sums fall from 2-12), three dice (sums fall from 3-18), and four dice (sums fall from 4-24). With one die, there are 6 equally likely outcomes; each sum from 1-6 will occur, on the average, 16.7 percent of the time. With 2 dice there are 36 possible sums; with 3, 216; and with 4, 1,296 possible outcomes. Note how the distributions become more normal (as in Fig. 3-1) as the number of outcomes increases. In all cases, the percentages add up to 100 percent. These percentages are, in fact, *probabilities* of occurrence that sum to 1.0 (i.e., certainty) in each distribution; for example, it is certain that the sum of any toss of two dice will be between 2 and 12.

mental data is normal, then very useful and convenient methods may be applied to analyze the information.

Measuring Probability: Levels of Significance

To begin with, the area under a distribution of values includes all possible outcomes of an experiment—or at least all the outcomes that were obtained in that experiment. In the case of tossing two dice, the distribution shown in Figure 3-2 includes in the area beneath it all the sums that can possibly be obtained in throwing dice. The probability that any value will fall somewhere within this area is designated 1.0, that is, it is certain. If the dice were thrown a great many times, the sums would be distributed exactly as shown in Figure 3-2. Not only would the sums range from 2 to 12, but they would appear with the same relative frequency as that shown in Figure 3-2. However, suppose that in a particular run of 36 tosses, we obtain the distribution shown in Figure 3-4. On inspecting the dice, we might conclude that they were biased, "weighted" to make lower sums

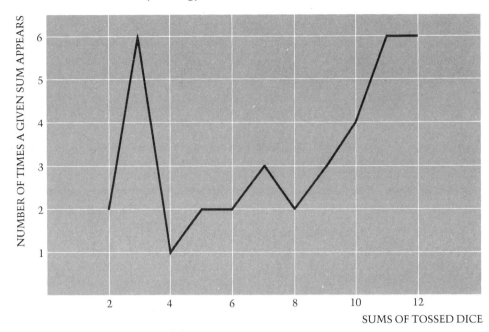

Figure 3-4. A biased distribution of sums obtained from a limited number of dice tosses. The distribution obtained when a very (infinitely) large number of tosses are made is shown in Fig. 3-2; with a small number of tosses, highly irregular distributions are possible.

more likely to appear than higher ones. However, it is also possible that, by chance, this particular run of 36 tosses resulted in an unusual distribution. Before choosing one of these alternatives, one must know what the probability is of obtaining such an odd distribution when many sets of 36 tosses are thrown. That is, one must know how frequently sets of 36 tosses will distribute themselves in the way shown in Figure 3-4. In the final analysis, any decision that the event (the distribution) was "too unlikely" or "not too unlikely" to be caused by chance will be arbitrary. Science has adopted two standards in cases like this—both strict, but one a little more liberal than the other. They are called the 1 percent and the 5 percent *levels of significance.* Briefly defined, these conventions state that an outcome will be considered to be caused by chance if chance alone would allow the outcome to occur on 1 percent (very severe) or 5 percent (less severe) of the observed occasions; that is, if the chance-probability is either 0.01 or 0.05.

Measuring Probability and Variance

Events that are normally distributed have well-defined probabilities of occurrence. The likelihood that any value will depart from the mean, or average value, decreases for values that are further and further from the mean. The spread of values around the mean (the area under the curve) divided by the total number (N) of values is called the *variance*. It is the average area filled by all the deviations (*dispersions*) of values around the central (mean) value of the distribution. As a measure of area, the variance is found by squaring the deviation of each value from the mean, adding together all of these squared deviations and then dividing this sum by the total number of cases. The equation for computing the variance is as follows:

$$V = \frac{\Sigma(x - X)^2}{N}$$

V = variance
Σ = summation
x = each individual score
X = the average or mean
N = the number of events or measurements

Scientists obtain another useful statistic by taking the square root of the variance. This measure, called the *standard deviation* (S.D.), is computed as follows:

$$\text{S.D.} = \sqrt{\frac{\Sigma(x - X)^2}{N}}$$

The *standard deviation* is a measure of variability that has certain specific properties. For the normal distribution, the probability that an outcome will have a value within +1.0 standard deviation of the mean is 0.34; that is, the frequency with which normally distributed variables fall within one S.D. of the mean is 34 percent. Another way of stating this is that 34 percent of the area under the normal curve (34 percent of the variance) is occupied by values falling within 1.0 S.D. of the mean. Figure 3-5 shows the relationship between percent variance and the number of standard deviations away from the mean. The entire variance adds up to 100 percent —which corresponds to a probability of 1.0. In other words, these percentages may be used as measures of probability.

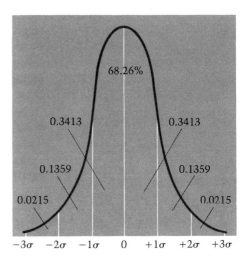

Figure 3-5. The normal probability distribution. Variables distributed normally will occur with frequencies described by this distribution. Departures from the average (indicated by "0" on the abscissa) become less likely. Values within ±1 S.D. from the mean occur 68.26 percent of the time. (After Guilford, 1956.)

When one compares sets of data obtained under different conditions and looks for the effects of the common independent variable, one must find the *degree of overlap* between the obtained distributions, or how much of the *variance* is shared.

It is important to understand that a mere difference in means is never enough to allow us to conclude that there are nonchance effects. Such differences must always be considered within the context of variance. In fact, two distributions can have identical means and still be significantly different, or they can have very different means and not be significantly different. Figure 3-6 shows conditions under which such interpretations could occur.

There are, of course, many different procedures for interpreting experimental findings statistically, but these methods are beyond the scope of an introductory study. It is sufficient that the beginning student realize that statistics are indispensable in research.

MEAN, MEDIAN, AND MODE

Can Statistics Lie?

People sometimes say that statistics can be made to tell any story one would like to hear. This is nonsense. Certain statistical methods, however,

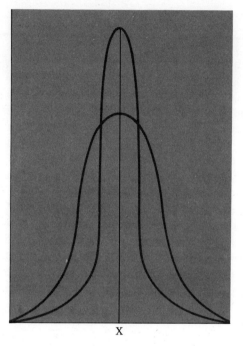

Figure 3-6. The distributions shown at the left describe outcomes with the same average value but with different variances. The curves shown at the right reflect distributions with different means but with the same variance. The shaded area on the right represents significant overlap. To determine whether two sets of observations, or measurements, come from the same statistical population, it is necessary to measure both the means and the standard deviations.

may be misapplied because they are not ideally suited to describing certain kinds of events. We can choose the average or mean as an example. Suppose a mayor declares that under his leadership average earnings in the community have increased by $3,000 in one given year. Does this mean that every family now receives $3,000 more than they did in the previous year? Or could it mean instead that the mayor has given his aides increases of $20,000, and that these raises have expanded the average by $3,000? In such a case, we should know the variance of income in the community. That is, if the mean had changed but the variance had remained the same, we would know immediately that the increase could not come from a small number of very large changes, in this case, pay raises. Even without knowing the variance, however, we could assess the mayor's claim by asking him whether the *median* income had changed and whether the *modal* income had changed. (See the discussion below for definition of median and mode.) If numbers are arranged in order, from high to low, one number, the median, will divide the distribution in half. For example, in the set of ordered numbers—(11,9,4,3,1)—the number 4 divides the set. There are two numbers that are greater and two that are less than 4. In this case, 4 is the median. If we had an even number of entries, for example—(8,7,5,3,1,0)—we would take the midpoint between the numbers in the third and fourth position, 5 and 3. Again, 4 turns out to be the median. As we can see from this example, if we were dealing with the incomes of 1,000 families and if the only real changes were in high raises to a few of these families, the median would not change much at all. That is, the salaries toward the middle of the distribution would remain unchanged; only those at the top would show a significant increase. While the median identifies the midpoint of a distribution, the mode identifies the value that occurs most frequently in a distribution. For example, in the set—(8,7,7,9,7,13)—the mode is 7. In the example of the mayor's community, the *modal* value of incomes, the level of earnings that most people receive, may not have changed either.

Common Relationships and a Typical Experiment

Most of the relationships discovered in psychological research fit into a small number of basic types. These tend to be mathematically simple, so that they can be represented without using very complicated equations. We have already noted one type, the *normal distribution* (which has a complex equation). It describes a relationship that occurs frequently in science. If you were to plot the frequency with which heights occur in an adult population on a scale of height expressed in inches, the normal distribution will be yielded. We can say, then, that the frequency-distribution of height is a normally distributed function of height—the labored way of saying "height is normally distributed." Other commonly observed relationships are those designated as the linear, logarithmic, and exponential, which are named after the equations that describe them.

We can illustrate the topics covered so far by describing an experiment. Here we want to find out, using three different strains of rats, the effects of rewarded practice on the number of errors made in a maze. We will run ten rats from each of the three breeds. Every rat will be run at the same time of day after the same number of hours after its last feeding. Each will receive the same amount of reward at the end of the maze. The [hypothetical] results are shown below on a graph that plots the independent variable (the number of rewarded trials) and the dependent variable (number of errors). We call the different strains of rats the *parameters* of the problem. Thus, the title of our experiment will be: "The Effects of Rewarded Practice on Maze-Learning by Rats with Strain as a Parameter." Our experiment reveals that practice has very sudden effects on the performance of Strain A, very gradual effects on the performance of Strain B, and almost no effect on the performance of Strain C (see Figure 3-7).

ORIGINS AND DEVELOPMENT OF EXPERIMENTALISM

The preceding survey has introduced you to a number of new terms and methods. The impression that you received surely fits what most people consider psychology to be. After all, people will say, what *could* it be but

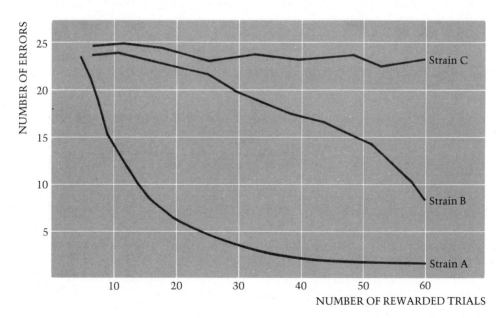

Figure 3-7. Hypothetical data indicating genetic factors in the acquisition of behavior.

an experimental investigation of the variables that are responsible for perception, learning, and the other psychological subjects of inquiry.

But when people learn that the first laboratory devoted to psychological research alone was not established until 1879, they may be surprised. After all, Archimedes did experiments thousands of years ago. Galileo and his followers were busy with research in the seventeenth century. Why did those interested in psychological issues set out to investigate them experimentally only a hundred years ago? Why was it that scholars did not accept the possibility of a valid *experimental psychology* until the middle of the nineteenth century? What allowed nineteenth-century philosophers to adopt this new perspective? We must look back to the sixteenth century for the answer. Renaissance science had a significant effect on sixteenth- and seventeenth-century philosophy. Aristotle, as we noted in the last chapter, made science submit to logic. As the Renaissance undermined Aristotle's scientific pronouncements, one of the consequences was a critical reevaluation of Greek philosophy in general. Some of the skeptics tried only to reconcile newly discovered facts to the old dogmas. But to others, a complete break with ancient ties seemed essential. Of these, one of the most important was Francis Bacon (1561-1626). He wrote in his major work, *Novum Organum:*

> For while men are occupied in admiring and applauding the false powers of the mind, they can pass by and throw away those true powers, which, if it be supplied with the proper aids and can itself be content to wait upon nature instead of vainly affecting to overrule her, are within its reach. There was but one course left, therefore,—to try the whole thing anew upon a better plan, and to commence a total reconstruction of sciences, arts and all human knowledge, raised upon the proper foundations. (Bacon, *Novum Organum*)

To Bacon, the "proper foundations" were those of observation and experimentation, which would bring about a knowledge of general laws through the steady accumulation of facts. Bacon was an early spokesman for England's empirical philosophy, and the first great spokesman for the modern *inductive* method of science. Scornful of the *rationalism* passed on by Thomas Aquinas from Aristotle, Bacon pushed knowledge closer to sensation and further away from opinion. "I leave to the syllogism and these famous and boasted modes of demonstration their jurisdiction over popular arts and such as are matter of opinion . . . in dealing with the nature of things I use induction throughout. . . ." His form of reasoning, however, was not the kind of clever combining of "self-evident" truths that adds up to a new insight. Instead, Bacon insisted on "a form of induction which shall analyze experience and take it to pieces. . . ." By "experience" he meant not a mental process, but a sense-event—an observation common to all who look or listen or touch. He realized, however, that the senses can distort or fail to detect reality. Therefore, the senses need "helps," the most important of which were *experiments*. In other words, Bacon proposed the method of *controlled observation* as the route to truth: "the office of the sense shall be only to judge of the experiment, and that the experiment itself shall judge of the thing."

Two of Bacon's younger contemporaries, Kepler and Galileo, published their influential works before Bacon's *Novum Organum* (1620). Bacon's *The Advancement of Learning* (1605) predated not only Kepler's first two *Laws* (1609), but also Galileo's open acceptance of the Copernican theory (1613), which was already 90 years old when *Novum Organum* was written. These dates are important in that they show that the revolutions in sixteenth-century science and philosophy occurred independently, yet during the same period of time. Bacon was not inspired by Galileo's successful observations, nor was Galileo spurred to observe the heavens as a result of reading the *Novum Organum*. Both men, along with Kepler, were products of the Copernican revolution. Bacon's revolt was more against scholastic philosophy than against astronomy. This is because scholasticism was emphasized more in England and astronomy more so on the European continent.

Bacon's *Aphorisms* listed the problems to be solved before science could advance. First, he wrote, science must distinguish "between certain empty dogmas, and the true signatures and marks set upon the works of creation as they are found in nature." The dogmas arose from the "wits." Bacon points to their limitations and distortions:

> The human understanding is of its own nature prone to suppose the existence of more order and regularity in the world than it finds. . . . Hence the fiction that all celestial bodies move in perfect circles; . . .
>
> The human understanding is unquiet; it cannot stop or rest, . . . Therefore it is that we cannot conceive of any end or limit to

the world; . . . this inability (to stop) interferes more mischievously in the discovery of causes: for although the most general principles in nature ought to be held merely positive, as they are discovered, and cannot with truth be referred to a cause; nevertheless the human understanding . . . still seeks something prior in the order of nature.

But by far the greatest obstacle to the progress of science . . . is found in this—that men despair and think things impossible.

Finally, he anticipated the hatred that society would show toward Freud: "And for things that are mean or even filthy . . . whatever deserves to exist deserves also to be known. . . ."

Bacon did not directly influence his contemporaries in their scientific research. William Harvey (1578-1657) was Bacon's physician after the *Novum Organum* had been published, but it is difficult to say that Harvey's research on the circulation of blood was inspired, in any way, by the system Bacon had developed. Much later, Robert Boyle (1627-1691) would acknowledge Bacon's influence on the research methods he used in his study of the gas laws. Bacon's most important contribution, however, was to establish a mode of thought at Cambridge, which spread to Oxford, and which made possible the ultimate victory of English empiricism at these English universities. He launched the empiricism that was developed further by Thomas Hobbes and taken to its height by John Locke.

In addition to the change in attitudes caused by Bacon and his followers, the nineteenth-century scientist could look back to Copernicus, Kepler, Galileo, and Newton and be encouraged by their brilliant achievements. By 1800 scientists believed without doubt that the universe ultimately would be completely understood. Moreover, since the time of Descartes, the science of physiology—especially neurophysiology—had grown. This development seemed to mark the end of many cherished beliefs. One example is the idea that the soul has an instantaneous effect on the body. Philosophers in the tradition of Plato and Kant had argued that the action of the soul, since it was inspired by God, occurred equally and instantly throughout the entire body. This concept was such a "received truth" that in the great Johannes Müller's *Handbook of Human Physiology* (1834), the author asserted that without question nervous transmission is too rapid to be measured. Within a few years, Müller's own student, Hermann von Helmholtz, not only measured nervous conduction, but found that it was surprisingly slow—moving only at the rate of 80 miles per hour. A century earlier, Galvani had discovered the electrical basis of Descartes' "animal spirits." Clinical neurologists had collected overwhelming evidence to support the view that the mind and the brain were the same—and brain was something that could actually be touched. In other words, while philosophy still seemed tied to the same ancient issues, such as the concern with the "mind," science in the nineteenth century promised progress. No problem seemed to be beyond the range of science, no question beyond its methods.

In this age of scientific optimism, the French philosopher Auguste Comte (1798-1857) offered a "positive" philosophy, soon to be labeled *positivism*. It was Comte who actually coined the term *sociology*, which represents the "science of society." He expressed the spirit of his time with a declaration that has often been called his "Law of the Three Stages":

> From the study of the development of human intelligence, in all directions, and through all times, the discovery arises of a great fundamental law. . . . The law is this: that each of our leading conceptions—each branch of our knowledge—passes successively through three different theoretical conditions: the Theological, or fictitious; the Metaphysical or abstract; and the Scientific or positive. . . . In the theological state, the human mind . . . supposes all phenomena to be produced by the immediate action of supernatural beings. In the Metaphysical state . . . the mind supposes . . . abstract forces. . . . In the final, the positive state, the mind has given over the vain search after Absolute notions, the origin and destination of the universe, and the causes of phenomena, and applies itself to the study of their laws. . . . What is now understood when we speak of an explanation of facts is simply the establishment of a connection between single phenomena and some general facts, the number of which continually diminishes with the progress of science. (Comte, *The Positive Philosophy*)

We can sense the optimism of this period even more strongly by looking at the "laws" of thinking that the English philosopher John Stuart Mill set forth in his *System of Logic* (1843). The book was written by Mill when he was just in his thirties; the vigor of youth is thus more apparent in it than the thoughtfulness he showed later in his famous essay *On Liberty* (1859).

In *System of Logic*, Mill sets forth those rules by which experimental science can discover objective truth. He is clearly uneasy in the shadow of David Hume's skepticism, which tells us that no matter how often B has followed A in the past, there is no *logical* reason to assume that B will follow A again. Mill is uneasy for two reasons. First, he cannot deny successfully Hume's argument—nor can we. Second, as an empiricist, Mill had to demonstrate that all our knowledge, especially our scientific knowledge, is based on *induction*. *Deductive* knowledge, favored by the idealists, takes the form of "spontaneous insights"—for example, Pythagoras' theorem or Newton's gravitational law. By using deductive reasoning, we will discover the general principle that unifies varied events with a concept. Mill, as an empiricist, had to show that what appeared to be deductions were generalizations derived from experience, not creations of the mind. The *System of Logic* fails to prove this, but his arguments are among the most persuasive ones on this issue.

After proving to his satisfaction that induction—predictions or generalizations based on past experience—is the essential, if not the only, form of knowledge, Mill lays down the laws of inductive science. The laws are given in the form of *methods*. Some examples of these methods are discussed below.

The Method of Agreement. This law concerns what we have already noted as *consistency*. If a scientist thinks he has shown that A causes B, then every occurrence of A should produce B. The identical operations should produce identical results. Where several results follow from several previous events, Mill's method of agreement is intended to show which event causes which effect. Thus, if A,B,C are always followed by a,b,c, and if A,B causes a,b, then, C must be the cause of c.

The Method of Difference. Suppose that whenever A,B,C, and D are present, a,b,c, and d are also present. We then introduce F,G,L, and V and observe that a,b,c, and d persist. That is, adding F,G,L, and V resulted in no difference. However, we now introduce E, and e occurs. We can now conclude that the difference between a,b,c,d and a,b,c,d,e was caused by E and not by the other factors (F,G,L, or V).

Method of Residues. If we find that A,B,C,D result in a,b,c,d, and we discover further that A,B,C causes a,b,c, then we can conclude that D causes d.

Method of Concomitant Variation. Though this method is similar to Mill's other methods, this one has the added requirement—a quantitative change in one variable must produce a change in another variable that is similar in amount, direction, and in the time of occurrence. Thus, if ABC causes abc, *and* AB(2 × c) causes ab(2 × c), then C causes c.

In one form or another, every experiment is ultimately based on one or more of these methods. One experimenter, for example, might use the method of difference. He first instructs an observer to press a button as soon as a light is shown. Everything is done to keep the environment *constant*. Background light and noise, the alertness of the observer, his distance from the light, the color of the light, the mechanical resistance of the button—these are just a few of the factors that must be controlled. When they are, the experimenter finds that the time it takes for the observer to react remains very similar on each of many repeated trials. Now, suppose the experimenter varies only one factor: the intensity of the light that is shown. It is found that responses are reliably faster at the brightest intensities and reliably slower at the dimmest. In other words, the *differences* in reaction time are due to brightness.

One of the most intriguing discoveries in astronomy was made through using the method of residues. Kepler's laws of planetary motion and Newton's gravitational laws had been proven correct by many careful observations. There was, however, one exception. The planet Uranus deviated ever so slightly from the path and the speed predicted for it by Kepler's and Newton's laws. There was, in other words, a *residual* effect—something left over when all the theoretical calculations had been made. According to the law of residues, there had to be some *cause* for the deviation. Astronomers predicted that another planet that had not been detected was influencing Uranus. After painstaking calculations, mathematicians and astronomers decided where this hypothetical planet must lie. As a result of their efforts, the planet Neptune was discovered.

You now have some sense of the major philosophical issues that underlie modern psychology and of the experimental method and outlook that are applied to contemporary psychological scholarship.

SUMMARY

In this chapter, we have examined the general nature of experimental science and have shown how it differs from mere observation. Experiments are undertaken in order to discover functional relationships between variables. The type of relationship that science explores is the *cause*. Using statistical analysis, such relationships can be tested to determine their reliability. It should be noted that the guidelines for experiments were set forth by John Stuart Mill, whose *methods* still regulate the way in which research is done.

The first three chapters have served as an introduction to the *foundations* of modern psychology. That is because they have provided a definition of the subject, a review of the timeless issues to which the discipline of modern psychology has been devoted, and an examination of the experimental methods that have been applied to these issues. We will now examine some basic mechanisms and processes that we must understand before our knowledge of human psychology can advance beyond mere speculation. In the next chapter, we will review *neuropsychology*, a specialized branch of psychology that explores the *biological* foundations of psychological processes.

SUGGESTED READINGS

BEVERIDGE, W. B. *The Art of Scientific Investigation*. New York: Random House, 1957.

This is a nontechnical summary of some of the formal properties and intuitive elements of scientific inquiry. Professor Beveridge takes recourse frequently to biographical material drawn from the lives of great scientists. In successive chapters, he elucidates the role of intuition, reason, and strategy, and the conduct of experimental work.

PLUTCHIK, R. *Foundations of Experimental Research*. New York: Harper & Row, 1968.

This is an excellent introduction to experimental design and basic statistics. Professor Plutchik draws his examples from a wide variety of psychological settings. His coverage of psychophysics and the nature of measurement in general is clear and thorough.

Human Psychology: The Universal Elements

CHAPTER

4

Neuropsychology: An Overview

HISTORICAL SKETCH

Aristotle classified the faculties of the soul as "the nutritive, the desiring, the perceptive, the locomotive, and the thinking power." It was chiefly through the seventeenth-century philosophy of René Descartes that the *soul* and the *mind* were considered in biological terms. Descartes applied the Copernican model, which viewed the universe as a mechanism, to the behavior of biological systems. He theorized that there were forces that infiltrated the muscles, thereby causing them to move. These forces, or *animal spirits,* were controlled within the brain and released in amounts and directed to the muscles according to the nature of the incoming stimuli. Descartes suggested that the *pineal gland,* located in the center of the brain, was the valve that controlled the flow of these spirits. Following his religious principles, he said that the soul controlled the pineal gland itself. To Descartes, only the soul distinguished man's behavior from that of animals or, for that matter, from that of inanimate machines.

The empirical philosophers had argued that all knowledge was a result of sense perception. Descartes' psychological theory held that behavior was merely the outcome of physical forces set in motion by such sensory events. The empiricists had set forth a process by which perception worked—the formation of associations by repetition and contiguity. What was needed was a mechanism that would connect perception with behavior. Descartes' mechanisms, however, did not serve. His animal spirits could not be tested experimentally. The issue, for the most part, remained a philosophical one until 1786, when Luigi Galvani (an eighteenth-century Italian physiologist) observed that an *electrical* stimulus applied to the leg of a frog resulted in contractions of the leg muscles. With that observation, neurophysiology (that branch of physiology dealing with the nervous system) was born.

In the years that followed Galvani's discovery, there was a great controversy over why the frog's leg twitched. Galvani thought his observations indicated that there was animal electricity, much as Franz Mesmer in 1766 had thought that the hypnotic trance came from a flow of animal magnetism from him to his patients. In a particularly ingenious experiment, Galvani suspended a frog's leg by draping its sciatic nerve over a brass hook. When the frog's foot touched a strip of silver, the leg was found to kick repeatedly. Each kick broke the electrical circuit between the leg and the silver strip by breaking the contact between the two and thus ending the stimulus. When the stimulus was removed, the leg dropped back down, so that the foot again touched the silver strip, thereby closing the circuit and causing stimulation.

The assumption that animal electricity existed was somewhat shaken by the physicist Alessandro Volta's invention of an electric cell—a pile of silver and zinc plates separated from each other by wet cardboard sheets. This Voltaic pile, built in 1800, produced electricity using only inorganic elements and thus caused suspicion about Galvani's theory. From Volta's point of view, Galvani's frog was simply a poor substitute for wet cardboard! Nevertheless, many physiologists still held to the idea that living tissue, indeed, produced electricity. By Galvani's time, anatomists had charted the largest nerve pathways joining the brain to the parts of the body. Descartes' materialistic and mechanistic form of biology required such a system of nerves. And it was reasonable to think that animal electricity was the mechanism that made the system function. For a time, this electricity was almost as hard to pin down as the animal spirits of Descartes. However, soon after Volta's discovery, a means of measuring direct currents was invented. In 1841, using such a new galvanometer, the physicist Carlo Matteucci reported the current of rest in animals. He observed that current flowed between the surface of a muscle and a region deep inside it, even when the muscle was at rest. This finding led directly to a *polarization* theory of tissue-generated electricity, advanced by the German physiologist Julius Bernstein in 1866. Many of the essentials of his theory have not been altered significantly. What follows is a discussion of the modern version of neural activity based on the original ideas of Bernstein, with some important additions.

MECHANISMS OF NEURAL ACTIVITY

The Neural Impulse

Figure 4-1 is a schematic drawing of the basic unit of the nervous system —the neuron. Structurally, it consists of tentacle-like *dendrites*, which connect with the body or *soma* of the cell. A filament-like axon extends from the soma toward the dendrites of another nerve cell. Like other cells in the body, the neuron (the nerve cell) is composed of a combination of organic and inorganic substances. Unlike other cells, however, the neuron responds to stimulation in such a way as to provide the organism, man included, with all of the information it will ever have.

The normal course of information flow in the neuron is from the dendrites to the soma to the axon. The neuron itself is electrically "charged," or polarized, at all times, whether stimulated or not. This charge results from differences between the electrical properties of the axoplasm and those of the environment outside of the axon. That is, there is a difference in electric *potential* between the material contained within the neural membrane and the material outside of the membrane. This ever-present charge in the unstimulated state is called the *resting membrane potential.*

While there are many substances in the axoplasm (see Figure 4-2) and in the surrounding medium, those chiefly responsible for the resting potential are sodium (Na^+), potassium (K^+), chlorine (Cl^-), and certain negatively charged proteins. The ($+$) and ($-$) signs indicate that the elements exist as *ions*. That is, they are electrically charged as a result of an excess

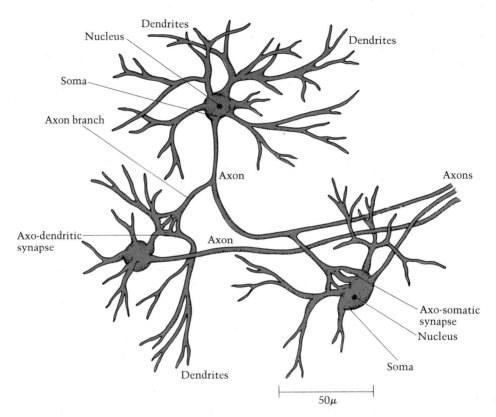

Figure 4-1. Interconnecting neurons. Shown are the cell body or *soma*, the *axons* and *dendrites*, and the synaptic space (*axodendritic synapse*). Size is indicated by a 50-micron (50 millionths of a meter) calibration mark. (After Milner, 1970.)

(negative charge) or a deficiency (positive charge) of electrons in their atomic structure. If the elements were combined into molecules, they would be electrically neutral salts, such as NaCl (sodium chloride) and KCl (potassium chloride), in which each (−) charge would be balanced (neutralized) by each (+) charge. If these major components were bonded into molecules, neurons would have no resting potential. Figure 4-2 shows that, within the composition of the axoplasm, there is an abundance of K^+ relative to the K^+ that is outside of the membrane. The medium outside the membrane has more NA^+ than the axoplasm itself. The smaller

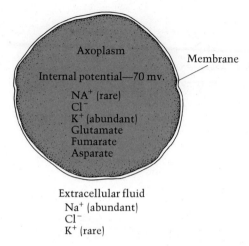

Axoplasm

Internal potential—70 mv.

NA+ (rare)
Cl−
K+ (abundant)
Glutamate
Fumarate
Asparate

Membrane

Extracellular fluid
Na+ (abundant)
Cl−
K+ (rare)

Figure 4-2. Concentrations of major ions within the cytoplasm and in the fluids outside the axon. Within the axoplasm, potassium ions (K^+) are in abundance and sodium ions (Na^+) are relatively rare. In the surrounding (extracellular) fluid, there is a high concentration of sodium and relatively little potassium. The large negatively charged protein ions cannot pass through the membrane; during rest, the membrane is relatively impermeable to sodium. Thus, the unequal distribution of ionic charges across the membrane leads to a potential difference of −70 millivolts on the inside relative to the outside.

ions (NA^+, K^+, Cl^-) distribute themselves unequally because the large proteins cannot pass through the membrane. The overall excess of Na^+ ions covering the outer surface of the membrane and the relatively high concentration of large, negatively charged proteins inside the axoplasm produce a resting potential of the membrane surface that is *positive* with respect to the axoplasm underneath (see Figure 4-3). The value of this difference in charge (electric potential) in the resting state is usually seventy-thousandths of a volt, or 70 millivolts (mv). If there were no large protein molecules in the axoplasm, K^+, Na^+, and Cl^- concentrations would quickly establish an equilibrium, or balance of charges, by diffusing through the membrane. But because the membrane will not allow the proteins to migrate outward, nor allow the Na^+ ions in the surrounding medium to migrate into the axoplasm, an equilibrium is never established. However, when the nerve is stimulated, *membrane permeability* is altered, and Na^+ ions rush in. This influx of positively charged ions makes the axoplasm more positive. As the sodium enters the axoplasm, it displaces potassium into the medium outside the membrane. However, after stimulation, the membrane is still permeable to potassium, which now reenters the axoplasm. The sodium is thereby "pumped" out, thus restoring the resting potential. It is possible to measure the time it takes for these changes in electrical potential to occur, beginning with the onset of stimulation. In Figure 4-3, such a measurement is shown graphically.

Actually, at the point of maximum change, the charge becomes slightly

Figure 4-3. After the application of a stimulus, the resting membrane potential is altered. Membrane permeability to sodium increases rapidly. As the Na$^+$ ions rush in, the axoplasm becomes more and more positive. At the peak of sodium conductance, the membrane potential reaches values of about +50 millivolts, an overall change of 120 millivolts relative to the −70 millivolts resting level. Soon (1/2-1 millisecond), conductance to sodium becomes zero and sodium is actually pumped out of the axoplasm. The membrane potential proceeds in a negative direction again, actually overshooting the resting level. This overshoot is occurring because sodium is being expelled faster than potassium is being returned. Thus, for a short time, until the positively charged K returns, the axoplasm is more negative than during rest.

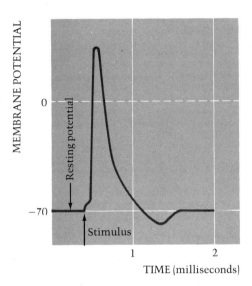

positive, finally returning to the resting level. This series of events, from rest to response to return to rest, is called the *neural impulse*. It is one letter of the alphabet with which life's experiences are written.

Several key terms are used to describe the neural impulse. Since the resting potential is caused by a polarization of + and − charges across the membrane, the neural impulse is described as the result of *depolarization*. If something happened to increase Cl$^-$ concentration within the axon or the Na$^+$ concentration outside the membrane, the neuron would be in a state of *hyperpolarization*. We should note that a stimulus must have a certain strength to produce an impulse. That is, the neuron has a *threshold* (or lower limit) that must be exceeded. Furthermore, a short period of time always passes between the application of a stimulus and the response of the neuron. This is called the *response latency*. After the neural response has passed, there is a short period of time during which the neuron will not respond to further stimulation no matter how intense it may be. This interval is called the *absolute refractory period*. Slightly later, a neural response can take place if the stimulus is strong enough. This interval is called the *relative refractory period*. During the absolute refractory period, the neuron's response threshold is infinitely high. During the relative refractory period, the threshold is high, but stimuli of very great intensity will initiate impulses.

The neural impulse occurs either at full strength or not at all. This is called the *all-or-none law* of neural conduction. Once it has started, the impulse travels the whole length of the axon at full strength. Each section of the axon excites the section after it so that the impulse moves in much the same way as a flame does down the wick of a candle.

Saltatory Conduction

Many axons have a fatty covering called the *myelin sheath,* which serves as an electrical insulator. This myelin jacket breaks at each millimeter along the axon. At these breaks (*the nodes of Ranvier*), the axon membrane is bare. It is at these nodes (Figure 4-4) that potassium and sodium exchange can occur across the axon membrane. Between the nodes of Ranvier, this exchange is impossible. The myelin acts as an electrochemical barrier. Thus, electrical conduction along myelinated fibers is like water running through a hose that had pinholes at fixed distances along its length. With slow-motion photography, you can see a sequence of springs rising at fixed intervals along the hose. In conduction in myelinated axons, the all-or-none impulse is recreated at each node of Ranvier. Between the nodes, the axon's surface (the fatty myelin surface) is electrically inactive. This kind of node-to-node conduction is called *saltatory* (from the Latin, *saltare,* meaning to skip). Saltatory conduction is far more rapid than conduction in axons without myelin sheaths.

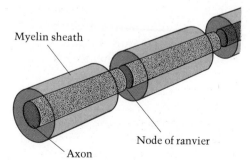

Myelin sheath

Axon

Node of ranvier

Figure 4-4. Myelin covering the axon. At each millimeter, the myelin is interrupted, exposing the underlying axon membrane. The interruptions are referred to as *nodes of Ranvier.*

Graded Conduction

The all-or-none law of neural impulses applies to axons (fibers). A different type of transmission occurs in dendrites. There, electrical fields are generated, again each one exciting a neighboring region. But, the strength of this activity diminishes as it spreads. That is, conduction is *decremental*. Moreover, the strength of the neural activity here depends upon the strength of the applied signal. A weak stimulus will elicit a weak electrical response; a stronger stimulus, a stronger response. Such responses are called *graded*. Contrary to the all-or-none binary properties of the neural impulse, this activity has an analog (or continuous-change) nature.

Neural Transmission

The ultimate destination of neural events, if they are to be used in perception and behavior, is the central nervous system (CNS), which consists of the brain and the spinal cord. In the journey from sense organs around the body to the CNS and from the CNS to the muscles and glands, neural information passes along many separate neurons. Though this information must be transferred from one neuron to the next, the neurons do not actually make physical contact with each other. That is, the end branches of one neuron do not touch the receiving dendrites of the next. The space between the two is called the *synapse* or *synaptic space*. The transfer of activity from one neuron to the next thus requires a chemical substance that will make the connection. Such substances are called *transmitters*. The terminal branches of each axon contain small pockets, or *vesicles*, which secrete transmitter substances into synapse. The transmitter moves across the synaptic space and depolarizes the dendritic branches on the other side. These respond in a gradual, graded fashion. Once enough depolarization has occurred, impulse activity begins in the axons connected with these dendrites.

There are probably several types of transmitter substances, but the neurochemistry of the synapse remains obscure. At *neuromuscular* junctions—where axons meet at a synapse with muscle fibers—the transmitter is *acetylcholine* (ACh). Certain post-synaptic effects are inhibitory, or hyperpolarizing, in that they raise the threshold of post-synaptic dendritic or post-synaptic membranes. Thus, there are *excitatory post-synaptic potentials* (EPSP's) and *inhibitory post-synaptic potentials* (IPSP's). Their mechanisms are still not fully understood.

If signals are to be controlled, there must be a mechanism that can stop transmission across the synapse even after it has started. Again, the mechanism is a chemical one, in this case involving enzymes, substances that aid chemical reactions in the body. At the neuromuscular synapse, secretions of the enzyme *acetylcholinesterase* (AChE) break down, or neutralize, acetylcholine and thus make the synapse silent with respect to signal processing. When the AChE is reabsorbed, the synapse will once again be ready for stimulation.

In view of the discussion above, the nervous system can be defined as a complex electrical network whose principal function is to allow *chemical* events to occur rapidly over great distances. The neural impulse supplies the energy needed for secreting and reconstituting chemical substances. These then form more or less permanent chemical codes. Each dendritic branch and each soma is almost enclosed in a web of axonal terminations. Each synapse may contain any one of many chemical transmitters whose effects may be excitatory or inhibitory. Thus, an enormous number of possible outcomes can await even the simple linkage of two neurons. If one considers the combination of both graded (dendritic) and all-or-none (axonal) activity, the incredible number (multiple billions) of functional units in the system, and the different states of activity each unit may be in when stimulation occurs, one comes to respect the awesome capabilities of the nervous system.

NEURAL ORGANIZATION

Despite the incredible number and variety of neural units, the nervous system is well organized structurally. The system as a whole can be divided into a small number of subsystems. We can make these classifications in terms of localization, function, the types of neurons, the organs of origin or destination, and so forth. Each of these methods of classification gives us insight into the nature of the nervous system. Perhaps the most convenient method is the one based on the overall functional characteristics of the various structures.

Functional Neuroanatomy

The major functions of the nervous system include (a) sensing environmental changes, (b) associating these changes with information already stored, and (c) initiating appropriate responses to environmental conditions. The word *environmental* refers to events occurring both within and around the organism. Broadly speaking, the functions of the nervous system are those of *detection, discrimination, association, action, feedback,* and *storage.*

Sensory, or *afferent*, fibers bring information to the central nervous system (CNS). Impulses from the CNS are sent to the muscles and glands of the body through motor, or *efferent*, fibers. All of the afferent and efferent units that are not part of the CNS make up the *peripheral nervous system* (PNS). That part of the PNS that acts mainly on smooth muscle (in the heart, the viscera, and the blood vessels) and on the glands (especially the endocrine glands) is called the *autonomic nervous system* (ANS). Because the ANS plays a unique role in emotion, it will not be considered until Chapter 11.

Afferent and efferent information flow is brought about by large collections of fibers (axons) and cell bodies of neurons. In the CNS, the paths formed by these collections of parallel fibers are called *tracts.* Tracts end on groups of cell bodies that, in the CNS, are called *nuclei.* The fiber bundles in the PNS are called nerves, and the peripheral bundles of cell-bodies are called *ganglia* (the plural of ganglion). Thus, the pathways of the entire nervous system involve tracts in the CNS and nerves in the PNS that connect with various nuclei (CNS) and ganglia (PNS). Since most tracts and nerves consist of myelinated fibers, regions in which these structures are numerous are white (myelin is a whitish, fatty substance). Nuclei and ganglia, which are composed of cell bodies, lend a gray cast to those regions where they are common. Thus, the gray matter and white matter of the CNS show the abundance of nuclei and tracts respectively.

The Bell-Magendie Law

In the materialist tradition founded by Descartes, scientists struggled to uncover the working parts of the human machine. In the years that followed Galvani's discovery, extensive neuronatomic studies were made. Independently, both Sir Charles Bell (in 1811) and François Magendie (in 1822) showed that sensory and motor functions occurred through completely separate structures in the spinal cord. The Bell-Magendie Law, based on dissections of spinal nerves, declared that all sensory information enters the cord on its *dorsal*, or back, surface while all motor signals exit from the cord's ventral, or front, surface.

The dorsal roots swell before entering the spinal cord. This "bulge" exists because those cell bodies that receive information from afferent fibers are grouped outside of the cord. These groups of peripheral cell bodies are referred to as the *dorsal root ganglia*. In Figure 4-5, you will see the relationship between signals coming in to the dorsal roots and those exiting from the ventral roots.

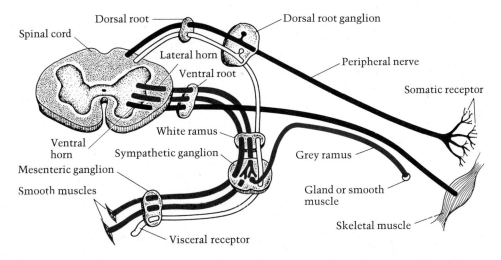

Figure 4-5. Sensory and motor roots of the spinal cord. Impulses from the periphery enter the cord on its dorsal surface while signals from the brain exit from the cord on its ventral surface and proceed to muscles and glands. The cell bodies of the dorsal root are placed outside the cord and give rise to a bulge, or swelling, called the *dorsal root ganglion*. Sensory nerves deliver signals to the cord. Within, these impulses can initiate activity in spinal motor neurons by way of internuncial connections. This is the basic mechanism for spinal reflexes. Other impulses are passed up to the brain through ascending spinal pathways. Commands from the brain which pass down the cord exist at various levels and initiate activity in muscles and glands.

The Nativistic Bias of Neuropsychology

Physiological psychology, an invention of the nineteenth century, began with a strong nativistic bias. This orientation had four principal sources. One was the Bell-Magendie Law, described above, which supported the argument that sensation and action were preplanned, at least in their anatomical design. This law did not try to uphold the formal, philosophical doctrine of inborn ideas, but it did make it easier for scientists to think in nativistic terms.

The three other sources of nativistic bias were (a) the concept of the *reflex arc*, (b) the *Law of Specific Nerve Energies*, and (c) the theory of *localization of function* in the cerebral cortex. Each of these ideas will be discussed briefly in the following sections. Collectively, they encouraged scientists to view the nervous system as an elaborate, wired system that confronts the environment in a specific and relatively unchangeable way. Along with Darwin's theory of natural selection, these four principles produced a climate of nativism in which certain theories would go unchallenged—theories of instinct and "race," and even modern concepts of the inevitable power of biological forces. In ancient times, people were thought to be the way they were because of the fates. The nineteenth century considered people to be mere products of their neurological fate. It is not surprising that Freud, whose theories we will examine in Chapter 10, would proclaim that "anatomy is destiny."

The Reflex Arc

By 1850, investigators were refining the mechanistic Cartesian model and were replacing philosophic conjecture with experimental observation. One of the most outstanding of these early neurophysiologists, Marshall Hall, observed that "if, in the decapitated trunk of . . . animals, we irritate a toe or other part of the foot . . . this extremity is immediately withdrawn" (Herrnstein and Boring, p. 303). Hall undertook many studies of the "spinal system," all of which pointed to this *reflex action* of the spinal cord. By stimulating a peripheral afferent nerve, one could stimulate the action of the efferent nerve that supplied the same region of the body. The anatomical basis of the *reflex arc* is graphically shown in Figure 4-6.

The axonal branch of the dorsal root has a synapse with a ventral (efferent) neuron at the same spinal level. Exciting this ventral, or motor,

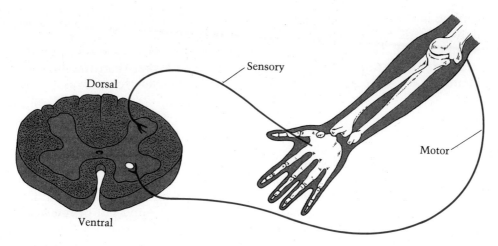

Figure 4-6. Schematic illustration of spinal reflex mechanism. Impulses from the left hand are delivered to the sensory root of the spinal cord. An internuncial neuron brings these signals, initiated by a painful stimulus, to motor fibers at the same level in the cord. The motor outflow results in withdrawal of the limb. The brain is not necessary for these reflexes.

neuron leads to the withdrawal of the limb. The dorsal-ventral connection is made by an internuncial neuron—one that links sensory and motor neurons—within the cord. Hall's work demonstrated that many reflexes were handled completely at the level of the spinal cord. Since they still occurred in a decapitated animal, the brain was not involved. Such reflexes are called *spinal* reflexes. Others, however, do involve the CNS, especially those that help maintain posture and balance.

The Law of Specific Nerve Energies

One of the great physiologists of the early nineteenth century was Johannes Müller. He summarized in his *Handbook of Human Physiology* many of the facts known in his time about neurophysiology. As a good Kantian, Müller tried to incorporate these findings into a nativistic context. His efforts are embodied in the Law of Specific Nerve Energies. It states that the experiences that result from stimulation do not depend on the physical properties of the stimulus, but on the specific nerves that are stimulated. Each nerve contains the potential (the energy) for a specific conscious experience. Thus, if the optic nerve is stimulated (whether by light, electric shock, heat, or any other means), the resulting experience will be visual. This law which has remained substantially valid, supports the Platonic–Kantian emphasis on the perceiver, rather than the environment, as the source of experience. Man "sees" what his nerves report.

Localization of Functions

Just as each nerve seemed to contain the energy for a particular sensation, many early nineteenth-century scientists viewed each of the major regions of the brain as the source of specific psychological functions. The Greek physician Galen (ca. 150 A.D.) had taken the mind out of the heart (where many ancients had located it) and placed it in the brain. Descartes treated the brain as the principal organ of cognition and behavior—the hydraulic system through which the vital spirits rushed and pushed the fluids of experience and action. The more materialistically-oriented English and Scottish empiricists also speculated on where the conscious faculties (perception, reason, judgment, and memory) resided in the brain. Apparently, sufficient clinical and experimental evidence was available by 1825 for the anatomist Franz Joseph Gall to declare that ". . . the different regions of the brain are devoted to different classes of functions; and that finally, the brain of each species of animal, man included, is formed by the union of as many particular organs, as there are essentially distinct moral qualities and intellectual faculties." From his Kantian perspective, Gall thought that moral qualities and intellectual qualities were innate and that the amount of these qualities was proportional to the size of the brain mass associated with them. So inspired, Gall declared that by carefully feeling the bumps and valleys of the skull, one could judge the relative amounts of morals and faculties present in the individual. His influence created the science of *phrenology*, which sought to identify psychological strengths and weaknesses in people by feeling the skull! (See Figure 4-7).

Gall's phrenology did not die easily. Because of its founder's reputation and zeal, logic alone could not undermine its principles. However, experiments were undertaken to assess the effects of surgically removing selected brain regions. These *ablation* studies challenged Gall's extreme beliefs, but they also supported the view that certain functions were *localized* within certain brain structures.

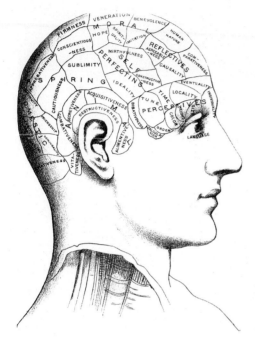

Figure 4-7. Phrenology head showing the regions of human capacities. *(The Bettman Archive)*

Collectively, the concepts of the reflex, the Law of Specific Nerve Energies, and the localization of function have dominated the history of the young science of physiological psychology. Each has entered the classical areas of psychology—sensation, perception, learning, memory, cognition, and emotion. In the chapters that follow, we will look at the more important physiological aspects of these processes.

THE LIMITATIONS OF PSYCHOPHYSIOLOGICAL METHODS

The basic methods of psychophysiological research include (a) clinical observation, (b) surgical ablation, or destruction of brain regions, (c) electrical stimulation and recording, and (d) chemical alteration and analysis. Various combinations of these are often used. Each in its own way has been of value in identifying the neural correlates, or related aspects, of certain psychological processes. Each, however, also is limited both in its applications and in its ability to provide truly *general* results.

Clinical Observation

Certain perceptual, cognitive, and emotional disturbances appear with neurological ailments. The clinical study of these psychological disorders has helped in identifying certain relationships between structures and functions in the nervous system. Brain tumors in the visual cortex do lead to visual defects. Tumors of the hypothalamus, a structure at the base of the brain, have been known to exist in extremely overweight patients. In this respect, clinical findings in neurology and neurosurgery have often provided broad hints for basic research. But no neural science can be based upon such findings. Nature is a very clumsy lesion-maker. It is rare, indeed, for a patient to suffer from brain pathology in only one small region, or for the neurosurgeon to be sure that that is the only region involved. Typically, tumors and other pathologic processes last for a long time, involve scattered parts of the CNS, and become complicated by the many abnormal conditions that usually accompany any serious disorder. Moreover, few patients or their families ever agree to contribute the corpse for scientific study after death. Thus, clinical observations such as memory loss or incoordination or generalized seizures, which are themselves very rough descriptions, must be correlated with surgical findings such as "tumor in temporal cortex" or "cerebellar degeneration" or "blood clot near thalamus." Without detailed studies of the brains and careful descriptions of the behavior defects, any information forthcoming is almost useless. When a patient does assign his body to science upon his death, matters are complicated by the time that elapses between surgery and the post mortem. Any damage could have been a result of the surgery or could have occurred after the surgery without any connection to the original condition. In any case, the damage discovered in a post mortem has not been linked with behavioral problems. Thus, clinical observation is, at best, a clue but never a key, to understanding relationships between the brain and behavior.

Surgical Ablation and Destruction

Brain tissue is highly interconnected, both structurally and functionally. One piece cannot be removed without affecting the system as a whole. Deficiencies that reliably follow the ablation of a given region are suggestive—not conclusive—of a relationship between structure and function. In addition, ablative research is essentially endless. There is almost no limit to the combinations of structures and amounts of tissue that can be removed. For example, an occipital lobectomy (removal of the visual cortex) leads to visual deficiencies in monkeys. This finding alone does not indicate the number of other regions whose removal will create the same effect.

Electrical Stimulation and Recording

There are two types of stimulation and recording techniques: the *macroelectrode* method, which stimulates or samples large numbers of neural cells; and the *microelectrode* method, which involves only one or a few cells. The former technique is limited in ways similar to those involved in ablative research. The latter is obviously restricted by problems of selection and representativeness. Each technique omits most of the nervous system from its analysis.

Chemical Alteration and Analysis

Like the foregoing methods, neurochemical studies can examine only a few of the many substances that make up the biochemistry of the CNS. By and large, the chemical methods require brains that have been removed and homogenized or made into a smooth mixture. Little research has been done (and, at present, some cannot be done) on living organisms. The research that has been done has been limited to introducing into the brain or into the veins various agents that might influence metabolic processes. The results of such studies are suggestive but not definite.

Collectively, the above methods have allowed scientists to make a number of very challenging assertions about the physiological bases of psychological events. It is still not clear, however, that the soul (or mind) is an enlightened machine. The machinery has turned out to be rather more complicated than the radical materialist philosophers of the eighteenth and nineteenth centuries had anticipated.

TENTATIVE CONCLUSIONS

Has a century of physiological psychology been successful in putting the controversy among nativism, empiricism, and materialism in a clearer perspective? Now that the brains and nerves of cats, rats, monkeys, and human beings have been examined, can we conclude that the mind is but the storage place for experience, or that it is endowed with innate ideas, or that it is merely an expression of neural activity? The answer to these questions is a resounding no. It is important for us to recognize why this is so, or at least why such a skeptical response is defensible. We might begin with the cave man as neurologist!

We might comfortably deny that the cave man had a written or even a spoken language; we might insist that he was cognitively impoverished and educationally disadvantaged, but we must admit that he could learn. Otherwise, we would not be discussing him here. Without taking sides in the associationist-cognitivist debate, we can agree that he learned, at least in part, through association. Granting this, we surely can imagine occasions on which he fell from a tree, tripped on a rock, slipped on a banana peel, got into a fight, or attacked a larger animal. Experiences of this sort would unavoidably lead him to conclude that the *head* is a very special part of the body. We learn this as children as did the cave man. He certainly knew that blows to the head, falling on the head, and sickness or pains in the head reduced his ability to do certain things; for example, to stay awake, to see clearly, to find his way back home, to keep his balance, or to recall where he was the day before.

Though such primitive insights are far removed from the theories and data developed by modern science, they do represent a kind of localization-of-function hypothesis. In the mind of prehistoric man, the hypothesis might go something like this:

I hit lion on left foot and lion bites my hand.
I hit lion on back and lion bites my nose.
I hit lion on head and lion lays down and goes to sleep.

All this story intends to convey is that there was no need for electrodes, scalpels, and special cages for testing rats if we only wanted to know whether or not the brain had anything to do with perception and action. Anyone who has ever had too much to drink at a party or who has received an anesthetic before surgery, knows that a healthy nervous system is *necessary* for psychological activities. However, this fact does not answer the more interesting question of whether or not a healthy nervous system is *sufficient* for psychological activities. Are the neurons all we need to know about in order to understand why we are the way we are? A pencil or some other writing tool is necessary to write a note, but a writing instrument is not enough. We also need something to write on, something to say, and a way to say it. The materialist assertion is not, in the last analysis, a scientific assertion but a philosophical one. The ultimate test of it will not be experimental but analytical. That is, there will be no experiment (nor can there be) that will prove that the mind is located in the brain. There can only be *arguments* defending the position that, for every event we call psychological, there is a *prior* event that must occur in the nervous system before the psychological event can occur. Even if all such arguments are analyzed and found to be true, we will still only be able to say that those events called psychological are connected to those called material, that is, neural in a causal way. However, such statements can never be more than statements of fact—statements about the way things are, not the way they must be, or will be, or even have been.

What is the role of physiological psychology within the nativism-empiricism issue? The answer to that question can be found in the foregoing discussion. Since we cannot locate an *idea* in the brain, we have no way of knowing whether that idea is innate. Even if we did discover a neural event that was perfectly correlated with a cognitive event, we would still be hard-pressed to decide which came first or whether one could exist without the other. In short, physiological psychology has provided answers to experimental questions, but not all questions are experimental. In the final analysis, the mind-body question is not experimental.

SUMMARY

In this chapter we have reviewed neuropsychology and its roots, both in history and within the context of the mind-body problem discussed by the philosophers. We have also examined the anatomy of the human nervous system, the mechanism of the reflex, and the concept of localization of function. This chapter, then, provides you with something like a map. It shows you the paths that information follows from the outside world to the inside world of the brain. We will proceed now to examine that special type of information-processing called *perception*. By studying perception, we might understand more clearly the limitations of experience, the laws that govern our experiences, and the mechanisms that serve our experiences. In the chapters that follow we will be returning often to the biological principles and processes discussed here.

SUGGESTED READINGS

BORST, C. V., ed. *The Mind/Brain Identity Theory*. New York: St. Martin's Press, 1970.

   This paperback edition contains seminal papers on the mind-body issue and serves as an excellent introduction to the philosophical dimensions of the problem.

FULLER, J. L. *Motivation: A Biological Perspective*. New York: Random House, 1968.

   Dr. Fuller provides a brief summary of biologically oriented views of human motivation. His effort is clear, critical, and nontechnical.

McCLEARY, R. A. and MOORE, R. Y. *Subcortical Mechanisms of Behavior: The Psychological Functions of Primitive Parts of the Brain*. New York: Basic Books, 1965.

   The authors present a simple statement of relations between limbic system structures and motivation and emotion. The book is nontechnical and short.

ROBINSON, D. N. *The Enlightened Machine: An Analytical Introduction to Neuropsychology*. California: Dickenson Publishing Co., 1973.

   This is a brief analysis of the mind-body issue in relation to contemporary research and theory in physiological psychology.

WOOLDRIDGE, D. E. *The Machinery of the Brain*. New York: McGraw-Hill Book Company, 1963.

   Dr. Wooldridge is an eminent figure in the engineering sciences and he brings this expertise to bear on an understanding of brain function. His writing is concise and as nontechnical as possible, given the topics chosen.

CHAPTER

5

Perception: The Problem of Experience

THE MODERN PSYCHOLOGICAL APPROACH: AN OVERVIEW

Perception is one of the basic psychological concepts that is of primary interest to contemporary psychologists throughout the world. It is a vast issue, indeed. In the broadest terms, perception refers to the full range of experiences of which animals and human beings are capable. In this sense, it embraces art, feelings, and even memory, since to recall something is to recreate a previous experience. Neither psychology nor any other discipline could possibly examine perception in such broad terms. There would just be too much ground to explore; one would never be able to decide where to begin. Moreover, as a discipline in search of general empirical laws, psychology would benefit only slightly from an attempt—ultimately a futile one—to study every single instance of perception.

Having decided not to try to assemble a list of every conceivable per-

By inspecting the following abbreviated list, we can appreciate the enormous number of interesting and important questions that result from these divisions and subdivisions:

1. What effect does brightness have on color vision?
2. Does a person's culture affect the formation or expression of visual illusions?
3. What is the smallest amount of light energy that the human visual system is able to detect?
4. Does visual sensitivity change during the course of a single day?
5. Can an animal adapt to an environment that is visually distorted?
6. How quickly must two flashes be presented for an observer to detect only one flash?
7. How many separate targets can an observer keep track of within any given period of time?
8. How quickly does the visual system adapt to a new level of illumination?
9. Is this rate of adaptation the same for all colors, shapes, and sizes of stimuli?
10. Do basic visual functions reveal sex differences?
11. At what age do children begin to recognize different faces?
12. Are all the basic visual functions present at birth? For example, does an infant have color vision?
13. What is the smallest object that can be detected by a human observer?
14. How long does an afterimage last, and what does this image depend on for its strength?
15. Why does the moon seem larger on the horizon than it does higher in the sky?

Questions of this sort can be multiplied almost endlessly. They can also be (and have been) raised in relation to the other senses.

ception and the conditions that give rise to it, the psychologist must find a basic rationale for including certain instances of perception while excluding others. Further, it is necessary for the psychologist to classify perceptions so that every *major class* of perceptions is examined, even though every instance of perception is not.

One of the more obvious ways of dividing the subject into major classes is to treat each sensory system separately. Thus, the psychology of perception, as studied in modern times, is classified in term of *vision, hearing, touch, olfaction* (the sense of smell), *gustation* (the sense of taste), and *kinesthesis* (the muscle sense that tells us the position of our limbs in space, the tension in our muscles, and other information concerning the movements and positions of our bodies).

Each of these major divisions is divided further. For example, vision

INFORMATION-PROCESSING

Let us use information-processing as an example of one subdivision of the sensory systems. Under this heading, we can reasonably include investigations that seem very different from each other, such as:

1. The effects of *attention* on the detection of signals.
2. The rate at which separate tone-bursts must occur before they are perceived as a continuous tone.
3. The number of letters and words that one can eliminate from a message and yet still preserve all the useful information.
4. The effects of stimulating one sensory system (for example, vision) on the sensitivity of another (for example, touch).

Though these investigations seem to cover very different topics and though the experimental arrangements for each will be different, the results of such studies can all be grouped under the heading, information-processing. In each case, we are trying to determine the observer's ability to process stimuli.

is in itself a vast subject. Entire volumes have been devoted to color vision, visual acuity, depth perception, photochemistry, visual anatomy, visual illusions, the development of visual functions, and differences in the vision of various animal species. To a lesser extent, all of the other sensory systems also offer many subordinate topics.

It is clear, then, that simply classifying the different sensory systems does not make the subject more manageable. Studying perception as a whole is an impossible task; studying vision as a whole is also impossible. Therefore, an even finer classification has been adopted. Studies of vision, for example, are grouped under some major headings: detection, discrimination, adaptation, illusion, and information-processing. This is not a complete list, but it does show how the once overwhelming subjects of perception and vision have now been tamed by an orderly system of classification.

Many of the important studies undertaken in the twentieth century could have been done in ancient times. In fact, many of our modern discoveries *were* anticipated by our ancestors, though they were not as inclined to experiment as we are. For example, we know that when one sensory system is stimulated, the sensitivity of the other systems may be reduced. Shakespeare, too, recognized this fact:

> *Dark night that does from the eye his function take,*
> *the ear the better sense does make.*

The difference between Shakespeare's insights and contemporary findings is, of course, the difference between a personal observation and a systematic examination—the difference between common sense and empirical laws.

The ancients did not study perception experimentally, nor did any other age until the nineteenth century. As we have noted before, this statement is to be understood in several ways. First, experimental science itself was invented relatively recently. Second, for any serious investigation of perception, one must have fairly sophisticated equipment. Then, too, one must have methods suited to the particular subject to be studied. In this last requirement stands the chief obstacle in the way of an experimental psychology of perception. How does one *measure* experience? For an answer, we turn to the work of the German physicist, Gustav Fechner (1801-1887).

FECHNER AND "PSYCHOPHYSICS"

Gustav Fechner was a man whose shifting interests revolved around a central theme—the uniformity of nature. He made his earliest contributions in theoretical physics, and his research on direct current won him recognition in that field. His work reached a turning point when he was blinded—irreversibly, it was thought—as a result of an experiment that involved direct observation of the sun. After his recovery, he was inspired —with almost religious zeal—to explore the uniformity of mental and physical nature. Fechner believed that mental events were only different aspects of physical events, and that the relationships between the two forms could be unearthed experimentally. He presents his position clearly in his book *Elements of Psychophysics:*

> Sensation depends on stimulation; a stronger sensation depends on a stronger stimulus. . . . Even before the means are available to discover the nature of the processes of the body that stand in direct relation to our mental activities, we will nevertheless be able to determine to a certain degree the quantitative relationship between them. (Fechner, *Elements of Psychophysics*, p. 10)

Fechner called this science of mental-physical relationships *psychophysics.* He advanced three general methods for determining psychophysical relationships which we will now examine.

The Method of Just-Noticeable-Differences

This method, often called the *method of limits,* is used to determine the smallest difference a practiced observer can detect when comparing two stimuli. For example, a subject is given two cans, designated as A and B, and of equal weight. On each trial, the experimenter adds small weights to one of the cans. The observer must report when that can appears to be "just heavier" than the other. The more weight that must be added, the less sensitive is the observer. The measure of sensitivity is thus the *reciprocal* of the required weight. A just-noticeable-difference (jnd) of 2 pounds, for example, would imply twice the sensitivity as one of 4 pounds.

The Method of Right and Wrong Cases

This procedure is like the method of limits, but it measures differences that are too small to be measured by the first method. For example, cans A and B may be made only very slightly different in weight. When the weight of can A is very different from that of can B, the subject is always right. But what if the difference in weights is very slight? The subject's sensitivity to such a small difference is measured by taking the reciprocal of the difference at which half the subject's judgments are right and half are wrong. Since this procedure usually involves making repeated judgments of two stimuli presented at the same time, it is often called the *method of paired comparisons.*

The Method of Average Error

Suppose a subject is asked to add or subtract weights from can A in order to make it weigh 3 pounds. Through many different trials, he will make some average error. The reciprocal of this error is a measure of his sensitivity. Since this method requires the subject, rather than the experimenter, to perform the necessary operations, it is often called the *method of adjustment.*

Weber's Law and Fechner's Law

Scientists had attempted to measure human sensitivity long before Gustav Fechner did his pioneering work in the theories and methods of psychophysics. Astronomers were especially interested in the subject because their discipline rested almost entirely on the accuracy of their observations. In *Elements of Psychophysics* (1860), which launched this new field, Fechner traced the history of this early interest and included in the book many of the findings that had been accumulated. The most impressive research had been done by the German physiologist Ernst Heinrich Weber (1795-1878) in the nineteenth century.

Weber had conducted numerous studies of sensitivity to weight and touch and of auditory (pitch) sensitivity as well. In spite of differences among the tasks and among the sensory systems, Weber observed that his data were surprisingly consistent. On all tasks and for all the senses he investigated, he found that the ratio of a comparison stimulus to the standard stimulus with which it was compared was constant for the just-noticeable-difference (jnd). That is, if the subject required a 1 pound difference in weights to call the comparison just heavier than a 10 pound standard, he would need a 2 pound difference before he could distinguish the comparison from a 20 pound standard. This principle can be stated mathematically:

$$\Delta S/S = C \text{ (for the jnd)}$$

ΔS is the difference between the comparison and the standard stimuli.

S is the amount of the standard.

C is constant at the point at which a difference is detected.

Fechner called this equation *Weber's Law*. Of course, the Weber ratio did not apply in every case or for all possible values of S, but Fechner was encouraged by the considerable range over which the law was valid. What bothered him was that all the equation could do was determine *sensitivity*. What Fechner sought was a law of sensation itself—a mathematical relationship between physical and psychological change.

Using Weber's Law as a base, Fechner made certain assumptions that simplified the equation and obtained a law for the growth of sensation known as *Fechner's Law:* $R = K \log S$. The law states that sensation is proportional to the logarithm of stimulation. From the time the law was originally formulated, it has encouraged research on sensation. The law has been challenged often—now and then, successfully—but the psychophysical methods themselves have remained intact. Psychology owes a great debt to Fechner for his contributions. In thousands of experiments conducted since 1860, the promise of *Elements of Psychophysics* has been largely fulfilled. There *are* reliable relations between experience and physical stimuli. Sensation can be measured, and the simple features of the response of the senses to stimulation are now a matter of record.

In his attempt to show that all experience is a series of elemental sensory responses, Fechner would confront the same opponents in science that the English empiricists had faced in philosophy. In tying experience to stimuli, Fechner would be challenged by those psychologists who insisted that experience is as much a *product* of consciousness as a *cause* of it. Fechner focused on sensation; his later critics responded with a psychology of *perception*. We can distinguish between these two perspectives by examining what each one considers to be its validating evidence. The evidence gathered by Fechner and by his followers in the century since his death, is an enormous catalog of *psychophysical functions*. These are relationships between specific aspects of a physical stimulus—such as intensity, wavelength, duration, and area—and the observer's measured ability to detect changes in these properties. This large body of data is not especially exciting, unless one is interested in the details of the senses themselves. However, the work is based on general philosophical assumptions that are interesting and significant to an understanding of psychology today. We will now review some of the major findings.

MAJOR PSYCHOPHYSICAL RELATIONSHIPS

The empiricist view of sensation implies that the nature of any experience is found in the physical properties of the stimulus. From an empiricist's perspective, therefore, it makes sense to assess sensation bit-by-bit and to construct a general theory of experience from the many stimulus-sensation relationships that are discovered. The theory would then be refined and reworked until a general theory of mental activity was found. A large number of experiments have been conducted following this orientation. They all fall under the heading of sensory psychology, and they all use modified forms of Fechner's methods.

THRESHOLDS: A MEASURE OF SENSITIVITY

The dependent variable in all sensory research is sensitivity; the independent variables are the physical properties of the stimuli. The two types of sensitivity studied are the observer's ability to detect a stimulus, and his ability to detect a *change* in the stimulus. The measure of an observer's sensitivity to the *presence* of a stimulus is called the *absolute threshold*. The measure of sensitivity to the difference between stimuli is called the *difference threshold*. Absolute thresholds mark the ability of a sensory system to *detect* stimuli; difference thresholds describe the system's ability to discriminate among stimuli. In point of fact, the distinction between absolute and difference thresholds is largely a semantic one. The former is a measure of the smallest amount of stimulation; the latter is a measure of the smallest *difference* in amount. Both are really measures of discrimination, because both are relative to a standard. For example, the absolute threshold for vision is the smallest amount of light energy that can be seen relative to absolute darkness. This, after all, is really a measure of the ability to discriminate a difference between darkness and non-darkness.

An infinite number of physical stimuli are able to affect sensation. However, it is not necessary to sample even a fraction of the possible combinations of stimuli in order to discover psychophysical relationships. The psychophysicist, or sensory psychologist, views stimuli as a physicist does. In spite of the staggering number of different stimuli, all of them can be ordered into a small number of categories. Thus, the stimulus may be photic (involving light), acoustic, thermal, electrical, or a combination of these, but it is still viewed as varying only in terms of the distribution of energy in time and space. Fechner hoped to uncover the fundamental relationship between these aspects of physical stimuli and the experiences that result from them.

Selection of Sensory Stimuli

The eye sees much more than the man does; the ear hears so much more. The senses are bombarded by an endless flood of environmental events, but man can respond to only the tiniest fraction of the total. At the outer edge of experience—the eyes, ears, skin, tongue, and other sensory systems—the mechanisms of detection are extraordinarily sensitive. They can respond to an overwhelming number of changes in the environment. But the behaving organism itself—with large muscle masses to move, with limbs that tire, with a brain that needs time to sort and code the innumerable messages—can use only a few of these changes in the task of *adaptation*. Much of what is detected by the sense organs, is, of necessity, "filtered out." The filter, however, is not an arbitrary one—it does not simply eliminate some fraction of the incoming information. The mother who sleeps through the loud noise of an alarm clock may awaken instantly to the subdued cries of a child in another room. *Sensory filtering*, in other words, is selective. The term used to describe the selectivity of sensory filters is *attention*. To be attentive, the organism must be able to draw distinctions—to evaluate differences—among the varied signals that affect the senses. Attention is active, not passive. It involves not only selectively responding to a narrow range of events, but also selective *nonresponding* to other events. To engage in attentive behavior, the organism must be able to assign values to environmental occurrences. To some extent, therefore, attention depends on the existence of memory—some record of the importance of events in the past.

There is, however, another form of selective filtering which is the result of the physical or physiological nature of the sensory mechanisms themselves, and not of attention. An analogy that is helpful in understanding this type of filtering is one that involves the system of loudspeakers used in radios, television sets, and record players. These speakers are so constructed that they vibrate maximally to a range of frequencies. The material of which they are made will respond only over some desired range. The "tweeter" (a loudspeaker designed for the production of high frequency sounds), for example, is smaller and more rigid than the "woofer" (designed for the production of low frequency sounds). In combination, these two speakers provide a total *system response* to a broader range of frequencies than either could accommodate alone. Such speakers are said to be *tuned* to certain frequency ranges. In very much the same way, the responses of sensory systems are determined by the tuning of the elements included in them. A sense organ will respond only to those events which fall within that physical range to which it is tuned. Different senses are tuned to different classes of events, all of which, however, can be said to have certain common features.

Common Features of Sensory Stimuli

The term *amplitude* is used to characterize the displacement of stimuli in space. Words such as *size* and *area* are used to depict the extent of spatial displacement. But, in referring to sound, amplitude means the displacement of air molecules in space, or in any other medium. Such displacement always requires a certain amount of time. A representation of changes in amplitude as a function of time is called a *waveform*. Figure 5-1 shows graphically the spatial displacement of air molecules as a function of time.

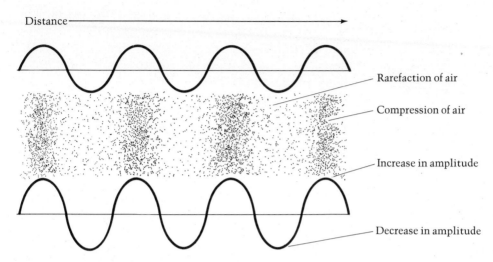

Distance →

Rarefaction of air

Compression of air

Increase in amplitude

Decrease in amplitude

Figure 5-1. The motion of air molecules creating sound. As the molecules become more compressed, the amplitude of the sound increases. As the density of molecules diminishes (rarefaction), sound intensity lessens. The "pitch" of the sound is determined by the frequency with which phases of compression and rarefaction occur.

Positive (+) and negative (−) amplitudes result from the fact that sound is produced by the compression (+) and rarefaction (−) of air molecules comprising the medium through which the sound is transmitted. This figure shows a waveform which begins at zero, passes through a maximum at 1 millisecond (msec.), a minimum at 2 msec., and then returns to zero at 2.4 msec. Tones consist of a large number of waveforms which repeat themselves at regular intervals. Each one of the waves, proceeding from rest through a maximum and a minimum and back to rest, is called one *cycle*. The number of cycles that occur within 1 second is the measure of frequency. For example, the frequency of a tone whose cycles are completed every 0.0025 seconds is 400 cycles per second (cps) or 400 Herz.

Instead of one tone, suppose we use a complex stimulus that consists of several tones, each different in its amplitude and its frequency. See Figure 5-2 where three such tones are plotted. Tone A reaches peaks at +2 and −2, and one cycle takes 4.0 msec. Thus, the frequency of tone A is 250 cps and its peak-to-peak amplitude (using arbitrary units) is 4. Tone B completes one cycle in 2.0 msec. Its frequency is 500 cps and its peak-to-peak ampli-

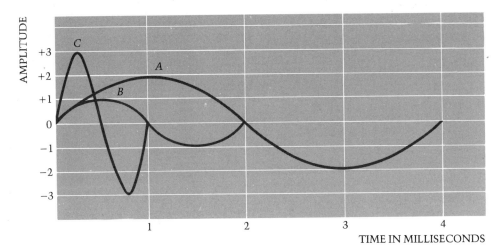

Figure 5-2. A complex tone consisting of three different frequencies. Wave A has the lowest frequency; B, an intermediate frequency; C, the highest frequency. Such a representation of amplitude *vs.* time is called a *waveform*.

tude is 2 units. Tone C has a frequency of 1,000 cps and a peak-to-peak amplitude of 6 units. We will now see how this complex sound can be represented in another way by examining Figure 5-3 where three tones are depicted. Instead of plotting three waveforms, we now plot the ampli-

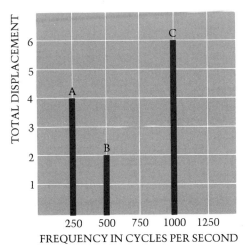

Figure 5-3. *A spectrum.* This is a replot of the waveforms shown in Fig. 5-2. In this figure, amplitude is plotted against frequency. Tone C reveals the greatest amplitude, tone A the next greatest, and B the least.

tudes present at each frequency. This representation of the three tones is an example of what is called the *spectrum*. If the units were units of power, this figure would be called a *power spectrum*. If the units were expressed in terms of acoustic energy, it would be an *energy spectrum*.

Sound is only one form of energy. It is mechanical in nature, because it involves the vibratory displacement of molecules through some distance. Light is a form of *electromagnetic* energy, produced by the vibratory motions of both an electrical and a magnetic field. As with sound vibrations, these electromagnetic vibrations can be of very low or of very high frequency. The full range of frequencies which describes the domain of electromagnetic radiation is called the *electromagnetic spectrum*, shown in Figure 5-4. In this figure, you can see how small a portion of the spectrum is occupied by visible light. You can also see how the frequency of electromagnetic vibrations determines the color of light, in the same way that the frequency of mechanical vibrations determines the pitch of sound. Figure 5-4 also indicates the reciprocal relationship between frequency and wavelength. All other things being equal, the higher the frequency of motion, the less the distance moved in any single cycle. Thus, the length of the path along which a vibratory wave moves shortens as higher vibratory frequencies are reached. When talking about light, it is more customary to use wavelength rather than frequency. Visible light is that consisting of electromagnetic waves whose lengths fall between 360 and 760 millimicrons (mμ). (A micron is a millionth of a meter; a millimicron is equal to one thousandth of a micron or a billionth of a meter).

In view of the foregoing discussion, one can see that the experiences which concerned the empiricists are governed by two factors: the physical limitations of the sense organs and the selective filtering (memory and attention) of the observer. The physiology of the senses will be discussed later in this chapter and learning and memory in the following chapter. For now, we will examine the senses psychophysically. Psychophysics stresses the characteristics of the sense organs. It will be helpful to examine the kinds of data that are obtained from psychophysical studies. The following summary is selective, attempting only to communicate the general features of sensory processing. It is examined here both to reveal the changes undergone by empirically-oriented psychology and to underscore the precision with which at least some aspects of human psychology can be estimated.

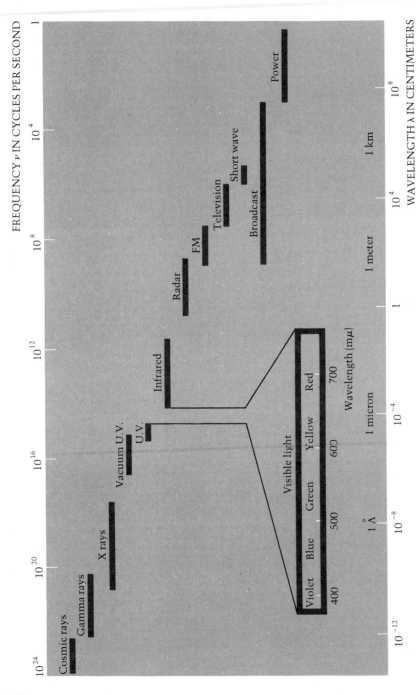

Figure 5-4. *The electromagnetic spectrum.* In this figure, the entire spectrum of electromagnetic radiation is shown. The relationship between frequency and wavelength is reciprocal; the longer the wavelength, the lower the frequency. *Visible light* is found only in a very narrow region of the spectrum. The longest wavelengths of visible light are about 750 thousandths of a millionth of a meter; i.e., 750 millimicrons. At longer wavelengths, infrared, radar, and broadcast radiation are found. The shortest wavelengths of visible light fall into the range of 360-400 millimicrons (violet). Below this range are found ultraviolet, X-rays, gamma rays, and cosmic rays. Certain organisms, like the honeybee, have visual sensitivity well into the ultraviolet regions of the spectrum. (After McKinley, 1947.)

VISION

Visual sensation results from contact between electromagnetic radiation of a certain wavelength and the eye. The absolute threshold of vision is the smallest amount of such radiation sufficient for an observer to detect its presence on a greater-than-chance basis. The psychophysical determination of the absolute threshold usually involves a modified method of limits. The subject's task is to state, from trial to trial, whether or not he sees flashes of light against a dark background. A graph can be drawn of the percent of flashes "seen" (or the frequency of seeing) against the amount of energy in the flashes. Much of the light is reflected away by the cornea and lens of the eye, so that only a fraction of it actually reaches the light-sensitive retina. A quantum is the smallest unit of light energy. If about 5 to 10 quanta get to the retina, the subject will report the presence of light (Hecht, Schlaer, and Pirenne, 1942). Thus, the human visual system is amazingly sensitive.

From the Weber ratio, one might conclude that the difference (Δ) in luminance (L) necessary for human perception of a differing light (L) would yield a constant fraction (C), that is, that $\Delta L/L = C$. This is approximately so at moderately high intensities, but it breaks down when dim lights are employed. Figure 5-5 shows the relationship between luminance (L) and the size of the Weber ratio ($\Delta L/L$) for flashes of different duration (from 2 msec. to 500 msec.) The ratio is smaller for lights of greater duration—that is, sensitivity is greater the longer the flash. It is also clear that the ratio is valid only for luminances above some critical value.

Spatio-Temporal Difference Thresholds

The absolute threshold and difference threshold considered so far describe sensitivity as a function of energy, ignoring that energy's distribution in space and time. Measures of the latter answer questions concerning how far apart multiple stimuli must be to be discriminated as separate. In informal philosophical terms, we are asking whether man can ever "know" a rapidly changing reality: whether the mind can keep pace with fast changes; whether we can perceive small separations between events in time and in space.

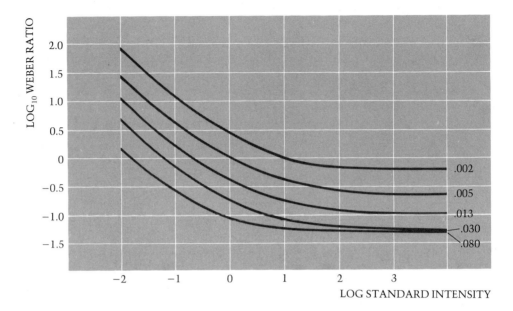

Figure 5-5. The ratio of change (ΔI) to initial or standard intensity (I) is plotted against I. The duration of comparison flash is shown in seconds for each curve. Weber's Law states that ΔI/I = C. If valid, the law would require all curves to be parallel with the abscissa. This condition is met from about 1.0 $\log_{10}$ on, but not at lower intensity levels. (After the data of Graham and Kemp, 1938.)

Acuity

The spatial separation required for a subject to discriminate between two stimuli is a measure of visual acuity. In measuring visual acuity, it is helpful to specify the separation between the two stimuli in angular terms rather than in inches or in feet. In using angular measures, one can account for both the distance between the observer and the stimuli, and the separation between the stimuli. Figure 5-6 will help to clarify this point.

Flicker

The temporal separation necessary for each stimulus in a sequence to be seen separately is a measure of the visual system's ability to resolve

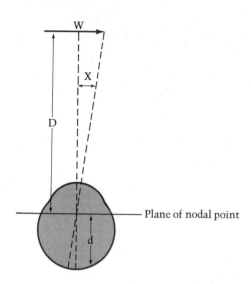

Figure 5-6. Determining visual acuity and the visual angle. The subject is presented with a black bar on a white surface. The width of the bar is W. The distance between the eye of the subject and the surface on which the bar appears is D. A triangle is formed with W as its base and D as its altitude. The angle X is the *angular* size of the object. Visual acuity is the inverse of this angle in minutes. Suppose the angle X was 2° (120 minutes). Then, if this were the narrowest bar the subject could see, visual acuity would be expressed as 1/120 or 0.0083. A person able to discriminate a 1° bar would have twice the visual acuity of this subject. The rays from the bar intersect within the eye at a point indicated by the line passing across the eye in the figure—the *nodal point*. The distance from this point to the retina is referred to in the figure as d. The actual size of the stimulus on the retina is given by dW/D.

in time. Many factors control visual-temporal sensitivity. One important measure of this threshold defines the rate at which a sequence of identical individual flashes becomes "fused" into a continuous light. Three stimulus properties play a major role in determining the *critical flicker-fusion,* or *c.f.f., threshold.* These are the size of the flashes, their color (wavelength), and their intensity. All other things being equal, as the size of the stimulus increases, higher rates of flicker are able to be discriminated.

At low brightness levels, color is a very important determinant of c.f.f. Maximum sensitivity (highest rates of perceived flicker) occurs with blue light (short wavelength), and poorest sensitivity with red light (long wavelength). At greater brightnesses, maximum sensitivity is obtained with yellow light, and this sensitivity is reduced when wavelengths longer or shorter than yellow are employed.

The c.f.f. increases with brightness. At very low levels, fusion occurs at flicker rates of 4 or 5 flashes per second. At very high luminances, flicker can still be seen at rates as high as 50 to 60 flashes per second. Over a rather broad range of brightness, the relationship between c.f.f. and log intensity is linear.

Masking

When only two flashes are employed and the subject's task is to determine whether he sees two or one, about 20 msec. must separate the offset of the first from the onset of the second for both to be seen (Hirsch and Sherrick, 1961). However, if the second is larger and brighter than the first, then only the second is seen at an interval of 20 msec. or even one of 150 msec. (Raab, 1963). This phenomenon is called backward masking. When three stimuli are presented in succession, with each successive one larger than the one that precedes it, the third masks the second and the first again becomes visible. Note how closely spatial and temporal characteristics are interrelated in determining visual sensations.

Color Vision

Another classical area of investigation in visual psychophysics is concerned with color vision. It is known that below a specified level of brightness, human vision is achromatic, that is, cannot distinguish colors. With enough light, a subject with normal color vision will be able to make about 180 distinctions of color over the visible spectrum, between wavelengths of 360 mμ to 760 mμ. The difference between two spectral stimuli necessary for discrimination depends on the region of the spectrum in which the stimuli occur. This relationship is seen in Figure 5-7. Note that the smallest percent difference is in the region of the spectrum corresponding to yellow.

If one ignores color recognition and is concerned instead with brightness only, the effects of wavelength are considerable. In experiments to determine brightness as a function of wavelength, the method of adjustment is usually used. The subject is presented with light A, whose wavelength and brightness (luminance) are fixed by the experimenter. Light B appears adjacent to A, and its wavelengths are also set by the experimenter. The subject's task is to vary the brightness of B, until A and B appear identical in brightness. The resulting data reveal the effectiveness of different wavelengths in producing brightness. This effectiveness is referred to as *relatve luminosity*. At relatively high luminances, light of 550 mμ wavelength (yellow) appears brighter than light of any other wavelength; its relative luminosity is 100 percent. At very low luminances, the highest relative luminosity is found at 490 mμ (blue-green). In Figure 5-8,

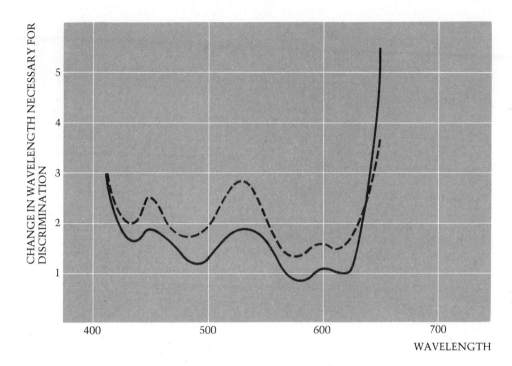

Figure 5-7. Wavelength discrimination in man. Data from two subjects showing the change in wavelength necessary for discrimination of a change at different regions of the spectrum. (After the data of Laurens and Hamilton, 1923.)

both the low-luminance (*scotopic*) and high-luminance (*photopic*) luminosity functions are plotted.

An interesting consequence of the relative luminosity of different colors is that blue flowers appear brighter than yellow ones in the moonlight, whereas the yellow appear brighter in sunlight. This simple observation reveals a basic feature of the human visual system.

The Duplex Nature of Vision

By examining Figures 5-7 and 5-8, it becomes clear that at least two processes are involved in visual information-processing; one that functions at low levels of luminance and one that occurs at higher levels. These two processes suggest the presence of two different visual mecha-

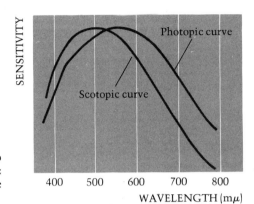

Figure 5-8. Sensitivity of human vision to lights of different wavelength. The scotopic curve is obtained in very dim light; the photopic curve in brighter light.

nisms in the retina. One is the rod mechanism, which is sensitive to the very lowest amounts of visible light, but is not sensitive to color. The other is the cone system, which cannot detect light at the lowest levels of visibility, but which can detect color vision. Because of this division of labor, the retina is called a duplex structure. It contains about 125 million rods and about 6 million cones. The cones are most plentiful in the center of the retina, decreasing in the periphery. Rods are absent in the very center (the *fovea*) of the retina and become more and more abundant further into the periphery. Because of this, peripheral vision is much better at night than is foveal (central) vision. For the same reason, however, peripheral vision is achromatic (insensitive to color).

As an instrument for detecting and discriminating various distributions of electromagnetic radiation, the visual sense is truly extraordinary. It responds selectively to minute variations in the brightness, duration, size, repetition rate, and wavelength of visible light. Visual psychophysics provides a precise and detailed catalog of how sensation will change as each of these stimulus characteristics is altered. If the state of adaptation (to darkness or to some level of brightness) is specified, the visual response to physical stimulation becomes predictable.

HEARING

All of the senses, within the context of psychophysics, are evaluated in terms of absolute and difference thresholds, spatial and temporal resolution, adaptation effects, and so forth. In hearing *(audition)*, the audible spectrum spreads from about 16 cycles per second (cps) to about 18,000 cps. As the visual absolute threshold depends upon the wavelength (frequency) of light, so the auditory threshold varies as a function of frequency. Frequencies between 1,500 cps and 3,000 cps can be heard at lower sound amplitudes than frequencies below or above this range. A plot of the relationship between threshold intensity and sound frequency is shown in Figure 5-9.

Another type of graph can be drawn to describe frequency discrimi-

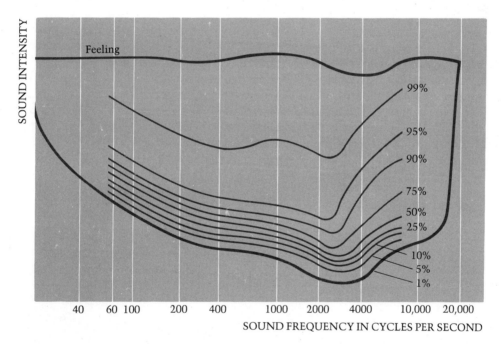

Figure 5-9. The relationship between sensitivity and frequency. Sound intensity is plotted on the ordinate. These values represent the intensities necessary for subjects to detect the sound as a function of frequency. Greatest sensitivity is found in the region 2000 to 4000 cycles per second. Here, the lowest intensities are still heard. The different curves describe the percent of a normal population able to hear the various tones. Thus, 99 percent of the observers can hear all tones from 60 to 10,000 cps if intensities are between 100 and 110 decibels. However, only 1 percent of the subjects can hear sounds below 40 cps, no matter how intense they are.

nability at different points along the spectrum, or difference thresholds for sound frequency. Again, the Weber ratio $\Delta f/f$ is smallest (that is, sensitivity to frequency differences is greatest) in the region of 1,500 to 3,000 cps.

Just as the sensory correlate of light frequency is color, the sensory correlate of sound frequency is pitch. Similarly, loudness is the auditory counterpart of brightness. The absolute loudness threshold, in the region of maximum sensitivity (1,500 to 3,000 cps) is astonishingly low (about 0.0002 dynes pressure per square centimeter against the eardrum). Thus, very little force has to be exerted on the eardrum for the listener to detect a break in silence, to "hear" something.

The *auditory flutter-fusion threshold* (a.f.f.) is a measure of temporal resolution in hearing. However, in hearing, a.f.f. drops when intensity is increased above some moderate level. The auditory flutter-fusion threshold is much higher than the critical flicker-fusion threshold; the a.f.f. reaches values in excess of 1,000 "flutters" per second. Thus, resolution in time is greater in hearing than in vision, whereas spatial resolution in space is far keener visually. An indication of the relatively poor localizing abilities of human hearing is provided in Figure 5-10, which shows the "cone of confusion" within which spatially separated sounds are not correctly located.

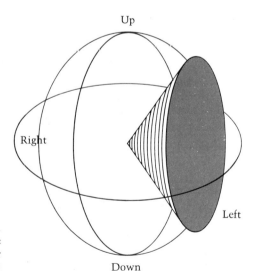

Figure 5-10. Volume of auditory confusion. Acoustic stimuli occurring within the shaded area will be confused as to their spatial location. (After E. B. Newman, 1948.)

Temporal factors, too, play an important part in auditory sensations. The experience of pitch depends strongly upon the length of exposure. A pure tone of 1,000 cps will be heard as a "click" if it is presented for only 1 msec. This is because 1 msec. of a 1,000 cps tone allows the occurrence of only one cycle, which is not enough for the sensation of pitch. It is clear that over a limited range, pitch is a function of both frequency and continuance in time. Similarly, pitch can be affected by intensity. Tones of equal frequency but different intensity will create different sensations of pitch. Generally, as intensity is increased, the sensed pitch increases; that is, over a certain range, the hearing sense confuses variations of frequency and intensity.

SOMAESTHESIS

Somaesthesis (soma = body; aesthesia = feeling or sense) refers to those sensations that occur in response to stimulation of areas on the body's surface. The somaesthetic senses include touch, pressure, pain, and temperature. Thus, most of what is classified under the heading *somaesthesis* is really descriptive of the "skin sense." In principle, however, somaesthesis includes other body senses, such as visceral pain, body temperature, and blood pressure, to all of which man is sensitive in varying degrees. But for obvious reasons, these internal sensations have proved resistant to measurement and to experimental manipulation. The skin senses have received considerable research attention, though not nearly as much as vision or hearing. This relative neglect is the result of both the apparently greater significance of vision and hearing to the life of man and the difficulty of obtaining reliable means of producing and quantifying somaesthetic stimuli.

The absolute threshold for touch may be defined as the smallest amount of pressure (weight per unit area) necessary for an observer to detect its presence on his skin. The value of the absolute threshold varies substantially over different regions of the body; for example, from 2 or 3 grams per square millimeter on the fingertips to more than 30 grams per millimeter on the back of the forearm (Bartley, 1958). Systematic analyses of the effects of stimulus area, duration, and amplitude on the absolute threshold of touch have yet to be conducted with sufficient rigor and reliability for inclusion. It would appear that the same skin region may sense touch, cold, warmth, and pain depending upon the nature and intensity of the stimulus. However, it also seems to be true that different regions of the skin are much more likely to sense one of these four sensations more acutely than the other three. Of course, if stimulated with great enough intensity, a pressure region will yield the sensation of pain. Yet the pain threshold varies a great deal from region to region, as does the nature of the stimuli that will give rise to pain sensations. Similarly, the qualitative feature of pain depends upon the region stimulated. Thus, excessive stimulation of a "touch" area leads to a different pain sensation than that produced by excessive stimulation of a "warmth" area.

There is still controversy over what the effective stimulus is for touch, for pressure, and for pressure-type pain. You are usually not sensitive to the clothes you wear, despite the fact that they constantly exert pressure on the skin. This may be interpreted as the outcome of adaptation or "fatigue" resulting from constant stimulation; other explanations are also possible. In their studies of touch and pressure thresholds, Nafe and Wagoner (1941) found that the effective stimulus was not simply the physical weight of a stimulus, but the rate at which skin was deformed by it; the sensation depended upon the rate of change rather than upon the absolute amount of stimulation. This fact is not unique to skin sensations; it may be argued that all sensation depends upon change from some initial "steady state" of stimulation.

The sensations of warmth and cold can be elicited by mechanical stimulation of certain skin regions. There are, so to speak, warm and cold spots on the skin whose activation determines the sensation independent of the variety of stimulus used. In fact, if a cold spot is stimulated by a hot object, the resulting sensation is paradoxically that of cold! The reverse effect, however, has proved to be much more difficult to obtain.

The skin surface shares properties similar to those of the basilar membrane of the inner ear. It is capable of responding differently to small changes in the frequency, intensity, duration, and size of vibratory stimuli that are applied. In fact, the skin is such a good "ear," that within the appropriate range of frequencies, an individual can learn a substantial "cutaneous vocabulary" (a vocabulary pertaining to the skin). Blind patients have been given "tactile sight" by stimulating large areas of skin with complex patterns. As a duration-discriminator, the skin is capable of distinguishing one event from another when the events differ by as little as 50 msec. Intensities, as expressed by the amplitude of mechanical vibrations, can be distinguished with differences as small as 10 millionths of a meter (Geldard, 1957).

OTHER SENSES

The full range of human experience involves more than visual, auditory, and somaesthetic sensations. Movement of the body produces stimuli that are basic to useful behavior. *Kinaesthesis*—the sensitivity to limb position and muscle action—is of obvious importance. Taste (*gustation*) and smell (*olfaction*) sensations provide man with experience essential to his survival and integral to his self-gratification. Finally, the *vestibular sense,* the sense by which man knows the position of his body in space, is crucial to posture, to walking, and to precise behavior. These sensations were first studied and are better understood within a physiological context. Such neurological complexities, however, cannot be covered adequately in a text devoted to the introductory elements of psychology. But vision, hearing, and somaesthesis were first and most completely studied psychophysically; in fact, it was in response to psychophysical findings in vision, hearing, and touch that much of the research in sensory physiology was undertaken. In the other senses, psychophysical data are relatively sparse and have often followed in the wake of physiological research.

SOME THEORIES OF SENSATION AND PERCEPTION

It is clear from these findings that the contemporary psychologist possesses reliable and accurate measures of basic sensory processes. And these measures are not limited to the human senses. There is an active field of research today called animal psychophysics in which conditioning techniques are employed to determine absolute and difference thresholds in a variety of species.

The question that survives these findings, however, in one form or another, is: "Is this all there is to the subject of perception?" That is, can we be confident that the methods and assumptions that have led to these findings will be effective in providing us with a scientific understanding of complex perceptions?

This is one of the most important issues, not only in modern philosophical psychology, but in a larger context that we call the history of ideas. Every age has wrestled with the validity of *reductionism*—the belief that all events, no matter how complex, are ultimately *reducible* to simpler elements. It is important to review reductionism in the context of the psychology and physiology of perception and to see how skepticism regarding psychophysics led to one of psychology's most significant schools —*Gestalt psychology*.

The Sensationist's Assumptions

Perhaps the most convenient way to analyze the assumptions of nineteenth-century *sensationist psychology* is to list what we must take for granted if the general point of view is to be valid.

There Are Sensations.

This assumption is most fundamental and, it would seem, most obvious. People universally acknowledge their experiences. They see, hear, touch, taste, and smell objects around them. Yet even this assumption can be challenged. The philosopher George Berkeley (1685?-1753), for example, actually presented arguments that raise very serious objections to the assumption that sensations refer to real objects.

If we follow Berkeley's reasoning, we can assume that man never senses objects as such, but only the perception of the objects in his mind. That is, he doesn't "see a house"; he only experiences the brain's activity when a house is placed before his eyes. This must certainly be true since the house itself does not pass through the eyes and into his brain. But if this *is* true, then can man ever be *sure* that a house actually exists? That is, how does he know that the activity of his brain is caused by the house? Berkeley's answer is that man cannot be sure; all he can know is what is in his mind—the *experience*, not the house. This argument has never been settled, but for scientific purposes, it has been put aside. Remember that in Chapter 1 we discussed the fact that a principal requirement of science was intersubjective agreement. This particular requirement is satisfied, for example, when every person who knows what a house is says he sees a

house when a house is presented. So this most fundamental assumption—
that there are sensations—must be accepted as valid if any science is to be
deemed possible.

Sensations Are Caused by Stimulation

This statement means that a person "sees a house" because the light
reflected by the house stimulates his optic nerves and the nerves in turn
activate certain brain regions in a particular way. Fechner's experiments
and his "law" have already been presented in evidence. Reported sensations
grew in strength as the intensity of a stimulus was increased. However,
while it may be true that sensations are *often* the product of stimulation,
it is not necessarily the case that they are *always* or *only* the result of
stimulation. For example, the house Mr. Smith dreams of is not in physical
space, before his eyes. It may not be any house he has ever seen or ever will
see. This is true of many things people imagine, and we now begin to
understand some of the difficulties that nineteenth-century sensationists
were faced with.

The Human Observer Can Report His Sensation

Fechner and those guided by his research and theory applied the
reasoning of physiology to problems that existed in the new science of
psychology. The human observer was treated as a large nerve, so to speak,
and his reports of experience were given a status quite like that of a neural
response. This analogy was, of course, simplistic. The human observer
brings to any setting a history of experiences unlike anything a single nerve
can incorporate. However, the psychophysical experiment is conducted in
a way that tries to eliminate these complications to the greatest possible
extent. The observer's reports are restricted to "yes" and "no"; the stimuli
are reduced to the simplest form. When these conditions prevail, the assumption seems valid: the observer's reports are closely related to the
responses obtained from sensory nerves when the same stimuli are presented. Thus, at least generally, the observer can report his "sensations" if
these sensations are no more than neural consequences of stimulation.

Experience Is No More Than the Accumulation of
Elementary Sensory Events

It is this assumption that led to the label *elementarism*: the notion that any experience, no matter how complex, was no more than a combination of basic sense-events. Given this attitude, it is not surprising that so much of the early research in psychology tried to separate experience into its various parts, to determine the *structure* of consciousness. The scientific climate of the nineteenth century contributed to this effort. In chemistry, for example, the periodic table produced an analysis of the most complex compounds into their elementary components. In biology, the taxonomists were able to assign the extraordinarily varied forms of plant and animal life to a relatively small number of identifying categories. And physics, of course, had succeeded (so it was believed) in reducing the complexities of the heavens to a small number of elementary principles. The most important factor was the decision to treat psychology as an experimental subject. Once that decision was made, it led inescapably to a study of perceptual "elements." Since a scientist could, for example, measure the absolute threshold in vision but could not measure "beauty," the former was at first studied by psychologists while the latter was left to those concerned with aesthetics. If this were the case, there would not have been a quarrel. After all, if a group of scholars decide to measure visual thresholds and ignore "beauty," they are free to do so. But something happened to take this distinction out of the context of mere taste and move it into the realm of philosophy. What was added was the contention that beauty was, after all, no more than a combination of elementary sensory events and that it could be reduced to these sensory events through experimentation. It was around this point that opposing points of view began to form.

The Truth of Sense and the Sense of Truth

The earliest analysis of the relationships between knowledge and sensation appears in Plato's dialogue *Theaetetus*. The name is taken from the young scholar who debates with Socrates on the nature of wisdom. In the course of their conversation, Theaetetus takes refuge in the authority of the great Sophist, Protagoras, who taught that *Man is the measure of all things.* Accordingly, what is true is what the individual perceives to be true; what is known is what the individual learns through personal experiences.

In short order, Socrates shows the absurdity of this position. If it were true, why would "a pig or a dog-faced baboon, or some other yet stranger monster which has sensation" not be the measure of all things? How could anyone with normal vision and hearing ever be in error? How could anyone know what he remembers since, in remembering, we recall events that no longer appeal to our senses?

As in most of the *Dialogues,* Socrates attempts to show that truth and knowledge are *ideas* and that their validity is not dependent upon sensory proof. While he accepts the possibility that man is the measure of all *sensible* things, Socrates rejects any suggestion that all truths are sensible. In Chapter 2, we developed this position and saw how it was supported by certain mathematical propositions. Recall, for example, that the truth of Pythagoras' theorem is established not by the eyes but by the implicit logic of the mind. This same kind of evidence was later revived in the nineteenth century by antagonists of the empirical point of view. However, since these claims were raised in connection with how we acquire knowledge of the sensible world, the antiempiricist position was more specific than Socrates' position. It was limited to the questions of perception, and it offered the following points in opposition to those sensationist assumptions discussed above.

Are There Sensations?

There are sensations, but only in the sense of *transactions.* That is, the observer is not a passive receiver of stimuli. He possesses an active mind that operates according to rules. These rules determine the effects of stimulation. Accordingly, every sensation is the result of a transaction between physical stimuli and mental dispositions. Using this view as a base, the important subject for psychological study is not the content of sensation but the *act* of sensing. Proponents of this view created what was called *act psychology,* and they emphasized the role of *attention, expectation,* and *meaningfulness* in determining experience.

Are Sensations Caused by Stimulation?

Because every experience is the product of a *transaction,* it makes just as much sense to say that sensations are caused by stimuli as to say that stimuli are caused by sensations. The mind will experience what it is *prepared* to experience. The final representation of "reality" is a mental one, and this is only very loosely determined by the "physical reality" of the stimulus.

Can the Observer Report His Sensations?

The observer can report a great many things. If all he is asked to report is whether A is brighter than B, he will do so. But such demonstrations fail to disclose completely the full fact of experience. For example, a camera will report the appearance of an orchestra, but will tell us nothing about the experience produced by a symphony.

Is Experience No More Than a Combination of Elementary Events?

This statement is clearly not true. Our concept of *triangle* is not simply the combination of our separate sensing of three lines. There is an infinite number of ways of presenting three lines:

Only the last satisfies what we *know* is a triangle and we know this *immediately;* that is, not by comparison or measurement or even visual analysis. Instead, we call the last figure in this series a triangle, because it answers certain mental criteria.

SENSATION AND PERCEPTION: THE EMPIRICIST-IDEALIST CONTROVERSY

In the last decade of the nineteenth century, the empiricist-idealist controversy was moved to the laboratory, and it has thrived there ever since. The earliest laboratory studies were conducted by those who established *Gestalt psychology*, a psychology of form (*Gestalt*) and organization. Fechner's psychophysical studies of *sensation* were the experimental version of empiricism; the Gestalt psychologists, in examining *perception*, created an experimental form of idealism.

The Phi Phenomenon

In 1912, Max Wertheimer published results of a study he did in vision conducted with two of his graduate students, K. Koffka and W. Köhler. The demonstration is a simple one. The subject, exposed only to darkness, is presented with laterally displaced lights, A and B, as shown in Figure 5-11. Each light is turned on and off in the sequence ABABABAB. Different intervals between A and B are chosen and the subject reports what he sees. Wertheimer found that over a range of intervals, the subject experiences not two flashing lights, but one light that moves left and right in pendular fashion. Wertheimer called this *apparent movement* or *phi* (phenomenal movement). *Phi* is not simply a response to stimulation; it is the creation of a stimulation that is not present in the stimulus. It is not an element of sensation; it is a perception. The subject imposes an order, a form (*Gestalt*), upon the physical reality. Therefore, he is not a passive receptacle of stimulation, but an active organizer of stimuli. His *perceptions* determine what reality really is for him.

The *phi* phenomenon has been found in experiments involving hearing and touch and even may take place in taste and smell. Stimulation of sepa-

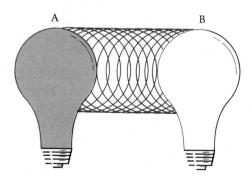

Figure 5-11. Apparatus for Phi phenomenon. As lights A and B are flashed alternately, an illusion of motion is created. The lights appear as a single light, moving back and forth in a pendular motion.

Figure 5-12. The Müller-Lyer illusion. The top arrow appears to have a longer center segment than the bottom arrow.

rate regions of the skin result in the perception of a single object moving along the skin when the two separated stimuli are presented at proper intervals. (In this setting, *phi* is called the *tau effect*—to distinguish touch and vision.) Similarly, two sounds from separate sources may be perceived as a single moving sound when the intervals are properly chosen.

In vision, certain trade-offs among spatial separation, temporal separation, stimulus area, stimulus duration, and stimulus intensity may be made to produce *phi*. Thus, the same *phi* can be obtained by exchanging distance apart and time apart.

Illusions

The *phi* phenomenon was the first in a long and continuing series of perceptual effects offered as challenges to the elementaristic view of experience. Many illusions which are illustrated here have been studied within the context of Gestalt psychology.

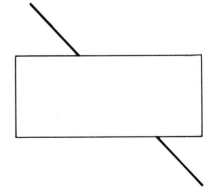

Figure 5-13. The Poggendorf illusion. The line entering the rectangle from the upper left corner of this figure appears to enter at a higher plane than the segment that exits at the bottom right of the rectangle.

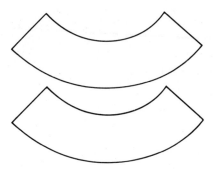

Figure 5-14. The Jastrow illusion. Are these two forms the same size? Which appears larger?

Figure 5-12 presents the *Müller-Lyer illusion,* in which the lower line segment (B) appears shorter than the one above (A), despite their exact physical equivalence.

Figure 5-13 illustrates the *Poggendorf illusion.* The exit line on the right appears displaced downward relative to the entrance line on the left. Using a ruler, the observer can see that the two segments are, in fact, in the very same linear path.

Not only may equalities appear different, but inequalities may appear identical. An illustration of this is shown in Figure 5-14, called the *Jastrow illusion.*

Illusions may not only involve distortions of what is present, but they

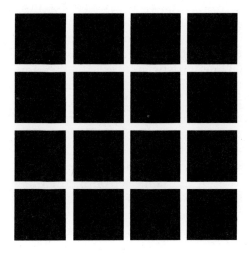

Figure 5-15. Hermann's grid. Note that visually there appear to be dark spots in the intersections of black and white.

may also involve the creation of "stimuli" that have no physical reality at all. In *Hermann's grid*, for example (see Figure 5-15), dark spots appear everywhere in the white spaces that enclose the black squares. The dots, of course, are in the perceiver—not in the figure.

There are many other illusions, some of which play a significant part in our daily perceptions. The so-called *moon illusion* is illustrative. The moon appears much larger on the horizon than at its zenith, despite the fact that its angular size on the retina is the same in both instances. If we did not have independent means of determining the distance between earth and moon, our perceptual bias would force us to conclude that the moon changes either in size or in distance under the two viewing conditions. It is interesting to speculate about the possible illusions of which man is ignorant, and how these illusions might be responsible for his current attitudes about the world and himself.

Perceptual Constancies

When an observer sees an acquaintance, his estimate of the height of that person is independent of the viewing distance, despite the fact that the retinal image of the acquaintance becomes smaller at greater distances. The fact that many features of a stimulus remain unchanged even under drastically altered conditions of observation is referred to as *perceptual constancy*. An observer will perceive a saucer on a table as round, even though the retinal image cast by the saucer is oval. If, however, the observer does not know what the object is, this shape constancy will not occur.

Size, shape, and color constancies have been cited by Gestalt psychologists as further proof of the nonelementaristic nature of perception. They have emphasized the role of the perceiver in many different observational settings. For example, if one places a photograph of someone who is well known to the observer in one field of a *stereoscope* (an optical instrument through which two pictures of the same object, taken from slightly different points of view, are viewed, one by each eye, and producing the effect of one single picture of that object, with the appearance of depth or relief) and an inverted picture of the same person in the other field, the fused image often appears right-side-up and is easily recognized. This does not happen when photographs of unknown persons are used (Engel, 1958). Similarly, if one eye receives "emotionally acceptable" material and the other receives "objectionable" material, the former will dominate the observer's perception (Engel, 1956).

Depth Perception

While seldom treated as an illusion, depth perception, too, is not easy to reconcile with sensationism. The retinal surface upon which light falls is two-dimensional and yet, when slightly separate images of an identical scene fall upon corresponding retinal loci, the fused image is seen in three dimensions. Furthermore, the effect is easily achieved stereoscopically. It can be shown that an observer cannot distinguish between "real" and stereoscopic depth. His absolute and difference thresholds are the same in both cases, or very nearly so, and his perceptions are reported as identical (Berry, 1948).

George Berkeley wrote extensively on the cues for depth perception (Berkeley, 1709). The most prominent of these are binocular convergence, interposition, size, and retinal disparity. Objects are seen as closer or as approaching when maintenance of focus requires a convergence of two eyes. Objects are viewed as retreating or as being further away when focusing involves a divergence of the eyes. Similarly, when one object obscures another, the former is perceived as being nearer than are smaller objects. Finally, any object that casts slightly dissimilar images on the two retinae is seen as existing in depth. Because size and interposition cues can act upon one eye alone, it is possible to perceive depth monocularly (involving the use of only one eye) though this experience is perceptually barren when compared with binocular observations. While Berkeley specified the cues for depth perception, it is still an intriguingly Gestalt-like ability, given the geometric paradox posed. How do we re-create depth from the two-dimensional events on the retina? Furthermore, since modern research has produced evidence of depth perception in the infant (see Chapter 8), Berkeley's empirical account does not fully settle the question.

Perceptual Organization

Additional support for the active role of the perceiver in all experience is found in the tendency to structure and organize ambiguous stimulus material. It is the view of Gestalt psychology that certain fundamental

Figure 5-16. Do you see youth or age in this figure? Initially, only one may dominate. However, once both the young girl and the old woman can be detected, the appropriate "set" allows the observer to go from one to the other at will.

processes within the individual control the qualities of experience. These processes all work to simplify, order, and shape the perceptual outcomes of physical stimulation. A popular example is shown in Figure 5-16. Depending upon the expectancy or "set" adopted by the observer, either an old woman with a large nose or the profile of a young girl will be seen. The ambiguity of the form allows the exercise of perceptual organizing tendencies. In the absence of detailed cues, the perceiver projects an order into the stimulus material. Tests have been fashioned, in this Gestalt tradition, which attempt to assess the basic features of personality by studying the organization imposed upon materials that would otherwise be meaningless. The Rorschach "ink blots" are illustrative of such tests.

Perceptual Adaptation

When light enters the eye, it passes through the lens and is turned upside-down on its journey to the retina. When Kepler looked through the back of an eye that had been removed from an animal, he saw an inverted world. The retinal image always depicts reality upside-down. To test whether or not this inversion of reality was necessary for correct perception, Stratton (1897) equipped one eye with a lens system that inverted the world around him while he kept his other eye covered. Stratton's research was conducted in the 1890s and by contemporary standards, it left much to be desired. However, he did demonstrate that after one week of continued inverted vision, one could adapt almost completely to these altered circumstances. Subsequent studies, performed on both man and lower organisms, have provided us with conflicting results. Man is able to adapt at least partially to the most severe optical distortions; overly mechanistic and empirical expectations are challenged by such an ability. If sensory systems are reporting to the organism what is "out there" and if this information is so severely transformed, then how does perception make the necessary corrections?

Significantly, lower organisms have an impossible time with situations to which man adjusts easily. In a series of ingenious experiments, Sperry (1943) surgically rotated the eyes of newts (salamanders) through 180 degrees. This produced the same effect anatomically as Stratton's inverting lenses produced optically. The newt's fate, however, was not as favorable as Stratton's. Food placed to its left led to responses to its right. No amount of training seemed to allow adaptation to this alteration of visual space. Newts are chameleon-like in their ability to modify skin color. With inverted eyes, they were found to alter their colors in response to lights from above rather than to the background conditions of the aquarium floor, as they normally would. Spinning in circles, perceptually confused, Sperry's newts lived out their lives without the slightest hint of adaptation.

Perceptual Isolation

Few laboratory demonstrations point to the active and inner nature of perception more than studies of perceptual isolation or, as it is sometimes called, sensory restriction. When subjects are maintained in homogeneous environments for prolonged periods (hours, sometimes minutes), various physiological and intellectual effects appear. When deprivation is especially severe, hallucinations may occur. Studies have involved the immersion of blindfolded and immobilized subjects in tanks of water kept at body temperature. In the absence of any sensory stimulation, the subjects soon experience self-produced perceptual phenomena.

STRATTON AND THE NEWT

The remarkable aspect of Dr. Stratton's experiment (really a demonstration) is not that he was able to adapt to the inverted world; this, after all would require only extensive practice. Rather, in time, Stratton perceived the inverted world as "normal." That is, the prismatic distortion became transformed into what we know as "natural."

This ability of the human being to reconstruct an ordered perceptual world under conditions that would overcome less developed species cannot now be explained. Dr. Stratton's nerves, we may conclude, did not rearrange themselves. His brain and sense organs did not turn themselves upside-down. Rather, his perceptual systems must have entered a new *functional* state, while remaining structurally the same. Even a poor analogy may clarify this point. An ordinary desk calculator contains a number of elements that do not change once the calculator is made. When we press the "+" key, all subsequent entries are added. When we press the "−" key or the "×" key, the *functions* performed upon subsequent information are different. That is, a system with hard-wired structural features still can provide a variety of different—even reverse—functions.

Whether the Stratton effect is limited to vision is not known. Would it be possible, for example, for someone to listen to tape-recorded messages played backwards and, with practice, to be able to hear the correct message? Probably not. When we reverse the world optically, all the physical relationships remain constant. Language, however, is not merely the physical relationships among sounds, but the semantic and grammatical relationships among words.

Arousal and sensory diversity appear to be as much a need of the nervous system as food is for normal physiology. In their absence, brain waves become slower and more irregular, subjects become anxious, their biochemical elements are altered, and their sensitivity is reduced. Language becomes impaired, as do abstract reasoning, dexterity, numerical skills, and verbal learning. All of these effects can be produced usually within two days of initial confinement. These effects would appear to warrant further skepticism in the face of sensationistic theories of perception.

Perception and Attention

Standing in a crowded and noisy room, an individual can carry on an intelligible conversation only by shutting out the distractions around him. This ability in its own right suggests a certain conscious control over sensation. But even more interesting is the fact that the individual will hear his own name uttered in a far corner of the room, even though he has heard no other part of that distant conversation. This so-called *cocktail party phenomenon* manifests itself in many different forms. It is one more effect that is difficult to treat in purely physical or sensationistic terms. The relevant stimulus in this instance is not intensity but rather, meaning.

One of the clearest and most suggestive studies of the active nature of perception was conducted by Colin Cherry (1953). Subjects were equipped with earphones designed so that a different tape-recorded message could be played into each ear separately. The subject was instructed to *shadow* one of the messages. That is, when instructed to shadow the message to the left ear, he had to repeat, word by word, the recorded message as he heard it. In a shadowing task, one must speak along with the speaker much as a translator does when he provides a running translation. Under these conditions, Cherry found that subjects could shift from right ear to left ear at will. However, when the subject shadowed a message to one-ear, he was entirely oblivious to all information delivered to the other. When subsequently questioned, the subject could not recall when the sex of the speaker had changed in the unshadowed message or even when the language had changed from English to French. In this experiment, Cherry adequately demonstrated the role of selective attention in perception. He left no doubt that conscious man is something far more than a passive receiver of sensory stimuli.

SENSATION AND PERCEPTION: A MODEL

There are two seemingly contradictory facts about the human senses that lead us into the most modern approaches to the problem of experi-

SHADOWING AND THE BRAIN

The listener who shadows information delivered to the left ear is generally oblivious to anything said in the other ear. In some cases, however, as when the nonshadowed information is highly meaningful and the shadowed information highly repetitious or redundant, there is recall of the nonshadowed information.

Research has also been conducted to determine how responsive the brain is to nonshadowed signals during a shadowing task. The figure below shows that while the subject is engaged in shadowing, the brain does not respond to repeated "tones." Note that the figure contains three panels and presents the brain responses recorded from the left hemisphere (LH) and the right hemisphere (RH) of a human subject. Each box contains three traces. In each box the center trace is the *average* response of the brain to the presentation of tone signals on 65 separate trials. Above and below the center trace are the *variances* associated with these average responses. Note that under the TONES ALONE condition, there are clear and sharp responses from both hemispheres. The same is true under the CONTROL condition which required the subject to read aloud as the tones were presented. However, under the SHADOWING condition, there is no defined brain response to the tones.

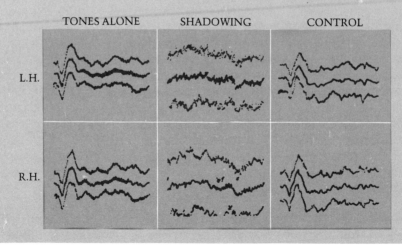

ence. First, the sense organs are exquisitely sensitive. Second, people—as opposed to their sense organs—are often surprisingly insensitive. In other words, as men and women walking about and experiencing our lives, we fail to notice or to observe accurately many events that are well above the threshold of sensory capacity. We will examine first the facts of our sensitivity.

Using our two most informative senses, vision and hearing, we enjoy nearly limitless sensitivity. The smallest physical quantity of light is the *quantum*, and experiments have shown that under the proper conditions, if as few as two or three quanta arrive at the receptor-level of the human retina, the observer will report the presence of light. In other words, for all practical purposes, we may treat the visual apparatus as almost perfectly suited to the task of detecting the presence of light. In hearing, our capacity is also great. The effective stimuli for hearing are molecular vibrations (typically, in air). Again, experiments have shown that the amount of vibratory energy necessary to cause neural responses in the auditory system is only slightly greater than that produced by *Brownian motion*—the random movement of molecules in a closed chamber and the smallest amount of acoustic energy that can be physically measured. In terms of absolute sensitivity, the human visual and auditory systems are not merely as good or better than any existing instruments, but are as good as any *conceivable* instruments. That they are not perfect is the result of two factors, one physical and one psychological. The physical limitations of our sensory apparatus are not limitations of sensitivity but limitations of range. While it is true that the visual system can detect the presence of just a few quanta, it can only detect those particular quanta whose frequencies fall within a given range. These frequencies correspond to the subjective experience of color, which occurs only within a very narrow region of the full spectrum of quantum frequencies. The region within which we can detect quanta is called the *visible spectrum*, and it runs from the very highest frequencies that produce the experience of blue to the lowest frequencies associated with the experience of red. Higher quantum frequencies (for example, ultra-violet) and lower quantum frequencies (for example, infra-red) are invisible to us. Thus, while we are extraordinarily sensitive within the range of visible light, we are totally insensitive beyond that range.

A similar physical limitation exists in hearing. Within a range of vibration frequencies (the audible range), we are able to make fine discriminations and to detect very low levels of acoustic energy. This range extends from approximately 20 cycles per second to approximately 20,000 cycles per second. Our sensitivity diminishes the closer sounds get to these limits, and beyond these frequencies, we are completely insensitive.

Of course, the human sensory apparatus is not unique in being limited physically. Any instrument designed to detect signals or to discriminate between different signals must be designed to operate only over a given range. Typically, the broader the range over which the system is designed to operate, the less sensitive the system is at any point within that range. There is an unavoidable trade-off between range (or what technically is called *bandwidth*) and sensitivity (or what is technically called *resolution*). The wider the bandwidth the poorer is the resolution. In vision, we pay the price of narrow bandwidth, and in return we possess great resolution.

It was noted that there are two limitations imposed upon the senses, and we now turn to what we call the psychological limitation. This can be most generally identified with the terms *attention* and *motivation*. Later (in Chapter 11) we will explore theories and research concerned with attention and motivation. For now, however, it is instructive to discuss them within the context of the bandwidth-resolution relationship described above. In this context, we might tentatively view attention as a kind of *selective filtering* and motivation as analogous to *gain*. By *gain* we mean the sort of function that an amplifier serves in a detection system. By *selective filtering*, we mean the ability of the observer (perceiver, detector, sensor) to select a portion of the total available bandwidth and to operate entirely within that portion. For example, the observer may be engaged in delicate surgery that requires the full utilization of visual sensitivity. Through attention, (that is, selective filtering) the visual system is taxed to the fullest, and the result is that the surgeon is relatively insensitive to sounds in the operating room, to a tight-fitting pair of shoes, to the odor of alcohol, or to the aftertaste of morning coffee. His insensitivity to these other stimuli is not based on a failure of the sense organs, but rather on a redirection of attention or—according to the model we have been using—a restriction in total bandwidth for the purpose of improving resolution in one of the "channels."

Our total environment acts upon us constantly, and the result is that all of our sense organs are under continuous stimulation. Odors are everpresent; our body surface is stimulated by clothing, by wind, by gravity; sounds are abundant; and a dazzling assortment of colors, lights, and shadows are before our eyes. Concentration would be impossible if we had to keep track of each of these events, moment by moment. Instead, on the basis of practice and experience (learning), we come to screen out—unconsciously, it seems—all but a few "relevant" environmental signals. The work of Cherry and the "cocktail party effect" cited in the foregoing discussion are but two examples of our capacity to selectively filter relevant stimuli. To illustrate the role of motivation in this process, we will now turn to the discussion of a recent technique for measuring thresholds, a technique quite different from Fechner's three psychophysical methods. As a result of this technique, we recognize that even such a basic measurement as the absolute threshold cannot be made in the absence of assumptions about learning and motivation.

Is There a Lower Threshold?

The data presented thus far describe the great sensitivity of the human sense organs. However, when psychophysical measures of sensitivity are compared with physiological measures of sensitivity, a significant difference is usually found. Generally, the directly stimulated receptor or nerve responds at energy levels well below those required for reliable verbal reports.

Initially, this discrepancy was attributed to complex filtering mechanisms designed to limit the total amount of information arriving at the central nervous system. It was assumed that neural responses to very weak signals competed with larger events in the nervous system and thus were lost in the "noise."

It is, indeed, the case that filtering of peripheral impulses occurs. But the amount of filtering can be modified by altering the subject's attentiveness and also by changing what is called his *response criterion*. This criterion is the rule the observer follows in reporting the presence or absence of a signal. He may adopt a very high criterion, so that he only reports a signal when he is absolutely certain it is present. In fact, traditional psychophysical methods impose high criteria upon the subject. He is instructed not to guess and to report only those signals that are clear. This traditional approach has been challenged recently by analytical techniques that were first developed in the fields of radar and sonar detection.

In designing a radar system, the engineer must strike a compromise between great sensitivity and high "false-alarm" rates. If the system is designed to detect and report every signal, no matter how weak, there will be numerous instances of meaningless reports (for example, birds, snowflakes, leaves, and the like). Such a system at a commercial airport would make traffic control impossible. Instead, the radar operator requires a display of airplanes in his area. He needs a detection system whose sensitivity is great enough to ensure the detection of relevant targets but whose standards are set high enough to prevent the reporting of false (noisy) signals. The difficulty inherent in any detection system is that measures taken to increase the rate of correct detection lead to inescapable increases in the probability of false alarm. On some occasions, the properties of the noise will resemble those of the signal. In order to prevent completely the possibility of ever reporting noise as a signal, the system would have to report *nothing* all the time, including on those occasions when signals were present.

Detection systems can be improved, however, by providing them with information about the physical properties of the signal and the noise. One source of radar interference, for example, is the echo effect from nearby buildings and mountains. The system can be designed to filter out all echoes from stationary objects and to report only moving signals. Moreover, it can be programmed to assign priorities to various signals on the basis of their velocities. Thus, a signal traveling at 600 miles per hour and providing a reflecting surface that is 200 feet long will be reported as an airplane with 0.99 confidence. A signal traveling at 40 miles per hour with a length of 10 inches may be reported as an airplane with 0.001 probability. In other words, the system can be governed by a kind of "payoff" program in which certain classes of events are reported unfailingly while others are reported either infrequently or not at all.

In the final analysis, the decision comes down to distinguishing between events consisting of noise alone and those consisting of a signal plus noise. Noise is everywhere: in the transmission, in the reception, in the amplification, in the decision process itself. The decision task involves a comparison of N with S + N, and the response criterion is simply the physical difference between these two quantities.

The situation for the human observer in a psychophysical experiment is much the same. Energy transmitted to him contains noise. His ever-active nervous system creates an intrinsic noise with which incoming signals must compete. He, too, is basing his reports upon the difference between N and S + N. To measure his sensitivity, it is necessary to assess his response criterion. That is, his failure to report a signal may not be due to any sensory limitation but, instead, to the adoption of a relatively high response criterion. A representative technique for determining his criterion is as follows:

1. The subject is told that at various times during a ten-second period a pure tone of very low amplitude will be presented against a background of continuous acoustic noise.
2. The ten-second interval will be divided into five two-second sequences, with each two seconds indicated by the onset of a light. A panel consisting of five lights (A,B,C,D,E,) is placed before him.
3. At the end of ten seconds, he is to report during which light (A,B,C, D,E,) the tone was presented.
4. He is then to rank-order his guesses as to which other intervals it may have been.

In this task, the observer may say, "I think the tone occurred during C. If not, it occurred during B; if not, then during D; then E; then A." Since there are five possibilities, the likelihood that the subject could simply guess correctly is 0.20 on his first response. He now has one chance in four (0.25) of guessing correctly. Then he has one chance in three (0.33), one in two (0.50), and one in one (1.0).

What has been discovered in experiments of this kind is that observers perform significantly better than chance at all levels of "guessing." By giving multiple choices and encouraging guesses, the experimenter establishes progressively lower and lower response criteria. The observer, who may believe he is guessing, is actually reporting the presence of signals much weaker than any reported under conventional (high-criterion) psychophysical conditions.

The research and perspective associated with the above information are contributions of modern signal detection theory. Using these methods, it has become possible to bring verbal report data into line with basic physiological data. The sensitivity of the observer is found to approximate what is obtained in studies of neural and receptor sensitivity. In fact, under appropriate conditions, the observer is so faultless in his detection of low energy levels that it is worth raising the question, "Is there a lower threshold?" Carefully measured, the human senses approach operating levels that border on what is physically possible.

SENSATION AND PERCEPTION: A REVIEW

The characteristics of perception appear to depend upon the observer to a far greater extent than strict empirical hypotheses would predict. These characteristics seem to defy reductionistic and elementaristic explanations and demand that any complete description of human experience go well beyond a simple specification of stimulus variables. The description must include the nature of the observer, his prior experiences, his expectancies, his innate characteristics, and the complex features of the immediate context in which his perceptions occur. Why do friendly faces appear larger than hostile ones (G. H. Smith, 1953)? Why, in social situations, do women appear to remember (re-perceive) names and faces so much better than men (Witryol and Kaess, 1957)? Complex perceptions depend upon variables that are not embraced by the mere "physics" of stimulation. Among the most significant of these variables is the perceiver's past experiences—what he has learned and how he organizes what he has learned, topics that will be discussed in the next chapter. Let us now summarize what has happened within experimental psychology to the older empiricism-nativism controversy as it pertained to the problem of perception.

First, as a result of modern research in sensation and perception, it is clear that no extreme form of empiricism can be valid. Even if we granted that all we know, we know from experience, we would still have to accept the fact that what we experience is determined by (a) the physical constraints under which the senses operate, (b) certain native features of the sensory systems that result in the tendencies to organize incoming stimuli and to treat various aspects of these stimuli in a preferential way, (c) the psychological processes of attention and motivation which, have not, as yet, been shown to be merely the result of experience.

Second, there is a definite trend away from the terms *sensation* and *perception* and a decided trend away from treating the two as distinct. Currently, the accepted practice is to discuss *information-processing* instead of sensation or perception. And this is not merely the substitution of a new label for the same old arguments. Instead, information-processing implies the interaction between characteristics of the stimulus and the observer, and with respect to the latter, there is full appreciation of the importance of past experience, hereditary factors, cultural variables, moment-to-moment shifts in attention, characteristics of the neural mechanisms involved, and so forth.

Finally, modern approaches to the problem of experience are not anchored to the assumption of *statics*, but are committed to the study of *dynamics*. That is, we no longer view sensory systems as instruments created by nature to do this or that during the entire life of the organism. We recognize that early experiences, subsequent learning, the demands of the situation, diet, culture, age, and other factors, all influence even the most elementary features of sensory processes. As a result of this liberalized view, the nature of perception has become far more resistant to explanation than the early empiricists could have imagined. The optimism of the nineteenth century led to a large number of experimental investigations. These, in turn, have raised serious reservations about the very optimism that inspired the research. Optimism has become realism; a realism telling us that very little can be learned about human beings as *psychological* beings when they are only studied one-system-at-a-time. Science, too, must accept the trade-off between bandwidth and resolution. In order to appreciate the full sweep of human psychology, we must forfeit the accuracy and comforting precision that comes from narrowing our attention to one or another of our features. Expressed another way, when we restrict our investigations to thresholds in vision, we can expect to learn much about the eye but not very much about the beholder.

No chapter on perception would be complete without a review of research concerned with the neuropsychology of perception. This research is within the tradition of philosophical materialism, and it seeks to establish the biological determinants of experience.

THE NEUROPSYCHOLOGY OF PERCEPTION

Sensory Codes

Given the great variety of human experiences and human behavior, it is natural to wonder how the nervous system processes incident energy and initiates appropriate behavior. In vision, for example, what are the neural codes by which man experiences changes in brightness, color, size, and form? From a physical point of view, all stimuli can be defined in terms of the spatial-temporal distribution of energy. Within this context, the physiological psychologist is concerned with those neural codes that allow the organism to discriminate intensity, duration, wavelength, area, and related properties of stimulation.

As the *intensity*, or amplitude, of a stimulus is increased, the discharge frequency of nerve impulses also increases. In fact, the relation between stimulus intensity and impulses per second tends to follow Fechner's Law—at least in vision. Figure 5-17 is based upon electrical recordings taken from the optic nerve of the frog during the presentation of lights of different intensity. Impulse frequency is seen to increase linearly as $\log_{10}$ intensity is increased; $F = (f) \log I$, where F is impulses per second.

Different nerves are especially sensitive (tuned) to different forms

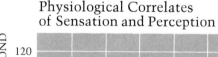

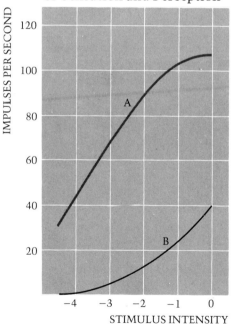

Figure 5-17. The relationship between rate of neural "firing" and the intensity of stimulation. Curves A and B indicate impulse rates under two different conditions. The very high rates shown in curve A occur immediately after the application of the stimulus. The rates in curve B occur after the fiber has been responding 3.5 seconds. The B curve reflects the effects of adaptation. (After the data of Hartline and Graham, 1932.)

of stimulation. For example, certain fibers in the optic nerve are found to be more active when red light is delivered to the retina than when blue light is. Certain fibers in the auditory nerve respond more to high frequencies (pitch) than to lower ones; others, to lower more than higher ones. Similarly, there are fibers in the olfactory nerve that are greatly activated by one type of odor and not at all by another. Thus, the distinction among various *qualities* of experience is based upon what Müller called the *Law of Specific Nerve Energies*. However, microscopic examination of these different nerve "types" often fails to reveal any anatomic differences at all! How do nerves of essentially identical composition come to produce widely differing experiences? There are two principal answers to this question. First, different sensory nerves (optic, olfactory, acoustic) are activated by different elements. The optic nerve consists of fibers whose cell bodies reside within the retina. These cell bodies are activated by electrical events in the rods and cones—themselves activated directly by light. The arrangement is the same in all sensory systems. Initially, incident energy (light, heat, touch, "odor," and so on) is converted to an electrical signal by a *transducer*, a device that is activated by one form of energy (such as light) and responds with a different form of energy (such as electricity). Then the different fibers carrying coded information terminate in different regions of the brain.

Color Vision

One illustrative sensory "quality" is color vision. In vision, the rods and cones are transducers—responding to light first photochemically and then electrically. Sensory transducers must convert all stimuli to electrical (neural) signals. Color experience depends upon the presence of different photopigments in the retinal cones. Certain cone photopigments are decomposed more by light in one range of wavelengths than by light in another range. How the photochemical decomposition leads to an electrical response is not yet known. The mechanism of transduction has not been discovered. It is known, however, that at least three chemically different photopigments are present: one whose maximum response is to reddish light, one whose maximum response is to greenish light, and one to bluish light. These *spectral peak responses* are shown in Figure 5-18. It is also known that these photopigments are synthesized from, among

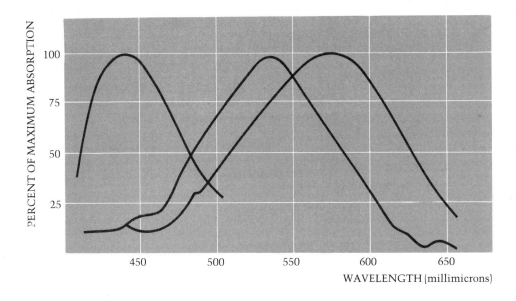

Figure 5-18. Spectral absorption by photopigments in the retinal cones of the monkey. Three distinct "peaks" are apparent; one occurs in the blue region of the spectrum, one in the green, and one in the red. Note the considerable overlap in the photochemical reactions of the three types of cones. (After the data of MacNichol, 1964.)

other things, vitamin A, whose absence in the diet can lead to color vision deficits.

The presence of three color receptors agrees with the old Young-Helmholtz trichromatic theory of color vision. This theory was based on the fact that a full range of color experiences can be obtained by mixing only three primary colors (red, green, and blue). The theory contends that all spectral vision is the outcome of a combination of only three color-sensing processes. However, certain color-blind individuals who are insensitive to green (deuteranopes) or red (protanopes) can see yellow, which is presumed to be the outcome of the activation of the red and green process. Furthermore, when color stimuli are reduced in size, they are no longer perceived as colored. This phenomenon of *small-field dichromatism* is interesting because the color experiences drop out in pairs: red and green at one size, blue and yellow at another size.

Such effects cast doubt upon the trichromatic theory as advanced by Young and Helmholtz.

An alternative theory, advanced by Ewald Hering in the nineteenth century, accommodates the foregoing effects quite well. Hering proposed an *opponent-process* theory that assumed that color mechanisms functioned as antagonistic pairs: red-green, blue-yellow, black-white. Stimulation of one member of the pair inhibits the other. Fatiguing one member has the effect of exciting (disinhibiting) the other. Thus, overexposure to red (R) results in a green (G) afterimage, the so-called *complementary* afterimage. Similarly, fatiguing blue leads to a yellow afterimage. Hering's theory easily accounts for the ability of the green-dichromat and the red-dichromat to see yellow. It also provides a ready explanation for the paired loss of color found in small-field dichromatism.

The major problem with the opponent-process theory was always the failure to obtain physiological support. Recently, this shortcoming has been rectified. Figure 5-19 presents a sketch of the retina and the arrangement of cells fom the rods and cones to the optic nerve. Using microelectrodes (tip-diameter = 20 microns), experimenters recorded electrical activity in the ganglion cells while presenting lights of varying color. They found that the same cell would respond positively to one wavelength and negatively to the complementary one. That is, they found physiological evidence for the existence of an opponent process. One of their records is presented and explained here in Figure 5-20.

It has been suggested that different nerves that are more or less physically identical result in qualitatively different experiences because (a) they are activated by different transducers and (b) they terminate in different regions of the brain. The optic nerve is no exception. Each of its [million] fibers bears a definite relationship to a number of retinal rods, cones, and bipolar cells (see Figure 5-19). As it proceeds back from the retina, its fibers terminate on a collection of cell bodies near the thalamus. This receiving station within the brain is referred to as the *lateral geniculate nucleus* (LGN; *nucleus,* because it is a collection of cell bodies in the CNS). Different color sensations are coded in LGN. Certain cells are stimulated more or less depending upon the level of activity in the fibers terminating on them. Finally, each region of LGN sends fibers back to the visual cortex of the brain. This arrangement is shown in Figure 5-20. Within the lateral geniculate nucleus, evidence supporting an opponent-process theory has also been found. De Valois et al. (1958) has developed

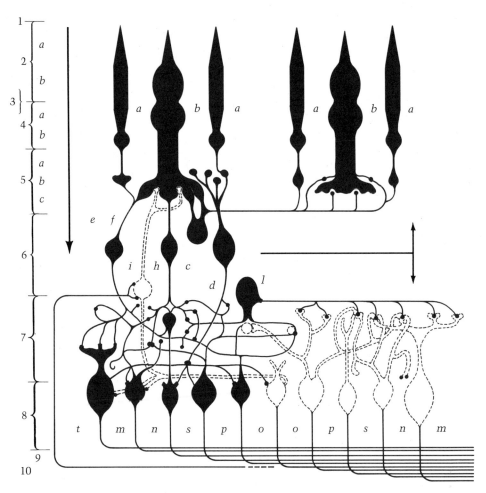

Figure 5-19. A cross-section of the retina. The numbers on the left indicate different layers of the retina. The arrows indicate the direction in which the nerve impulse travels. The rods (*a*) and cones (*b*) transmit their excitation through the various kinds of bipolar cells (*d, e, f, h, i*), sometimes across the retina through horizontal cells (*c, l*), to the ganglion cells (*m, n, s, p, o*), and on through the optic nerve (layers 9 and 10) to the optic nuclei and the visual cortex. (After Polyak, 1941.)

techniques for recording from single cells within LGN while delivering lights of various wavelengths to the immobilized animal. The cells always

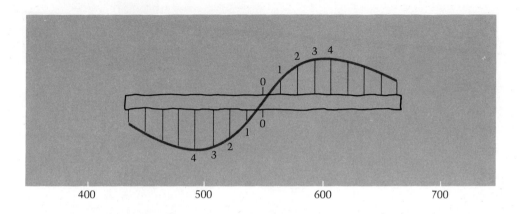

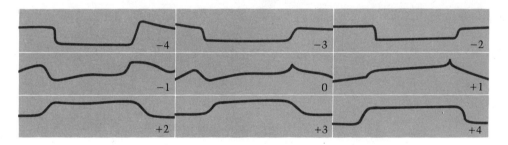

Figure 5-20. Opponent-processes in the retina of the fish. The trace appearing at the top of this figure shows the amplitude of electrical charges resulting from stimuli of different wavelengths. Charges have negative polarity in the region between 400 and 500 millimicrons; charges have positive polarity in the region from 600 to 700 milli-microns. The actual charges in polarity corresponding to 0, +1, +2, +3, and +4 and 0, −1, −2, −3, and −4 are shown in the boxes that appear in the lower part of the figure. Because of its shape, the top trace has been called the S-potential. (After the data of MacNichol and Svaetichin, 1958.)

display some activity, even when no stimulus is applied. Cells have been isolated that reveal an increase in activity in the presence of one range of wavelengths and a decrease in activity when wavelengths of a complementary composition are presented. For example, a given unit may, in the absence of stimulation, emit 200 impulses per second. When red light is presented, the response of the unit may increase to 300 impulses per second. When green light is applied, the unit's response may drop to 100

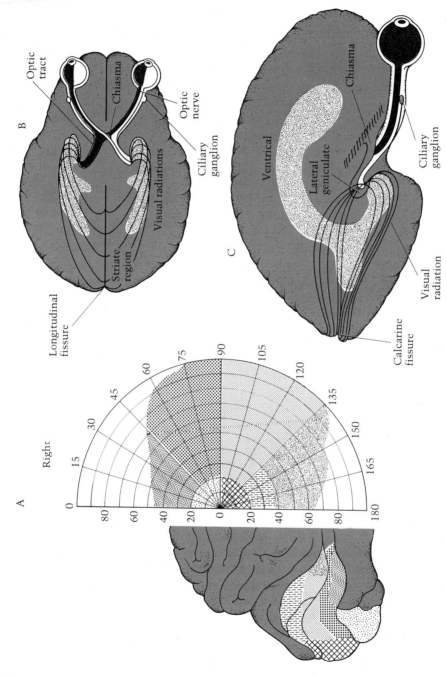

Figure 5-21. Visual pathways from the retina to the visual cortex. Note the point-to-point projection of fibers from specific retinal areas to specific cortical regions. (Figures A and B after Fox and German, 1936; Figure C after Holmes, 1945.)

impulses per second. Such a unit is labeled +R −G to indicate a positive response to red and a negative response to green. Research of this kind has also uncovered −R +G units as well as both +B −Y and −B +Y units where effects are found in the blue and yellow regions of the spectrum (see Figure 5-21). Analogous units have been discovered in the visual cortex as well. Thus, the physiological basis of color vision would appear to involve two distinct processes, one that is photochemical and described by a Young-Helmholtz type of theory and another that is neurophysiological and best described by a Hering-type opponent-process theory. In the final analysis, each specific region of the retina comes to be represented in a specific region of the visual cortex. There is point-to-point organization in the visual system from retina to cortex, as illustrated in Figure 5-21.

Pitch

Different fibers in the auditory nerve are attached to different transducers in the inner ear. These transducers (hair cells) lie along the basilar membrane as is shown in Figure 5-22. As air presses against the eardrum, three small bones (ossicles) in the middle ear are caused to vibrate. These vibrations set up fluid vibrations in the inner ear as illustrated in Figure 5-23. The basilar membrane sweeps up and down through its fluid medium. The hair cells are stretched and relaxed accordingly. The consequence of this deformation is the initiation of an electrical response. As with photochemical decomposition in the rods and cones, the hair cells' response is a graded (D.C.) one which—by means not fully understood—initiates all-or-none impulses in the auditory nerve. Different regions of the basilar membrane are displaced more by certain frequencies of sound than by others. High frequencies cause greater displacement at the narrowest portions of the membrane; low frequencies, at the widest. Thus, pitch is initially coded according to the region of maximum displacement along the basilar membrane. This phase determines which hair cells (and, therefore, which fibers) will be stimulated. The auditory nerve fibers travel from station to station with their information finally deposited in the temporal cortex of the brain. That frequencies are broadly represented in the cerebral cortex—and not just in the temporal lobe—can be seen in Figure 5-24. At each successive station, frequency "tuning" becomes progressively sharper. Thus, almost all of the basilar membrane responds to any sound;

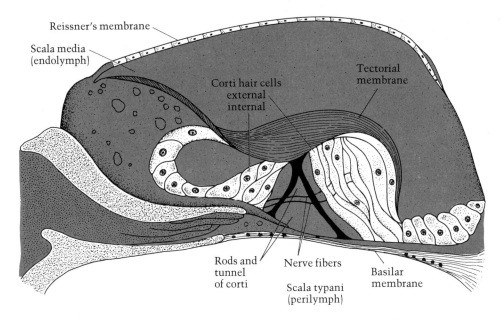

Reissner's membrane
Scala media (endolymph)
Corti hair cells external internal
Tectorial membrane
Rods and tunnel of corti
Nerve fibers
Scala typani (perilymph)
Basilar membrane

Figure 5-22. Structures of the inner ear. Note hair cells extending from the basilar membrane to the tectorial membrane. Fluid vibrations in *scala tympani* (the chamber in which the hair cells are located) incite motion in the basilar membrane. The hair cells are thus placed under tension and respond electrically to this tension. Impulses are then initiated in the nerve fibers, which pass into the brain as a bundle, the *auditory nerve.* (After Davis et al., 1953.)

certain fibers in the auditory nerve, to only a range of frequencies; cells in the auditory cortex, to but a few frequencies.

Olfaction

Different chemicals give rise to distinctly different odors. It is still not clear how such experiences are coded, though Amoore et al. (1964) have advanced a compelling theory. They have obtained evidence suggesting that the molecular shape of certain chemicals "fit" the shape of olfactory receptors that line the nasal passage. Figure 5-25 depicts this theoretical compatibility between molecular shape and receptor shape. Presumably, the "fit" results in coded receptor discharges. While the mechanism is unknown, the theory does account well for a broad range of odors.

In olfaction, as in vision and audition, receptors transduce information into an electrical signal which, through bipolar cells, leads to neural impulses in the olfactory nerve. This information is carried to structures buried deep in the *temporal lobes*, structures that are highly developed in organisms that depend upon the keenness of their olfactory sense for survival.

Olfactory adaptation to continued stimulation occurs with great rapidity. Even the most noxious odors fail to be detected after a relatively brief period of exposure. It is not clear why this should be the case. Perhaps because of the condition of the food that man's ancestors had to eat (rotten and aged), selection pressures favored those whose olfactory sense adapted soon enough to allow eating.

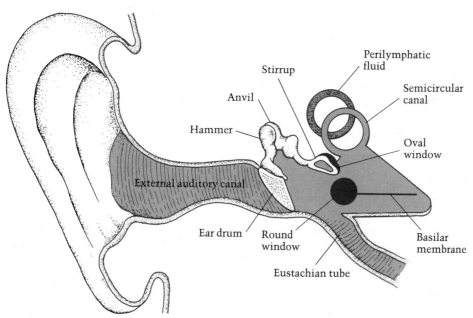

Figure 5-23. Schematic representation of basilar membrane within the fluids of the cochlear duct. Oscillations in the bones of the middle ear (hammer, anvil, and stirrup) are translated through the oval window to the fluids of the inner ear. Undulations of the basilar membrane result. (After von Békésy, 1935.)

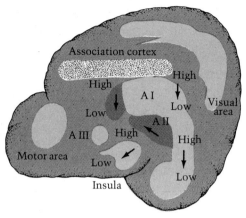

Figure 5-24. Regions of the cortex of the cat that respond electrically when sound is delivered to the ears. In some areas, there is a spatial organization for sounds of different pitch. Where the words *high* and *low* appear, the cortical areas respond most to high and low pitches at these loci and to intermediate pitches in between. Secondary visual areas and motor areas also respond to auditory stimuli. AI, AII, and AIII refer to the three well-defined hearing areas of the cat cortex. (After Woolsey, 1960.)

Taste

Taste depends heavily upon olfaction as is evidenced by the tastelessness of substances when the nostrils are clamped closed. In man, the taste (gustatory) sense is less sensitive than it is in many other species. As with olfaction, it has been difficult to specify the relevant dimension of the

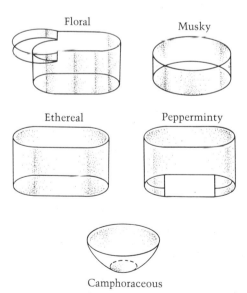

Figure 5-25. Receptors in the olfactory epithelia. These receptors may be "shaped" to receive molecules with compatible shapes. (After Amoore, 1964.)

stimulus. Currently, the sensations of sweet, sour, salty, and bitter are viewed as the outcome of different patterns of activity in different taste receptors. Fibers have been isolated in the cat's taste (glossopharyngeal) nerve that respond to certain stimuli and not to others (Cohen et al., 1955). The general findings from recent research are summarized in Table 2.

TABLE 2.   Response of Taste Fibers in the Cat's Glossopharyngeal Nerve

Solution Applied to Tongue	Water Fiber	Salt Fiber	Acid Fiber	Quinine Fiber
Water	yes*	no	yes	yes
Salt	no	yes	yes	no
Hydrochloric acid	no	no	yes	no
Quinine	no	no	no	yes

*"Yes" refers to the appearance of patterned responses following the application of the four agents.

Perceptual Codes

A number of phenomena were discussed earlier that appeared to defy empirical reductionism. These included some of the "illusory" stimuli generated by Gestalt psychologists. Over the years, physiological phychologists have been especially interested in uncovering the mechanisms that underlie these perceptual events. To a degree, they have been somewhat successful.

Lateral Inhibition

Reference was also made earlier to backward masking. Figure 5-15 demonstrated the peculiar "dots" on the Hermann grid. These phenomena are the outcome of special features of neural organization within the retina. It has been shown by H. K. Hartline and his associates (Ratliff, Hartline, and Miller, 1963) that in the primitive eye of the crab (Limulus), visual cells exert inhibiting influences upon their neighbors. For example, if unit *A* in Figure 5-26 is stimulated, its fiber will discharge at a rate such as that indicated. However, if adjacent unit *B* is then stimulated, activity in fiber *A* will immediately decrease. Matters are further complicated by the fact that a third unit, which inhibits unit *B*, will thereby disinhibit unit *A*. It is still not clear how such events occur, but they do serve the vital function of image-sharpening. Figure 5-27 shows the blurry image formed on the retina by the lens. This coarse "optical" image is refined by neuroelectric inhibition as illustrated in the figure. The dark spots in Hermann's grid are also the result of inhibitory effects produced at boundaries between regions of high and low excitation.

Form and Motion Perception

The Gestalt psychologists were quite emphatic about the role of "good form" in visual perception. They drew attention to the subjective appeal of certain types of geometric stimuli (circles, ovals, squares, vertical and horizontal arrangements, and so forth). Recently, evidence has been obtained suggesting a physiological basis for form and motion perception.

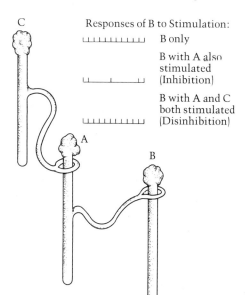

C

Responses of B to Stimulation:

⊔⊔⊔⊔⊔⊔⊔⊔⊔   B only

B with A also
stimulated
(Inhibition)

B with A and C
both stimulated
(Disinhibition)

A

B

Figure 5-26. *Inhibition:* Activation of B can be reduced or terminated by activation of A. *Disinhibition:* Activation of C reduces activity in A, thereby releasing B from inhibition due to A.

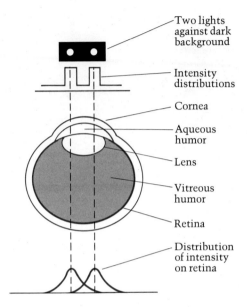

Figure 5-27. Two bright lights against a dark background create sharp distributions of light intensity, but by the time the light passes through the various structures and fluids of the eye, the retinal image is blurred.

It has been shown, for example, that the retina of the frog contains cells that respond (a) only to movement, (b) only to moving "contours" or "edges," or (c) only to changes in velocity (Lettvin et al., 1961). Similarly, in the visual cortex of the cat, Hubel and Wiesel have isolated unique cells that respond on the basis of visual stimulus motion, shape, and slant (Hubel and Wiesel, 1959). Moreover, these specific *receptive fields* are present in kittens prior to any visual experience. Figure 5-28 illustrates and describes receptive fields in vision.

There are, of course, many perceptual phenomena that continue to elude both empirical (reductionist) explanations and the search for physiological substrates. Yet more is known about the physiological mechanisms of sensation and perception than about any other psychological process.

SUMMARY

In this chapter, we have examined the physiology and the capacities of the major sensory systems. We have reviewed the methods employed to measure these characteristics and the variety of functional relationships between stimulation and experience. We have seen, also, how perceptual

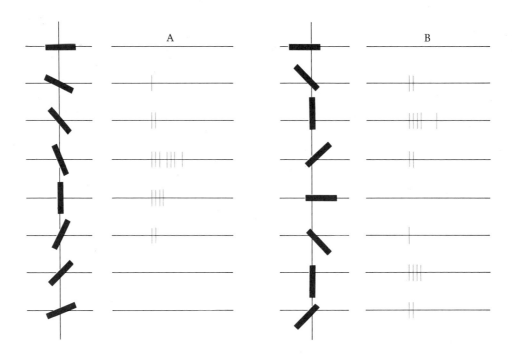

Figure 5-28. Part A of this figure shows a rectangular bar of light rotated clockwise while imposed upon a receptive field. Note how particular positions lead to increases in the firing rate of the neurons in visual cortex. In part B, one end of the rectangle of light is kept on the center of the receptive field as the light is oriented in different directions. Increased firing is observed with the light oriented in the vertical direction. In these and other experiments, scientists have discovered a remarkable degree of motion specificity and geometric specificity in visual stimuli capable of eliciting responses from single cells in the visual cortex. (After the data of Hubel and Wiesel, 1959.)

illusions, adaptation, isolation-effects, prismatic distortion, "shadowing," and the like challenge reductionism. Clearly, the rich perceptual world of human beings involves more than piece-by-piece additions of sensory "elements." Perception is affected by characteristics of the person-as-a-whole and not merely by his sense organs. In the next chapter, we will examine those psychological processes that are affected by and that, in turn, affect perception. Learning, cognition, and memory—the processes by which the past influences the psychological present—are all factors to be considered. We will see once more the continuing conflict between the schools of empiricism and nativism and the manner in which contemporary psychology is attempting to resolve it.

SUGGESTED READING

DRÖSCHER, V. B. *The Magic of the Senses.* New York: E. P. Dutton & Co. 1969.

Mr. Dröscher, an engineer by training and a science writer of great skill and imagination, has assembled a large number of intriguing facts about the senses of animals. His book contains photographs of great interest and clarity which penetrate the private worlds of many species. His descriptions of physiological processes are unambiguous and remarkably accurate.

GELDARD, F. A. *The Human Senses.* New York: John Wiley & Sons, 1953.

Professor Geldard offers a concise summary of basic laws and principles uncovered in sensory research. His treatment of the cutaneous sense is especially informative.

GREGORY, R. L. *Eye and Brain.* New York: McGraw-Hill Book Company, 1966.

This is certainly one of the finest treatments of the psychology and gross physiology of vision and visual perception ever written for a general audience. It is filled with excellent figures and photographs to complement the fluid clarity of exposition.

TOCH, H. and SMITH, C., eds. *Social Perception.* Princeton: D. Van Nostrand Co., 1968.

This anthology contains 25 original research papers concerned with the complexities of the perceptual process in social settings. The roles of personality, sex, culture, and motivation upon social perception are included.

WEINTRAUB, D. J. and WALKER, E. L. *Perception.* Belmont, Calif.: Brooks/Cole Publishing Co., 1966.

This is a monograph-size summary of several key areas of perception. Illusions, constancy phenomena, depth perception, and color vision are discussed lucidly and illustrated clearly.

CHAPTER

6

Adaptation by Learning and Memory

CONTEMPORARY APPROACHES

The contemporary psychologist is probably more influenced by the "psychology of learning" than by any other area of study. With increasing frequency, older psychological terms are being replaced by those drawn from studies of human and animal behavior: "behavior therapy," "behavioral management," "behavioral control," "behavioral science." Today more than at any previous time, the psychologist studying pigeons and rats, the psychologist treating children suffering from phobias, the psychologist assisting city planners, and the psychologist counseling married couples can talk to each other with similar terminology and can base their conclusions on evidence obtained with similar methods. If society after the impact of Freud could be described as the "age of anxiety," then contemporary society may well be called the "age of performance." The emphasis has shifted dramatically from interest in the deep motives and hidden causes underlying our behavior to the more immediate influences of the environment on our conduct.

The popularity alone of behaviorism has not been strong enough to account for this transition. We must look instead to the failure, actual or perceived, of alternative explanations and methods. As we shall see in Chapter 10, traditional theories of personality—the theories of Freud and his followers in the psychoanalytic movement—tried to provide an understanding of why we feel the way we do, why we have the desires we have, why it is so difficult to avoid anxiety, frustration, depression, and hostility. The explanations were, and still remain, complex, largely based on subconscious experience. As a result, a cloud of mystery has always surrounded the traditional explanations. Part of the success of behaviorism can be understood as the result of its appeal to one's common sense and common experience. Behaviorism has taken the mystery out of feelings and has made our desires and conduct more obvious. Whereas in 1920, a psychologist might have explained maternal behavior as the direct expression of an instinct, the psychologist today is more likely to describe those elements in the environment that will evoke that collection of behaviors referred to as "maternal." Whereas in 1930, a psychologist might have told an anxious patient that he had failed to come to grips with the resentment he continued to harbor against his dead father, the contemporary therapist is more likely to deal with the patient's *behavior* that seems to lead to feelings of fear.

One major characteristic of this altered perspective is that it is *pragmatic*, more concerned directly with cause and effect. Less and less does the psychologist attempt to arrive at a deep understanding of the patient's problems; instead he tries to help make his patient more *effective* in his day-to-day dealings with people. The traditional "Know Thyself" has been replaced by "Get the Job Done." It should be noted that this change in the therapeutic point of view has been most apparent in the United States.

In addition to the pragmatism that is a basic feature of behaviorism, there is another reason for modern psychology's shift in emphasis: more traditional therapeutic approaches did not produce the expected results. They also promised to make a patient's performance more effective. That is, the person who entered therapy a half century ago was also encouraged to believe that if the therapy succeeded, he would be more successful in his daily activities. Because of this explicit or suggested therapeutic outcome, society generally came to view psychology as an enterprise able to *do* something, not just as mere theory. As a result, when fifty years of psychological theorizing failed to create a nation of happy and productive citizens, many found it more logical to turn to the behavioristic approach for the answer.

This is not to say that Freudian psychology is passé or that theories of personality are no longer valid. Instead, there is an attempt on the part of "nonbehaviorists" to reconcile their own theories to the findings, methods, and general orientation of behavioristic psychology. Increasingly, references to Freud are used more historically than authoritatively. The term *instinct* is used far more in the figurative sense than the literal sense. *Motives* are discussed in behavioristic terms. The *unconscious* gradually passes from the classroom to the social setting of a cocktail party.

In this chapter, we will trace those developments that resulted in the acceptance of behaviorism. We will also review the methods of behavioral science as well as the implications of the findings that have been uncovered by these methods. We will then outline the more significant sources of opposition to the behavioristic approach, and will conclude with an analysis of memory, psychology's approach to it, and several of the firmly established physiological mechanisms that underlie behavior.

SOCIALIZATION

Consider a science-fiction account of a society of intelligent beings who live in a way that violates every cherished principle of human conduct. Members of this society habitually cheat and steal from each other. Children are abused and abandoned. The aged are neglected and left to die. The most tragic events are greeted with indifference or laughter. Every gesture of human decency is absent in social interaction. Expressions of even the most elementary concern for others are utterly lacking. The only moral principle—if one can call it that—is the principle of personal survival.

It is chilling to discover that such a description is not fictional, but a sketchy outline of the society of the Ik, an African tribe studied and recently described by the anthropologist Colin Turnbull in his book *The Mountain People* (1973). For two generations, the Ik have been accumulating a record of conduct that is nearly incomprehensible to civilized communities. How is this record of behavior to be understood?

The temptation is to dismiss the Ik as "primitive," but this would do no more than assign them another name. Given more thought, we might account for the behavior of the Ik in terms of the harshness of their environment: a mountain tribe struggling to scratch out of the rocks the barest necessities. Giving them the benefit of the doubt, we may conclude that their conduct is deeply disturbing to them, but they really have no other alternative. The fact is, however, that there is not the thinnest strand of evidence to suggest that the Ik are at all remorseful. There is not the barest evidence of guilt or reluctance on their part. To the contrary, it appears that underneath a selfish and indifferent exterior, there is a remarkably selfish and indifferent interior. At this point, the Ik would have as much difficulty understanding the behavior of a good Samaritan as civilized people have in comprehending the Ik.

Turnbull lived for nearly a year with the Ik. In that time, he observed that the callous and selfish disregard for one another was nearly total. He recalls only one instance of genuine human feeling. A very old woman had stumbled into a deep crevice. She was utterly ignored by all except those who stopped to laugh. She did not scream for help since, as an Ik, she had no reason to expect assistance. Given her age and the climate, she would have died soon. Turnbull rescued the woman and when she was safe, he observed that she was crying, something virtually unknown among Iks. When he asked her why, she explained that his actions reminded her of bygone times when people helped each other.

Terms such as *primitive* and *backward* have little explanatory value, but it is obvious that advanced civilizations provide greater opportunity for moral instruction than life among the Ik does. At first glance, it might seem reasonable to attribute the Ik's ignorance of compassion to a lack of systematic and self-conscious ethical training. After all, Americans normally do not laugh at the disabled, nor do they ignore the suffering of their children or friends. Nevertheless, the inclination to dismiss the Ik as victims of an environment devoid of moral lessons must be suspended. Several illustrations will show why.

A Study of Obedience

In 1963, Stanley Milgram reported the results of a study involving residents of the greater New Haven, Connecticut, area. Newspaper advertisements invited male volunteers to earn $4.50 per hour as research assistants in studies of learning and memory conducted at Yale University. Of those replying to the advertisement, forty were selected, ranging in age from twenty to fifty years and drawn from a variety of unskilled, skilled, business, and professional workers. Appointments were set up and each volunteer arrived alone. An accomplice of Milgram behaved as if he, too, were a volunteer.

The experimenter explained to the naïve subject and to the accomplice that very little was known about the role of punishment in human learning; that is, whether it was beneficial or detrimental, whether it was best administered by young people or by older people, and so on. Two participants were told that one of them was to serve as a "teacher" and the other as a "learner" in an experiment requiring the learner to master a list of words. In the actual experiment, a list of pairs of words was presented, for example, *bird-town, candy-ink,* and other word pairs. Once the list had been presented, the teacher began again, this time presenting only the first member of the pair (*bird-*), and the learner was to respond with the second (*-town*).

A "fixed" lottery guaranteed that volunteers would always be "teachers" and the accomplices would always be "learners." The learners were strapped into chairs (reportedly to reduce excessive movement) and were connected to an electric shock source. In an adjoining room, the teacher was given an instrument with a dial. The dial readings went from 15 to 450 volts. The "teacher" was told that each dial position would increase the shock by 15 volts. Also, signs on the instrument read, "SLIGHT SHOCK," "MODERATE SHOCK," "STRONG SHOCK," "VERY STRONG SHOCK," and "DANGER: SEVERE SHOCK," The instructions to the teacher were straightforward; begin administering shocks when the learner makes an error and increase the shock by 15 volts for every error after that. In other words, by the time the learner reached twenty errors, he was receiving what appeared to be very painful shocks. The learner-accomplice was well drilled in the number of errors he was to make. Moreover, when enough errors had occurred to lead to a shock of 300 volts, the accomplice was to pound on the wall but not attempt to provide a correct answer. More loud pounding was to follow 315 volts, and if shocks greater than this were administered, the learner was to remain absolutely quiet.

Before undertaking this experiment, Milgram had taken a poll of students and colleagues at Yale to learn what they expected the results to be. Nearly all agreed that only a very small fraction of "teachers" would continue to administer dangerously intense shocks to another human being—especially after hearing him pound on the wall and apparently too much in pain to speak.

The results of the experiment failed to confirm the prediction. Every teacher increased the shock intensity to at least 285 volts (INTENSE). Indeed, twenty-six teachers (65 percent) raised the level to maximum, 450 volts, 15 volts past the point indicated as DANGER. Some volunteers refused to continue after the learner pounded on the wall; most were extremely anxious. Many broke into uncontrollable giggling. If one refused, the experimenter would say, "Please go on"; or "It is essential that you continue"; or, finally, "You have no other choice, you *must* go on." Sixty-five percent of the teachers carried the "experiment" through to its grizzly conclusion.

Kitty Genovese and the Bystanders

At 3:00 A.M. one morning in the populated area of Kew Gardens, New York, a young woman was attacked. She fought valiantly and screamed constantly for half an hour until her assailant finally stabbed her to death. Thirty-eight people, aroused by her cries, were brought to their windows. In the thirty minutes it took to kill her, no one came to her rescue, no one tried to discourage the killer, and no one even telephoned the police.

This event precipitated a series of imaginative experiments designed to uncover some of the factors that determine whether people will help each other under certain conditions. One crucial determinant of what an individual does when confronting someone in distress is what others do. Naïve subjects, for example, have been called in to participate in a study, an interview, or a marketing survey. That is, they are invited to volunteer under a pretense. During the interview, the interviewer leaves for a moment and enters an adjoining room. Minutes later, a loud crash is heard and the interviewer shouts painfully that she has been hurt. What does the person in the other room do? In one study of this kind, 70 percent of all "interviewees" attempted to help (by either entering the room or at least telephoning for assistance) *if they were alone*. However, *if there was another person present* who (by previous instruction) behaved in a passive and an aloof way in response to the crash, the "interviewee" often followed suit. In fact, all but 7 percent of the subjects did nothing (Latané and Darley, 1970).

Prisoners and Guards

In 1971, the psychologist Dr. Philip Zimbardo appeared before the California House of Representatives' Committee on the Judiciary. The Committee was hearing testimony pertinent to prison reform. Zimbardo's testimony included a presentation of major findings uncovered in an experiment on prisons. The study attracted seventy volunteers.

Groups were randomly assigned the categories of "prisoner" and "guard." All were paid $15 per day. The "guards" worked in 8-hour shifts. The "prisoners" were actually apprehended at their homes by a police car, booked at the police station, and then brought blindfolded to the "prison" where "they were stripped, deloused, put into a uniform, given a number, and put into a cell with two other prisoners . . ." (Zimbardo, 1971).

The experiment had been scheduled for fifteen days, but because of the incredible series of events that began almost immediately, it was terminated after six days. Many guards quickly began to torment prisoners who, in turn, became demoralized, servile, and, in some instances, hysterical and acutely depressed. All bonds among the prisoners dissolved. Apathy and selfishness replaced concern and altruism. Supposedly "civilized" men had been transformed into barbarians; the prisoners were engulfed in fear and hate; the guards were consumed by their own power.

THEORIES OF SOCIAL MAN

The brief review of research findings by Zimbardo may be compared with Turnbull's observations of the Ik. In light of these results, it is not so easy to dismiss the Ik as "uncivilized," devoid of "Westernization" or reduced to "barbarism." The Ik can only be understood within their specific social situation. They exist as a tribe confronted by an austere environment. The daily necessities of life are hard won. Their culture is a culture of competition; their religion, a religion of survival. They are neither "mutants" nor, necessarily, the products of a morally bankrupt education. To argue otherwise would leave us without an explanation for the behavior of Milgram's "experimenters," the "bystanders" of Latané and Darley, and Zimbardo's "prisoners" and "guards." The subjects in these studies were not different genetically or culturally from any other group of American citizens. In religious belief, formal education, socioeconomic status, and general family backgrounds they were nearly a representative sample of the nation as a whole.

This is not to suggest that these subjects were "Ik" using another name. Indeed not. Milgram's subjects were nearly overcome by guilt and worry. Kitty Genovese's neighbors were shamed by their conduct. Zimbardo's "guards" were at a loss to account for what they *subsequently* considered to be unthinkable behavior. Thus, there is at least one fundamental difference between the Ik and the subjects in these studies: the latter suffered regret. They considered their actions to be wrong. They attributed them not to a rejection of the moral lessons of a lifetime, but to being disarmed by *the situation* they were placed in.

Since the dawn of philosophy, scholars have attempted to explain the nature of social man. Their writings have covered the full range of human activity, for whether one is concerned with law, family, war, art, science, music, or literature, the human experience is not understandable when removed from the context of society. Human history is a history of interpersonal transactions. These may involve no more than two people or they may involve the influence of an entire age upon posterity. But no matter what the number, the occasions and creations of significance will always be found in a *social* context. It is not surprising, therefore, that so much of traditional philosophy takes the form of social theory. The philosopher has two domains of interest: the physical universe and "human nature." When he turns to the latter, he becomes, *ipso facto*, a social theorist.

The importance of Turnbull's study of the Ik and the social-psychology experiments described in the foregoing is twofold. First, they help people understand the extent to which situational factors can control social conduct. But more importantly, they raise grave questions about the validity of those philosophical assumptions that form the very core of Western thought, or at least that portion of Western thought that is usually employed in teaching children how and why to behave. It is profitable to outline these assumptions and to examine them in light of research in the social sciences.

Nature-Nurture

Most philosophical views of social man are distinguishable from each other in terms of the relative importance given to experience and heredity. Some theorists—such as Aristotle and Thomas Aquinas—begin with the

"Man Is Basically Good"

Two of Plato's *Dialogues* are especially useful in illustrating optimistic assumptions about human nature. In his *Protagoras* Plato describes young Hippocrates thumping at Socrates's door early in the morning. Socrates learns that he has been so rudely awakened because of *good* news—Protagoras has come to town! After gently reproaching Hippocrates for being so excited ("Has Protagoras robbed you of anything?"), Socrates finally lets him explain that his excitement is based on the fact that Protagoras will answer all their questions.

In his good-natured way, Socrates agrees to take his student directly to Protagoras's quarters so that both may have all their questions "answered." The dialogue that ensues between Socrates and Protagoras covers much ground, but it centers on whether or not virtue can be taught. Initially, the Sophist (Protagoras) assures all those assembled that it can. Socrates begins his probing by asking Protagoras to define *virtue*. Is it one or many things? Why may virtuous men have wicked sons? Is virtue no more than happiness or the "good" or power?

Plato's position on these matters is clarified in a second dialogue, *Meno*. Here, too, Socrates is found criticizing the education provided by the Sophists. He defines the role of education as one of awakening the soul so that it may direct the student to a virtuous life. At this point, Meno teases Socrates with a common paradox: if a man knows something, he need not inquire about it; if he does not know it, he does not have any basis for inquiring. This, according to Meno, should make the acquisition of virtue impossible in that one either has it or, if one is lacking (a knowledge of) it, has no clue to search for it.

Socrates solves the paradox by quizzing Meno's servant, a youth who has had no formal education. By carefully ordering questions and by drawing simple geometric forms in the sand, Socrates shows that the servant understands the relationship between the diagonal of a square and its area. That is, while initially unaware of this knowledge, the servant can be led to acquire it. The knowledge exists as a capacity of the soul that is realized by education.

The Platonic notion is that virtue is an innate characteristic of all human beings, one requiring cultivation but always present as a human capacity. It is not taught, it is drawn out. It is not implanted in the young, it is simply nurtured.

Since Plato's time, this view of man has been defended often. One notes it in such sayings as, No child is born bad, as well as in the fully developed ideals of humanistic philosophers such as Jean-Jacques Rousseau.

Manes and the Great Struggle

In the third century A.D., the Persian philosopher-mystic Manes (also called Mani and Manicheus) preached of the great and eternal struggle between Spirit and Matter, God and Satan, Good and Evil. He saw man pulled in both directions, each vying for the soul, each dwelling within the soul.

One form or another of *Manicheanism* is found not only in many religions (Gnostic Christianity, Zoroastrianism, Buddhism), but also in social theory. The poet Dante (1265-1321), a father of the Italian Renaissance, defended monarchy as the only form of rule able to control man's "natural" tendencies toward vice, greed, and aggression. Three hundred years later, in *Leviathan*, Thomas Hobbes (1588-1679) described man's fear of a violent death—his need to avoid the "natural" assaults of his fellow man—as a principal justification for totalitarian rule. He believed that only Leviathan, the super-state, could control the "natural" human appetites of greed and vanity.

Hobbes recognized the role of life's general circumstance in creating destructive competition. In this respect, he was articulating a form of *situation ethics* according to which the rules of conduct are created not by some "higher law" but by the necessities and realities of the situation. Thus, the Hobbesian environment contains Manichean Good and Evil only in the sense that, in any environment, there exists competition among the inhabitants. This view is an obvious forerunner of Charles Darwin's "survival of the fittest," but with an essential difference. For Hobbes, the differences among people due to their respective native endowments, are small, even insignificant. Indeed, were the differences great, competition would be *less* keen and social hierarchies would develop quite naturally. It is only because every person is really at the mercy of every other person that all must invest their individual powers in the supreme authority of the sovereign.

The Manichean element in Hobbes does not exist in the idea of good and evil "spirits," but in his belief in the inevitable conflict between vanity and safety, between the desire to *have* and the fear of *losing*.

Another version of Manicheanism appeared in the nineteenth century as an inescapable tension between pleasure and pain. Accordingly, the social theory of *utilitarianism* was advanced. Put briefly, it was a doctrine of happiness. The ultimate standard in all matters of government, ethics, morals, and interpersonal affairs is the standard of "the greatest good for the greatest number."

assumption that man *by nature* is a social animal. There is a *native* disposition to assemble and live in social groupings, with an aversion to solitude. Others—such as Thomas Hobbes, John Locke, and David Hume—consider the social affiliations of man to be the result of the dangers of solitary living. Faced with constant challenges from a cruel and difficult environment, individuals seek security in numbers. However, in seeking the protections of a society, they must forfeit certain individual liberties. That is, they must transfer certain individual powers and rights to the group as a whole. This transfer takes the form of a *social contract*. It need not be a written agreement or a formal constitution. It may only be a collection of common understandings shared by all members. To ensure that people will comply, the group or society uses the threat of punishment for violations.

For all practical purposes, the social conduct predicted by *nature* theories are much the same as those predicted by *nurture* theories. Each theory allows the full range of behavioral possibilities. Thus, murder can be "explained" just as well by assuming the murderer is "naturally" evil as by assuming he has not been "nurtured" properly. At the level of common sense, there is not much to choose between these competing accounts. Putting practical purposes aside, however, there are great differences between a society organized on the assumptions about "human nature" and one that accepts the possibility of perfecting man through education. A society that believes man is naturally wicked will create methods of control and punishment. The society will tend to be repressive and suspicious. But a society that considers man to be naturally good will be more open, approving, and liberal. A society that rejects the notion of innate goodness or innate evil—that is, one that places the responsibility for social conduct in the hands of parents and educators—will sway back and forth between liberalism and repressiveness: As behavior becomes lawless, freedoms will be constrained; as order is restored, laws will be relaxed.

All of the foregoing discussion means that for those seeking a just, happy, productive, and creative society, it is important to know the merits of the "nature" and "nurture" positions. Their validity must be analyzed if effective practices and institutions are to be established. One does not build a concert hall for those who are deaf from birth, nor does one fill a birdcage with water. By knowing that nature has denied some people the ability to hear and others the ability to swim, a society spares itself useless expenditures of money and hope. Similarly, if a society ceased teaching children to read because after a week or two no improvement was observed, that society would burden itself unnecessarily with a generation of illiterates.

These examples are offered to establish the importance for any society to know about the psychology of its members: to know what is possible, what is probable, what is virtually inevitable. Most people would agree, for example, that universal literacy is possible except for the severely retarded. Most would also agree that increases in life expectancy are probable. Finally, nearly everyone agrees that death is inevitable. But how about crime, war, prejudice, corruption, envy, madness, mercy, and love? Is any one of these inevitable? Or always possible? Or highly probable?

We can return now to the Ik, to the obedience studies, and to the California "prison" experiment. What lesson can be learned from these observations? The lesson takes the form of questions. In light of the Ik and in light of these other studies of compliance and obedience, we may ask:

1. Can one argue that a proper education in "moral principles" is enough to ensure moral conduct?

2. Can one maintain that man, in his social conduct, is "naturally good" or "naturally evil"?
3. Is the individual's history of rewards and punishments enough to allow a prediction of how he will behave in a given situation?

We will turn now to the *behavioristic* approach to these questions.

BACKGROUND OF BEHAVIORISM

How is "learning" to be understood? The proverbial "wisdom of the ages" has had little trouble in defining it: to learn is to come to know something. But this is merely defining the word *learn* with a different word, *know*. While common-sense definitions have always been inadequate, man has still mastered enough of the principles of learning to use the process to his advantage. That is, the common man's *practical* wisdom has anticipated much of the psychology of learning. Ancient families reared their children and ancient teachers schooled them. Hannibal's elephants responded to the stick, and pharaoh's slaves worked themselves to death. In the Middle Ages, when written contracts were rare, learning principles were put to special uses. On their wedding day, the young couple would round up small children to witness the ceremony. They would ply them with sweets and toys and excessive displays of affection so that as long as the children lived, they would remember that fateful day when X vowed to love, honor, and obey Y (Coulton, 1931). Then there was a man who required a witness to the sale of certain properties. As he concluded the transaction he immersed his son in scalding water, ensuring that until his dying day, the boy would recall every detail of the negotiation.

Implicit in these practices was the assumption that human behavior was shaped by pleasure and pain. It is the same assumption that, in the more philosophically self-conscious period of nineteen-century England, formed the framework of Jeremy Bentham's utilitarianism. But it was not until the age of experimentation that such an assumption would find itself represented in laboratory investigations.

Today, many psychologists view *behavior* and *psychology* as essentially the same. Furthermore, as strict empiricists, they accept behavior itself as no more than the consequence of *learning*. To those not conversant with the history of psychology, such a perspective seems oddly restricted, even strange. In order to understand this modern attitude, it is necessary to explore briefly the conditions that helped to create it.

Behavior and Learning

The first laboratory devoted by title and by intention to psychological research was established at Leipzig in 1879 by Wilhelm Wundt. Wundt's training was in physiology, and for a time he assisted Hermann von Helmholtz, a nineteenth-century German physicist. Wundt was a man of great industry, and he was privileged to spend his early career in a climate filled with spectacular achievements. Charles Darwin had published *The Origin of Species* in 1859. Shortly before, Helmholtz had measured the speed of nerve-impulse conduction and thus placed the "animal spirits" in the domain of natural science. Gustav Fechner's *Elemente der Psychophysik* had appeared in 1860, and within a decade Fritsch and Hitzig would demonstrate the ability to produce movement in a living animal by stimulation of the brain. All these contributions aroused Wundt's imagination. His philosophical education had cultivated an interest in the most complex psychological questions, but the scientific spirit of his time made him impatient with purely philosophical methods of investgation. Only a new and distinct discipline could hope to combine the questions of philosophy with the methods of science. This new discipline was called *experimental psychology*. Its subject was *consciousness*. Its methods were the same psychophysical methods used by Fechner. Its perspective was structural, in the tradition of physics. Wundt's goal was to determine the elements of consciousness and the laws by which these various elements were related.

The early days of the Leipzig laboratory were marked by almost frenzied productivity. Hand-chosen, carefully instructed subjects were exposed to a variety of stimulus materials—visual, auditory, tactile—and were called upon to *introspect*, to reflect upon their experiences, and to report them accurately to the experimenter. Tentatively, the contents of the conscious mind were divided into three categories: *sensations*, *images*, and *feelings*. Sensations were viewed as simple empirical outcomes. Images were but the recollections of sensations. And feelings were the emotional correlates of experience and recollection. Rather crude models based upon association theory were developed to account for observed relations among the three. Reaction time was a popular measure of the speed with which sensations developed. More complex tasks were developed to assess more complex interactions.

It is in the tradition of Wundt that the color blue is found to be "cool" and the color red "warm." It is in the same tradition that certain facial expressions are discovered to communicate specific feelings, that complex decisions are reported to require a longer time, and so on. Wundt and his students were as tireless in their efforts as they were hopeful in their outlook. But as months of research developed into years, it gradually became evident to many that the Wundtian catalog of consciousness would never be a complete one. A prize student at Leipzig, E. B. Titchener, left there to found a laboratory and a new movement at Cornell University. This movement was called *structuralism,* and while it was intended to be a departure from the psychology of Leipzig, it retained much of the flavor of Wundt's work. The focus was on the structure (contents) of the mind; the method was still introspection; the results were a collection of even more data that confuse rather than clarify the issue of consciousness.

With impatience, scholars in America reacted rapidly to Titchener's form of German psychology. The most organized reaction was located at the University of Chicago, and the principal antagonist there was John Dewey. The Chicago school saw the search for mental elements as unnecessary and unending. Impressed both by Darwin's writings and by advances in the neurological sciences, the Chicago philosophers emphasized function over structure and mechanisms over contents. But even this alternative movement, known as *functionalism,* failed to rescue the young science from the confusion surrounding its methods and objectives. One of John Dewey's students elected himself to set things in order. His name was John B. Watson, and he is credited with founding the school of American *behaviorism.*

Not a man to waste words, Watson accused all of the psychology before his own as being a form of mentalism (a doctrine which states that objects of knowledge have no existence except in the mind of the perceiver), empty, opinionated, and metaphysical. He referred to concepts such as the mind as "ghosts" and to methods such as introspection as subjective and pointless. To Watson, a science can study only that which can be observed, and as far as psychological matters are concerned, all that can be observed objectively is behavior.

Watson's behaviorism was mechanistic and associationistic. The mechanism by which behaviors are acquired is the *conditioned reflex* (Chapter 8). The process of acquisition is repetition. Of the organism's *innate*, or inborn, tendencies, Watson admitted only three: rage, fear, and love. All other feelings spring from these and through conditioning.

Watson's psychology was little more than a neo-Cartesian study of *reflexes*, with some modern touches provided by the Russian physicist, Ivan P. Pavlov. Few contemporary psychologists would identify themselves as "Watsonian" behaviorists, and no one would attempt to use his barely adequate data to support such imposing assumptions. But he did—perhaps more in argument than in fact—challenge the way psychologists viewed their science. His criticisms were more valid than his alternatives, and his arguments were sounder than his methods. He made his contemporaries feel not only angry, but also guilty—guilty over pretense, guilty over ornateness. He immodestly preached about the virtue of modest objectives, and voiced passionately the need for objectivity.

While avoiding some of the arrogance of Watson, behavioristic psychology today owes much of its flavor to him. This school of thought can be summarized as follows:

1. The subject matter of a scientific psychology is the behavior of organisms.
2. The behavior of greatest interest is that which promotes survival, that is, *adaptive* behavior.
3. Adaptive behavior is acquired by experience, and its strength or durability is to be found in its consequences, in the rewards or punishments it provides.
4. Psychological variables, no matter how complex, can finally be reduced to measurable patterns of behavior.
5. "States" such as consciousness and entities such as "mind" have no place in an objective natural science. To make them available for study, they must be translated into observable elements of behavior.

We can now explore the application of these ideas to psychological research. What develops is a behavioristic model, a schematic diagram indicating the relationship between behavioral modification and environmental modification. The focus is on *learning*, which to the modern behaviorist is the process by which the activity of the organism accommodates the requirements of its environment. We must keep in mind that the laboratory findings that follow are merely illustrative of the larger behavioristic vision.

Associations

Recall that in advancing his empiricism and associationism. Aristotle posed certain "laws" by which sensory experiences were learned and remembered. To *repetition*, *contiguity*, and *similarity*, Locke and Hume added, through inference, *reward* and *punishment*. But it was not until the influential writings of Jeremy Bentham that the English empirical (philosophic) psychologists made "utility," "happiness," and "pleasure" integral features of their theories of behavior. James Mill and his son, John Stuart Mill, were both disciples of Bentham, and each expressed his influence in their psychologies. But neither was an experimentalist, and as with sensation, the laboratory investigation of learning began not in the country of its philosophic roots, but instead in Germany.

In 1885, Hermann Ebbinghaus published the results of the first research conducted on learning and memory. In his paper, he expressed impatience with the "anecdotal" foundations of associationism and with science's continued ignorance of the essential nature of the learning process.

Ebbinghaus began his research with a concept both ancient and unchallenged: material is best learned when repeated most often, and ideas become associated when their elements occur together in place and time. Given these "truisms," Ebbinghaus was determined to assess quantitatively the relationship among contiguity, repetition, and learning. (It should be pointed out how much Ebbinghaus was influenced by the assumptions of Fechner's psychology.) His measure of learning was to be *time required for errorless recall*, and he appreciated how crucial it was to select proper material to be learned. He rejected poetry, prose, and conversational verbal material because of their built-in associative characteristics; he needed a learning task unbiased by previous experiences. Since virtually no form of language was guaranteed to be "experience-free" (nonassociational), Ebbinghaus invented a meaningless language that he called *nonsense syllables*. These were formed by the juxtaposition of consonant-vowel-consonant, for example, *veg, mib, cav, wul, foj*, and so on.

There are very many possibilities of which only few (*cat, dog, top*) have any meaning; these, of course, were not used.

Placing a large number of nonsense syllables on separate strips of paper and drawing them randomly from a drum, Ebbinghaus constructed sixteen-syllable lists and measured the time required for him to learn the lists sufficiently well to be able to reconstruct, in order, all sixteen items. Over a nine-month period, he memorized many such lists, always testing his memory twenty-four hours after the original learning process took place. He also determined the time required for the complete relearning of the originally learned and partially (or completely) forgotten lists. Ebbinghaus's measure of associative strength (learning) was the time saved between original learning (OL) and relearning (RL). Thus, $S = OL - RL$, where S (savings) is the measure of associative strength that existed at the completion of OL.

As with Fechner, Ebbinghaus's great contribution is not the enduring nature of any general law he advanced, or even the accuracy of his data when compared with more recent findings. What Ebbinghaus accomplished was to put the issue of learning and memory in experimental perspective; to place these once-philosophic processes in the domain of natural science. Ebbinghaus-type "memory drums" are still used in studies of human learning, as are the very nonsense syllables he used nearly a century ago. Moreover, *savings* continues to be a popular measure of original learning —or, at least, a useful measure of memory retention.

In his experiments, Ebbinghaus found that with repetition, syllables became not only more strongly associated with those immediately before and after, but also with syllables further removed from one another on the list. The number of confusions in recall decreased with the number of these interspersed items; however, with little repetition, the errors were quite numerous. But in all cases, the closer together two syllables were (the greater the *contiguity*), the greater was the association between them, and the more frequently repeated, the greater the savings and the fewer the errors on recall.

While probably unaware of Ebbinghaus's results, Mary Whiton Calkins undertook research that introduced the method of "paired-associates" to the study of human learning (Calkins, 1896) (see p. 210). The subjects she used were presented with consecutive pairs of stimuli, one member of which was a color and the other a number. She systematically varied the frequency of certain pairs in a long chain of presentations; for ex-

ample, green-55, brown-82, green-55, red-15, blue-43, green-55. . . . In another series, a particular color was followed by an unusual ("vivid")
number, such as a three-digit rather than a two-digit number. The results of
Calkins' studies indicated that repetition was the most important determinant of learning. In a long series, the recent pairs were remembered
the best and the earliest pairs, the next best. That is, in serial learning,
recency and *primacy* affect associative strength. Calkins also drew attention to the role that "vividness" played in the formation of associations.

The research done using nonsense syllables and paired-associates is
substantial and has uncovered many of the variables that influence human
learning and memory. Some of these will be considered shortly. Here it is
necessary to complete the picture of early "associationism" by sketching
the psychology of animal learning.

DARWIN AND THE PSYCHOLOGY OF ANIMAL BEHAVIOR

We live in a time so comfortable with the Darwinian view of biology
that it is difficult to appreciate the revolutionary nature of that theory as
perceived by nineteenth-century Europe. While the ancient philosophers
had anticipated Darwin, as they did nearly every modern scientific theory,
no one had ever documented the principle of evolution with a precision
even approaching Darwin's.

His famous voyage on the *Beagle* brought him into contact with a vast
assortment of animal and plant forms that, at first glance, seemed to occur
haphazardly. The principle that finally unified this diversity—the principle
of *the survival of the fittest*—was impressed upon Darwin after his reading of a treatise on economics written by Thomas Malthus. Malthus,
making crude estimates of the rates of birth and death as compared to
likely agricultural capacities for production, concluded that, all other things
remaining equal, human beings were increasing in number at a rate that
exceeded the rate at which food could be produced. In his famous *Malthusian prediction*, he concluded that man would starve to death and
vanish as a race were it not for the effects that war and pestilence had
on the population. It was in these grim speculations of Malthus that
Darwin discovered that strand with which he could connect his observations of plant and animal diversity: those forms survive that have de-

veloped characteristics suitable to the demands of their environments. The two laws that governed survival were those of *natural variation* and *selection*. Darwin's theory of natural variation was particularly inventive since the science of genetics had not yet been developed. Even without this, he was able to set forth a theory very much like a mutation theory of evolution; from one generation to the next, small but decisive differences occur in the offspring. Some of these differences are irrelevant; others are counterproductive. But others make it easier for the animal or plant to obtain its requirements for living. These variations are *selected* by nature in the statistical sense; the challenges of nature "select" certain types for survival and, because of this fact, these types prosper in number, producing more of their kind.

Darwin's extension of this theory to man was bold, in both a positive and a negative sense. And while contemporary science tends to accept the main premises of Darwin's theory of the evolution of man from lower forms, there are still certain facts that remain unexplained. For example, the fact that tool use occurs *before* digital development of the hands (paws) is puzzling within the Darwinian context. Then, too, there is the question of the survival value of human language and the startling abruptness with which it occurs. Still, as with Ptolemy, Darwin allows us to bring a large number of otherwise unconnected facts together. No competing theory comes close to his in this respect. Darwin's theory was received with great enthusiasm by the developing science of psychology in the nineteenth century. In his two major works, *The Origin of Species* and *The Descent of Man*, he provided the major facts that support his theory of evolution. In *The Expression of the Emotions in Animals and Man*, it may be said that he established what we now call *comparative psychology*. Collectively, these three works permitted psychology to operate on the following premises:

1. There is no *essential* discontinuity in the progression of animal forms. Structural differences merely reflect the effects of environmental selection. Each structural change is designed to meet some functional necessity, but all the differences are understandable within the evolutionary-survival scheme.

2. Survival—the universal tendency of all living systems—is achieved in different ways. Yet the superficial differences between the fish's fin, the

bird's wing, and the human arm should not make us think that different laws are involved. One has been selected by the demands of aquatic life, one by the demands of aerial life, and one by the demands of terrestrial life.

3. Any "trait," any action, any process we observe in animals must be investigated in terms of the function it serves for the animals. If, in fact, it serves none—that is, if it is *vestigial*—either it will disappear in later generations or, indeed, the species itself will disappear.

It was not long before the impact of Darwin's theories found expression in experimental psychology. As the nineteenth century ended, the concern of the young science of psychology was with "associations" and the "contents of the mind." Through Darwin's influence, it made sense to examine these "associations" in many "minds," including those of lower animals. According to the theory, as simpler versions of ourselves and as specimens easier to control in a laboratory, animals might provide us with a simpler and clearer picture of the laws according to which our own associations are formed and of the functions that they serve.

The first psychological research concerned with associations in animals or "animal intelligence," was conducted by E. L. Thorndike (1898). Experimenting with cats in a "puzzle box," such as that shown in Figure 6-1, Thorndike recorded the time required for them to escape by pulling on on a looped rope, which allowed the cat to reach a piece of fish.

Thorndike observed that there was a marked reduction in escape time

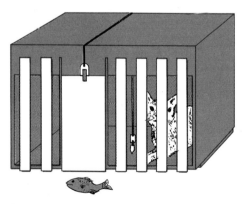

Figure 6-1. Thorndike's apparatus for studying learning in cats. Pulling a string attached to the door of the cage allows the cat to lift the door and escape to get a piece of fish placed outside the cage. Although primitive, this apparatus permitted Thorndike to study the general effects of practice on performance.

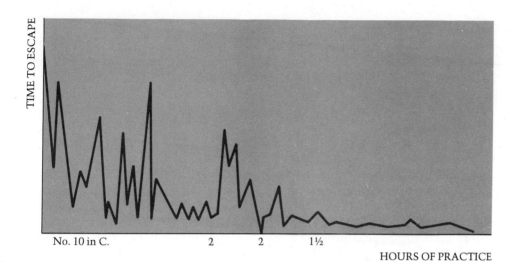

Figure 6-2. The first animal learning curves. The data from one of Thorndike's cats are plotted to show the amount of time the cat took to escape as a function of the number of hours of practice. There are many fluctuations in performance early in training. Soon, very rapid and consistent success occurs.

over successive trials. Representative data are offered in Figure 6-2, the first animal *learning curves* to appear in psychology.

From such investigations, Thorndike formulated a law of behavior that was really little more than a formal statement of ideas advanced by Locke and Hume, which were quite fashionable since Bentham's "pleasure principle." Thorndike's law—later called the *Law of Effect*—stated simply that associations that lead to reward are strengthened and those that result in punishment are weakened. That is, the strength of associations depends upon their effects. From this apparently self-evident statement, an experimental discipline arose within psychology, one which continues to dominate research in learning.

Collectively Ebbinghaus, Thorndike, and the early associationists created a *psychology of learning.* It was concerned with stimulus characteristics, reward, punishment, and practice as they influence the acquisition and modification of behavior. Since that time, a technical language has evolved with which psychologists can describe these variables and their effects.

Drives and Drive Reduction

The concept of drive has varied considerably in the history of psychology. Generally it is used to represent those states or conditions of an organism that result in changes in behavior. One view is that drive is an energizer of behavior; another view is that it directs behavior toward certain ends.

The status of drive in psychology is similar to that of gravity in physics: while it is not material but only hypothetical, its assumed existence allows one to understand a number of effects. Thus, drives are said to intervene between some condition of the organism, such as starvation, and some resulting behavior, such as the search for food. The term *drive* is referred to as a *hypothetical construct*, invoked to represent the complicated processes that link the internal environment of the organism with its overt behavior. Drives are assumed to be states of disequilibrium in the organism: insufficient food for cellular metabolism, overstimulation leading to tissue damage, and so forth. It is further assumed that the organism is equipped with regulatory mechanisms with which to maintain balanced physiological processes. The word used to summarize all of these regulatory events is *homeostasis*. Drives tend to compete with homeostatic processes, and learning is the adaptive feature of behavior by which homeostasis is restored. According to this view of the organism (including man), *learning is a means of reducing drives*. In this sense, it is a restatement of the Law of Effect. A further exploration of some of these concepts is offered in Chapter 10.

Cue

If a caged animal is deprived of food, his tissue demands are not met and a "hunger drive" is said to exist. If, under these conditions, a ball is rolled into the cage, no matter what the animal does, the hunger drive is not reduced (assuming he does not eat the ball!). If, instead, meat is introduced into the cage, the animal can reduce the drive through appropriate behavior (eating). Thus, meat and ball are cues, but meat is the only *relevant* cue for the hunger drive.

In any setting, there are many different cues, each signifying different things. Through learning, certain cues come to be associated with the reduction or increase of certain drives. Their presence allows the organism a means of altering a given drive level. That is, the cues are stimuli that allow the organism to distinguish (discriminate) rewarding from nonrewarding or punishing environments. Cues that "signal" the availability of reward or punishment are called *discriminative stimuli* and are abbreviated S^D; cues that have neither rewarding nor punishing significance are abbreviated S^Δ (Δ is the Greek letter *delta*).

Response

Response is any musculo-skeletal behavior (movement) of the organism that has the ability to modify the environment or that can acquire that ability. In the simplest sense, it is an observable part of the organism's total behavior. The responses of greatest interest are those that allow the organism to manipulate or operate upon the environment. These are called *operant responses*, or *operants*.

Environment

Technically, of course, *environment* is a term that can cover just about anything. For the behavioral psychologist, however, environment is limited to those characteristics of the world around the organism that change in response to the organism's behavior and that are, in turn, capable of altering behavior. One can also appreciate that cues and the environment are characteristics of the organism. For example, hunger is a change in the internal environment of the organism and it leads to visceral cues. Moreover, every response results in cues arising in the organism, and each change in the external environment leads to new external cues, serving as signals for adjustments in behavior. In other words, all of the processes involved are continuously changing and are interdependent.

Learning

A common-sense conception of learning assumes that the organism has come to possess knowledge that it did not have before. But to be scientifically useful, a definition must lend itself to measurement and to systematic manipulation. That is, the scientist must define learning in terms that permit demonstrations, measurement, and control. While, undoubtedly, learning does involve many complex internal processes, these processes are not readily apparent. From the perspective of the behavioral psychologist, learning occurs only when there are observable consequences. Consistent with this view, learning may be defined as a change in the probability of a response to a particular cue—a cue that was previously neutral in its effects upon behavior.

This definition can be applied to the study done by Thorndike. The cue is a looped string and is an S^D (a discriminative stimulus whose presence signals the possibility of escape). The response (pulling the string) is *learned*, because the probability of its occurrence is increased by particular changes in the environment.

Reinforcement

Reference to changes in the probability of a response is an attempt to acknowledge that a certain connection in time has come to exist between some S^D and some behavior (R). If Thorndike's cats never received food after their escape from the box, string-pulling behavior (R) would not have shown the same change in probability of occurrence in the presence of the S^D. The basic principle of drive-reduction theories of learning is that rewarding changes in the environment strengthen the temporal connection between S^D and R (that is, the connection is *reinforced*). Stimuli such as food, water, and the removal of pain, which alter the probability of a response to an S^D, are defined operationally as *reinforcers*. The strengthening of this connection should not, however, be viewed as a "backward" effect. Further discussion of this point is necessary here.

A criticism often directed against the concept of reinforcement is that it requires *effects* to be responsible for their *causes*. That is, how does reinforcement strengthen events that occur before it? How, for example, does a loud horn work backward in time to keep a child from stepping into the street in the future? What this criticism fails to appreciate, according to the behaviorist, is that on subsequent occasions, the stimulus is no longer only the street. It is the street *plus* the emotional responses conditioned by the pairing of the *horn* with the *street*.

Primary and Secondary Drives and Reinforcements

There are several internal and external environmental conditions that must be satisfied if the organism and its species are to survive. Opportunities for food, water, copulation, and shelter are essential. Their absence creates what are called *primary drives,* a reduction of which is termed *primary reinforcement.* If the otherwise "neutral" features of the environment are reliably present under conditions of primary drive, frequent repetition will result in responses to these previously neutral features. Such responses will be very similar to those obtained under conditions of primary drive. Similarly, by repetition and contiguity, certain stimuli—themselves insufficient to reduce primary drives—will acquire reinforcing properties if their presence is necessary for obtaining primary reinforcement. Thus, there are *secondary drives* and *secondary reinforcers.* Because these secondary drive and drive-reinforcing characteristics must be learned, they are sometimes referred to as acquired drives and reinforcements. An advertisement featuring a person wandering in the desert in search of a beverage may elicit a sense of thirst in a viewer. This is done by presenting an array of stimuli that, for the viewer, have constituted the conditions under which the primary drive of thirst will occur. The man whose food, water, and shelter are made available to him only in the presence of money will come to treat money as a strong secondary reinforcement. Similarly, if the money made available to him requires a certain "image" on his part, then articles of clothing, style of life, model of automobile—almost anything—may have secondary reinforcing properties.

Measuring Reinforcement Variables

Attempts to quantify the drive-reduction model of learning have often involved systematic variations of drive levels. The two most frequently employed conditions have incorporated hunger and pain (shock). In these cases, magnitude has been defined respectively as (a) number of hours of food deprivation and (b) shock current.

In a representative study of hunger effects, Kimble (1951) measured the speed with which rats would push open a door to get food. It should be noted that response speed (*latency*) has been used often as a measure of the "strength" of learning. Figure 6-3 indicates how running speed (the reciprocal of latency) varies under different degrees of hunger. These results support an "energizing" interpretation of drive.

Further understanding of drive effects requires more specific study of drive levels during learning and during subsequent performance. It has been shown that organisms will learn a task in fewer trials when very hungry rather than when only moderately hungry. Generally, they will also perform better, at a time subsequent to original learning, if they are under high-drive conditions.

The major reinforcement variables are the amount, the delay, and the regularity of reinforcement. That is, the rate of learning depends upon the interval between response and reinforcement, and the reliability with which reinforcement is correlated with responding. Performance is also affected by the magnitude of reward.

Amount of Reinforcement

Zeaman (1949) recorded the speed of runway-running in trained rats under conditions where the amount of food at the end of the runway was

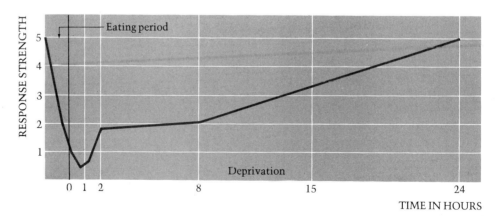

Figure 6-3. The role of hunger in behavior. During the eating period, the animal's strength of response drops markedly. At this point, food deprivation is initiated. As it progresses, the animal's strength of response again grows. (After the data of Kimble, 1951.)

changed. Rats trained to receive .05 grams and others trained to receive 2.4 grams were tested under conditions that reversed the amounts for the two groups. Profound changes in latency (performance) resulted, as shown in Figure 6-4. This effect of shifting the amount of reward after initial training is especially interesting. Animals trained on large amounts of food work far less energetically when shifted to lower amounts, a so-called *depression* effect. Animals initially trained on small amounts of reward display a substantial increase in their behavior when shifted to larger amounts, an effect that has been called *elation.* Such effects have been used to understand further what in ordinary language is called *incentive;* large rewards presumably have more incentive value than smaller ones. At the root of incentive value is, of course, discrimination learning. Typically, the animal's long history of food reinforcement has associated the amount of reward with the rate and with the duration of drive reduction. After all, the onset of hunger is a function of the amount of food consumed prior to the initiation of deprivation. Interestingly, however,

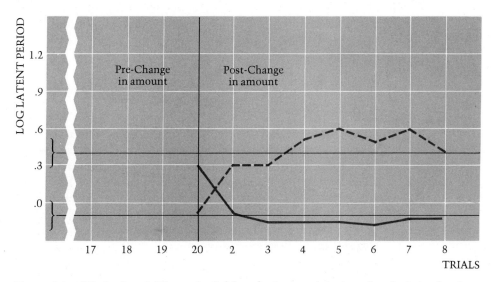

Figure 6-4. "Elation" and "depression" following changes in the amount of reward. Animals that are used to one amount of food reward show a great reduction in response strength when a smaller amount of food reward is introduced. Animals given an increased food reward show a great increase in response strength. (After the data of Zeaman, 1949.)

the magnitude of reward seems to have little effect upon problem solving, although, as can be seen in Figure 6-4, it does influence response strength or speed. That is, while the animal's performance is affected, learning is not.

Delay of Reinforcement

The variable of delay of reinforcement can be manipulated as an experimental test of the associationist's concept of contiguity. The research question is concerned with how close together in time response and reinforcement must be for the latter to affect the former. It turns out that, at least for lower organisms (rats, cats, and so on), intervals between response and reinforcement must be in terms of seconds if learning is to occur. For example, if a rat is to learn to press a lever in order to obtain a pellet of food, the delivery of food must follow the bar-press within 5 to 10 seconds, or the rat will never learn the pressing response. It has been found that longer delays are less interfering with monkeys, and man can accommodate very long delays. It would be interesting to determine the maximum delays of reinforcement at which learning still occurs from infancy to adulthood.

Regularity of Reinforcement

The last major reinforcement variable, and in some respects the most intriguing, is regularity of reinforcement. It is not necessary for every response occurrence to be reinforced for that response to be learned. If a hungry rat receives a pellet of food every time he presses the lever, he will acquire lever-pressing behavior in fewer trials than a rat reinforced for, say, every third response. Generally, the greater the regularity of reinforcement, the more rapidly learning occurs. However, if one is concerned with the durability or persistence of learned behavior, the role of regularity becomes surprisingly complex.

Persistence or durability of learning implies the resistance of learned behavior to *extinction*. If a rat has learned to press a bar to obtain pellets and is subsequently no longer rewarded, the rate of bar-pressing will ultimately decrease to the pretraining (low) level. This reduction in response probability as a result of nonreinforcement is called *extinction*.

The most extensive studies of extinction and reinforcement regularity have been undertaken by B. F. Skinner (1938) and his students and collaborators. It was he who provided the term *schedules of reinforcement* to describe the various ways in which animals could be reinforced. The major varieties of reinforcement schedules are:

1. Continuous reinforcement (CRF).
2. Fixed ratio (FR).
3. Fixed interval (FI).
4. Variable ratio (VR).
5. Variable interval (VI).
6. Mixed (VRFI, FRVI, and so forth).

The CRF schedule provides a reinforcement for every appropriate response: each time the bar is pressed, a pellet of food is delivered. With FR reinforcement, every *n*th response is reinforced: for example, with FR 5, every fifth bar press results in a pellet. Under FI reinforcement, the first response after *n* minutes (since the preceding reinforcement) is reinforced. An FI-2 schedule requires that the animal wait two minutes from the last reinforcement before pressing the bar again. No response during that interval is rewarded. VR and VI schedules allow reinforcement on a variable (random) basis. For example, VR 8 dictates that, on the average, one out of every eight responses will be reinforced, but there is no way of telling which one it will be. Thus, the animal may be reinforced twice in succession and then be nonreinforced for the next 18 bar-presses. With VI-3, successive reinforcements will occur at three-minute intervals on the average. But on one occasion, the effective interval may be ten seconds; on another, five minutes.

Skinner devised a novel means of collecting and displaying data from animals "taught" to bar-press. His now-famous "Skinner box" is depicted in Figure 6-5. Also shown is a cumulative recorder and the strip chart on which response events are recorded. The cumulative recorder is simply a rotating drum and a pen deflected by one unit each time the bar is pressed. The drum rotates at a constant speed, and the cumulative record provides a written history of bar-pressing over the duration of the animal's training. The "hash" mark indicates the delivery of a pellet.

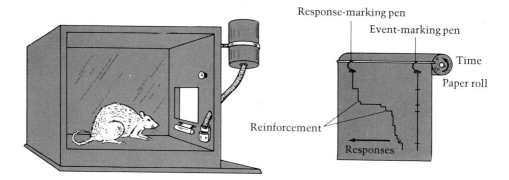

Figure 6-5. On the left of this figure, a rat works diligently to secure food pellets. Pressing the bar activates a feeder that releases a food pellet through a tube into a small well. Note, to the right, a *cumulative record*. Each press of the bar moves an ink- pen up one notch as the rolled paper flows continuously. Hash marks indicate when food reward is provided. The slope of the record indicates the rate at which the rat is responding. (After Reynolds, 1968.)

If the animal never pressed the bar, the record would show no deflection over time. If bar-presses occurred every 60 seconds, the record would look like that shown in Figure 6-6. When the deflection reaches the top of the trace, the pen resets.

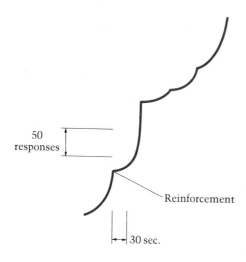

Figure 6-6. *Schedule effects.* Animals placed on a fixed-interval schedule will emit most responses just before the required elapsed time. As the animal learns the interval schedule, a regular "scallop-shape" cumulative record emerges. (After Reynolds, 1968.)

The effects of different schedules of reinforcement upon response rate are illustrated in Figure 6-7.

The animal's training cannot begin with high ratio or interval requirements, since extinction would occur before learning! Rather, CRF is used to train a reliable bar-pressing response. Gradually, (during successive sessions), CRF gives way to a low FR (FR 2 or FR 3); then, to higher and higher FR's; then, to a high VR. Once the animal has acquired this high VR behavior, extinction may never occur. That is, no matter how many responses fail to secure reward, the animal will continue to bar-press. Since VR reinforcement provides no cue as to when reinforcement should occur, the animal has no basis upon which to cease responding ("hoping"). It is not surprising that VR performance has been called "gambling" behavior. In general, behavior acquired under conditions of irregular

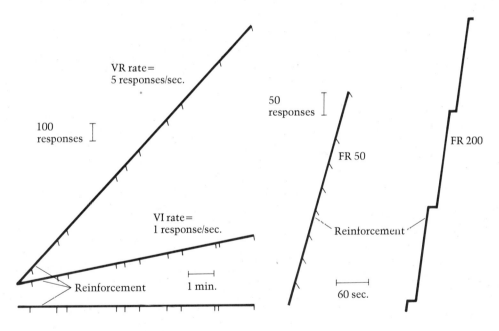

Figure 6-7. *Schedule effects.* Variable ratio and variable interval effects are shown in the traces at the left and fixed-ratio effects are shown at the right. Note how the slopes (rates of responding) can be altered through the use of different schedules of reinforcement. (After Reynolds, 1968.)

reinforcement (VR, VI, or VRVI) is extraordinary resistant to extinction; for all practical purposes, some schedules may result in unextinguishable behavior. The common-sense view of the need for consistency in training is not supported by the effects of irregular (partial) reinforcement.

Generalization and Discrimination

Once the organism has come to respond reliably in the presence of a particular S^D, responses will be made to other stimuli which, while not

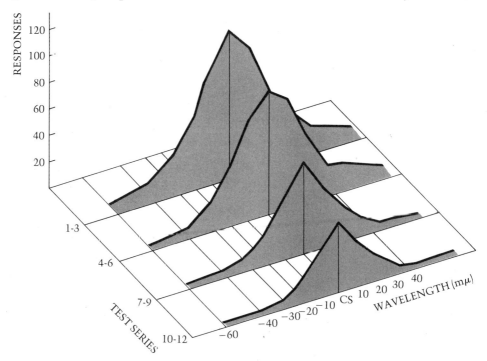

Figure 6-8. *Extinction and generalization.* As extinction proceeds, from the first three sessions (1-3) to sessions 10-12, responses from pigeons diminish, while remaining highest to the conditioned stimulus (CS). As the test stimuli become more and more different from the color of the CS, the response rate falls off progressively. (After the data of Guttman and Kalish, 1956.)

identical, are similar to the S^D. For example, if a rat is given food pellets for bar-pressing in the presence of red light and given no pellets when pressing in the absence of red light, he soon learns to respond only when red light (S^D) is present; he has discriminated between S^D and S^Δ conditions. However, should an animal so trained be exposed to orange or green light—or any color light at all—responses will occur at rates higher than those to S^Δ but lower than those to S^D. The process by which those stimuli physically similar to an S^D (Hume's *resemblance*) share its response-controlling properties is referred to as *generalization*. Discrimination and generalization, while opposing processes, are both crucial to behavioral adaptation. A driver must respond differently (discriminatively) to a red traffic light than he does to a red candy wrapper. Similarly, he must be able to treat ten single dollar bills, two fives, and one ten the same. Discrimination endows behavior with the characteristics of precision and accuracy, while generalization allows efficiency and flexibility.

With training, generalizations can be made progressively narrower, progressively more discriminating. Illustrative of this is the research in animal psychophysics by Guttman and Kalish (1956). Pigeons, originally trained to peck a colored key of a specific wavelength, displayed considerable generalization in the subsequent test series. While they responded most to the training color, they also responded to hues as much as 40mμ higher and lower in wavelength than the S^D. During extinction, the generalization gradients became flatter, as is shown in Figure 6-8.

Discriminative Stimuli and Secondary Reinforcement

The operational definitions of secondary reinforcement and S^D are different, but these two types of stimuli can share certain basic properties. Operationally, a reinforcer is any stimulus that the animal will work to secure (a positive reinforcement) or to avoid (a negative reinforcement). Again operationally, a discriminative stimulus (S^D) is any stimulus whose presence signals the availability of reinforcement. It has been shown that an S^D may come to function as a secondary reinforcer in its own right. If pellets are available only when a light (S^D) is on, the animal will work to turn on that light; the S^D now has secondary reinforcing properties.

Reward and Punishment

There has been a continuing controversy over the relative advantages of reward and punishment in the control of human behavior. Behavior shaped by negative (aversive) stimulation can be remarkably resistant to extinction. Moreover, very few negative reinforcements may be necessary. A case in point is *avoidance conditioning* (Sidman, 1953). The animal is shocked at certain intervals unless a bar is pressed. After only several successful avoidances, the animal will continue to press the bar, often thousands of times. On a common-sense level, the only way the animal can tell whether shock will still occur if bar-pressing ceases is to risk receiving a shock. Generally, this experiment is one the animal prefers not to conduct. Avoidance conditioning usually involves an S^D (such as light) followed by a punishing stimulus if the avoidance response is not made.

Such avoidance conditioning was once viewed as paradoxical, because surprisingly few reinforcements were necessary for the establishment of extraordinarily persistent behavior. An explanation for this phenomenon has been given by Solomon and Wynne (1954). The S^D, according to their view, elicits strong internal stimuli of a negative nature. These include changes in heartbeat, blood pressure, blood chemistry—a whole group of visceral changes that form the biological basis of fear. Each avoidance response successfully reduces the intensity of these internal stimuli; in other words, the response is fear-reducing. Since we know these "emotional" responses can be conditioned with very few reinforcements, it is not surprising that avoidance behavior becomes so persistent with so very few reinforcements.

By and large, punishment variables are sensitive to the same parameters as the variables of reward, although shifts in the amount of punishment generally do not lead to elation and depression effects (D'Amato, 1969). Shifts from punishment to nonpunishment, however, have been reported to yield particularly marked elation effects (Azrin, 1963). Similarly, delay of punishment retards the learning of appropriate escape or avoidance behavior just as delay of reward retards reward-gaining behavior (Fowler and Trapold, 1962). Interestingly, punishment may be used as an S^D for reward, so that organisms will work *for* punishment in order to secure reward, offering a model of *masochism*.

Pain, of course, is not the only form of aversive stimulation. The

CONDITIONED AVOIDANCE

The organism lucklessly facing a "conditioned-avoidance" paradigm has the forces of both biology and strategy to contend with. First (as described by Solomon and Wynne) the conditioning procedures lead not only to *operant* responses, such as limb-withdrawal, jumping, or running, but also to conditioned *reflexes* of a visceral nature, such as increased heartbeat, changes in blood pressure, muscle tone, respiration, and the like. This latter class of reflexes is associated with what is normally called "anxiety." Thus, in order for the tendency to respond to be weakened, *both* components (the operant and the visceral, or "Pavlovian") must be diminished. Furthermore, *strategically* the organism is in a peculiar position, for in order to discover whether the punishing stimulus will continue to follow the signal, the organism must risk being punished! The situation is analogous to one in which a person has been shocked by an exposed electrical wire and is not sure whether the right fuse has been removed. In order to learn if it has, another shock must be risked. Circumstances such as these produce persistent "avoidance" behavior, which can endure long after the removal of the aversive stimuli that were initially responsible for the behavior in question. Political history also offers grim evidence of the effectiveness of "avoidance conditioning." The government that executes or tortures the first protesting citizens often can control entire populations by doing no more than presenting the threat of similar treatment.

mere withholding of rewards also has negative properties. Animals accustomed to finding food in the goal box will become highly agitated when they are confronted with a "bare cupboard." This agitation has been treated as a "frustration" effect (Amsel, 1962) and has interesting parallels in our daily lives. It is also important to note that the effects of delayed reward and punishment depend on where they occur in the chain of behavior. For example, if an animal begins to run down a runway and is repeatedly delayed in the middle, on subsequent trials, he will run more slowly from start to middle but more quickly from middle to end. This frustration effect is viewed as the consequence of "thwarting."

One frequent question concerns the proper application of reward and punishment and the proper occasions for nonreinforcement. Several generalizations from available data can be offered in response to this question. Because of the fear-inducing properties of punishment, behavior controlled by conditioned avoidance or maintained by aversive stimulation may well contain emotional components that compete with desired outcomes of behavior. Learning academic material in the interest of avoiding punishment may be as efficient as, or more efficient than, learning the same material in an attempt to secure reward. However, while the amount learned may be the same, the student may also learn—by stimulus generalization—to fear or to avoid the circumstances of learning, for example, school. Under different circumstances, where it is essential to terminate undesirable behavior quickly (such as drunken driving), the application or threat of the application of punishing stimuli may be warranted. Detailed discussions of reward and punishment are available (Logan and Wagner, 1965; D'Amato, 1969).

IMPLICATIONS OF THE BEHAVIORISTIC MODEL

The research we have just examined has been concerned primarily with learning by rats and pigeons. The tasks have been intentionally simplified—bar-pressing, key-pecking, solving mazes, running down runways—for purposes of objective measurement. But hidden by these simplifications and disguised by the choice of experimental animals is a general theory of behavior. The name most commonly associated with this theory is B. F. Skinner. Skinner has not only led the major technical innovations in the field of operant conditioning but through his novel, *Walden Two* (1959), and his social treatise, *Beyond Freedom and Dignity* (1974), he has established himself as the major spokesman for modern behaviorism as a *social* science. Using the principle that a scientist should not be held responsible for the fiction he writes, we will not examine *Walden Two* but, instead, concern ourselves with *Beyond Freedom and Dignity*.

If one expression can aptly summarize a complete point of view, then "No Praise—No Blame" is the essence of *Beyond Freedom and Dignity*. It is Skinner's argument that since all actions are determined by reinforcement, the individual is not free and is not, therefore, accountable for his actions. That man may think he is free to choose one automobile over another is no different from a rat "thinking" he is free to make a left turn in a maze. Once the relevant reinforcement history is analyzed, both choices are seen to be inevitable. Thus, human achievements are no cause for praise and human failures are no cause for blame.

Consistent with the historic flavor of behaviorism, Skinner finds little merit in spending time on questions about the mind, desire, dignity, personality, consciousness. Human history is a record of behavior. It is only behavior that threatens or rescues a troubled society. In our affairs with other human beings, we are concerned only with their behavior toward us. We can never know what is in their minds; we can only witness and be affected by their conduct. This has always been the case, but according to Skinner, it is only recently that we are able to do anything about it. As a result of developments in behavioral psychology, we are, in Skinner's view, finally in a position "to engineer" desired forms of social conduct. Moreover, punishment is unnecessary. By establishing the proper "contingencies" of reward (that is, the conditions that must be satisfied by the individual if he is to be rewarded), we can regulate human behavior to any necessary degree.

Many have found Skinner's argument satisfactory, and some have even established "operant communities" in which children are reared along these lines. Others have rejected his thesis as either grotesque or ridiculous, or both. As with any proposal so grand in scope, Skinner's must be evaluated along several different lines. These include the philosophical, scientific, and practical implications of such an approach to human behavior.

Philosophically, there is little in Skinner's position that was not fully anticipated by the nineteenth-century *utilitarians*, notably Jeremy Bentham and John Stuart Mill. The latter—an ardent defender of the rights of the individual—would have blushed at the idea of molding anyone by conditioning, but he certainly accepted the role of rewards and punishments in cementing our "associative bonds." On this purely philosophical plane, the view of man as shaped by positive and negative reinforcers is an old one. It is as old in practice as parenthood and at least as old in theory as Aristotle.

Scientifically, Skinner has developed these ancient philosophical ideas to the point where behavioral control is remarkably complete. His ping-pong playing pigeons are extraordinary to watch. Yet, as we observed in Chapter 1, the ability to predict and control is not the *only* criterion of validity in science. In addition to accuracy, the scientific statement must also be *consistent* with other things we know to be true and it must have a degree of *generality*. A psychological law that was true for pigeons but not for chimpanzees would be very limited. In terms of consistency and generality, Skinner's position is less than adequate. It is not consistent with many experimental analyses of the determinants of learning, as we shall see later in this chapter, and it does not seem to be generally valid as we shall see in our discussion of language (Chapter 7).

ENVIRONMENTALISM, NATIVISM, AND "SITUATIONISM"

The research of Professors Zimbardo, Milgram, et al. raises fundamental questions about the ability of both nativistic and empiricistic psychologies to explain human behavior. Note in the studies of obedience and of the "prisoners and guards" that the behavior of the participants was controlled by the social context and that this behavior was, or at least seemed to be, at variance with the lifelong lessons that members of our society must learn. Zimbardo's experimental subjects were drawn from socioeconomic ranks usually identified as having strong Judeo-Christian roots and commitments. Milgram's subjects were working-class and white-collar people, reared, one would suspect, to behave in a civilized and humanitarian way. Yet under the pressures of the moment, the majority of the subjects exhibited behavior of which neither we nor the participants themselves would approve. In other words, the variable that seemed to account for the behavior was neither the prior "reinforcement history" nor "heredity," but rather the "demand" characteristics of the *situation*.

It is unfortunate and perhaps somewhat revealing that little is known about those subjects who did not comply in the Milgram studies and those who were largely immune to the "situation" presented in Zimbardo's research. Psychological research tends to confine itself to large effects and has traditionally displayed a certain degree of impatience toward exceptions.

Practically, Skinner's plan for society is not impossible. Indeed, a good deal of social control has been achieved by principles like his for centuries. But if the behavioristic conception of man is incomplete, any social program based on this conception will fall short, and it will fall short by an amount that is proportional to its degree of incompleteness. To the extent that human conduct is regulated by the rewards and penalties that guide a rat through a maze and to this extent only, human psychology and rodent psychology are essentially the same. The great epoch of human achievement seems to suggest that more is involved, but this cannot be proven here. All we can do in the present context is consider several experimental lines of evidence that suggest that the behavioristic model is incomplete. Let's turn our study to *cognition,* a process as different from association-learning as perception is from sensation. And in order to keep our analyses comparable, we will not examine complex cognitive functions in man. Instead, we will examine the behavior of the same animals upon which behaviorism bases its arguments.

Behaviorist theory, illustrated in the preceding pages, states that the behavior of organisms is unpredictable before learning and that all learning is the consequence of reinforcement effects. Individual differences, according to this view, are the result of differential reinforcement histories and can be eliminated by the application of new reinforcement schedules. It considers such attributes as "personality," "attitudes," "beliefs," and "motives" to be learned and to be learned through the application of reinforcement. Let us see.

Cognitive Processes in Learning

Cognitive theories have drawn support from two general sources. The first is the part of the empirical-associationist tradition that questions the need for reinforcement in learning. The second and more influential source is the nativistic-idealistic tradition that points to the role of instincts and insights; the former challenging the very foundations of empiricism and the latter rejecting any theory of behavior based on the idea that knowledge grows gradually merely as a result of rewarded practice.

The drive-reduction theory presented earlier has dominated the psychology of learning almost since the time of Thorndike and surely since Skinner's earliest writings. Integral to this view of learning is the role of reward and punishment in the formation of "associative bonds." Despite the seemingly self-evident nature of this assumption, certain findings have emerged that bring forth some reservations and that tend to support a cognitive alternative.

Latent Learning

If hungry rats are presented with repeated exposure to a maze containing food in the last compartment, their errors (entries into blind alleys) will progressively decrease in frequency from one day to the next. If well-fed rats are placed in such a maze, their error-frequency remains high day after day. However, if—say, on the seventh day—these well-fed animals are starved and then placed in a food-providing maze, their performance comes to match that of the continuously rewarded group with startling rapidity (Blodgett, 1929). These effects are shown in Figure 6-9. Note that the high error-rate of the well-fed (nonreinforced) rats drops sharply with the first introduction (on the seventh day for Group II and on the third day for Group III) of *hunger and food reward* conditions. The obvious implication of these data is that learning was occurring during days one

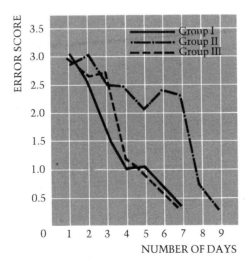

Figure 6-9. *Latent learning.* Group 1 received food reward in the maze from the first day of training. Group 2 received reward for the first time on day 4; Group 3, on day 8. Note how performance improves immediately after the introduction of reward for the first time. Presumably, animals in groups 2 and 3 were *learning* before the introduction of reward but their *performance* only reflected this learning when reinforcers were added. (After the data of Blodgett, 1929.)

through nine, but was revealed in performance only after the introduction of incentives. E. C. Tolman (1924) referred to this unobserved learning as *latent*. Influenced by the Gestalt theorists, Tolman argued that learning is the formation of *cognitive maps*—mental pictures of a frequently confronted environment. By repetition, the organism develops an awareness of objects and their positions and relations through cognitive processes. However, while these cognitive maps are being formed all the time, they cannot influence behavior until they acquire a significance. The various turns in the maze become, in Tolman's terms, *significates* or *local signs* when they are attached to rewarding or punishing circumstances.

Sensory Preconditioning

A modified type of this latent learning is suggested by research done in preconditioning. An animal, fully fed and resting in his home cage, is presented repeatedly with a flash of light followed by a brief tone. After several thousand such pairings of stimuli distributed over many days, the animal is trained to jump a barrier as soon as a light is flashed in order to avoid a shock. Once the animal has learned to make the avoidance response every time the light is flashed, a tone is substituted for the light. The preconditioned animal responds to the tone as if it were the light. The interpretation of this finding indicates that the nonreinforced flash-tone presentations had been learned. That is, the association was formed without the use of reinforcement.

Latent Extinction

Explicit in the reinforcement psychology of learning is the need for a response (behavior) to occur if it is to be shaped by the application of rewards and punishment. Extinction, according to the model, requires the occurrence of behavior in the absence of reinforcement. In an interesting series of experiments, Beck and Doty (1957) conditioned and extinguished flexion (the act of bending) responses in animals rendered incapable of movement by certain biological procedures. Paired stimuli—signal followed by shock—were presented frequently to the paralyzed animal. The investigators found that, subsequently, when the animals were capable of movement, they made the flexion response to the signal. Similarly, by presenting treated and trained animals with the signal *not* followed by a shock, the flexion response was extinguished when treatment effects were reversed. That is, extinction of unexecuted responses occurred. This latent extinction is difficult to interpret within the context of traditional (Thorndikean) reinforcement psychology.

LATENT EXTINCTION

It is unfortunate that studies of *latent extinction* have been rare. Even the few studies done have not been treated to the necessary replications, despite the fact that the phenomenon seriously challenges one of psychology's most durable principles—that of *sensory-motor association*.

A workable approach to the phenomenon requires the introduction of a procedure that effectively eliminates the motor component in conditioning but leaves the sensory systems unaffected. One way of achieving this is to inject the conditioned animal with a paralyzing agent (for example, Flaxadil) that has no harmful effects on sensitivity. Let us say that the animal has been conditioned to withdraw its right forepaw when a bell is sounded. Now the animal is reversibly paralyzed and, during the period of paralysis, is given frequent presentations of the same stimulus. Under these circumstances, the classical associationistic theory predicts that the conditioned response (limb-withdrawal) will remain as strong as ever since motor events that do not occur cannot be extinguished. Cognitive theories, however, predict otherwise. These theories tend to attribute "mental" events to experimental animals, assuming that the animal "knows" the shock no longer is following the bell even though this animal is unable to move. What the study by Beck and Doty indicates is that extinction occurs whether the response does or not, as long as a conscious organism has the opportunity to perceive that the association between the conditioned stimulus (bell) and the unconditioned stimulus (shock) is no longer in effect.

Insight

It is usually stated or implied in reinforcement psychology that learning involves the gradual, continuous strengthening of association; that reinforcement by reinforcement, the connection between stimulus and response becomes stronger and stronger. This hypothesis is challenged by a range of learning phenomena classified under the term *insight*. Wolfgang Köhler, the famous Gestalt psychologist, provided the classical demonstration of insight learning in apes (Köhler, 1925). A hungry ape is able to reach through the bars of his cage and obtain a banana. The banana is moved out of reach, and the ape is given a stick. After some predictable trial-and-error behavior, the ape soon learns to reach with the stick and pull the banana close enough to grab it. Then the banana is moved twice as far away, and the ape is given two separate sticks that can be joined to form one stick long enough to reach the banana. Köhler observed that under this condition, the ape spends some time grunting, pacing, and otherwise "cogitating." Then, without engaging in any practice, the ape spontaneously joins the sticks and obtains his banana! Köhler stressed the spontaneity—the *discontinuity*—of this behavior and stated that it resulted from the emergence of a cognitive solution—an *insight*—on the part of the ape. Presumably, the ape was running through the possible solutions covertly and acted upon the one that seemed most likely to work. This covert "thinking" is called *vicarious trial and error* (VTE).

Learning Sets

If a subject is given extensive discrimination training in which many different S^D—S^Δ pairs are used (such as the symbols Δ *vs.* $\square$, O *vs.* X, and so on), it is found that the greater the number of different problems the animal solves, the fewer the number of trials are needed in solving subsequent problems. The animal learns to learn, or forms a *learning set* (Harlow, 1949). Analogous to Tolman's "cognitive map," the learning set is viewed as a mental state that allows the classification, ordering, and ranking of cues based on limited but relevant experience. An illustration of learning-set data is shown in Figure 6-10. This figure depicts

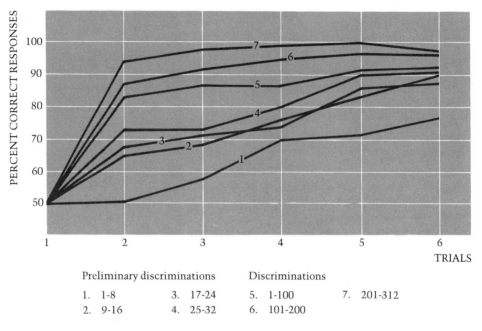

Preliminary discriminations   Discriminations

1. 1-8   3. 17-24   5. 1-100   7. 201-312
2. 9-16   4. 25-32   6. 101-200

Figure 6-10. *Learning sets.* As monkeys learn more and more discriminations, the speed with which they can learn new and different ones increases. They are "learning to learn" or forming "sets" by which to solve problems drawn from a given genre of problems. (After the data of Harlow, 1949.)

percent correct responses as a function of the total number of different problems the animal (monkey) has solved. Each curve relates the effects of the set on a different trial in the learning series. Thus, after solving 50 problems, the animal is correct on the second trial with a new problem about 60 percent of the time. After 450 problems, the monkey's second-trial success figure is nearly 100 percent.

Transposition

The more elementaristic proponents of the psychology of learning argue that reinforcement strengthens the connection between specific responses and specific stimuli. Thus, while generalizations occur, they are distributed normally around a maximally effective stimulus—the S^D. It is predicted, according to these views, that relations between stimuli and behavior will become progressively weaker as the stimuli become increasingly different from those used in original learning. However, certain Gestalt-type studies do not support this prediction. For example, an animal can be trained to jump at a light gray card rather than a darker gray card in order to obtain food. Once this has been learned, two new cards are substituted: one, the same shade as the original S^D and one brighter than the S^D. Does the animal now jump at the stimulus initially associated with reward, or is his behavior guided by a "brighter than" cue? Many investigators report that animals learn to respond to *relations* rather than to absolute stimulus values. That is, the animals *transpose* cues. A popular example of transpositional learning can be found in music. One can learn a melody in one key and have no trouble recognizing it when played in another key, despite the fact that the physical properties (frequencies) of the sounds are changed. In transposing from one key to another, the relations among notes are preserved, and it may be argued that it is the relations that are learned.

Transposition requires an explanation more complex than those offered for discrimination, learning, and generalization. Pavlov attempted to explain stimulus generalization on the basis of *cortical irradiation*, the spread of activity from that part of the cortex directly activated by the stimulus to the immediately neighboring regions. Using this view, the only form of generalization that can be accounted for involves stimuli that are represented in specific cortical regions. This condition is not met for changes in stimulus intensity and for many other stimulus dimensions, all of which reveal generalization gradients. Neurophysiology has failed to support Pavlov's irradiation as the mechanism of generalization, and studies of transposition challenge the concept with behavioral (perceptual) exceptions. (A key paper is that of Lashley and Wade (1946), and an excellent review is offered by Kalish (1969).)

SOCIAL LEARNING AND COMPARATIVE PSYCHOLOGY

The experiments conducted within the behavioristic context are usually limited to a single species of animal, and they examine relatively simple sequences of behavior. The settings have little in common with the environments in which animals and people normally function. This is not to say that general laws do not exist, laws that remain valid when applied to situations that differ from those in which the laws were discovered. Rather, one wonders whether other lawful relations exist that can *only* be observed in more natural settings.

The science that studies animal behavior in natural settings is called *ethology*. It is only recently that attempts have been made to incorporate the "realities" of the ethologist's world into the laboratory of the behaviorist. It is of interest to note that prior to the time when behaviorism dominated experimental studies of animal behavior, there was great activity in *comparative psychology*. For example, in the 1947 edition of *Encyclopedia Britannica*, the section on comparative psychology is almost as long as the section on *psychology* itself. From the date of Darwin's *The Origin of Species* until the late 1940s, ethologists and comparative psychologists seemed to be converging on a common point, and Darwin's influence was felt equally by both. The ethologist confined his studies to the field and relied principally upon naturalistic observation. The comparative psychologist tended to bring nature into the laboratory and measure "elements" of behavior and differences across species in a more exacting way. In spite of these differences in methods, the two specialties shared a common outlook: that natural selection and heredity had created unique adaptive mechanisms and that each successful adaptation resulted from a mixture of instinct, learning, and the peculiarities of the environmental situation. Where today's behavioral psychologist might examine schedules of reinforcement with a single rat in a Skinner-box, the comparative psychologist in the 1930s would study the effects of one rat's eating upon the eating behavior of another rat. Indeed, in one such study (Harlow, 1932), rats did eat far more after observing other rats eating, even though the observing rats had been fully fed in advance. This *social facilitation* effect was described in terms of the rats' "actively competing with each other." Similar results have been obtained from mice, chickens, and monkeys and have been found in studies of sexual activity and nest building as well. Moreover, since the results were found using animals reared in isolation, they cannot be explained solely in terms of "imitative" learning.

In Chapter 9 we will explore instinctive patterns of behavior more fully. However, of importance here is this one question: What happened to comparative psychology from about 1945 until very recently?

COMPARATIVE PSYCHOLOGY: AN HISTORICAL PERSPECTIVE

Psychology in the tradition of behaviorism is an *empirical* psychology. It emphasizes environmental determinants, and as a result, it has been less than cordial to *nativistic* (genetic) explanations of behavior. In addition to its empirical character, behavioristic psychology is *hedonistic*—it reduces useful behavior to a search for rewards and an aversion to punishment. Accordingly, some form or other of the Law of Effect has dominated its theories, and there has been no reason to assume that any other "law" is necessary when dealing with different species; that is, all species must eat, drink, reproduce, and avoid tissue-damage, and any species that can learn, learns according to these rewarding or punishing events.

Why the vast majority of American psychologists adopted this attitude in their approach to animal behavior is not clear. One reason, derived from the social influence on social science, is found in the universal repulsion scholars felt toward Nazi propaganda and practice. The genocidal program of the Nazi party caused an immediate suspicion toward any science that concerned itself with "genetic differences," "native endowments," "natural tendencies." The experience of World War II left little sympathy for genetic explanations of psychological characteristics. In America, where egalitarian principles were historically enshrined—at least on paper—this kind of reaction was especially intense. Then, too, the war created an age of engineering in which any problem, no matter how intricate, would admit of "technical" solutions. This, after all, is the enduring corollary of environmentalism. Since, "if the price is right" we can do all things, why should rats be different? And, finally, psychology was eager, often desperate, to establish itself as a *science,* and this required, it was thought, precision, control, and predictive power. These were the very promises of the operant-conditioning method.

Again, times are changing. Gradually, psychologists and others have come to believe that every assertion of inherited *difference* is not a disguised suggestion of *superiority.* Also, as we observe animals building nests, chattering away at each other, selecting mates, feeding their young, swimming against insurmountable odds, we come to recognize that something more than "conditioning" is involved. Animals can do many things without the aid of either parents or experimental psychologists. Finally, psychologists are more secure in their efforts, in large measure because of the many contributions of behavioristic psychology. Being more secure, they are willing to take more chances, willing to leave the safe predictability of the rat laboratory and venture forth into the organized chaos of "real" animals and "real" behavior. And when they find that a rat eats more after watching another rat eat, they are even willing to discuss perceptual-cognitive determinants of behavior. Watson would not applaud this development, but Darwin would have no argument with it. (Darwin had even theorized about the *games* animals play!)

MEMORY

The experiences of life can be adapted for use only to the extent that they can be recalled at some subsequent time. In the absence of memory, learning is but the passing, random adjustment of responses to a new condition. In the absence of memory, perception is but the dazzling sense of a change in the environment. Memory provides meaning. It is the context in which all new experiences vie for the organism's attention. It is the basis of the concept of causation; effects become orderly only through an awareness of their antecedents. It is the fuel for consciousness, the substance of reflection.

At a scientific level of understanding, the concept of memory resists simple definition. Common-sense views are invariably nominalistic. They define memory with new names rather than explain it in terms of principles, mechanisms, and lawful dependencies. According to such views, memory is "recalling," "remembering," "knowing," "recollecting," "having a knowledge of the past." Not only are these words mere substitutes for the word *memory* but they have a rather human-sounding quality, which makes them seem out of place when applied to the behavior of lower organisms. Does the nestbuilding robin have "a knowledge of the past"? Is the rat at the junction of the Y-maze "recollecting"?

To escape the bind imposed by natural language, scientists tend to express the nature of memory in terms that are neither ambiguous nor mentalistic. For obvious reasons, the particular conceptualization they have of memory depends on their concept of learning. Clark Hull, whose theory will be discussed in Chapter 10, proposed that each reinforcement causes an increase in habit strength (sH_R). Within his system, the unit of learning and the unit of memory are indistinguishable:

> Whenever a reaction R takes place in temporal contiguity with an afferent receptor impulse . . . and this conjunction is followed closely by the diminution in a need . . . there will result an increment . . . in the tendency for that stimulus on subsequent occasions to evoke that reaction. (Hull, p. 71)

In stating this *Law of Primary Reinforcement,* Hull defined learning (reinforced practice) as a permanent change in the internal environment of the organism. A new neural connection or predisposition to respond has been established. Since such associative bonds are exclusively a function of the number of reinforcements (n), they are permanent. Once n events have occurred, sH_R is at a specified and essentially immutable level. Forgetting, for all intents and purposes, does not occur. Rather, the likelihood that the fixed level of sH_R, will ever again materialize in behavior depends upon many variables. Hull's index does not contain an entry for memory. He does, however, discuss *reminiscence.* If an animal learns a habit (running down a runway for food) whose strength after repeated trials is at some level, it is often the case that after an extended period of nonpractice, the vigor (speed) of the response is greater. This reminiscence phenomenon (an enhancement of responses following "empty" time) can be explained on the basis of diminished inhibition. Continued practice leads to high levels of "inhibitory potential." Rest leads to its decay. Thus, not only is the passage of time not harmful to learning, it may actually be helpful.

If forgetting does not occur in Hull's system, it is necessary to provide a mechanism by which once-learned and always-remembered responses fail to recur. Hull accounts for such phenomena in his discussion of *experimental extinction.* A given environment has "paid off" n times, creating X units of habit strength. At a given drive level, all other things equal, the animal's tendency to respond is Y. Now, this response *(R1)* which may be bar-pressing, no longer results in reinforcement. The competing behavior *(R2)*, which involves *not* pressing the bar, increases in strength with each unsuccessful emission of $R1$. Aided by the build up of inhibition, a point is reached where $R2$ is more likely than $R1$. In the Hullian system, forgetting is not the passive loss of once-learned information, but the active participation of a competing response. This is really a kind of conflict model of forgetting and presents interesting analogies of the Freudian idea of repression, as we will see in Chapter 10.

Theories of Forgetting

Hull was compelled to recruit active processes to account for a weakening of memories because numerous studies had indicated that the mere passage of time did little to reduce the strength of associations. Thorndike had advanced a *Law of Disuse* by which unpracticed habits were assumed to weaken. This was a *trace-decay* theory of forgetting, whose history dates back at least to the time of Aristotle. Its principal tenet is that experience somehow creates a "trace" in the brain that, if unreinforced by repetition, weakens with the passage of time. Ebbinghaus, in his classical studies of (his own) memory, did much to popularize this view in psychology by demonstrating progressively poorer recall (less savings) of nonsense syllables over a period from twenty minutes to one month. But, in 1924, Jenkins and Dallenbach showed that if sleep intervened between the learning of lists of nonsense syllables and tests of recall, errors of retention dropped sharply relative to performance under continuous waking conditions. An influential paper by McGeoch (1932) followed in which the role of time per se was seriously questioned. In its place, *interference* was advanced as the chief cause of forgetting. Interference theories of forgetting are based on the contention that memories are not weakened, but that the acquisition of new information competes with the recall of older information. An extension of the interference model holds that learned material also works in a forward direction and interferes with the acquisition of new information. These two processes are called *retroactive* and *proactive interference*.

Retroactive Interference (RI)

The usual approach to the study of RI involves the following steps:

1. Subjects learn to associate a number of words in list *A* with words in list *B*.
2. A retention interval elapses.
3. Subjects are now required to learn to associate a new list of words (list *C*) with the original words in list *A*.
4. Subjects are retested on the *A-B* (original) associates.

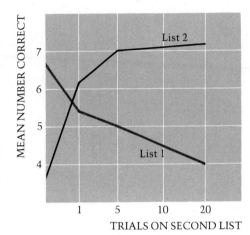

Figure 6-11. Interference in verbal learning. An example of *retroactive interference* is depicted on this graph. As performance on a second list improves, the retention of material learning on the first list deteriorates. (After the data of Barnes and Underwood, 1959.)

The results of studies of this kind show marked reductions in the retention of *A-B* associations when interpolated material (*A-C*) is introduced between original learning and tests of recall. An illustrative experiment is that done by Postman and Riley (1959). Subjects practiced *A-B* lists either 5, 10, 20, or 40 times. Interfering (*A-C*) lists were also practiced to all of these extents. Thus, there were 25 combinations of *A-B: A-C* degrees of learning. The major finding was that *A-B* retention was enhanced by increasing the strength of original learning and diminished by increasing the strength of *A-C* learning. Similar data are given in Figure 6-11, which shows the progressive decline of *A-B* (list 1) retention as the number of learning trials on *A-C* (list 2) is increased. In good Hullian fashion, increases in the strength of one set of responses are matched by decreases in that of a competing set.

Proactive Interference (PI)

Studies of PI take recourse to methods analogous to those used in RI, but with different temporal relations among lists and tests.

1. The subject learns lists *A-C*.
2. The subject then learns lists *A-B*.

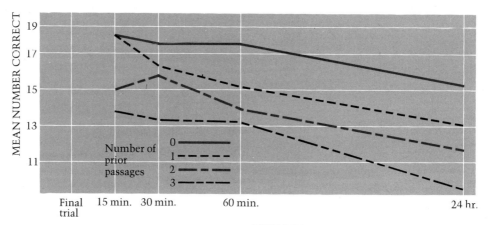

TIME BETWEEN LEARNING AND TESTING

Figure 6-12. *Proactive interference.* As the number of prior lists learned increases, the recall of recently learned prose passages diminishes. Moreover, retention of knowledge becomes systematically poorer over longer retention intervals. (After the data of Slamecka, 1961.)

3. A retention interval elapses.

4. The subject is tested on *A-B*.

The detrimental effects on *A-B* retention produced by the original learning of *A-C* are measures of PI. Illustrative data of this are given in Figure 6-12. This figure shows that retention of new (*A-B*) material is poor as retention intervals become greater and as the number of prior passages is increased.

One of the variables that can confound research of the kind cited above is that of *rehearsal.* It is often difficult to control what the subject does during the retention interval. Even when this interval prescribes specific activities, such as reading prose aloud or solving mathematical problems, some rehearsal still may be possible. Moreover, since both the interference and the trace-decay theories of forgetting postulate effects that occur soon after the acquisition of new material, experiments involving long retention intervals may be insensitive to short-term phenomena. A very important study designed to examine these possibilities was conducted by Peterson and Peterson (1959). Subjects were shown single-consonant syllables (for example, QFZ) and, immediately after saying the letters, were given a number (such as 305). They were instructed to begin counting backward by threes as soon as the number was given. At a certain time after they began counting backward, a signal was flashed. This was the cue for them to report the letters. Their backward counting was keyed by a metronome, and recall intervals were thus timed to consist of 3, 6, 9, 12, 15, or 18 seconds. Backward counting was intended to preclude or at least to limit rehearsal. Each of twenty-four subjects was tested eight times. Average frequency of recall is shown in Figure 6-13 as a function of the retention intervals.

Note the immediate decay in retention even at the shortest interval (3 seconds), and its continuous reduction thereafter. By 18 seconds, recall is negligible. These results underscore the presence of what has come to be called *short-term memory* (STM). It is viewed as a process distinct from *long-term memory* (LTM). The latter may persist over a period of decades. The former is viewed as a transitory process during which new material may be evaluated for possible long-term storage.

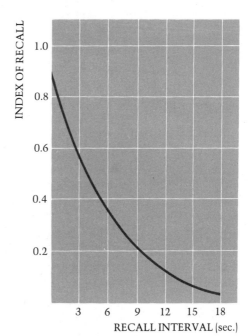

Figure 6-13. A measure of *short-term* memory. Subjects receive a brief presentation of material and immediately are required to begin counting backwards by 3s. At different times in the retention interval, they are tested for recall. Note the dramatic deterioration of recall over the first 18 seconds. (After the data of Peterson and Peterson, 1969.)

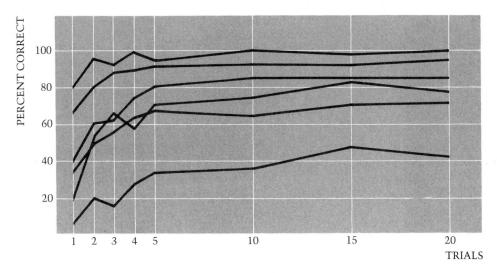

Figure 6-14. Information increases with frequency of exposure. Moving from the top of this figure to the bottom, the curves are based upon (1) 25 msec. exposures of English words, (2) 20 msec. exposures of English words, (3) 25 msec. exposures of Turkish words, (4) 20 msec. exposures of Turkish words, (5) 15 msec. exposures of English words, and (6) 15 msec. exposures of Turkish words. (After the data of Hershenson and Haber, 1965.)

Perceptual Short-Term and Long-Term Memory

This type of sensory STM is revealed in studies involving more complex (perceptual) stimuli as well. Hershenson and Haber presented subjects with both English and Turkish words for durations of 15, 20, or 25 msec. and measured the probability of perceiving as a function of the number of repetitions. Their interesting finding was that percepts grew in clarity with increasing repetitions. That is, even on the early trials in which nothing was "seen," presentations were providing useful information. The results are summarized in Figure 6-14. It should be noted that with very brief presentations, increases in repetition are not sufficient to bring recognition to a high probability. That is, some critical amount of information is necessary per presentation for a given probability of recognition. Moreover, there is no simple reciprocity between frequency and duration. One cannot, for example, reduce duration by one-fourth (20 msec.) and compensate for this by adding 25 percent more presentations. This would suggest, therefore, that the mechanisms activated by the duration of a stimulus and by the frequency of presentation are either different or are affected differently. Using a language common to the computer sciences, the different effects of duration and frequency may be viewed as describing the "read-in" and "storage" capacities of the system. Since very significant improvements occur with only a 5-msec. increase in duration, the system must have a very high read-in rate. That is, it must be able to integrate successive "bits" of information very rapidly.

In Figure 6-14, you will note that the recognition of Turkish and English words is enhanced by roughly comparable degrees by increases in duration, although, at a given duration, recognition of English is decidedly better than recognition of Turkish. This would imply that while the read-in is independent of the familiarity or meaningfulness of the material, the "read-out" or verbal report does depend on such variables. While comparable, the range of change produced by increasing the duration of Turkish words is greater than the range of change produced when the duration of English words is altered. For an English-speaking subject, there is more meaning in English words. A dynamic read-in mechanism could be specified to account for such effects. This hypothetical device must change its read-in properties according to the information content of the stimulus. That is, for ambiguous material, the read-in rate is slowed down. The material is sampled less frequently but for a greater duration per sample. On the other hand, unambiguous material is sampled at a high rate, but each sample is of a very brief duration. In order for a read-in mechanism to be so adjustable, it must have feedback from LTM; that is, it must have a memory core capable of assigning degrees of informativeness to inputs. The recognition of English words in the Hershenson-Haber study is nearly perfect after a few presentations of 25 msec. each. Recognition of Turkish words never rises above about 85 percent. Presumably, longer exposure durations would bring this recognition rate to the level attained with English words.

The evidence for at least two separate memory processes (STM and LTM) extends well beyond what has already been presented. There are now many studies that show that in paired-associates learning, short-term interference effects are produced by material *acoustically* similar to the learned associates, while effects upon LTM are greatest when interfering materials are used that are *semantically* similar to what has been learned (Conrad, 1962; Baddeley, 1966). In fact, studies are in such agreement on this point that one could advance two laws of retroactive interference: (a) *verbal material in STM will be harder to recall when interpolated learning involves acoustically similar items; (b) verbal material in LTM will be harder to recall when interpolated learning involves semantically similar items.*

Positive and Negative Transfer

There is a difficulty posed by the paradoxical nature of the two laws of retroactive interference stated above. If memory interference is greatest when practice during the retention interval involves similar material, how does learning or memory ever occur? On a trial-to-trial basis, stimulus conditions are always changing so that the animal and the human subjects invariably are exposed to similar *but not identical* circumstances. In verbal learning and memory, these very conditions produce interference, whereas in all other learning they appear to be a permanent fixture of the learning context. This paradox was resolved by Osgood (1949) and rests on the nature of positive and negative transfer. His explanation may be stated as follows:

1. When conditions vary (as they must, in some way, from trial to trial) from one learning task to the next but response requirements are kept constant (bar-pressing, key-pecking, left-turns), *positive transfer* occurs. That is, this experience will facilitate the learning of similar tasks. The degree of positive transfer (measured as savings) will increase as the new situations are more and more similar to the original learning context.
2. When conditions remain essentially constant from one learning task to the next but response requirements change, *negative transfer* occurs with a strength proportional to the similarity between the original and the new response requirements.

A typical example of the latter is the successive learning of two mazes. The physical appearance of alleys and culs is the same from the rat's perspective. The first requires a sequence of left and right turns: LLRLRRRLLLR. The second requires RRLRLLLRRRL. With new response requirements imposed by nearly identical stimulating conditions, negative transfer occurs. That is, more trials are necessary to learn the second maze than if the first had not been learned at all. A similar challenge occurs in verbal retention. New responses (associates) must be learned to words that were initially paired with other words. Retroactive interference ensues, and its magnitude increases as either the acoustic (for STM) or semantic (for LTM) similarity between old and new increases. Multilingual people often find themselves confusing Italian and Spanish words much more frequently than they confuse either with German words. A career as a sculptor would be of greater benefit to an aspiring surgeon than would years of practice at bricklaying.

Persistence of LTM

While it is not clear how long STM is or even how many separate memory systems there may be, it is apparent that LTM can persist for the entire lifetime of the organism. Even the pigeon, conditioned to peck a key for food and then removed from the experimental chamber for four years, will spontaneously engage in this once-learned behavior when original conditions are restored (Skinner, 1950). A man may cease to practice a habit of childhood, such as bicycle riding, and many years later discover very little loss of proficiency. When the memory task is simple (recognition), retention may be perfect over intervals of years. For example, one may readily recognize that a face has been seen before, though it may only have been seen once many years before. As the task becomes more difficult, LTM is less perfect. This can be demonstrated with nonsense syllable paired-associates learning (Figure 6-15). Subjects have nearly perfect *recognition* of syllables presented during learning. They do not freely *recall* all of the learned syllables as well. Relearning becomes more difficult with elapsed time and with an *anticipation* task. In these facts, too, one realizes the multiple forms of memory. Recognition, recall, and reconstruction are all affected differently by time, by interference, and by situational factors. It is against the background of these complexities that physiological psychologists, biochemists, and neurophysiologists have struggled to identify the biological mechanisms of memory.

NEUROPSYCHOLOGY, LEARNING, AND MEMORY

Any biological theory of memory must be able to propose plausible mechanisms that can accommodate the following facts.

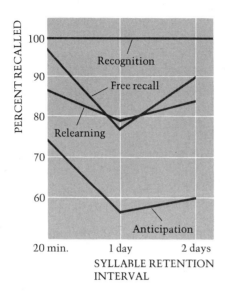

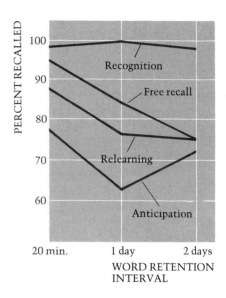

Figure 6-15. The retention of syllables (on the left) and words (on the right) over short and long retention intervals. Peformance de- pends upon the kind of retention required. (After the data of Postman and Rau, 1957.)

1. *The stability of reinforced behavior over long periods of time even after extended periods of nonpractice.* In this regard, a biological theory of memory should be able to respect the effects of schedules or reinforce- ment by which partially reinforced behavior is more resistant to extinc- tion than is continuously reinforced behavior.

2. *The one-direction tendency of reinforcement effects and the fact that an optimum interval exists between responses and reinforcements in the formation of associations.* In Pavlovian conditioning, it has proved to be almost impossible (there are several reported exceptions) to effect *backward* conditioning. For example, repeated pairings of UCS (food in the mouth) followed by CS (bell) will not produce the CR (conditioned salivation). In operant conditioning the same appears to be true. Nagaty (1951) has demonstrated this adequately. Four groups of hungry rats were trained to depress a rod immediately upon its introduction through the wall of the cage. Training consisted of delivering food pellets two seconds after the rod-press. After this training one group was maintained

on this same condition, one group was given pellets two seconds before the insertion of the rod, one group was given pellets twenty seconds before insertion of the rod, and one group was given no further reinforcement (behavior was extinguished). The behavior of all four groups is summarized in Figure 6-16. Rats rewarded two seconds after responding continued to emit responses as frequently as they did at the conclusion of original training. All other groups displayed a sharp decline in conditioned responding. Presentation of reward before the appropriate response had the same effect as withholding reinforcement entirely.

3. *The fact that identical response requirements in new circumstances result in* positive transfer, *whereas altered response requirements in similar circumstances result in* negative transfer. The facilitating and interfering effects of old and new learning upon each other point to complex memory processes. Retroactive and proactive interference (negative transfer) and retroactive and proactive facilitation (positive trans-

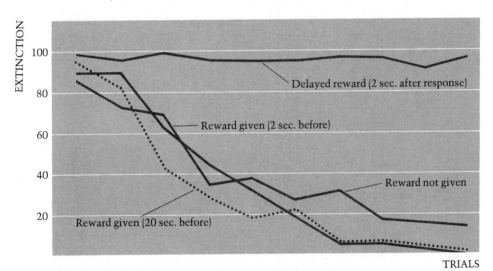

Figure 6-16. Extinction when reward precedes response by 2 or 20 seconds, when it follows response by 2 seconds and when it isn't administered at all. Note that with briefly withheld reward, extinction does not occur. However, extinction proceeds as rapidly when reward comes only 2 seconds before a response as it does when reward is withheld entirely. (After the data of Nagaty, 1951.)

fer) indicate that theories based on simple storage mechanisms will not be sufficient.

4. *The presence of at least two separate memory processes, one of a short-term nature and one of a long-term nature.* Studies like that of Peterson and Peterson clearly demonstrate the presence of some intermediary nonpermanent storage of recently learned material. Ultimately, a satisfactory theory of the biology of memory must be able to specify not only the mechanisms underlying these distinct phenomena, but also those that allow meaningfulness, prior knowledge, repetition, and stimulus duration to have the effects they do on both STM and LTM.

5. *The great variability of the intensity and vividness of memories.* Recollections are not of a yes-no nature. They vary in strength and detail. Proposed biological mechanisms must have the capacity to "code" experiences in a way that allows a full range of recalled details and the full range of vividness of recall.

6. *The selective nature of memory and, complementing this, the inextricable connection between attention and memory.* Biological mechanisms must be able to permit only selected features of sensory input data to be coded for long-term storage. Such coding requires feedback from what is already in LTM to some buffer store. At the same time, the organism's sensing behavior must be directed at more or less specific stimulus elements while "ignoring" other aspects, even though these may be highly distinctive physically.

Trace Theories

Mechanical metaphors have been set forth to account for psychological functions since the time of Descartes, and "memory" has not escaped their widespread application. The everyday observation that ease of recall increased with repetition led quite naturally to physiological explanations involving neural "traces" of one sort or another. Presumably, each repetition left a stronger trace of itself in the neural pathways. Different theorists proposed different trace mechanisms. Some postulated the presence of "reverberatory circuits," that is, neural events, once initiated, continued to recycle in small clusters indefinitely. Others contended that repeated stimulation of certain neural pathways produced anatomic changes in the neurons, making subsequent transmission easier. Relying on the age-old associationistic laws of repetition, similarity, and contiguity, early trace theorists all emphasized the necessity of afferent-efferent (sensory-motor) connections as the fundamental mechanism of memory. The writings of Pavlov and of Watson added substantial support to these ideas.

Karl Lashley (1924) conducted several experiments that put aside any hope of a simple afferent-efferent connection theory. Placing a blindfold over one eye of a rat, Lashley trained the animal on a simple visual discrimination task. Once the rat had learned to perform without error, the "naïve" eye was uncovered and the "practiced" eye was blindfolded. As expected, the rat went right on discriminating at the criterion level. Such perfect positive transfer violates the hypothesis of afferent-efferent connections. The optic nerve leading from the naïve eye received none of the stimuli necessary for discriminative behavior. That is, the afferent components were different during tests of retention than they were during original learning.

Having challenged the sensory side of the simple associationistic model, Lashley addressed himself to the efferent link. If selected regions of the motor cortex of a monkey are surgically destroyed, the limbs on the opposite side are immediately paralyzed, but function returns in time. Lashley performed such an operation and then trained monkeys to open boxes with their "good" hand. The paralyzed limb hung stiffly throughout this training. Once the animals gained proficiency at the task, the intact portion of the motor cortex was destroyed, thereby paralyzing the "good" hand. In a number of weeks, the initially paralyzed limbs had recovered function, and the animals were confronted with the same "latch" problem. With neither fumbling practice nor halting indecision, the monkeys competently opened the boxes and secured their just rewards. These effective limbs had never received practice on the task at hand. The efferent nerves involved in movement had not participated in the original learning but, again, complete transfer of training was observed.

Place Theories

The postulated connections between sensory and motor pathways proved incapable of accommodating findings such as those of Lashley. The phenomenon of transfer was their undoing. If the memory "codes" (en-

grams) were not in the pathways themselves, they must reside someplace in the brain. According to "place" theories of memory, patterns of afferent activity are stored in association areas of the cortex as are codes representing efferent output data. Repetition of similar stimuli, according to this view, will result in similar efferent commands. Lashley (1950) and Klüver (1942) did comparable damage to this hypothesis with the experimental technique of *cortical ablation.* Lashley, bit by bit, removed cortical regions, large and small, here and there, together and in stages, but could find no amount of combination that selectively affected the animal's memories. Klüver's fascinating study has been summarized by E. Roy John (1967):

> Klüver . . . conditioned monkeys to perform serial discriminations between the brighter of two lights, between two patterns, between two tones, and between two different weights. After the animals had learned all these discriminations, the associative cortex around each of the relevant primary cortical areas was extirpated. Following recovery from surgery, the monkeys were tested in each of these tasks and it was found that none of the discriminations could be performed. Klüver then retrained his monkeys to perform the discrimination between two weights, selecting the heavier. . . . During the retraining period, no further experience was given the monkeys in *any* of the other tasks. Once the discrimination of weights had been restored to its previous high level, the animals were again tested for retention of the performance of all other discriminations. . . . Klüver found that the monkeys were again able to discriminate between all the various visual and auditory stimuli for which differential performance had been abolished following surgery (John, p. 10).

Redundancy Theories

Because of the survival of memories in the wake of extensive surgical ablation, it is currently considered necessary to treat memory mechanisms as rather diffusely distributed processes occurring throughout the cerebral cortex or even the entire nervous system. The research done by Lashley and by Klüver indicates that the concepts of *mass action* and *equipotentiality* (discussed below) certainly apply to memory. According to redundancy models, memories are stored in many separate locations but, perhaps, preferentially. There are two feasible means by which such diffuse representation of information can be achieved. One is neuroelectric; the other, biochemical.

Neuroelectric Mechanisms

As in perception and learning, there are reliable changes in both the ongoing and the evoked electrical events in the CNS during successive stages of training. However, these altered electrical patterns do not have anything resembling the durability of LTM. Their time course is of a comparable duration to STM, and this fact has led to studies of the effects of electroconvulsive shock (ECS) upon memory. One of the earliest of these was reported by Duncan in 1949. Rats were trained to make either left or right turns to obtain food reward in a T-maze. After extensive training, reward was shifted to the opposite side. The experimental group was administered ECS following their successful reversal of habit, while control animals received no such ECS. The ECS itself is produced by clipping electrodes to each ear and passing a shock between them. Generalized convulsions follow, and it takes some minutes for animals to regain consciousness. Duncan found that ECS animals reverted to their old habit (either a left or a right turn) and attributed this to the amnesic effects of ECS. This interpretation was consistent with studies of human patients given shock therapy for schizophrenia. Amnesia for recent events is a common residual of these treatments.

Since Duncan's pioneering study, numerous investigators have reported memory loss of recently acquired behavior in animals exposed to ECS after learning trials. The interval between learning and ECS has been systematically varied, but reports of critical intervals have been highly inconsistent. Most studies indicate that if ECS follows training by more than an hour, amnesic effects are weak or absent. This has been taken to indicate that ECS disrupts the period of memory consolidation, that is, the time during which the contents of STM are "deposited" in LTM. While research of this kind is suggestive, the present picture is rather inconclusive. Studies often have failed to assess the possibly averse properties of ECS itself. Each study has tended to introduce some variation or another, making it difficult to obtain comparable results. Animals have varied in age, genetic composition, and sex. A wide range of tasks has been used. Learning criteria have differed. All sorts of ECS parameters (intensity, duration, waveform, and so forth) have been chosen. And finally, whatever the disruptive effects of ECS turn out to be, the retrograde amnesia involves only relatively recent experiences. Thus, mechanisms underlying long-term storage are not likely to be found in those neuroelectric events presently measurable. Even when all electrical activity in the CNS is terminated (which is possible by freezing animals to 0°C.), long-term memories are not erased (Gerard, 1963). The persistence of memory does not appear to require the persistence of neuroelectric activity.

Biochemical Mechanisms

At present, the biological theories of memory are becoming predominantly *biochemical* in nature. The trace for which Lashley searched all his life is now a molecule. A popular question today is, "What is the memory molecule?" The appeal of biochemical models is manifold. Chemical "codes" can be stored everywhere in the CNS, thus accommodating the inability of surgical removal of part of the brain to erase memories. Altered chemical states can persist indefinitely, and the facts of biochemistry leave ample room for both intermediary and final forms. Molecules that exist in abundance in neural tissue contain among their number some that are so large and complex as to allow an enormous number of modified versions (codes). Studies of gross changes in brain chemistry following enrichment and deprivation (Chapter 8) also are consistent with the implications of a biochemical theory.

The first in a growing list of molecular candidates was DNA. However, while ideally suited to the task of genetic coding, it seems to be less than desirable as a memory code. While it is big (it can consist of many, many possible atomic configurations) and self-replicating (by which local changes can be multiplied and distributed), it is remarkably resistant to change. Once formed (and presumably unique to each genetically unique individual), its molecular configuration may well be permanent. Analyses of brain-DNA following electroconvulsive shock (ECS), for example, indicate no change. RNA (ribonucleic acid), however, is amenable to change, occurs in high concentrations in brain tissue, and has self-replicating capabilities. Studies have been reported in which chemicals known to interfere with RNA metabolism have been injected directly into the brains of animals either before training or before tests of retention. Results have not been definitive. Prevention of RNA synthesis seems to affect learning more than recall (Dingman and Sporn, 1961), which could implicate it more in STM than in LTM. Other studies, involving drugs that increase the synthesis of RNA and proteins, have indicated greater resistance to the effects of ECS (Essman, 1966). These, too, would seem to suggest a role for RNA and certain proteins in STM.

Some of the most intriguing research on the biochemistry of memory is that which suggests a transfer of learning from one animal to another! In 1962, McConnell published a paper with the somewhat ghoulish title "Memory transfer through cannibalism in planarians." His study constituted the limiting test of molecular theories of memory. Planarians are flatworms with relatively simple nervous systems. They enjoy a kind of diffuse metabolic physiology and, if cut in half, will regenerate into two new worms. Despite their simplicity, they do offer two very favorable talents that bear on research in this area. First, they are conditionable. Second, they will eat other planarians as a steady diet. McConnell trained one group of planarians to solve a simple maze. Having learned the criterion, each one was then chopped up and fed to a naïve worm. Control recipients received "uneducated" donors. McConnell reported that recipients of trained planarians learned the maze significantly faster than control worms, which had received naïve donor worms! Understandably, the work of McConnell and his associates generated much excitement, astonishment, and skepticism. Attempts to duplicate the original finding have met with some frustration, and attempts to interpret the finding have taken a number of different roads. It is not clear, for example, whether actual memory is transferred in such studies or whether just some chemical stimulant is involved. Nor is it certain that the donors' accomplishment is really learning. The debate between McConnell and his doubters has been lively (McConnell, 1964; Halas, James, and Knutson, 1962) and is far from over.

At the present time, it is impossible to provide an integrated theory of learning and memory based upon the known biochemistry of the CNS and changes in this biochemistry according to experience. Empty correlations are abundant.

PHYSIOLOGICAL CORRELATES OF LEARNING AND COGNITION

Conditioning: Classical and Operant

The first general physiological theory of learning was advanced by Ivan Pavlov and was based upon the concept of the reflex arc (see p. 88). Pavlov's influential works were reported at the beginning of the twentieth century, by which time much of the basic anatomy and physiology of reflexes was known. Pavlov's important contributions all started from his remarkable observation of the susceptibility of reflexes to conditioning.

He was a physiologist who had spent many years investigating (and who received a Nobel prize for his studies of) the mechanisms of digestion. At one point he developed a method of collecting saliva from dogs by implanting a tube in the parotid gland of the cheek. Pavlov's initial interest was to analyze chemically the contents of the saliva at different times after placing different powdered foods in the dog's mouth. Very early in this research, he noticed that dogs would come to salivate *before* receiving food. The smell of food, the presence of the laboratory assistant who always brought them food, the sight of food—all of these conditions associated with food could elicit salivation. Pavlov took this observation and based an elaborate research program on it. He replaced the ambiguous conditions (assistants, sights, smells, and so on) with a stimulus that could be specified (a bell), and he systematically varied the number of bell-followed-by-food trials and the interval between bell and food. He found that just a few bell-food pairings were sufficient for the *bell alone* to result in the flow of saliva. In this experiment the food is called the unconditioned stimulus (UCS), and the salivary response to it is called an unconditioned response (UCR). The bell, which to be effective must be a reliable condition for food, is called the conditioned stimulus (CS), and salivation in the presence of the CS alone is called a conditioned response (CR).

Pavlov theorized that the frequent pairing of UCS and CS formed an association between CS and UCR by substitution; that is, CS came to represent UCS. Consistent with traditional empirical associationism, Pavlov's data indicated that repetition, contiguity, and similarity all increased the strength of this elicited response.

In the United States, Pavlov's contributions added impetus to the early behaviorism of John B. Watson, whose system attributed all human behavior to the compounding of elementary conditioned reflexes. Watsonian behaviorism was doomed by its extremism, and it was in its wake that the Thorndikean and Skinnerian approaches, emphasizing operant conditioning, became popular. Procedurally, the two forms of conditioning are achieved in different ways. The behavior in Pavlovian (classical) conditioning is in response to unconditioned stimuli that precede it; it is *respondent* behavior that is elicited by stimulation. The behavior in operant or instrumental conditioning *secures* the reinforcing stimuli; operants occur prior to the stimuli that strengthen them.

It is often aserted that operant conditioning taps the functional behavior of organisms—behavior that is adaptive and under organismic control. Pavlovian conditioning is seen as a "coupling" of visceral-glandular processes with stimuli. It is much closer to nineteenth-century "mechanistic" views of behavior than is operant behavior. Despite the differences, however, the two forms of conditioning do occur within the same organism, and each participates in the establishment of the other. The fact that two seemingly different procedures for conditioning exist should not imply a "Pavlovian" animal, distinct from a "Thorndikean" animal. It is the same animal and one of psychology's tasks is to unite the two fictional organisms within the one actual organism.

Schematically, the two conditioning operations can be differentiated as outlined in Figure 6-17. Together, the two embrace a broad range of

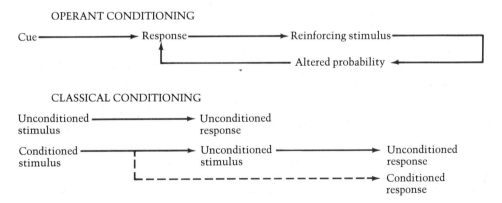

Figure 6-17. The basic paradigms for *operant conditioning* and *classical conditioning*. In operant conditioning, reinforcement follows behavior; in classical conditioning, reinforcement precedes behavior.

learning phenomena, and the Pavlovian system remains a watershed in the history of the physiology of reflex learning.

Learning and the Brain

The most dramatic alteration in the nervous systems of progressively higher forms is the elaboration of the head end of the organism (the process of *encephalization*) and the emergence of anatomically demarcated and subdivided cerebral hemispheres (*corticalization*). Because of the disproportionate mass of the great cerebral hemispheres in man and because of early clinical observations of the effects of injury to them, the pioneers in the psychophysiology of learning focused their attention on the cerebral lobes. Gall's phrenology was based upon their assumed functional distinctiveness. In large part, because of surgical convenience, the earliest research was restricted to them. Unfortunately, these reasons for focusing on cortical functions were not completely justified. Research seldom materialized into unequivocal statements regarding the cortical basis of learning. The most extensive early studies of localization of function were those of Karl Lashley. His major research technique was ablative surgery, which he combined with careful behavioral analyses—something that was lacking in nearly all of the neuropsychological research on learning before him.

Lashley's experimental subjects ranged from rats to monkeys. They engaged in maze-learning tasks of varying complexity as well as simple discrimination tasks. One of the better known discrimination tasks involved the Lashley "jumping stand," depicted in Figure 6-18. The animal is starved for a day or two and then placed on a stand in front of which are two or more stimulus cards. One of the cards contains a positive discriminative stimulus or S^D (a stimulus signaling the availability of reinforcement). The other contains an S^Δ (a stimulus signaling the nonavailability of reward). In Figure 6-18 the S^D is a triangle and the S^Δ is a square. Each time the animal jumps to the triangle, the card falls and food is made available. This simple setting allowed Lashley to study a wide range of learned visual discriminations—form, color, brightness, size, and the like.

Initially, it was Lashley's expectation that the learning that occurred in such a setting would be stored in some specific region of the brain, that the animal's solution would be neurally coded as some sort of an *engram* that would be localized specifically in a region of the cortex. Moreover, it seemed reasonable to assume that learning itself required some specialized

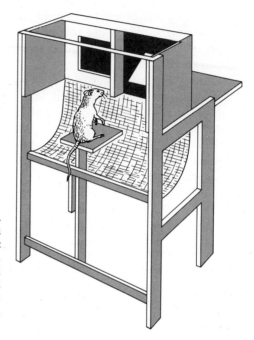

Figure 6-18. A Lashley jumping stand. Jumping at the correct stimulus results in the displacement of the card so that the rat can reach food on the table behind the card. The wrong response will cause the animal to bang into an immovable card and fall into the net below. (You may wish to read E. B. White's *The Door* for a comment on this.)

cortical structure whose removal prior to training would render the animal ineducable.

In hundreds of imaginatively conceived and carefully executed studies, Lashley removed various regions and amounts of cerebral cortex before training to determine their role in learning and after training to identify the locus of memory. The major conclusions emerging from these studies and from similar studies conducted by others are as follows:

1. There is no restricted region of cerebral cortex whose removal permanently eradicates information learned prior to surgery.
2. There is no restricted region of cerebral cortex whose removal precludes the ability to learn.
3. The degree of deficit produced by ablations tends to depend on the total amount of cortex removed and is relatively independent of the locus removed.
4. Deficits immediately following cortical ablations typically dissipate after a sufficient period of convalescence.

These findings led Lashley to propose two general properties of cortical organization. These were the principle of *mass action* and the concept of *equipotentiality*. By mass action, Lashley suggested that in learning and memory, the cortex functions as a whole, as an integrated and interdependent system of structures. It should be noted that this neuropsychological concept is in accord with the Gestalt view of mental processes. By equipotentiality, Lashley meant that many regions of the cortex have the potentiality for assuming those functions normally undertaken by other cortical structures. Removal of the latter results in a shift of functional responsibility. A unique property of cortical neurons and of CNS neurons in general is that they are nonregenerative. Once removed, they can never be replaced by new growth. Thus, equipotentiality cannot be explained on the basis of structural regencration. This perplexing state of affairs has been summarized by Sperry (1958):

> Cortical lesions produced initially in the expectation that whole blocks of memory and categories of experience and behavior would be wiped out proved in many cases to have so slight an effect on functional organization and memory as to tax the ingenuity of the investigator to detect any behavioral deficits.

Thus, while basic sensory processes such as vision and audition are rather selectively represented in specific cortical regions, more global capacities such as learning, cognition, and memory appear to have diffuse representation in the cortex. Because of this nonspecific cortical involvement, recent investigations have been expanded to include studies of neuroelectrical correlates of learning, biochemical correlates of learning, and subcortical mechanisms in learning.

Before moving on to these, we will put Lashley's research and theories in perspective. Superficially, he seems to have removed every possible argument in favor of localization of higher functions such as learning and cognition. But examining his research more closely, we recognize the following limitations:

1. The use of ablative surgery almost to the exclusion of any other method.
2. Restrictions of surgery almost exclusively to the cerebral cortex.
3. The use of behavioral tasks of a crude nature to assess abilities that depend on subtle fractional abilities.

Because of these limitations, Lashley was confronted with experimental findings that forced him to reject the classical ideas of localization of function. More recently, however, investigators have extended Lashley's procedures, have included a more sophisticated set of behavioral (learning) tasks, and have come to the conclusion that the classical view was not as trivial as Lashley would have us think. Some tasks—such as the delayed response task in which the animal must choose one of several alternatives after being shown which one is the correct one—are impossible for animals with very specific cortical lesions. Similar effects can be produced by highly restricted lesions introduced into *subcortical* areas such as the hippocampus. Thus, the question of localization of higher mental functions remains open. But it becomes increasingly apparent that specific regions of the brain are at least related to specific learning and memory skills.

Neuroelectrical Correlates of Learning

The central nervous system is never at rest in a living organism. Every region reveals ongoing electrical activity, often of a highly rhythmic nature. In 1929, Hans Berger applied electrodes to the scalp of human subjects and, with the aid of a high-gain amplifier, observed the presence of constant and rhythmic electrical waves of activity (alpha waves) that presumably originated in the cerebral cortex. In the waking subject, relaxed and reclining in a dimly lit room, these waves occurred at frequencies between 8 and 13 cycles per second. Berger called his recordings an *electroencephalograph* (EEG) and labeled the large regular waves the *alpha rhythm*. He noted that the presentation of light flashes or loud sounds or instructions requiring the subject to become alert would obliterate the alpha rhythm and lead to waves of lower amplitude and higher frequency. This phenomenon is referred to as *alpha blocking*, shown in Figure 6-19.

An enormous amount of research has been concerned with the EEG. Electroencephalography has become a very useful tool in clinical neurology. Certain characteristics of the EEG may be used to detect tumors, latent epilepsy, and infectious processes in the CNS. The alpha rhythm especially has enjoyed the attention of researchers because of its unique response to visual stimulation. It has been shown, for example, that the speed of the blocking response (alpha blocking latency) is reliably related to the intensity, area, and duration of visual stimuli (Robinson, 1966). While efforts to uncover relations between *rhythmic* EEG activity and

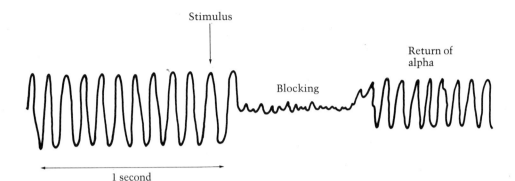

Figure 6-19. The *alpha rhythm* and *alpha blocking* are illustrated in the waking but resting subject. The dominant EEG frequency is in a range from 8-13 cps (the alpha rhythm). Presentation of a stimulus leads to a reduction in amplitude and an increase in frequency of the EEG (alpha blocking). But with termination of the stimulus or under conditions of prolonged, monotonous stimulation, alpha frequencies return.

learning by and large have failed, there is evidence to suggest a reliable relationship between nonrhythmic (D.C.) EEG changes and learning. This fact was first reported by Walter et al. (1964), who noted that the baseline voltage of the EEG gradually changed on those trials in which meaningful material was presented. For example, suppose a subject is told that if a certain stimulus (red light) is presented, he is to respond to the next visual stimulus, but if a blue light is presented, he need not respond to the next stimulus. In such a case, the red light creates an expectancy and is, therefore, meaningful. Using averaging computers, it is possible to add the small changes in brain activity that occur in response to each of these flashes. Since these brain responses are not ongoing but, instead, are produced by the flashes, they are referred to as *evoked responses* or *average evoked responses* (AER). What has been found is that, under conditions such as these, the overall AER to the meaningful stimulus reveals a substantial negative shift in the baseline electrical activity.

Biochemical Correlates of Enrichment

Since the central nervous system's electrical response to stimulation ends soon after the stimulus is terminated, it has long been assumed that the persistence of learned behavior (memory) is the result of relatively permanent changes in the biochemistry of neural tissue. There have been numerous tests of this assumption involving several research designs. One of the more frequently employed techniques is that of exposing genetically matched groups of animals to very different experiences. One group—an "enriched" one—is given daily learning trials, usually of the maze variety. A second, "impoverished" group is kept in home cages and denied an opportunity to learn. After two or three months of this regimen, the groups are sacrificed and their brains analyzed chemically and histologically. (Histology is that branch of biology dealing with the tissues.) Krech et al. (1960), who were pioneers in this research, have reported substantial changes in brain chemistry, brain weight, and overall neurohistology as a result of environmental enrichment.

Subcortical Mechanisms in Learning

Throughout the nineteenth and early twentieth centuries, a rather geometric view of the nervous system prevailed. Primitive skeletal reflexes were assumed to be the major function of the spinal cord. "Higher up," the medulla was assumed to mediate the vegetative (visceral) reflexes involving heart rate, respiration, and digestion. Midbrain was assigned the role of rather simple coordinations of sensory inputs. Finally, the great cerebral hemispheres were reached where reason, will, and consciousness resided. The preservation of learning and cognitive abilities in animals with massive cortical ablations was sufficient to challenge this hierarchic view of nervous organization. Scientists became increasingly intrigued by the functions of those phylogenetically older structures that lay beneath the cerebral mantle.

The model of learning advanced early in this chapter proposed the following chain of events: Drive → Cue → Response → Reinforcement → Drive Reduction. Cue identification requires *attention*. Reinforcement assumes the termination of some aversive condition. It is now known that subcortical mechanisms are directly involved in those processes implied by the terms attention, motivation, reward, and punishment.

Attention   All of the sensory pathways are represented neurally in the *reticular formation*. Beginning at the anterior portion of the medulla, this structure proceeds to the floor of the forebrain (below the cortex) as a net-like arching column of interconnected fibers. If stimulating electrodes are inserted into this reticular bundle and recording electrodes are placed on the cerebral cortex, it can be shown that reticular stimulation leads to a widespread desynchronization of ongoing cortical (rhythmic) activity. That is, something like alpha blocking occurs. Thus, there are portions of the reticular formation whose activity "arouses" the cerebral cortex. These portions constitute the *ascending reticular arousal system* (ARAS). There are interesting behavioral correlates of this action. If, for example, the ARAS of a sleeping cat is stimulated, the animal awakens abruptly, its ears prick up, its posture becomes stiff and poised, and the animal displays all of the responses usually associated with attention. Another function of ARAS is that of "screening" sensory information. Hernandez-Peon et al. (1956) recorded the response of a cat's auditory system to repeated "clicks" while monitoring the electrical activity in ARAS. In the resting state, the cat revealed reliable neural responses to each click. Then, a mouse was placed in front of the cat's cage. Activity in ARAS immediately increased and responses to the clicks were now greatly reduced. It would appear that in addition to generalized arousal, the separation of "meaningful" and "meaningless" cues is also mediated by activity with ARAS. This separation is, in fact, what attention usually implies. Unfortunately, many essential controls were missing from this research; therefore, we know less about the neurology of attention than we would have, if this experiment had been more extensive.

Attention is highly selective (specific), but the effects of ARAS on the cortex are quite diffuse. Thus, some structures other than ARAS must participate in directing and limiting attentional behavior. Most strongly implicated in this role are the various nuclei of the thalamus. Many fibers from the ARAS terminate in the thalamus. It is known that certain very specific pathways proceed from thalamus to restricted regions of cortex. At the present time, the neural mechanisms responsible for selective attention are assumed to be those that form a reticulo-thalamo-cortical pathway.

This descending reticular system has a major effect upon the amount and nature of information carried from the spinal cord to higher centers. One example is found in studies of pain. If a peripheral nerve in the leg of an animal is intensely stimulated, the usual train of events is: Peripheral Nerve → Dorsal Spinal Cord → Reticular Formation → Thalamus. However, if DRS is activated electrically while the peripheral nerve is stimulated, the thalamus does not receive the peripheral "pain" signals and the animal does not withdraw the stimulated limb (Hagbarth and Kerr, 1954).

A recent application of such findings involves the implantation of externally controlled electrodes into the "pain center" of the thalamus in patients with intractable pain. With the onset of pain, the patient delivers a brief "shock" to his own thalamic nuclei. Long periods of painlessness ensue without any other insensitivity developing. The aphorism about pain that suggests that "it's all in the mind" would appear to be valid, at least if the "mind" includes the thalamic nuclei, or vice versa.

Drive   To say that animals eat because they are hungry explains little. It fails to describe how animals "know" they are "hungry." It would make as much sense to say that animals eat because they want to. *What are the cues that give rise to eating behavior?* is a more fruitful question, and a partial answer to it is available. The *primary* drives (those that exist in the absence of conditioning) of hunger, thirst, copulation, and pain-avoidance originate peripherally. At one time, it was assumed that peripheral deficiencies or injuries were necessary for the creation of such drives. Cannon and Washburn (1912), for example, observed a reliable correlation between the peristaltic contractions of the stomach muscles and subjective reports of hunger. They concluded that the former were necessary for the latter. Other investigators demonstrated, however, that normal hunger cycles occur in animals whose stomachs were pharmacologically paralyzed or even surgically removed. Similarly, theories of satiation based upon a filling or distention of the stomach were challenged by the fact that animals whose food passed from the mouth out through a cannula without ever reaching the stomach tended to eat much less. In other words, hunger was reduced *by the act of eating.* Thirsty animals continue to drink even when liquids are placed directly into the stomach, presumably because dryness of the mouth and esophageal mucosa is aversive. Other peripheral theories focused upon "homeostatic" cues by which eating and drinking were assumed to occur in the presence of altered blood chemistry. Here, too, conflicting data were gathered. Intravenous maintenance of normal blood pressure, blood sugar levels, and various blood serum nutrients are not sufficient to terminate eating and drinking.

After the "peripheralists" had had their day, "centralist" theorists took over. Their view was (and still is) that the basic drives—independent of whatever peripheral conditions normally are correlated with them— are ultimately reducible to events within the brain. Beginning with the observation that some chronically overweight patients are found, on post-mortem, to have subcortical tumors, neuropsychological research has un-

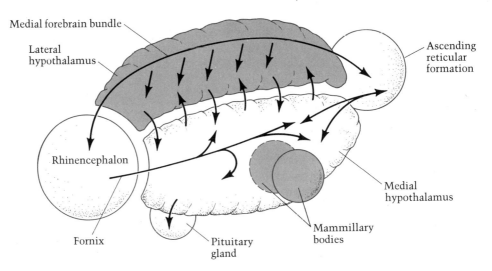

Figure 6-20 A schematic diagram of the hypothalamus and immediately associated structures. The arrows indicate the direction of information flow. (After McCleary and Moore, 1965.)

covered an impressive range of relations between subcortical stimulation and appetitive behavior. The specific structure implicated is the *hypothalamus*, which is schematically shown in Figure 6-20. If an electrode is inserted in the *lateral* hypothalamic nuclei, stimulation results in the animal's uncontrollable eating. With daily and prolonged stimulation, the rat will double or triple its weight. This compulsive eating is called *hyperphagia* and results are given in Figure 6-21. Stimulation of the *ventromedial* hypothalamus results in *hypophagia*, an absolute refusal to eat, with the usual consequence of death by starvation. Drinking "centers" overlap with the eating centers of the hypothalamus, although the inhibition of drinking has been more difficult to obtain through electrical stimulation. In both systems, however, there are antagonistic processes (what in color vision were called opponent processes), so that activity in a hunger area depresses the electrical activity in a satiation area. In fact, the same area can initiate either drinking *or* eating if stimulated chemically by adrenalin-like substances in one case or "anti-adrenalin" substances in the other (Grossman, 1960). Furthermore, since the hypothalamus sends fibers to the pituitary gland, hypothalamic activity can have profound effects upon hormonal

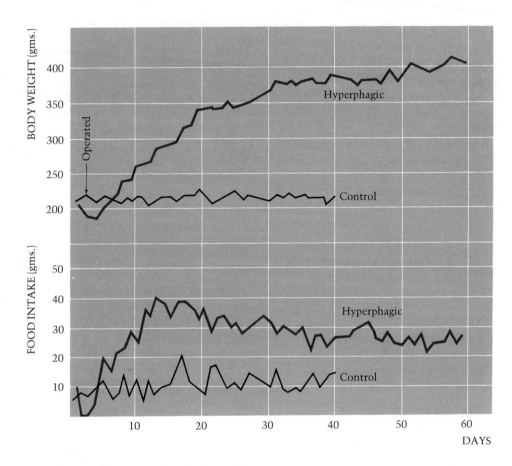

Figure 6-21. Changes in the body weight and the food consumption of rats whose ventromedial hypothalamus has been destroyed. Note changes relative to the control animals on whom surgery has not been performed. (After Teitelbaum, 1961.)

balance throughout the body. Hypothalamic discharges can also result in the pituitary secretion of gonadotrophic hormones, whose presence in the blood causes the secretion of those gonadal hormones that result in mating behavior. Thus, the hypothalamus appears to be important to the expression and satiation of sexual and appetitional (primary) drives.

Reward and Punishment   Bentham's "twin masters" of pleasure and pain operate well beyond the rather primitive needs for nourishment and pain avoidance. Life allows a grand assortment of delights and disappointments whose roots in hunger and copulation are usually quite indirect. In 1954, Olds and Milner reported a study of rats who were able to stimulate regions of their own brains by pressing a lever. Electrodes were placed in numerous locations. Specific centers were found that would lead to bar-pressing rates up to thousands per hour. Since their study, other investigators have used this intracranial self-stimulation (ICS) technique to "map" the areas of reward and punishment.

Numerous sites within the forebrain and midbrain lead to positive, negative, and both positive and negative reinforcing effects. Those areas that have the potential for both reward and punishment may be viewed as possible *conflict* centers. It should be noted that while ICS reinforcement does reveal schedule-of-reinforcement effects (see above) and does allow the establishment of secondary reinforcers by pairing neutral stimuli with ICS, there are important differences between ICS reinforcement and external reinforcement. For one thing, ICS-reinforced animals are extremely resistant to satiation; they cease self-stimulation principally out of exhaustion. The only external reinforcement with this property is pain-avoidance. Second, very often those centers associated with the highest rates of ICS are not the preferred ICS centers when the organism can choose which area to stimulate. Furthermore, it is difficult, if not impossible, to establish low response rates in ICS animals. Using food reward and a long FI (fixed-interval) schedule, for example, it is possible to train animals to pause for long durations between bar-presses. This is called differential reinforcement for *low* response rates, or DRL. The estabishment of DRL behavior using ICS has not been reported despite frequent attempts. Thus, while there are operationally definable centers of "reward" and "punishment" in subcortical areas, it is not yet clear that these rewarding states are the same or even similar to those produced "naturally."

In the natural state, the organism does not await the implantation of electrodes to eat or drink or sleep. Processes occurring within must somehow trigger activity in those brain regions that are responsible for initiating behavior. Recent research has shed some light on the mechanism by which brain regions may be activated by changes in the organism's general physiology. As has been mentioned, Grossman (1960) devised an ingenious method for stimulating very small areas of the brain with biochemical substances. He has shown that the same area may display an increase in activity when bathed in an adrenalin-like substance and a decrease in activity when bathed in an antiadrenalin-like substance. The significance of this research stems from its ability to account for the manner in which changes in blood chemistry may selectively turn on and turn off specific brain regions. Effects analogous to those found in opponent-process cells in vision have been found in brain regions associated with basic drives, for example, hunger and thirst. In these regions, local changes of a biochemical nature have effects similar to those produced by complementary regions of the visible spectrum—excitation and inhibition.

SUMMARY

In this chapter we have explored the adaptive capacities of organisms able to learn. We have noted that a broad range of behavior can be brought under experimental control through the application of rewards and punishments and that, to this extent, traditional associationistic principles are confirmed. We have also seen, however, some evidence to suggest that these principles are not sufficient to account for all reliable behavioral adaptations. The more advanced species, at least, possess *cognitive* capacities as well and, as a result, are able to abstract general features from the environment even when trial-and-error learning is not possible. Moreover, studies in social psychology have been reviewed that raise questions about the power of "reinforcement histories" to regulate behavior in demanding social contexts.

We have seen that adaptive behavior may be more than the formation of "associative bonds" and that memory and forgetting involve more than the passive collection or weakening of such bonds. These studies of learning and memory in animals and in human beings point in the direction of active and creative processes that are brought to bear on the environment by the organism. Thus, we must add to association the following elements —perception, organization, spontaneity, the psychological demands of the current context, and the past history of success and failure. Some of these factors have been examined in neurophysiological terms as well, and we are now in possession of a small set of reliable relationships between gross adaptive behavior and biochemical and electrophysiological events in the nervous system. We are not yet in possession of developed theories by which to explain these relationships. As of now, these relationships are little more than observed correlations.

Although findings from experimentation on both animals and human beings were reviewed in this chapter, we restricted our examination of performance to relatively simple tasks of the associative type. Even the "insight" studies involve little more than stringing together a few behavioral elements. Tasks of this sort do not test the merits of empiricistic versus nativistic explanations. We will move now to what may be the most complex event of all—language. From a behavioristic perspective, its importance derives from the fact that it is our most frequently emitted "operant." That is, within the adult human community, there is probably no intentional response produced as frequently as the use of language. And from the cognitive perspective, language is the crowning achievement of the educated mind. Therefore, if we are to judge a theory or system of psychology, we have no more discriminating test than that which calls upon the theory or system to provide a plausible account of language.

SUGGESTED READINGS

ADAMS, J. A. *Human Memory.* New York: McGraw-Hill Book Company, 1967.

This is a concise and excellent review of research findings in human (mostly *verbal*) memory. Dr. Adams' summary of theories is fair and quite readable.

BRUNER, J. S., GOODNOW, J. J. and AUSTIN, G. A. *A Study of Thinking.* New York: Science Editions, 1962.

This is a book anchored firmly to the cognitive traditions of the psychology of learning or, as the authors would put it, *information processing.* The introduction provides a summary of cognitive psychology's recent history. Chapters 3, 4, and 5 on concept formation are particularly relevant to Chapter 5 of this book.

CATANIA, A. C., ed. *Contemporary Research in Operant Behavior.* Glenview, Ill.: Scott, Foresman & Co., 1968.

Dr. Catania has assembled 60 readings in "Skinnerian" psychology covering, among other areas, aversive control, schedules, generalization and discrimination, and applications.

GUROWITZ, E. M. *The Molecular Basis of Memory.* Englewood Cliffs,
   N.J.: Prentice-Hall, 1969.

   Dr. Gurowitz has written a brief review of research on the biochemistry of memory. He gives a helpful introduction to basic neurochemistry
and then summarizes a number of recent studies. The book is satisfactory
for the beginning student.

LOGAN, F. A. and WAGNER, A. R. *Reward and Punishment.* Boston: Allyn
   & Bacon, 1965.

   Professors Logan and Wagner offer a concise summary of recent research comparing behavior control under positive and aversive conditions.
Traditional theories are discussed briefly. The accent is on data.

NORMAN, D. A. *Memory and Attention.* New York: John Wiley & Sons.
   1969.

   Dr. Norman has written and edited material which falls under the
"information-processing" model of memory. This volume is rich in research
findings and sophisticated in its treatment of theoretical issues. Chapter 8
(*Models of Memory*) is worth special attention.

CHAPTER

7

Language

WHAT IS LANGUAGE?

All definitions of language incorporate the concept of communication, and most require that the communication have an effect upon the behavior of other organisms. Those who avoid mentalistic terms do not include *intention* as a necessary feature of language, but at least intuitively, we can assume that any organism capable of linguistic behavior is also capable of choice. When the parrot announces, "Polly wanna cracker," it is not clear whether the bird, in fact, does want a cracker, but it seems that only through rewarded practice do such vocalizations become distinct and reliable. It is often said that this behavior is mere mimicry and not speech. However, it is not all that obvious how to distinguish between the two. By speech, one usually means the emission of unique patterns of sound capable of informing another person. "Polly wanna cracker" certainly answers this condition. When a master says, "Do you want to go out?" and his dog barks, is this speech? When his tail is pinched and the dog yelps, is this a cry of pain? Are mating calls intentional acts of vocal communication? Moreover, is it necessary that language be verbal in nature? Presumably, it is not, since many people have developed sign languages in which gestures and postural symbols serve quite satisfactorily as forms of communication. Recently, psychologists have exploited this fact in attempting to teach a chimpanzee to "speak" through sign language. In earlier studies, only marginal success was enjoyed in getting chimps to utter words. The ultimate size of their vocabularies seldom extended beyond a few words, and these were never used in grammatical sequences. Gardner and Gardner (1967), however, discovered a somewhat greater linguistic capacity in chimps by teaching sign language, such as that used by deaf people, for words. After about two years of training, the chimp "Washoe" gained command of some sixty signs and could emit several dozen in an attempt to obtain reward. Furthermore, sequencing was observed in which Washoe placed subjects, verbs, and adverbs appropriately in a sign language sentence.

Does Washoe know what she's "saying"? Is she to become another member of the community of speakers which, until now, has been restricted to man? Can meaning be assigned to the many sounds and signs that are emitted by one animal in the presence of others? And even if there is some meaning, is the animal aware of its meaningfulness? Is it the outcome of a cognitive process? Does the lion intend his roar to be frightening? Does the baby utter "ma-ma" in an attempt to draw its mother closer?

At present, it is entirely arbitrary to assign certain sounds to the categories of speech and nonspeech. But *language* is something else again, and it is this phenomenon that we will explore in the present chapter.

There is no attribute of life that suggests the discontinuity of evolution as much as human language. With it, man acquires a history, traditions are passed down, pacts are formed, feelings expressed, hopes entertained, images recalled, and creation made possible. It bears the relationship to civilization that a chisel bears to a statue. It is the key to consciousness and a possible path to immortality. Moreover, it is our most frequently occurring and inexhaustible behavior. It is estimated that a billion words are uttered in a lifetime, that a student who likes to talk with other people listens to 100,000 words a day in addition to the 90,000 he reads (Carroll, 1954). No wonder that the linguist B. L. Whorf (1956) called speech "the best show man puts on."

Oddly enough, the classical philosophers raised few questions regarding language, and perhaps because of this apparent disinterest, early psychologists did not include it in their list of experimental variables. In using introspective report, Wilhelm Wundt rather casually assumed that his subjects could verbalize their experiences. Freud recognized that language was both a means of communicating troubled conditions and, as exemplified by parapraxes, a possible symptom of those conditions.

Until recently, the scientific study of speech was largely the work of neurologists and neurosurgeons treating *aphasics* and *dysphasics*, whose inability to communicate verbally is symptomatic of brain damage. Because of its clinical orientation, even this research had little if anythng to do with the nature of language per se. Linguists, on the other hand, had developed a substantial catalog of structural properties of language (grammar, syntax, semantics), and anthropologists had recorded a host of linguistic nuances unique to various cultures. But until the 1940s, a true *psycholinguistics*, or study of the psychology of language, was hard to locate. Two pressures combined to stimulate enthusiasm for linguistics research in psychology. First, the growing interest in verbal learning and memory created a need for what may be called "semantic scales." Concern for variables such as meaningfulness and prior knowledge in influencing paired-associates learning led naturally to statistical studies of word frequency in language usage. Research programs were launched to determine such things as the number of associations that subjects could form in response to word x. Supplementing this trend was the psychometric craze of the war years, during which numerous objective tests of personality, interests, beliefs, concept formation, basic skills, and so on were fashioned. Preliminary studies were necessary to determine the linguistic composition of such examinations. Which words does an individual need to describe his feelings? Which words most sensitively discriminate people with respect to vocabulary? Which words are laden with significance for the neurotic?

The second major impetus to the creation of a psycholinguistics grew out of *information theory*. War and peace both require the accurate and rapid exchange of information over great distances and often in the presence of obscuring events (*noise*). World War II was no exception. Codes intelligible to speakers of many different languages were needed. Elaborate telephonic and telegraphic networks were designed to accommodate the greatest stream of communication the world had ever known. The engi-

neering triumph of information theory did not occur until 1949 (Shannon and Weaver), but the war effort made possible many of the facilities and projects that led to it. In barest outline, information theory is really a theory of decision-making whose central tenets are these:
1. All decisions, no matter how complex, can be reduced to one or more yes-no (binary) events.
2. Decisions are made possible by *information*, which can be treated as a *probabilistic* phenomenon.

The unit of information is the *bit* (binary digit), which is simply a measure of the *a priori* probability of an event. Information theory asserts that *there is no information conveyed by the occurrence of events whose likelihood is certain.* Thus, if one releases a shoe, there is no information transmitted by its falling to the ground. In a gravitational environment, objects heavier than air are certain to fall. One is not informed when the inevitable occurs. Accepting the view of information as the occurrence of uncertain events, it was possible to invent a measure of information based on the assumed binary nature of all control (decision) functions. In the simplest case, such as flipping a coin, only one of two alternatives can occur. The coin lands either "head" up or "tail" up. The *a priori* probability of "heads" is 0.50; of "tails" also 0.50; and of either one, 1.0; it is *certain* that either "heads" or "tails" will occur. Such either-or, 0-1, yes-no, two-valued outcomes convey the smallest unit of information (1 bit) when one of the two alternatives does, in fact, occur. The equation that allows a computation of information content is:

$$I = \log_2 \left(\frac{1}{P} \right)$$

where (I) is information in *bits* and (P) is the *a priori* probability of the event's occurrence. The equation preserves the reciprocal (inverse) relationship between certainty and information. For example, when $P = 1.0$, $I = 0$. That is, $\log_2 (1) = 0$. The use of a ($\log_2$) scale is based upon the binary nature of all events. Just as the $\log_{10}$ of a number is the power to which 10 must be raised to produce the number, the $\log_2$ of a number is the power to which 2 must be raised. For example, $\log_{10} (100) = 2$. That is, 10 must be raised to a power of 2 (that is, 10^2) to produce 100. Similarly, $\log_2 (4) = 2$; that is, $2^2 = 4$; $\log_2 (8) = 3$ (since $2^3 = 8$). When "heads" fall, one bit of information is conveyed:

$$I = \log_2 \left(\frac{1}{P}\right)$$

$$I = \log_2 \left(\frac{1}{0.5}\right) \text{ since the likelihood of "heads" is 0.5}$$

$$I = \log_2 (2)$$

$$I = 1 \; bit$$

Suppose, instead of a coin, one places four names in a hat, shuffles the names, and draws one. How much information is conveyed by that name?

$$I = \log_2 \left(\frac{1}{P}\right)$$

The *a priori* probability of any one name being drawn is 0.25. Thus,

$$I = \log_2 \left(\frac{1}{.25}\right) = \log_2 (4) = 2 \; \text{bits}$$

For each doubling of alternatives, there is a unit increase in information. Applying these principles to verbal communication allows a considerable increase in the efficiency of message-sending. For example, consider the message THE CAT IS CAUGHT IN THE TREE. Many of these letters are unnecessary for an accurate reception of the message. If the message were written THE C–T IS CAU––T IN T–– TREE, almost everyone conversant in English would be able to decode it for meaning. The receiver of such a message would insert the "A," "GH," and "HE" with certainty. The extent to which a message contains information unnecessary for accurate decoding is a measure of its *redundancy*. Written and spoken language are over 50 percent redundant in that more than half of the words (letters, syllables) used are not necessary for an accurate decoding of intended information.

There are numerous applications of information theory to language. Most important for our present purpose is that it fostered studies concerned with the *statistical* nature of language and it provided a theoretical context within which older data became more comprehensible.

SOME STATISTICAL PROPERTIES OF LANGUAGE

A most ambitious undertaking, in line with statistical descriptions, was reported by Zipf (1945) in his monograph *Human Behavior and the Principles of Least Effort*. Zipf examined lengthy passages of prose, newspaper writing, novels, and the Bible and discovered that the frequency with which words are used is inversely proportional to their length. Moreover, there is a linear relationship between the frequency with which a word is used and its meaningfulness (measured as the number of different meanings that can be assigned to it). These statistical attributes are shown in Figures 7-1 and 7-2. Zipf viewed such highly reliable relationships as indicative of the action of basic biophysical mechanisms that require language to be as effortless as possible. Somehow, language was structured in such a way as to "cost" the speaker as little as necessary. Adherence to the "principle of least effort" was found to be as great among the ancient classical writers, the Peking Chinese, and James Joyce as it was to cub reporters

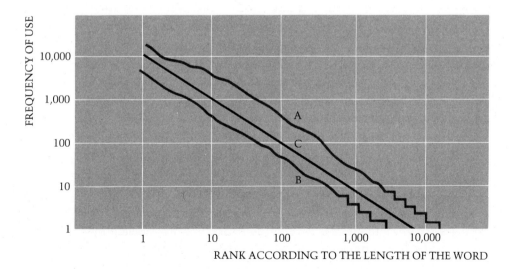

Figure 7-1. One of *Zipf's laws*. Curve A is derived from James Joyce's book *Ulysses* and B from samples of English newspapers. The straight line C is what results from the prediction that frequency of use and rank are perfectly negatively related. (After Zipf, 1949.)

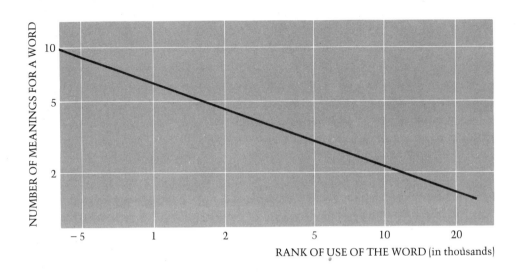

Figure 7-2. The greater the number of meanings a word has, the more it is used. Note the linear quality of the relationship. (After Zipf, 1949.)

laboring in New York. Neither time, context, culture, nor content appeared to affect these relationships.

To some, the findings of Zipf and numerous reports of the statistical properties of language suggested that the learning of language could be understood in the same terms as all other learning. In 1957 Skinner published *Verbal Behavior,* a text that advanced this view boldly and that caused much mischief in the emerging discipline of psycholinguistics. The book was reviewed by the linguist Noam Chomsky (1959), and since then psychology has been enlivened by a spirited controversy over the nature of language, an argument that is often called "the Skinner-Chomsky debate." As a debate, it has little of the drama created by Lincoln and Douglas and even less of the eloquence. Psycholinguistics is a new discipline, still getting its "sea legs." As such, its case is occasionally made polemically and with rather visible defensiveness. The student of science has an excellent opportunity to apprehend scientific growing pains by reading articles written by "Skinnerians" and "Chomskians." At the root of it all, the controversy is none other than the ancient argument between empiricists and nativists, a revival of the bouts between Plato and Aristotle, Locke and

Leibnitz, Kant and Hume. Today's adversaries have chosen impresssive company.

LANGUAGE AS VERBAL BEHAVIOR

The production of sound is made possible by the resonant properties of the vocal chords, which are activated by air forced over them. This expulsion of air from the lungs is controlled by the musculature of the diaphragm working in concert with that of the larynx. Whatever else it may be, speech is sound and, to that extent, is created by the same kind of neuromuscular events that underlie all other varieties of operant behavior. This is the point of origin of Skinner's *Verbal Behavior:* speech *is* verbal behavior. Initially, the newborn sputters, bellows, and grunts meaningless little sounds whose phonetic properties are determined by the physical features of the apparatus. Given the latter, certain sounds have a higher probability of occurrence than do others; for example, "bak" is more likely than "deoxyribose nucleic acid." The infant's world, for all its newness, is rather narrow. He "knows" pain, hunger, thirst, cold, and environmental change in that the neural connections necessary to signal such conditions are established. Beyond the crib, hopeful adults dutifully attend to the responsibilities of parenthood. Sooner or later, some event of an aversive nature impels the baby to screams and tears. Within moments, talcum powder, warm milk, a mother's caress, and gentle rocking replace the unpredictable irritating universe of new life. Crying is now more probable under similar conditions in the future. Furthermore, mother (and by *stimulus generalization,* father, grandparents, siblings, other adults) gradually gains effectiveness as a secondary reinforcer, that is, the baby will work to secure mother. Sounds seem to do the trick.

We will assume that the mother is responsible, motivated, and concerned. She knows that if baby is to reach college eighteen years later, he had better start learning things soon. Holding baby on her lap (another secondary reinforcement—for both of them) she says, "Ma-ma." Baby utters, "Brahghoo."

Mother: "Say 'Ma-ma' "
Baby: "Goo . . . hilerr"
Mother: "Say 'Ma-ma . . . Maah-maah' "
Baby: "Ah . . . mm"

This is close enough for the mother to pick up the baby, hold him close to her cheek, pat his back, and otherwise create pleasurable stimulation. The likelihood of responses such as "Brahghoo" and "Goo . . . Hilerr" is no higher than chance, but "Ah . . . Mm" is. Soon baby delivers a genuine "Ma-ma," and mother begins saving for college. An especially significant consequence of this process is that of raising the verbal *operant level*. That is, the baby will spend progressively more time engaged in verbal behavior for the simple reason that it proves to be substantially more effective in securing primary and secondary reinforcements than are competing or alternative responses. In the English language and most other languages, the number of sounds (*phonemes*) employed in creating all possible words is very small. In English, it is about forty-five. Phonemes are the juxtaposition of vowels and consonants in short sequences. Since the phonemes that dominate a language tend to be relatively easy to pronounce, by increasing the verbal operant level of the baby, it is more likely that useful phonemes will appear and, therefore, be reinforced. Phonemes themselves carry no meaning. In combination, however, they form *morphemes*, meaningful sets of phonemes, which, for the present, will be considered as synonymous with words. With merely forty to fifty phonemes, tens of thousands of morphemes can be constructed. That is, all of the words that comprise a language derive from combinations of a relatively small set of basic sounds. By selectively reinforcing certain combinations, the mother quickly establishes a small working vocabulary in the child. If she is clever, she can even arrange reinforcement contingencies in such a ways to make imitative behavior increasingly probable. The child must emit sounds of acoustic comparability to his mother's in order to obtain reward. The process is analogous to a pigeon's having to peck a key to increase the brightness of one light until it is just as bright as an adjacent one. Soon toys get names, self becomes "babe-ee," dog is "bow-wow," and so forth. Ultimately, selective reinforcement and the processes of discrimination and generalization act to create coherent speech. As a rat learns to turn left at one symbol, right at another, and to stop at a third, the child learns that speech starts with certain words (nouns) and proceeds with others (verbs, adverbs, and so on). He often omits articles and inflections ("Baby go now"). Further training permits the acquisition of "the" and the addition of "s," "es," and other appropriate inflections. By generalization, the learning of "The baby goes now" embellishes former utterances: "Daddy home now" becomes "Daddy's home now"; "He break toy" becomes "He breaks the toys." New morphemes—many of them wrong—appear as the child's reinforcement history urges him on to "discover" words. By reinforcing novelty in speech and ignoring excessive repetition, the probability of altered morpheme combinations is increased.

The foregoing, which in its broad essentials conveys the spirit of Skinner's position, has been put to various tests. Unaware that they are subjects in an experiment, people will increase their use of certain words during casual conversation when each occurrence is followed by a smile or an expression of interest on the part of their audience. Several studies of isolated children reared by mute parents reveal, predictably, the absence of all but grunts and groans in the vocalization of the children. Observation of general child-rearing practices also confirms the view that reinforced imitation and the steady application of rewards do much to facilitate the acquisition of a vocabulary. Not only are Skinnerian principles effective with children, but they work just as well with parrots, dolphins, and dogs, within the limitations of their "linguistic" proficiency. But as was emphasized in Chapter 1, a scientific explanation must be more than correct. It must also provide a more satisfying understanding than that offered by alternatives. One alternative to Skinner's view—one that essentially dismisses Skinner's whole approach—is that proposed by Noam Chomsky.

LANGUAGE AS STRUCTURE

Perhaps the best preparation for an introduction to "Chomskian" psycholinguistics is the retelling of an old joke. The essence of linguistic theories that rely on probabilistic determinants of verbal sequences is found in the law: *If an infinite number of monkeys type on an infinite number of typewriters for an infinite period of time, one of them is certain to type Hamlet.* To test this law, two psychologists were successful in suspending all practical encumbrances; they obtained both an infinite number of monkeys and an equally infinite number of typewriters and sheets of paper. Using very large stopwatches, they began to time the monkeys' efforts. Day and night, the tireless scientists marched up and down the infinitely long aisles, constantly vigilant for the first thread of simian literacy. Years, then decades, and even millenia elapsed. Then, 7344 years after the beginning of the experiment, early in the morning, one of the psychologists shouted,

"Wait! I think I have something." Sure enough, one of the monkeys had typed the line, "To be or not to be. That is the gavornick."

The most conspicuous limitation of treating language as verbal behavior and simply as the outcome of operant conditioning is that language seems to be too complex, variable, and unique in content and too systematic, lawful, and uniform in structure. The structure of language consists of morphemes and *syntax* (the rules governing the organization of morphemes). Together, morphemes and syntax constitute the grammar of a language. As Brown (1965) has pointed out, while dictionaries record nearly all permissible morphemes, the number of phrases and sentences that can be generated by syntax is infinite. There is no limit to the number of coherent and grammatically correct morpheme strings possible in a language. In his *Syntactic Structures*, Chomsky argues that the learning of simple rules of syntax will not allow the full expression of the grammar implicit in any developed language. That is, teaching the child that subjects precede verbs, articles precede nouns, adverbs follow verbs, and so on will not permit a prediction of the grammatical language used later. Moreover, a careful examination of parental responses to children's speech raises fundamental questions about precisely what is being reinforced. Typically, mother rewards correct content even though expressed ungrammatically, while she corrects (not rewarding) incorrect content even when expressed grammatically. This is illustrated in the following dialogue:

> Child: "Good baby I, mommy."
> Mother: "Yes, dear, you are."
> Child: "Mommy is bad."
> Mother: "No, no. That's not nice."

In addition to the application of reinforcement operations, the Skinnerian concept of *chaining*, as applied to language, has also been assailed by Chomsky. In animal conditioning, it is possible to arrange reinforcement contingencies such that each response serves as the S^D for a successive response. Thus, response chains are produced so that a rat may climb a rope to a basin of water, jump in, swim to the other side, ride a lift to the floor, run across an open space, and press a bar for food. Reinforcement of each "link" gradually leads to an elaborate chain. The process of chaining has been applied to the learning of rules of sequencing in language, that is, to syntax. The model suggests that each word becomes an S^D for the words (verbal operants) that follow. The child merely must learn that proper order is subject-verb-direct object. Response generalization will do the rest. But a sentence such as "Why are the boys fighting?" requires the selection of a verb (*are*) before the subject (*boys*) occurs in the sentence. Moreover, if the child is to learn syntax through conditioning, he would have to be able to identify each word with respect to parts of speech. How does he know a noun? What are its "S^D" features? Why does the parrot trained by a Russian to utter Russian phrases display no accent when later taught English phrases (Lenneberg, 1960)? Why do children in widely varying cultures that differ markedly in child-rearing practices acquire their mother-tongue so early and so similarly? Why has the *structure* of language remained so constant over ten millenia and across different cultures despite changes in most apparently relevant environmental variables? Chomsky sees only one way around these questions:

> It seems not unlikely that the organism brings, as its contribution to acquisition of a particular language, a highly restrictive . . . class of generative systems (potential theories) from which the grammar of its language is selected. . . . (Chomsky, p. 112)

In other words, the rules of grammar are innate! There is, to use Chomsky's term, a *universal grammar*. For some, this nativistic premise suffers all of the shortcomings already cited in Chapters 5 and 6. For others (Deese, 1970), the contention is embraced without reservation: "Because universal grammar is innate, the study of grammar occupies a central position in modern psycholinguistics studies" (Deese, p. 11). According to this hypothesis, the forces of evolution have created a human nervous system predisposed to communicate verbally in a structured way. While phonemes, morphemes, and styles of speech may depend on local or cultural habits, the "deep structure" of language is controlled by rules that are neurological in nature. In essence, Chomsky's *generative* theory of language is the application of Gestalt ideas to verbal communication. Somehow the organism is predisposed to organize, classify, and pattern its speech production. Chomsky's rules are thus organized neural networks participating in the reception and expression of symbolic material. They must function in such a way to generate grammatical, and only grammatical, speech once the necessary morphemes have been fed in. He invokes the concept of "critical periods" (Chapter 8), realizing that the generating mechanisms require time for maturation and that, if not exercised soon after maturation, these mechanisms probably will not ever function properly. So in general terms, his theory does no violence to what is already known about critical periods, early deprivation, and innate tendencies. In fact, had he included a role for imprinting, his theory of language, though more formal, would be nearly identical to Lorenz's theory of aggression (Chapter 9).

It would be unfair to suggest that the Chomskian explanation of language is reduced to the assertion that language is the way it is because there is a mechanism that makes it that way. He and his advocates and colleagues have offered imaginative and thought-provoking linguistic models that will, no doubt, lead to important research and insights. At present, however, the theory, for all of its formal elegance, remains more descriptive than analytic. It does offer a technique for classifying many structural features of language and a rather complex and indeterminate model for generating grammatical sentences. But the old "parts of speech," taught in schools since medieval times, also allow the classification of linguistic structures, and Skinner's pigeons are also a model for generating organized chains of behavior that obey specified rules. Skinner's approach is simple and, therefore, striking compared with the apparent complexity of language. Yet it is an approach that adequately embraces a large domain of behavior, and it is tempting to place language in its custody as well. Chomsky's is a theory of Byzantine ornateness and parliamentary order. There are rules upon rules at every turn. The theory matches the inscrutability of language but appears to be generalizable to nothing else in human behavior. Perhaps language is sufficiently special to warrant this exclusivity. But the history of science seems to forbode trouble for overly complex theoretical assaults on nature. Should language be governed by more rules than the heavens?

LANGUAGE AS A NEUROLOGICAL OUTCOME

In 1861, the French neurosurgeon Paul Broca was presented with a fifty-one-year-old man paralyzed on the right side and able to utter only the syllable "tan." The patient had a very serious history. As a child he was the victim of epileptic seizures, and by the age of thirty he had lost his speech (*aphasia*). Ten years after this, his right arm began to weaken and finally became paralyzed. Within four more years, he could not stand up. Six days after admission he died. The autopsy revealed a diffuse lesion over the right frontal lobe of his brain. The oldest portion of the lesion was in the third convolution of the frontal lobe. Its date of onset was coincident with the patient's aphasia. The region is shown in Figure 7-3 and has come to be known as *Broca's area* or the "speech center." Since Broca's time other regions of the cortex associated with symbolic communication have been identified. Some of them are also shown in Figure 7-3. Their integrity is necessary if the individual is to be able to receive, interpret, and transmit symbolic information. Lesions in different areas produce different effects, for example *agraphia* (inability to write coherent messages), *alexia* (inability to read), *acalculia* (inability to perform routine arithmetic operations), and *aphasia* (inability to communicate verbally). Each of these may be expressive (the patient cannot perform the act) or receptive (the patient cannot comprehend the act), or a combination of the two.

While the right side of the body is controlled by the left cerebral hemisphere and vice versa, the speech center is invariably on the left side, which is the dominant half for right-handed individuals. (Handedness is not a foolproof indication of cortical dominance, however.) Thus, there seems to be a place for speech control and some highly provocative studies have been made possible by this fact. There is a form of epilepsy in man that is produced by abnormal electrical discharges in a highly focalized region of the cortex. However, generalized seizures do not occur until similar discharges begin to appear in the corresponding cortical area in the other hemisphere. In some cases, medical approaches cannot control the spread of discharges from one hemisphere to the other and potentially fatal seizures ensue. Based on the animal research of Sperry (1964), surgeons attempted to prevent the development of the second and critical focus by severing the neural connections that join the two hemispheres. That is, they "split" the brain by cutting through the fibers of the corpus callosum. This operation has been a very successful treatment of this epilepsy. In addition, it has provided scientists with extraordinarily interesting experimental subjects—subjects in which the left side of the brain does not know what the right side of the brain is doing. If such a subject has visual material presented in the nasal field (temporal retina) of the left eye, the optic nerve fibers carrying this information project to the left occipital cortex. This is the dominant side in a right-handed individual and it houses Broca's area. Under these conditions, the subject reports what he sees. However, if material is delivered to the right occipital cortex, the subject cannot verbalize

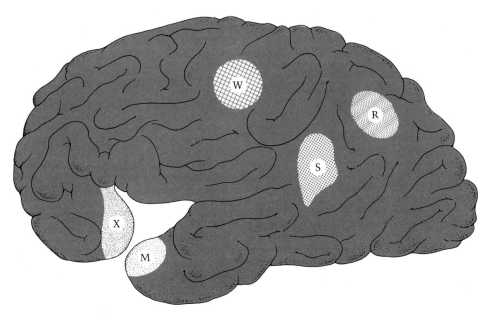

Figure 7-3. Brain regions associated with symbolic processes. W = writing; M = ability to recall melodies; X = singing; S = ability to understand spoken sound; R = ability to understand reading material.

what he sees, although it is seen as clearly as in the former case. With the corpus callosum sectioned, information in the right occipital cortex has no means of being represented in the speech area. The subject is visually agnosic; he can "see" but he cannot interpret verbally (symbolically) (Gazzaniga, Bogen, and Sperry, 1965). Predictably, agraphia was observed when the patients were required to draw (see Figure 7-3). In tests of tactile discrimination, patients could not verbally describe objects manipulated in the left hand. In summary, tasks requiring verbal mediation were disrupted when the pathways to Broca's area were disconnected.

LENNEBERG'S BIOLOGICAL THEORY

Findings from studies of the neurologically diseased have failed to support any simplistic structural theory of language; that is, there is no single brain locus that when disturbed leads predictably and irreversibly to language disorders. This fact has been used by some to disclaim attempts to understand language from a biological perspective. However, in 1967, E. H. Lenneberg published his *Biological Foundations of Language,* and this work has done much to rekindle interest in physiological approaches to the study of language.

In developing his case for a biological basis of speech, Lenneberg focuses upon a particular weakness in the behavioristic view, the problem of *serial order.* Behavioristically oriented psychologists traditionally explained complex chains (series) of behavior in terms of each unit response serving as the signal, or discriminative stimulus, for the next response in the series. According to this theory, long chains of behavior become connected, link by link, through the reinforcement of each member. Through rewarded practice, the organism emits the first response, and the sensory consequences of this action (such as stretched muscle movement) are sent back to the central nervous system where they are then used to trigger the next response element. In a 1951 treatise, Karl Lashley drew attention to the logical and the biological limitations of this explanation. Quite simply, there are too many instances of serial behavior in which the behavioral elements occur too close together for the sensory consequences of one to have the time to have a role in the initiation of the next. One example of this can be seen in playing a piano. Many musical pieces must be played so quickly that the interval between successive notes is entirely too short for the fifteenth response to have any modifying influence upon the sixteenth response. Lenneberg makes the same point in regard to speech. An adult has little trouble speaking 500 phonemes per minute, which is 7 to 9 per second. In order to articulate these sounds properly, a very large number of muscles must be controlled by an elaborate neural assembly. Certainly more than one hundred separate muscles arc involved in the formation of the various speech sounds. Each of the most frequently occurring phonemes imposes unique restraints on the respiratory physiology, the facial and oral musculature, the muscles of the neck, the muscles of the larynx, and so forth. Given these demands, it is virtually impossible to account for the fluidity of speech in terms of an element-by-element chain of associations. Instead, "the sequential arrangements of muscular events require preplanning with anticipation of later events; therefore, the occurrence of some events is contingent upon other events yet to come. This may be adduced as proof that sequencing on a neuromuscular level is not accomplished by an associative mechanism" (Lenneberg, p. 120). What Lenneberg means by "preplanning" is that the chain, as a chain, is initiated by some central brain mechanism. In this respect, his position is the neurological equivalent of Chomsky's generative systems.

Lenneberg hypothesizes that language, as all behavior, is the consequence of biological maturation and development. Behavior, after all, is a characteristic of all organisms, and there is no reason to assume that it is any less dependent upon physiology, maturation, and morphology than any other aspect of the organism. Language unfolds *when the time is right:* Why do children normally begin to speak between their 18th and 28th month? Surely it is not because all mothers on earth initiate language training at that time (Lenneberg, p. 125). Children begin to speak during this critical period because they now have the neural apparatus that is necessary for language. Integral to this apparatus is a mechanism for timing. One of the important characteristics of all languages is rhythm, the regular separation of phonemes by periods of silence. Because of the universality of rhythm in language, Lenneberg contends that a feature of the human brain is responsible, a timing "device" with a natural frequency of about 6 to 7 cycles per second. Evidence that the frequency is in this range is drawn from studies of speech intelligibility. If one is presented with chopped speech, it is found that the ability to repeat what is heard is poorest in this range. Moreover, the temporal pattern of normal speech also reveals cyclical events in this frequency range. Finally, those neurological diseases that interfere with speech often result less in mispronunciation than in the improper sequencing (timing) of speech sounds.

While Lenneberg considers language to be the outcome of maturation, he does not relate it to the same maturational processes associated with simple sensory-motor development. That is, the child needs more than the motor capacity to produce sounds—even phonemes—in order to produce language. Children, for example, can learn a few words before they are even able to walk, but at this stage of neural development they cannot build upon these words, they cannot utter sentences or even phrases. Indeed, children can comprehend language at an earlier time than they can produce it, which is further evidence for the separate development of language mechanisms in relation to general development.

Lenneberg finds additional support for his nativistic theory from studies of children reared in linguistically impoverished environments. Some of the cases were found in orphanages; others in homes where both parents were deaf and mute; others in which the children themselves were born deaf. While acknowledging that such extreme conditions do leave their mark on the subsequent language development of the child, he emphasizes the extraordinary degree to which the child's language proficiency is resistant to these conditions. In many instances, the onset of language is not even delayed by such circumstances and, when it is, the children are found to catch up with remarkable rapidity once they are placed in an enriched environment. The generalization that emerges from such studies is this: while certain speech habits are affected by environmental variables, the age of onset for language seems to be highly independent of even extreme environmental deficiencies. Children born blind show normal language acquisition; children born with diseases or infirmities that prevent the ability to speak come to comprehend language. In short, radical empiricism will find little to support it in the area of speech and language.

The cornerstone of Lenneberg's theory is the intrinsic rhythmic nature of the brain. He argues that the neurobiology of speech is not to be understood in terms of a particular brain locus or a particular part-to-part connection. Instead, speech is the consequence of a general property of brain function, a temporal property. The property is innate and the overall process is mechanical:

> There is, then nothing unscientific about the claim that a species-specific behavior pattern, such as language, may well be determined by innate mechanisms. . . . [T]here is just one peculiar mode of neural activity for aural-oral communication in man; if an individual communicates at all, or may be reached by communication, it is by virtue of this basic, unique, unalterable function. . . . During childhood the neural automata are activated by appropriate input, and the machine becomes operative; the incoming signals are processed through its unique type of operation and the emission of language responses are likewise generated by the operation of the same basic mechanism. (Lenneberg, 1967)

One cannot say how the future will treat Lenneberg's interesting hypotheses. As with Chomsky, his superficial assertion is that language occurs because "something within" allows it to occur. But both theorists are saying much more. They are emphasizing the singular role of genetically implanted mechanisms in creating the most complex of man's abilities.

SUMMARY

With this review of research and theory, you should be aware of the infant stage in which the psychology of language now finds itself. The status of contemporary wisdom can be summarized this way: man learns a lot of words because he has a nervous system geared to allow it. Of course, much more than this is known, as is evidenced by the contents of this chapter. But as with so much of psychology, there is a stark absence of unifying principles. The field seems divided between imaginative theorists with little to support their speculations and careful researchers with little to tie their diverse findings together. Theories on the horizon presumably will be less narrow than current ones. They will incorporate the facts of human memory and will rely increasingly upon relevant biochemical and neuropsychological research. Universal grammars will give way to more dynamic models, one may say more elastic models, which will stretch to accommodate the influences of learning, burgeoning memory, and, of course, heredity. Studies of the statistical nature of language will go beyond counting and curve fitting and progress to the level of basic postulates and corollaries. Information theory is commendable, but it would appear that psycholinguistics has got about as much mileage out of that theory as it can. Zipf's speculations, perhaps a bit too mechanical and rigid for the phenomenon of language, are also exemplary in the sense that they attempt to tie verbal behavior to principles applicable to all life processes. For now, language must be left as it was found, the key to consciousness but somewhat out of theoretical reach. It must be stressed, however, that the chances of a solution have increased—not diminished—as a result of the Skinner-Chomsky controversy. Each has walked away a victor, and the issues have been clarified in the process. In one respect, the conflict was artificial from the start. Skinner's *Verbal Behavior* attempts to delineate the determinants of *speech*. Chomsky's *Syntactic Structure* offers a theory of *language*. The former is concerned with behavior; the latter, with underlying processes. Skinner suggests what happens; Chomsky and Lenneberg, why it happens. Thus, they are offering explanations at different levels, and neither is necessarily wrong. A man blushes when he is embarrrassed. He blushes, too, because his blood vessels are closer to the surface of his skin, because his blood pressure is elevated, because his heart rate is increased, because his adrenal glands have been stimulated, because his sympathetic ganglia have responded. Events are produced by multiple agents, and each event viewed carefully enough turns out to be varied and complex. If the debate did no more than call attention to the number of levels at which language can be approached, it would be well worth the controversy.

SUGGESTED READINGS

CARROLL, J. B. *Language and Thought.* Englewood Cliffs, N. J.: Prentice-Hall, 1964.

Psycholinguistics moves so rapidly and in so many directions that a 1964 text is already somewhat dated. Professor Carroll's book, however, is exceptional in its clarity, brevity, and studious avoidance of doctrinal positions.

DEESE, J. *Psycholinguistics.* Boston: Allyn & Bacon, 1970.

Professor Deese accepts the Chomskian view unhesitatingly and then summarizes its features. The book is descriptive, but rather light on the side of data. It is excellent as an exposition of one opinion about language.

TERWILLIGER, R. F. *Meaning and Mind: A Study in the Psychology of Language.* New York: Oxford University Press, 1968.

Professor Terwilliger's review of psycholinguistic theories is comprehensive and excellent. His style is personal and readable. The chapter on language disturbances is very interesting.

The Psychology of the Individual

CHAPTER

8

Psychological Development: The Problem of Change

THE BACKGROUND OF PSYCHOLOGICAL DEVELOPMENT

Both empirical philosophy and common-sense philosophy insist that the environment works profound changes on the developing organism. Yet with equal conviction, philosophic and common-sense ideas have accepted genetic explanations of the differences among people to account for psychological characteristics. The present chapter will focus principally on aspects of human psychological development and will draw information largely from work conducted in the empirical tradition. In Chapter 9, we will then take up the matter of instinct and heredity.

There is no final answer to the taunting question, "If a tree falls in the woods and no one is there to hear it, does it make a sound?" We occupy an infinitesimal volume of the universe, and we are, no doubt, affected in one way or another by forces and events beyond our sensibilities. In one respect, we "know" only that for which we have invented words, but these words may be deceptions. All too often, in science as well as in everyday life, there is the tendency to assume that an event has been explained once it has been labeled, as if speechlessness were our only form of ignorance. The word *environment* has frequently gratified this tendency.

In the research done on lower animals, it is possible to control many of the conditions embraced by the term environment. But even in the laboratory, it is important to realize that each animal possesses an elaborate *internal* environment over which the experimenter is able to exert little control. The internal environment of an organism interacts constantly with the outside world. Behavior is only one consequence of that interaction. To speak of controlling the environment is really to overstate the case for the experimental setting. More properly, one specifies those aspects of the environment that are to be altered experimentally in some systematic way. It may be assumed that observed behavioral changes that correlate with these alterations are caused by the alterations only when other variables— those beyond experimental control—can legitimately be considered as inoperative, constant, or random. In studying developmental aspects, these limitations are particularly significant. Immature organisms, for example, might have the intellectual capacity to learn, but fail to perform because of inadequate locomotor abilities. This is a case of the internal environment— that environment beyond the experimenter's control—deciding the results before the research ever begins. Thus, in order to test empiricistic and nativistic alternatives by studying the very young, it is essential to account for those behavioral, sensory, perceptual, and cognitive changes that require *maturation*. Some of the oldest literature in developmental psychology was concerned precisely with this distinction between maturation and learning. An often-used example illustrates one attempt at this distinction.

The larval form of the salamander begins to swim relatively early in life. One obvious question is whether swimming is learned by the salamander or simply occurs once the necessary maturational processes are completed. Carmichael (1926) examined this question in the following way. He placed a group of young salamanders (not yet swimmers) in a chemical solution that, though not fatal, prevented motion. A second group of the same age was placed in fresh water. At the age when members of the second group began to swim, the first group was transferred to fresh water, and these salamanders, after a very brief period of recovery from the drug, began to swim as well. Clearly, swimming behavior required neither learning nor practice. All that was necessary was waiting for a sufficient amount of time to pass for those structures essential for swimming to mature.

Numerous studies and casual observation, as well, point to the critical role of purely maturational variables in a wide range of behaviors. However, the really intriguing psychological question is not concerned with swimming salamanders, climbing monkeys, or nest-building robins. Rather, psychologists are concerned with the *psychological* functions that may simply depend on maturation and that occur in the absence (or in the presumed absence) of learning.

To answer some of the questions about maturation and learning, psychologists have undertaken studies of infant organisms, including studies of human infants. William James alluded to the "great blooming, buzzing confusion" that birth brings to the infant, but maturation within the womb has also caused an elaborate system for detecting and reacting to stimuli. Because of the very limited behavioral capacities of newborn humans and other animals, and because of the absence of language in the human infant, it has been extremely difficult to obtain reliable psychophysical assessments of neonatal sensory capacity. This situation has been somewhat improved by recent developments in physiological recording techniques (Chapter 4), but even with these advances, there is still no body of literature that can claim to set forth a developmental psychophysics. Despite these gaps in available information, there are scattered but important findings that point to the presence of some surprisingly sophisticated perceptual capacities in the newborn baby.

Before turning to these, we should note that research with the newborn is hampered by unique obstacles. What the developmental psychologist is trying to determine is the nature and degree of abilities of a *psychological* nature. Simple tests of strength, coordination, reflexes, and the like are not enough. Rather, the psychologist must explore learning, memory, perception, motivation, and other complex processes that reveal themselves with adults in intricate behaviors of which the infant is simply incapable. In Chapter 5, for example, we discussed the minimum interval separating two flashes such that the observer would report the presence of both—the ability of the nervous system to resolve events in time. Adults can answer questions of this kind by saying "two" or "one" after being presented with pulses of light. Rats can press bars and pigeons can peck keys to tell us that they have distinguished between "two" and "one." But the one-day-old infant cannot say "two," nor can he master the motor control necessary to be a good bar-presser or key-pecker. Thus, the procedural problems involved boil down to this: How do we ask a one-day-old infant how many flashes he has seen? We can, of course, record his brain responses to the flashes, but these records permit only the loosest inferences about perception. Instead, we might condition some response (such as heartbeat) to a pair of stimuli, say flashes separated by two seconds. The procedure would involve taking the following steps:

1. First flash . . . two-second interval . . . second flash . . . one-second interval . . . loud sound (a loud sound will result in an alteration of heart-rate).
2. Single-flash . . . no loud sound.

Now, if these two conditions were presented often, we should find that the two-flash condition produces changes in heartrate even after we have no longer followed it with a loud sound and that the single-flash condition produces no change in heartrate. In other words, we have successfully *conditioned* heartrate to the two-flash condition. With this conditioned response now "built in," we can apply a range of test stimuli consisting of two-flash presentations in which the intervals between the two cover a range of values; for example, from 5 msec. (an interval too short for adults to distinguish the two flashes) to two seconds, a value well within the resolution limits of the baby's nervous system.

Studies of this type are uncommon in the area of infant or even child development. These are not easy experiments to conduct. The ability to condition itself is not a fully understood feature of neonatal psychology. That is, we are not safe in using a conditioned response as a measure of sensory capacity unless we are certain that the organism under investigation is conditionable. Finally, the newborn baby is a precious and delicate organism, not to be dealt with crudely. Understandably, new parents are not eager to turn their infants over to experimental psychologists for study. And on those occasions when the psychologist has at least limited access to the newborn infant, there are severe restrictions on the experimental procedures that can be used, on the duration of the experiment, and on the frequency with which the experiments can be repeated during the first weeks and months of life. It is for these reasons that we know far more about the psychology of the newborn monkey, rat, cat, and dog than we do about neonatal man. Indeed, while we have not subjected the existing literature to a count, it may be safely estimated that 90 percent of the research in human developmental psychology is based on the study of children. A small fraction of study has been concerned with infants, and very little involves those whose ages are below one month. This is particularly confining to psychologists concerned with constructing theories of human development. From the perspective of neurological development, for example, there is more growth in the first few weeks of life than in the following six months. Moreover, the most dramatic confrontation the child has with the environment surely must be in these first days. And while there will be a long period of psychological development to follow, the newborn baby does enter the world with an intricate developmental history behind him, a nine-month period of being carried in the womb, at the end of which he possesses an extraordinary nervous system, sensory apparatus, response mechanisms, and so forth. In fact, in terms of the number of neurons present in the brain, the newborn infant has almost as many as he will ever have. Maturation in the rest of the body will involve the multiplication of cells, growth by division. But in the central nervous system (CNS), maturation will be largely a matter of growth by growth, that is, neurons become larger rather than more numerous. Because of this, we are safe in assuming that the nervous system on day one contains at least the broad outline of features—what might be called the functional "blueprints"—that will establish the conditions of its own development. How unfortunate it is that we know nothing of what this system *knows* or whether it *knows* that it knows.

We know next to nothing about the newborn and only a little more about the aged. Therefore, it can be said that developmental psychology is strong in the middle and weak at the extremes. These two stages—early infancy and advanced age—are periods of profound change and are, therefore, potentially the most informative to theorists. To use a metaphor from geology, we are scientists dealing with volcanic eruptions and the migration of glaciers, and we are limited to thermometers that will respond to only a ten-degree range of temperatures.

Fortunately, we are in a position to sample certain aspects of neonatal (newborn) and geriatric (old age) stages of development by studying non-human organisms. There is now a small but growing amount of literature about learning and sensory function in newborn monkeys and cats. So far, senility in lower organisms has not captured the imaginations of many experimenters, but this too is bound to change in the future. Yet even when we have explored the neonatal and senile periods of lower animals, we still will have a difficult time generalizing these findings to human beings. The reason is simply this: the functional *psychological* superiority of man over all other animals is far greater than his physical, sensory, or behavioral superiority. Indeed, we are weaker, less sensitive, and less durable than many of the other existing species. Thus, when we examine the kidney or heart or liver of a chimpanzee, we are getting a reasonably good simulation of their human equivalents. But if we are concerned with language, thought, emotion, culture, politics, and other features that define human existence and that make the study of psychology something more than just theory, the chimpanzee may prove to be of very limited value. With this in mind, we can now proceed to review the kinds of developmental studies that have been possible despite the limitations involved.

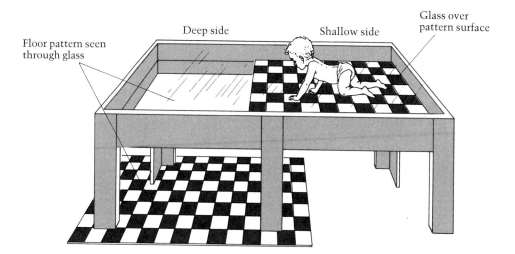

Figure 8-1. *The visual cliff.* On the left side of the table is a sheet of transparent glass through which the baby can see a checkerboard pattern on the floor below. On the right side, the patterned floor is just below the surface along which the baby is crawling. The visual "cliff" is formed at the border of the two sides where, perceptually, a sudden drop appears. This type of apparatus is used to study depth perception in very young children and animals. (After Gibson and Walk, 1960.)

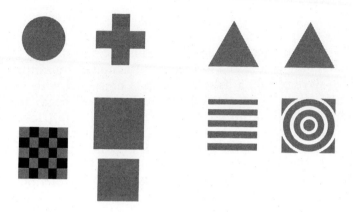

Figure 8-2. Stimulus patterns used by Fantz (1958) in studies of perceptual development. On each trial, the checkerboard (red and gray squares) is presented to the child along with a big or small plain square (which appears in this figure next to the checkerboard.) Even when area, color, and overall brightness are equated, Fantz finds that babies have decided preferences for certain forms.

PERCEPTION

E. J. Gibson and R. D. Walk (1960) have conducted a series of experiments on depth perception in very young organisms. Figure 8-1 depicts the "visual cliff" being approached by a six-month-old baby. The baby crawls along a checkered floor and reaches an edge. In fact, a transparent plastic sheet would prevent his falling, but he stops abruptly when the checkered pattern reveals a drop in height. This experiment indicates the presence of depth perception at a very early age.

R. L. Fantz (1958) and Jerome Kagan (1970) have developed a method by which infants are presented with different patterns while the experimenter records accurately the position of their eyes. Multiple patterns are presented, and the experimenter can determine which ones are "preferred" by measuring how long the baby gazes at each. Using patterns such as those depicted in Figure 8-2, Fantz has found that infants come to show decided preferences for face-like patterns by ten weeks of age or even earlier. These perceptual biases are evident when basic sensory cues such as area, intensity, color, and position are equated.

Imprinting

One of the most striking demonstrations of seemingly "built-in" perceptual preferences is revealed in the phenomenon of *imprinting*. If, within the first two days of life, a baby duckling is presented with an object that resembles the adult of its species, the duckling will begin to follow that object and will continue to do so during its adult life (Hess, 1964). This strong attachment, referred to as *imprinting*, is found in many species and suggests the presence of inborn perceptual organizations and their control over behavior. The time during which imprinting is possible—the so-called *critical period*—is brief, but the effects are lasting. Furthermore, the duckling can be imprinted to figures that resemble different species of ducks and will later show mating preferences for the wrong species.

The imprinting phenomenon itself appears to be more complex than was once assumed and more flexible than the earliest studies suggested. For example, Klopfer (1969) exposed ducklings to moving decoys—a plain one and one painted with lively colors. Both decoys were effective in eliciting the imprinting response, but in later tests, both groups of ducklings preferred the painted decoy. However, if the decoys were kept stationary in later tests, the ducklings would then prefer the model to which they had been imprinted initially. Describing his results, Klopfer suggests that, "It seemed that the act of following a decoy during the training period activated a preexisting perceptual bias" (Klopfer, p. 62). While imprinting as such has not been observed in human infants, perceptual biases do appear to be rather well developed.

Infant Conditioning

In the past decade, there have been an increasing number of studies concerned with the conditionability of the human infant. Operant conditioning of infants from three to five months old has been reported (Brackbill, 1958; Rheingold, et al., 1959) in which reinforcements consist of smiling at the baby, making "gentle" sounds, lifting the baby, and tickling. The research seems to indicate that discriminative behavior is possible at these very young ages. Within the first year of life, there is no doubt that the child can and does acquire a sizable behavioral repertoire. Which behaviors are the result of conditioning?

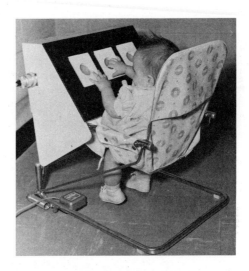

Figure 8-3. Discrimination learning in the infant. Lipsitt has developed apparatus like that shown in this photo to test the baby's ability to learn to discriminate "odd" members of a three-stimulus display, two of which are the same. (Photograph courtesy of Dr. Lewis Lipsitt.)

Lipsitt (1963) has studied infants through the use of apparatus such as that shown in Figure 8-3. The three panels allow the presentation of different visual material (colors, shapes, brightnesses). Three stimuli are presented, two of which are identical, such as two circles and a triangle or two crosses and a square. The infant's task is to respond to the "odd" stimulus by pressing an appropriate button, for which he receives a reward (such as the sound of a buzzer). Lipsitt's findings indicate that a type of concept learning takes place as early as eight months of age, when the child is able to solve the so-called oddity problem. Representative data from color discrimination studies are presented in Figure 8-4.

Vocalization

A number of investigators (Lewis, 1959; Rheingold, et al., 1959; Weisberg, 1963) have shown that as early as three months after birth, infant vocalizations can be reinforced by smiles, sounds, contact, and handling. If these neonatal sounds are primitive or elementary components of language, then the traditional operations of reinforcement and repetition would seem to be sufficient to create adult verbal behavior. That the nature of language may defy such explanation was discussed in Chapter 7. Once children do acquire language, the range of their intellectual abilities broadens considerably.

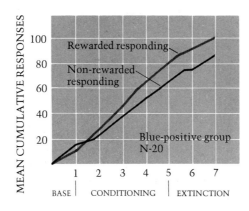

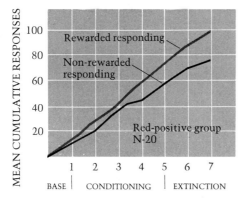

Figure 8-4. Color-discrimination learning in the infant. For the blue-positive group, blue stimuli lead to reward when responses are made while responses to red are not rewarded. For the red-positive group, these same conditions are reversed. As indicated by cumulative responses during conditioning and extinction, the young child can learn these discriminations. (After the data of Simmons, 1962.)

Basic sensory processes show only marginal variations after age five or six, and learning by operant conditioning shows results similar to what is found in adults. Among young children, however, considerable variations in operant conditioning are found. These individual differences are represented in the cumulative records obtained by Bijou and Baer (1963) in Figure 8-5. Their results were obtained by using the apparatus shown in Figure 8-6. The task in their study was to operate a control to maintain the "attention" of a puppet. Proper manipulation results in a "talking" puppet that moves and appears to look at the child. Comparisons between a "bold" and a "shy" child reveal considerable differences in the amount of operant behavior. From an empirical-reinforcement perspective, these differences are attributed to the fact that childhood comes at the end of an already

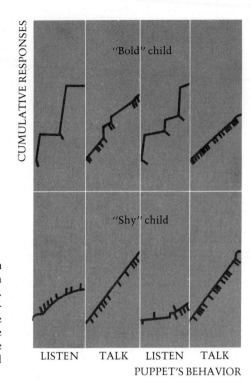

CUMULATIVE RESPONSES

"Bold" child

"Shy" child

LISTEN   TALK   LISTEN   TALK
PUPPET'S BEHAVIOR

Figure 8-5. Cumulative responses of a "bold" child and a "shy" child who can manipulate a puppet by operating a lever. The little hash marks shown indicate responses. The shy child spends most of the time getting the puppet to talk while the bold child spends his time making the puppet listen. (After the data of Bijou and Baer, 1963.)

Figure 8-6. The apparatus used to generate the data shown in Fig. 8-5.

lengthy reinforcement history, different for different children, and bound to create sizable individual differences.

JEAN PIAGET

Between approximately two and twelve years of age, there appear to be rather large transformations in the way children perceive the world and react to it. The renowned psychologist Jean Piaget, famous for his theory of cognitive development, has divided this period into a *preconceptual* (two-to-four-years-old) and an *intuitive* (four-to-twelve-years-old) phase of cognitive growth. A third stage, the final cognitive one, is reached at about ages twelve to fifteen. Piaget calls this the stage of *formal operations* (Inhelder and Piaget, 1958). It is important to examine Piaget's developmental theory, or certainly its general features. It departs from rigorously empirical psychologies of development in much the same way that Kant deviated from Hume. But even before Kant had accepted the challenge laid down by Hume, Leibnitz (1646-1716) had anticipated Kant's *Critique*. Leibnitz's nemesis was Locke, whose *An Essay Concerning Human Understanding* (1690) was the authoritative statement of the empirical position. Leibnitz had this to say of the *tabula rasa*, that intellectual void presumed to exist before experience:

> This tabula rasa of the philosophers means that the soul has by nature and originally only bare faculties. But faculties without some act . . . are also only fictions, which nature knows not. . . . For where in the world will you ever find a faculty which shuts itself up in the power alone without performing any act? . . . You oppose to me this axiom received by the philosophers, that there is nothing in the soul which does not come from the senses. But you must accept the soul itself and its affections. *Nihil est in intellectu, quod non fuerit in sensu, exipe: nisi ipse intellectus.* (Leibnitz, *New Essays*, Bk. II)

This maxim of Leibnitz's—"Nothing is in the intellect that wasn't first in the senses, except the intellect itself"—contains the starting point of Piaget's system. As Flavell (1963) has written:

> [Piaget] has tried to uncover the basic and irreducible properties of cognitive adaptation which hold true at all developmental levels.

These invariant and fundamental properties are to be found in the functional . . . aspects of intelligence; the functional characteristics form the intellectual core—in Piaget's words, the *ipse intellectus*— which makes possible the emergence of cognitive structures. . . . (Flavell, p. 41)

The *ipse intellectus,* the intellect itself, is that feature of the developing child that determines the way experiences will affect and otherwise modify his cognitive life. The two most significant functions of the intellect are *accommodation* and *assimilation.* The developing child is confronted by a great diversity of stimuli. His intellect, though primitive, must be able to accept a full range of environmental events. Simultaneously, these events must be assimilated: "Every act of intelligence . . . presupposes an interpretation of something in external reality, that is, an assimilation of that something to some kind of meaning system in the subject's cognitive organization" (Flavell, p. 48). Thus, the child must assimilate reality in terms meaningful to his cognitive structure while at the same time accommodating the facts of that reality. Piaget calls the state of equilibrium between the objective accommodation and the "cognizing" assimilation *adaptation.* The two processes are in reciprocal relation, with adaptation representing the balance. Through a constant dialogue with the world of reality, the cognitions of the child become structured in such a way that new experiences can be fit into older niches. These should be viewed as styles of organization based, in part, on classes of behavior. Thus, there is a sucking schema, a grasping schema, an observing schema, and so forth. The *schema* is not the behavior, it is a cognitive response to an environmental event, a response that leads to and guides behavior. In a sense, cognitive development is just the addition of new schemas, the modification of older ones, and their generalizations to new situations. In the Piagetian system, this cognitive development moves the organism through distinct stages.

Infancy to Early Childhood

In infancy, a condition of egocentrism prevails in which "the cognizer sees the world from a single point of view only—his own—but without knowledge of the existence of viewpoints or perspectives . . ." (Flavell, p. 60). Thus, unaware of his "self," the infant is trapped by his limited ability to assimilate knowledge creatively. Later, with increased sensory-motor development, the child views himself as an object, and his new schema allows new definitions, new perspectives, to be brought to bear upon older experiences. In drifting away from complete egocentrism, in tentatively treating his "self" as an object, the young child then becomes capable of far greater objectivity.

The final infant stages of sensory-motor development occur at about eighteen months of age. The child is now capable of representing sensory-motor problems symbolically. This is the last of the stages, characterized by a kind of inventiveness that in Gestalt terms is called *insight*.

Early to Middle Childhood

From about eighteen months to perhaps five or six years of age, the child is in a period of *preoperational thought*, during which cognitions of a symbolic nature are largely sensory-motor. Problem-solving, while often insightful, tends to be restricted to rather simple perceptual and locomotor behaviors; it is "an intelligence of action" (Flavell, p. 152). In terms of the categories previously cited in Chapter 2, preoperational thought is similar to practical wisdom, to "the pursuit of concrete goals of action rather than to the quest for knowledge" (Flavell, p. 152). At this stage, the child tends to fix his attention on very limited features of complex stimuli. His attention omits the subtleties of a scene or an object. This practice of centering on a single detail or a small number of details is called *centration*. The child's preoperational mental world is literal and binding. One illustration that has been given is that of a little boy wandering in the woods who, on seeing a snail every now and again, assumes that it is the same snail each time.

While capable of certain abstractions, the child's cognitions remain anchored to his primitive perceptions. For example, if he is confronted with a tall, thin cylinder, half-filled with beads, which are then poured into a shorter and wider cylinder, he will conclude that the number of beads has changed.

Middle to Late Childhood

Gradually, in middle childhood (approximately six to eleven years of age), the ability to treat reality in hypothetical ways develops. Problems such as the bead experiment noted above are minor, because the concept of *conservation* has been mastered: the number of beads is conserved no matter what the shape of the cylinder may be. The child becomes capable of logical thinking, the kind of hypothesizing that Piaget refers to as *concrete operations*. Now the child learns arithmetic, understands identities, groups very different objects into appropriate functional classes, and appreciates logical equalities and inequalities. He becomes a master organizer.

Early Adolescence

At this stage of development (approximately twelve to fifteen years of age), the child grows from the level of concrete operations to that of *formal operations*, "the crowning achievement of intellectual development . . . towards which intellectual evolution has been moving since infancy" (Flavell, p. 202). Formal operations go beyond the structured ordering, the arithmetic style of classification and judgment. Now the child can deal with complex propositions; not simply logical equalities and inequalities, but logical arguments.

The Nature of the Evidence

For Piaget, the stages of cognitive development represent what he calls "mental embryology." It is certain that rewards and punishment, as parts of the environment, are represented in the child's schema. However, the natural unfolding of cognitive capacities is viewed by Piaget as the legitimate subject matter of the psychology of learning. It is the fundamental process that determines behavior of interest.

Because of the assumed ubiquity of cognitions, Piaget and his followers avoid the kinds of experiments that will place artificial restraints on the cognitive process. Given the scope of Piaget's theory, there would seem to be little purpose, for example, in conducting studies of bar-pressing. Rather, the Piagetians observe children in relatively unstructured and natural situations. A Piagetian psychologist will, for example, listen to one child tell a recently learned story to another child and note how the egocentricity of the six year old is responsible for ambiguities and distortions in the telling. Or he will ask simple questions like, "Ernest has three brothers—Paul, Henry, and Charles. How many brothers has Paul? And Henry? And

Charles?" (Flavell, p. 277). Very young children do not see themselves as siblings and cannot understand aggregates in relation to one another. Thus, while the five year old has no difficulty in counting and distinguishing among three things, the *concept* of three cannot be used in answering the question. For Piaget, the cognitive processes determine all other psychological events. In language, therefore, one may observe the effects of cognitive structure.

Foundations and Implications of Piaget's Theories

We have already discussed the connection between idealist philosophy (that is, Leibnitz and the *ipse intellectus*) and Piaget's theory of cognitive development. But we must recognize that Piaget's psychology is more than a developmental psychology or a child psychology. Fundamentally it is an *epistemological* psychology, a psychology of *knowledge*. It is concerned with how we come to know the objective world, and how much of that world we can know. Putting aside experiments for a moment, we may view Piaget's writings as falling on the continuum that begins with Plato and passes through the Middle Ages to Descartes, Leibnitz, Kant, and Hegel. In the very same way, Skinner's implicit epistemology establishes him on that continuum dominated by Aristotle, Locke, Hume, Bentham, and John Stuart Mill. Of course, neither Piaget nor Skinner would accept the burden of defending all the ideas of the scholars with whom they have been identified. One doubts, for example, that Piaget accepts the existence of Leibnitz's eternal, indestructible *monads* that form the ultimate spiritual composition of the universe. One also doubts that Skinner shares Hume's skeptical view of the validity of scientific generalizations. But each must feel much more comfortable with the concepts of the philosophers mentioned with him than he would with those of the other.

Piaget's epistemology is best illustrated in his studies of conservation. The conservation tasks are numerous. We have already mentioned one: the child's ability to recognize that the number of beads poured into pitchers of different shapes remains constant (that is, the number is conserved). Another version of the task involves pieces of clay molded into various shapes. The child who understands the concept of *conservation* appreciates that whether stretched out as a sausage or rolled up as a ball, the *quantity* of clay is *conserved*. On the other hand, a younger child judges the amount of clay in terms of its existing shape. Indeed, the *constancy* effect discussed in Chapter 5 comes under the same principle. We recognize—if we know that Bob is 5'10" tall—that Bob is just as tall when we see him two blocks away as he is when he is walking next to us. Not only do we *know* that his height remains the same (is conserved), but we even *perceive* it as such in spite of the fact that his height visually reflected on our retinas diminishes with distance.

These studies of conservation are but the experimental version of an inquiry that, in one form or another, is very old. We discover it repeatedly in Plato's *Dialogues,* as when the question is raised, "Are Socrates and Socrates seated the same?" The basis of this question is the distinction between *true forms* (the *real* Socrates) and mere *appearance* (the *attributes* of Socrates). As Socrates walks about, ages, bends over, eats, shaves, gets sick, and so on, his physical, visual characteristics change dramatically. Yet, there is some essential feature that remains the same throughout these transformations. There is a *true* Socrates, which as the *Dialogues* labor to prove, is the *idea* of Socrates.

This discussion of *idea* versus *appearance* reappeared in the Middle Ages in a new form—the controversy between the *nominalists* and the *realists.* The realists argued that there were true classes of things, true *genera.* For example, there is something that is *horse,* and this *genus* is quite distinct from any particular horse and its specific attributes. The nominalists were skeptical about this. They argued that "horse" is merely a name (*nomen*) given to certain sensations, and when any thing gives rise to some number of these sensory attributes, we call it "horse." For the realists, the truth of a thing was the general idea of it, of which it was merely a particular instance. For the nominalists, the truth of a thing was merely the objective, sensory character of it, and when many things share certain of these objective properties, we *invent* a general class. This class is no more than a name, for example, "horse," and has no reality independent of the separate instances.

Clearly, the medieval philosophers were not concerned with horses. What directed these debates was the tension between *idealism* and *empiricism,* between *abstraction* and *sensation.* To the medievalist, there was a tremendous difference between a God known only through *experience* and a God whose reality was established by the *idea* alone of God. We can begin to discern the heat of this controversy by examining the sort of argument a nominalist might advance:

If the real world is caused by
God's will and the real world
is in constant flux, God's will
must be inconstant.

or

God is merely the name we use
for those features of nature
which influence our senses.

The modern psychological form of this controversy is found in the competing theories—*sensationist* versus *perceptionist*, *associationist* versus *Gestaltist*, *behaviorist* versus *cognitivist*. Piaget's studies of conservation have a direct bearing on this current version of the debate. We can list below the central elements of his findings in just this one area of conservation.

1. The appearance of a collection of balls changes with the shape of the pitcher into which they are poured. Similarly, the appearance of clay depends on the shape we give it.
2. At a certain age, the judgments of *number* of balls and *quantity* of clay are determined by shape. At an older age, these judgments are completely independent of shape. The older child knows that number and quantity are conserved throughout any spatial transformation.
3. Once conservation is demonstrated, it is found in many different versions of the same problem without the need for instruction. However, if the child cannot perceive the conservation of number and quantity but is trained to solve one such problem, he cannot solve different versions of it.

From these facts, we are forced to conclude that conservation is a concept; that it is not *taught*, at least in the Skinnerian behavioral sense; that it is a property of the cognitive-perceptual mechanisms and not some simple derivative of "conditioning." Analogous to the studies of transposition, it is a form of *relational* knowledge. This is the major thrust of

Piaget's epistemology. Cognitive capacities *unfold*. They require maturation of the nervous system. And while associational learning and conditioning are important, the ultimate nature of cognition cannot be explained in these terms.

Notwithstanding Piaget's very significant and influential writing, there is still substantial evidence to support the view that the learning that occurs throughout infancy and childhood can be explained in purely empirical-reinforcement terms. The empiricist's reaction to Piagetian findings is reserved; it has not been shown that reinforcement operations and practice were *not* the major variables in determining the different stages of cognitive development. The argument continues that Piaget would have to demonstrate that such stages would naturally unfold in children reared under the full range of possible environmental conditions. This debate is representative of the general controversy between environmentalists and nativists, and it has been responsible for an interesting and growing experimental literature concerned with early environmental influences on subsequent psychological development.

THE EFFECTS OF EARLY EXPERIENCE ON DEVELOPMENT

Enriched and Impoverished Environments

One of the earliest studies of the effects of environmental impoverishment was conducted by von Senden (1932). He gained access to patients blinded by cataracts since birth, who were given sight through surgery. What does an adult, reared in darkness, see once vision is acquired? The methods employed by von Senden were crude, and his findings have never been fully replicated. But what appears clear from his work is that these individuals do see whole forms immediately. They can discriminate differences in brightness and, perhaps, in depth. They certainly do not remain "blind." However, they do have great difficulty naming objects that may have become very familiar through touch. The overview of von Senden's research suggests that considerable perceptual competence is present in the newly sighted adult after a childhood of visual impoverishment.

It was not until the key ideas of Hebb were published in 1949 that von Senden's work and the utility of deprivation methods in the study of development gained research interest. One of the first to respond to the implications of Hebb's theoretical writing was Riesen (1947), who has conducted extensive research on the effects of early sensory deprivation in cats and monkeys. He found that kittens reared in environments that restricted movement showed subsequent deficits in visual perception. Moreover, monkeys reared in the absence of patterned light showed marked but reversible deficits in learning visual discrimination if deprivation was limited to the first several months of life, but irreversible incapacities if unpatterned environments were maintained for eighteen months.

Gibson and Walk (1956), using an enrichment rather than a deprivation variable, reared experimental rats in cages on whose walls were placed triangular and circular forms. Control animals were reared in cages with blank walls. At ninety days of age, the two groups were tested (operantly conditioned) for form discrimination requiring responses to one form and not the other. The difference in performance between the two groups is shown in Figure 8-7. It can be seen that early exposure, even in the absence of differential reinforcement, facilitates subsequent learning. Since this study by Gibson and Walk, there have been attempts to determine whether early enrichment is more effective than later enrichment, or whether early

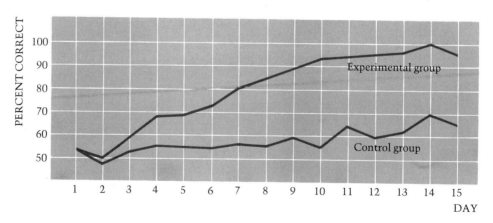

Figure 8-7. The effects of early enrichment. Experimental group animals were reared in home cages rich in geometric stimuli. Control group animals were reared in the absence of these stimuli. Subsequently, discrimination learning occurred. The data above indicate the difference in performance between the two groups. (After the data of Gibson and Walk, 1960.)

impoverishment can be compensated for by subsequent enrichment. The data are not uniform, and the question is still very much disputed.

Experimental Requirements

In testing the effects of early experience, it is of crucial importance to assess a broad range of perceptual-behavioral capacities. Two experiments can illustrate the need for care in this area. Tees (1967) reared mice in the absence of all sound until early adulthood. The mice were then tested for pure-tone discrimination and were found to be "normal." Tees then required a more complicated discrimination, the discrimination of tonal patterns: the mice were to respond to the tonal pattern high-low-high and not respond to low-high-low. Mice reared in acoustically varied environments had no difficulty learning this discrimination, but the acoustically deprived mice failed completely. Thus, while impoverishment may not lead to deficits in a relatively simple task, it is not proven that deficits are entirely absent.

A second experiment illustrating these complications grew out of the previously cited research of Riesen, who reported visual deficits in cats reared under conditions restricting movement. Held and Hein (1963) devised an ingenious experiment to test whether reduced movement, pure and simple, was the major factor in resulting deficits. They used apparatus like that shown in Figure 8-8.

Kitten A is free to walk circularly in a round chamber whose walls are striped in black and white. Kitten B is harnessed in such a way as to be moved passively by Kitten A. Both animals receive identical visual stimulation and both move equal amounts and at identical speeds. The only difference is that Kitten A moves actively, while Kitten B moves passively. After this rearing, the kittens were tested in a number of ways to determine differences in perceptual capacity. Tests indicated the superior ability of kittens in the A group: they avoided the visual cliff, while the kittens in the B group did not; A's blinked at an approaching object, while B's did not. The results supported the view that stimulation and movement were not sufficient specifications of the environment. Movement must be further specified (active or passive) in research concerned with the role of early experiences in subsequent capacity. It is interesting to consider this experiment in the same context as that of Klopfer that we cited earlier.

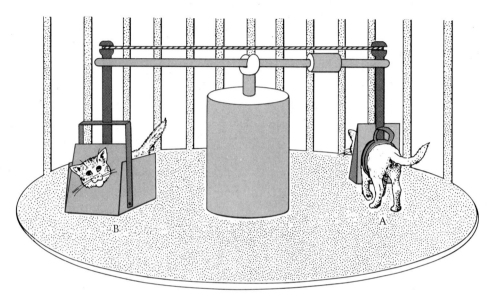

Figure 8-8. *The kitten carousel.* An actively moving kitten (A) and a passively moving kitten (B) are shown in this figure.   (Adapted from the *Journal of Comparative and Physiological Psychology*, 1963, 56, 873.)

Cultural Variables

In the real, nonlaboratory environment in which human development occurs, a complex collection of laws, beliefs, traditions, and expectations is obtained. It must come as no surprise, therefore, that a number of those perceptual-cognitive regularities observed in European and Euro-American cultures will be "violated" among peoples of the world whose heritage is quite different. For example, so-called primitive tribes have been found where their members fail to experience certain illusions as described in Chapter 5. Evidence exists suggesting that the "innate and universal" Piagetian stages of cognitive development may also be different and may occur at very different ages in different cultures. Trobriand Islanders, for example, who do not grow up in the highly "carpentered world" of America, perceive highly angular objects in a unique way (Campbell, Segall, and Herskovitz, 1963). The African bushwoman may not recognize her own child in a photograph. The Eskimo has many words for snow but not one for pineapple. Thus, there has been a growing tendency to resist absolute statements of "normal" developmental trends and to set forth, instead, a cultural relativism in assessing both the cultures and the perceptual-cognitive characteristics of their members. Here again, we note the tension between empiricistic and nativistic explanations. The adoption of cultural relativism is but an endorsement of the view that psychological development is principally a reflection of environmental influences. On the other hand, absolutism argues that certain psychological characteristics are innate, can be found in all people at approximately the same age, will appear under nearly any cultural or environmental conditions, and can be understood only in genetic terms.

This dispute is, of course, far from settled, and it is obvious that extreme versions of the nativism-empiricism perspectives cannot be correct. But experimental findings have been used to favor one position somewhat more than the other. We have already reviewed Piaget's theory of cognitive development, which is essentially nativistic and idealistic. Piaget insists that the stages of cognitive development are fixed, that they must be passed through sequentially, and that they appear in roughly identical form in all cultures examined. As we noted in Chapter 7, a similar case can be set up for language: it appears around the world in children of similar age, its underlying, deep structure is constant, and rewarded practice, while necessary for the development of vocabulary, has little or nothing to do with language as such.

In addition to cognition and language, the issue of *moral behavior* has also been subjected to empiricistic and nativistic interpretations. It will be instructive to examine the research and theory that proceed from this issue.

In the same way that Piaget's cognitive psychology is rooted in the Kantian tradition, so is his psychology of moral development. In 1932, Piaget reported the results of studies of the moral judgments of children of different ages. On the basis of his findings, he concluded that there are two stages of moral development, a *heteronomous* stage and an *autonomous* stage. Children from four to eight years of age were found to be in the heteronomous stage, the stage in which their moral judgments were based upon what others considered to be wrong, what others would punish them for doing. At this stage, ideas of right and wrong were based entirely on what an authority figure had declared. Older children, those who had reached the autonomous stage, judged right and wrong in personal terms and according to their own personal standards.

Piaget studied these stages through the use of children's reactions to pairs of stories. Here is one example:

SOCIALIZATION AND MORAL DEVELOPMENT

There is no universally accepted definition of morality and, therefore, no scientific definition that would permit easy experimental analysis or convincing experimental demonstrations. For Plato, what is moral is indistinguishable from what is truthful and just. It is not merely *doing* good things that, after all, can be done by accident; it is *wanting* to do what is good. Accordingly, one cannot be said to be moral solely on the basis of his conduct; intentions must also be known.

From the foundations provided by Plato, a traditional school of moral philosophy developed whose principal spokesmen were Saint Augustine, Descartes, and, ultimately, Kant. The basic axiom of this school is that the moral dimension of man is to be understood in terms of his *will*. Indeed, Kant views morality as synonymous with what he calls *the good will*. This perspective leads to Kant's famous Categorical Imperative:

Act in such a way that the maxim of your action
would be instituted as a universal law of Nature.

What Kant means by the *maxim* of an action is its *intent*, the *lesson* it teaches, the motive it springs from. For example, we avoid harming those weaker than we are—those who cannot defend themselves and who cannot retaliate in any way—in part, because we realize that if we can so treat those weaker than we, those who are stronger than we are can treat us similarly. *"Do unto others as you would have them do unto you"* is a biblical version of the Categorical Imperative. Were we to treat people only on the basis of their ability to defend themselves—that is, were we to adopt as morally acceptable the concept of survival of the fittest—the *maxim* of our actions would be "Might Makes Right."

The Categorical Imperative goes well beyond the primitive desire to

1. There was once a little girl called Marie. She wished to surprise her mother by giving her a nice piece of sewing. Marie didn't know how to use the scissors, however, and so she cut a big hole in her dress.

2. A little girl named Margaret took her mother's scissors while her mother

protect ourselves from assault and exploitation. We do not mistreat those weaker than ourselves merely because we want to avoid similar treatment at the hands of those stronger than we. We do not mistreat those weaker than ourselves because we know it is wrong. Accordingly, another version of the Categorical Imperative is this:

> Treat no man as merely a means to an end, but
> treat every man as an end in himself.

Kant was convinced that reason and an inner moral sense lead inescapably to the validity of this pronouncement. In other words, while moral instruction aids our moral development, the instruction is effective only because the mind is innately equipped to receive the instruction. Indeed, were we to attempt to teach a contradictory imperative, we would find, sooner or later, that our students would consider the maxim to be morally wrong. It would conflict with a feeling within, an internal moral light.

It is not surprising, in light of this opinion, that Kant concludes that the *rationally* perfect individual is, by that very fact, *morally* perfect. In the same breath, however, Kant acknowledges that there is no rationally perfect individual.

The important point here is that in the Kantian system, morality is to be understood in rational, emotive, and cognitive terms. It is to be treated as a feeling and as an idea. It is "learned" only in the sense that the child learns $2 + 2 = 4$; that is, once he learns the language and the notation, he is immediately impressed not merely with the fact, but with the *necessity* of the fact. The capacity to appreciate necessity is innate. While we can learn what *is* so, we can only know what *must* be so *a priori* (logically prior to experience).

was out. She didn't know how to use the scissors, and after playing for a while, she cut a little hole in her dress.

Children in the heteronomous stage considered both Marie and Margaret equally guilty since both would be punished for damaging their dresses. Older children, however, considered Marie far less guilty, since her intentions were good. For the older children, right and wrong were judged on the basis of what the character wanted to do, not simply on the basis of what the character did. Piaget's conclusion is that, at the stage of cognitive development when it is too early for the intellect to form its own moral rules, the child cannot distinguish between goodness and obedience. Later, the concept of what is good is based on the child's internal rules and may be completely indifferent to whether or not others will punish the child.

An extension and modification of Piaget's theory of moral development has been provided by Lawrence Kohlberg (1963) who classifies the evolution of moral judgment in six stages:

Stage 1 Premoral. The child (as with Piaget's heteronomous child) bases his judgments of right and wrong on anticipations of reward or punishment.

Stage 2 Conventional morality: At this stage, the child adopts judgments that conform to the standards of the people around him. He justifies his actions in terms of a desire to receive rewards and attain certain goals.

Stage 3 Good-boy: good girl. This stage is more complex than Stage 2 in that the behavior is intended to produce social acceptability and familial approval. Where Stage 2 behavior strives for fundamental rewards (for example, toys and candy), Stage 3 conduct is intended to produce good social relations with parents.

Stage 4 Peer-acceptability. In this stage, the child's desire to enjoy good relations with family is extended to his society-at-large, principally to his peers. By extension from the family context, the child regulates his conduct according to the dictates of authority in general: teachers, police, elders. At this stage, the child is still governed by the morality of approval, but approval is sought in a wider setting. Internalized moral rules are either absent or changing.

Stage 5 At this point, we find the child who could enter into those social arrangements we discussed in the preceding chapter under the heading *Social Contract* theories. This is the moral agent about whom Hume, Locke, and Rousseau theorized, an agent aware of the implications of the "golden rule," consciously avoiding abuse of the rights of others out of an interest in preserving his own rights.

Stage 6 This is the highest stage of moral development in Kohlberg's theory. Moral judgment is now guided exclusively by personal, internal standards of right and wrong. Neither obedience nor approval is able to distract the person from his awareness of which moral rule applies to the situation in which he finds himself. In this stage, which can be reached no earlier than adolescence, Kant's Categorical Imperative is recognized as necessary.

Kohlberg studies moral development with methods that are borrowed from Piaget. The child is given a story or, more typically, a situation in which someone violates a particular law or departs from conventional rules. The child is then asked to judge whether the action is right or wrong. In one example, we learn that a sick woman will die unless she receives a particular medicine. There is only one druggist in town, and he has discovered the medicine. It costs the druggist $200 to make the preparation, but he charges $2,000 to anyone who wants it. The sick woman's husband does everything he can to raise the money but can only raise $1,000. The druggist refuses to let him have the medicine even though the man pledges to work for the balance until his bill is completely paid. Later that night, the husband breaks into the pharmacy and steals the medicine.

Presented with this situation, children of different ages are asked whether the husband did the right or the wrong thing and why. From their replies, Kohlberg's six stages cited above take effect. At a premoral level, the young child judges the husband's actions to be wrong because he will be punished. At Stage 6, the adolescent judges the actions to be morally right because life has a moral claim that is more compelling than property.

Recalling the "guards," the "teachers," and the "by-standers" discussed in Chapter 6, we recognize that such compliance and obedience constitute Stage 3 and Stage 4 levels of moral development. Even the libertarianism of a John Stuart Mill would, according to Kohlberg's model, fail to rise above Stage 5. The John Stuart Mill-type liberal, who will not restrict the freedom of anyone unless that person threatens to do physical injury to another, the John Stuart Mill-type liberal who would not be a "policeman of the world," has yet to achieve Stage 6. Clearly, the Stage 6 moralist *would* be a policeman of the world at that point when some people in the world were treating others in an unscrupulous way.

Kohlberg's theory has been tested in different cultures, and its major predictions seem to be confirmed. That is, we do not find the various stages occurring in any other order but sequential order, and we do not find any of the stages in evidence unless the earlier ones have been completed. In other words, the child must have mastered the reasoning involved at one level before he can comprehend the principles involved at the next higher level.

Piaget and Köhlberg Or A "Situation" Ethics?

In reply to theories of moral development such as those advanced by Piaget and Kohlberg, empirically oriented theorists offer evidence similar to that given in Chapter 6. They ask, "Why did thirty-eight people watch Kitty Genovese die?"; "Why did the 'teachers' in Milgram's study proceed to deliver apparently intolerable levels of shock?" They point to studies that show increased physical assaults on dolls by children who have merely watched adults behave this way toward the dolls (Bandura, Ross, and Ross, 1961), to studies that show that when people are made angry in the presence of guns, they subsequently administer more shock (in the Milgram-type setting) than people made angry in the presence of neutral objects such as badminton rackets (Berkowitz and LePage, 1967). Collectively, these studies and observations are intended to reveal the *situational* determinants of moral behavior; determinants that are not the result of some fixed unfolding of an inborn moral sense, but are instead purely environmental and understandable in terms of learning and socialization.

Examining Piaget's theories and Kohlberg's theories in light of the above, we are confronted with the modern version of the controversy between *moral absolutism* and *moral situationalism,* between a doctrine of inborn ideas and one of radical empiricism, between a psychology of cognition and one of learning. The most prudent conclusion is that the issue remains unsettled. Moreover, it is not the kind of issue that is likely to be settled by experimental findings. If a child is raised at all, it is not likely that the child-rearing will, or even can, occur in a morally neutral environment. And to the extent that any moral judgment is the consequence of reason, there will always be an aspect of morality that is not attributable to mere habit or rewarded practice.

It is not uncommon in presenting the views of Kohlberg to confront an audience astonished that anyone at this late date would consider the moral dispositions of man to be innate. This astonishment is not confined to those familiar with the research of Zimbardo, Latané and Darley, Milgram, Bandura, et al. The layman also is impressed with the fact that moral mandates are violated as frequently as they are obeyed. But this is not the point that Kohlberg is trying to make. Those who contend that moral dispositions are innate are not referring to *conduct*, but to *judgment*; not to what we do, but to our moral evaluations of what we do. Thus, the fact that many people cheat on their income tax returns is irrelevant. What *is* relevant is that they judge this behavior to be wrong or, if not, to be justified according to specific moral principles.

The Ik, who constitute an apparent exception to the rule—an exception not in what they do but in their lack of remorse—may not be an exception at all. We might argue that the Ik now operate at a Stage 1 (premoral) level of moral awareness and that with guidance they will come to appreciate the moral deficiencies of their society. What we ask, following Kohlberg's line of reasoning, is this: Once the rational arguments for a particular moral judgment are advanced, do the Ik agree with the conclusions, follow the reasoning, and recognize the inadequacy of lower-stage alternatives?

In neither case does conduct settle the matter; neither the case in which everyone in the world agrees on a particular moral judgment nor the case in which everyone disagrees. The fact that everyone agrees does not make the judgment in question *absolutely* right; it just renders it universally acceptable. Thus, as with other versions of the nativist-empiricist controversy, the question of the origins of our morality cannot be answered either in the laboratory or in public opinion polls.

MATERNAL CARE

It has been shown that certain features of the environment of the developing organism can exert profound influences upon the emergence of psychological capacities. These influences are not limited to the perceptual-cognitive ones only, nor are the environmental requirements limited to those of simple stimulus enrichment and opportunities for simple learning. Over the past decade, H. F. Harlow and his collaborators have conducted numerous experiments with monkeys reared normally or in the absence of playmates or with "substitute" (surrogate) mothers or mates—surrogates which, in fact, are simply cloth dolls. Their major findings have been summarized recently (Harlow and Harlow, 1966).

Monkeys reared apart from all other monkeys are emotionally retarded. Their subsequent adult sexual behavior is abnormal and their interactions with other monkeys is limited and bizarre. If they are female and (forced to) bear children, maternal behavior is virtually absent. In all instances, these deprived animals are hyperexcitable, fearful, and generally barren of the necessary capacities for adaptive behavior. The introduction of a surrogate (a "cloth mother") may be sufficient to counteract only some of the debilitating consequences of motherlessness and the absence of play-mates. At the same time, even the motherless monkeys can come to be attentive mothers themselves with sufficient later experience. But by and large, the emergence of adaptively successful patterns of emotional behavior depends upon early interaction with other members of the species, contact with other infants, and contact that allows the learning of at least the basic emotional responses to the environment.

Not only does restriction impair adjustment but it largely affects the manner in which normal monkeys react to the isolation-reared animals. Adult females will almost always avoid isolation-reared males if they have a choice. Paired isolation reared monkeys fight more frequently. Thus, not only are they incapacitated themselves, but they also provoke the kind of behavior in other animals that only aggravates this incapacity.

More recently, H. F. Harlow has studied the extent to which the maternally deprived monkeys can be rehabilitated. While it is still too early to provide a definitive statement on the matter, it does seem that many of the social and emotional effects of maternal-social deprivation can be overcome by placing the once-deprived monkeys in the company of normal monkeys who are several months younger than the deprived animals. The reasoning behind the procedure is this: since maternal-social deprivation leads to arrested emotional development, the deprived animals could not be expected to benefit from interaction with animals of the same age. Instead, being emotionally and socially younger than their age would otherwise suggest, they can best adapt to a normal environment containing chronologically younger mates.

We must be cautious in generalizing Harlow's findings to the human situation. Not only is Harlow discovering a greater capacity for rehabilitation than was expected from his earlier research, but field studies of human populations have raised questions about the validity of the old view that the first years of life are overwhelmingly important. The Harvard psychologist Jerome Kagan reminds us repeatedly that in a number of South American and Mexican communities in which infant care is absolutely minimal—and in which the young children display a variety of learning deficits—young adults prove to be normal in every way. In other words, while deprivation does produce signs of retarded psychological development, these signs somehow disappear later in life. Such facts simply underscore the remarkable adaptive characteristics of human beings and their ability to overcome handicaps that might permanently incapacitate lower organisms.

From all that we have discussed, it would appear as if a normal setting and normal maturational (biological) supports allow psychological development to unfold as a consequence of the fateful "reinforcement history." This is the behavioristic explanation for all organisms and for all psychological attributes. In light of this, however, the philosophic questions still linger. Is there nothing determined *a priori* other than man's domination by Bentham's twin masters? Are the Piagetian stages present in all men, requiring only a permissive environment for them to unfold? Are the staggering differences among individuals to be understood solely within the context of operant conditioning? In response to these questions, scientists have examined the influences of heredity upon psychological processes. These genetic influences will be the topic of the next chapter.

AGING

A further appreciation of developmental processes demands, in addition to cross-cultural studies, more attention to the process of aging than psychology has given in the past. One of the most distinguished investigators in this area, James Birren (1964) has provided a systematic account of changes in a number of capacities over a broad range of ages. Representative examples all point to the rise and fall of function from infancy to

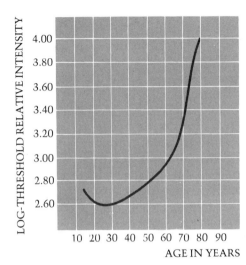

Figure 8-9. The absolute threshold of vision as a function of age. Note that from about 15 to 40 years of age, sensitivity shows little change. Beyond the age of 40, sensitivity diminishes, and beyond 70, sensitivity diminishes with great rapidity. (After the data of Birren, Bick, and Fox, 1948.)

senility. On such basic sensory dimensions as brightness thresholds and audibility (see Chapter 5), pronounced alterations occur, as those shown in Figures 8-9 and 8-10.

Data comparing children, young adults, and old people in relation to the conditioning and extinction of an eye-blink response are depicted in Figure 8-11. Both learning (to respond) and extinction (learning not to respond) are retarded in the aged sample.

Experimental studies of aging have included basic sensory processes (Figures 8-9 and 8-10), simple conditioning (Figure 8-11), and more complex cognitive functions (Figure 8-12). Also, the biographical method has uncovered the relationship between age and achievement in various disciplines (Figures 8-12, 8-13, 8-14, 8-15). These findings are presented here and are discussed in the figure captions.

On more complex cognitive tasks, the effects of age are again pronounced. Friend and Zubek (1968) have examined critical thinking ability in subjects from twelve to eighty years of age. Note their findings illustrated in Figure 8-12. An important question related to this data is: At what time in the developmental process are the capacities so cultivated and the negative effects of aging so minimal as to "optimize" the likelihood of creative expression? Obviously, there is great variability from one individual to the next in terms of the years of maximum productivity and creativity.

Trends, however, have been studied and the results are summarized in Figures 8-13, 8-14, and 8-15. From these findings, one would expect the greatest creative productivity from individuals between thirty and forty years of age.

It is important to exercise some reservation, however, in interpreting this data. Advanced age brings with it a downward movement of basic sensory and motor capacities. Tests designed to assess intellectual and cognitive functions must be free from bias in the sensory-motor domain. The problem in studying the psychology of aging is in this respect similar to that confronted in studies of the very young. Just as the latter can be confounded by maturational variables, studies of the aged can be influenced by physiological changes that do not affect psychological capacities directly but do affect the results—for example, fatigue, weakness, poor vision and hearing, and even aches and pains. There is also the problem of motivation; in many testing settings, the inducements to perform to one's fullest capacities may be irrelevant to the aged.

A final word should be added to the problem of dealing with the aged

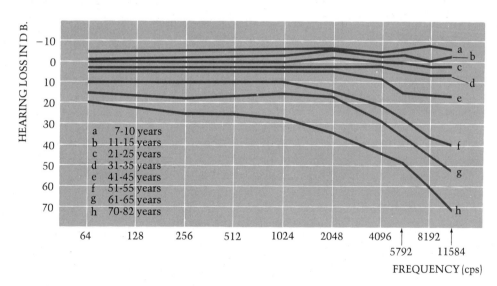

Figure 8-10. Changes in hearing with age. From the age of 40, a steady decline in auditory sensitivity is observed. Hearing loss is expressed in decibels (DB), a measure of acoustic power. (After the data of Graf de la Rosée, 1953.)

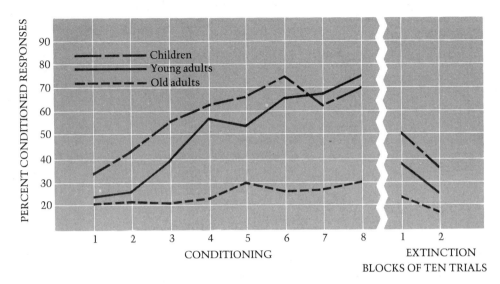

Figure 8-11. Conditioning and extinction as a function of age. As shown in this graph, children, young adults, and old adults show distinct differences in the formation and the extinction of conditioned responses. (After the data of Braun and Geizelhart, 1959.)

in psychological terms. Assessments of creativity, reasoning, and cognitive function often require the subject to abandon tentative hypotheses and turn to new evidence or new methods of solution. Similarly, common-sense assessments of mental ability often are based on characteristics such as flexibility, enthusiasm, and so forth. In these respects, the aged should not be held responsible for the arbitrary criteria of those who are younger. When a man reaches eighty years of age, he has enjoyed a prolonged reinforcement history in which certain behaviors have proven to be useful time and time again. Apparent inflexibility may be no more than a reluctance to change what has already led to success.

In this same connection, we must distinguish between the failures *of* the aged and the failures *due to* aging. The former may reflect no more than attitudes on the part of society about the ability of the aged to take on responsibility. In America in particular, where a veritable cult of youth has appeared, it is increasingly difficult for those past the age of retirement to obtain or retain positions of responsibility. This difficulty is not related—or very often is not related—to any physical debility, but to the purely administrative practice of not hiring or keeping on the payroll those over sixty-five years of age. In such instances, changes in personality, in performance, and in motivation cannot be readily attributed to "aging," but to the changes in one's lifestyle imposed as the mere consequence of becoming older.

SUMMARY

Psychological development reveals two interacting processes. The one is broadly defined as "experience," by which is meant the history of reinforcements, perceptions, and situations that have occupied the life of the developing organism. The second is broadly defined as "maturation," the structural and functional transformations that occur in the nervous system as the organism ages. While noting the strong (and obvious) influences of training on the young organism, we have also drawn attention to native processes that must be taken into account if we are to explain the dramatic changes that take place in the cognitive abilities of the developing child. Mere practice does not account for these changes nor does aging. Clearly

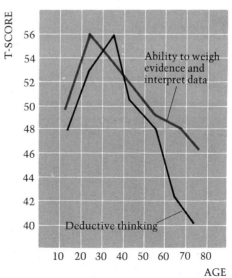

Figure 8-12. Estimated "thinking" ability as a function of age. Note that both forms of thinking appear to be carried on with maximum efficiency between the ages of 25 and 45. To the extent that it can be measured by tests, deductive thinking— the ability to distinguish particular cases from general principles—is greatest at about 40 years of age. (After the data of Friend and Zubek, 1958.)

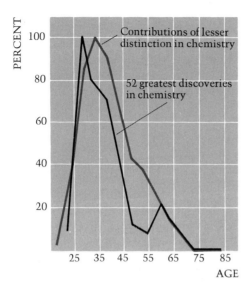

Figure 8-13. Major and minor contributions in chemistry by people of different ages. The findings suggest that the greatest contributions are made by people who are in their thirties. Motivation probably is reduced in those people who have not made such contributions by a certain age and even among some who have contributed. (After the data of Lehman, 1953.)

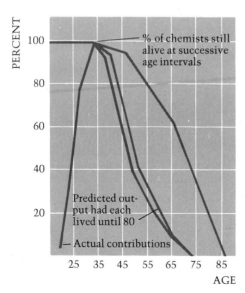

Figure 8-14. Scientific productivity and age based on contributions of chemists. Beyond the age of 35, productivity drops off quickly and remains significantly less of a fraction of the total productivity in the field. Again, many variables may be involved. For example, beyond 35-40 years of age is the time that many scientists accept administrative positions, have heavy family pressure, are confronted with illnesses common to middle age, and so forth. (After the data of Lehman, 1953.)

there is a built-in disposition to process information in specific ways, and under normal circumstances, this disposition becomes qualitatively (functionally) different from major "stage" to major "stage." Since we have proposed such native dispositions to account for the experimental findings, we will move on to examine the relationship between genetic and experiential factors. Therefore, we turn to *genetic psychology* and the concepts of instincts and traits.

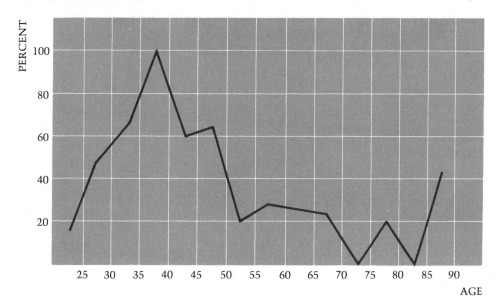

Figure 8-15. Contributions to medicine and the age of the scientist. The pattern above is similar to that observed in Fig. 8-14. It should be noted that Kant's *Critique of Pure Reason* appeared when he was 57; Locke's *Essay Concerning Human Understanding* appeared when Locke was 58; J. S. Mill's *On Liberty* was published when he was 53; Descartes was 48 when his *Principles of Philosophy* appeared. Thus, as the weight, durability, and generality of a contribution increase, so may the age of the author. (After the data of Lehman, 1953.)

SUGGESTED READINGS

ELKIND, D. *Children and Adolescents: Interpretive Essays on Jean Piaget.* New York: Oxford University Press, 1970.

Professor Elkind is an authority on Piagetian psychology. In this concise text, he summarizes Piaget's conceptions of the mind of the child and proceeds to discuss education, intelligence, reading, and so on within a Piagetian framework. The text is clear and the discussion thoughtful.

GIBSON, E. J. *Principles of Perceptual Learning and Development.* New York: Appleton-Century-Crofts, 1969.

Dr. Gibson's treatise is filled with theories and data concerned with perception and cognition. Some sections will tax the beginning student but her treatments of deprivation and enrichment, traditional theories, and imprinting are informative and require no special preparation.

9

Genetic Psychology: The Problem of Fixity

INTRODUCTION

The underlying themes dominating the preceding three chapters and presented fully in Chapter 5, as well, are those of *nativism* and *empiricism*. In Chapter 5, we learned that advanced species do not just passively receive stimuli, but actively organize and transform those stimuli that affect their sense organs. The creative aspects of perception cannot be dismissed as an effect of "past experience," since all past experiences are also influenced by these native tendencies. After all, the person who spends twenty years laying railroad tracks still sees the tracks converge at a distance, even though on the basis of "past experience" he certainly should know that they are parallel to each other. In Chapter 6 we looked more closely at past experience in the context of operant conditioning, classical conditioning, cognition, and "situationism." Again we observed that a radical empiricistic account simply is not completely supported by the facts. Then, in

Chapter 7, we discussed human language, which by all accounts resists every attempt at behavioristic reduction. Finally, in the last chapter, we examined the more significant findings in studies of human and animal development and again were impressed by the need for both empiricistic *and* nativistic principles. Now we are ready to address the nativistic proposition directly, to see how far an "instinct psychology" can take us in our attempt to comprehend the psychological nature of man. We all know that there are genes that control heredity, and we all have at least a general idea of "heredity." The major issue which we will examine in this chapter is that of the applicability of genetic principles to psychological processes and events.

Of the many features of Darwin's theory, the concepts of natural variation and selection were especially influential in nineteenth-century psychology. Sir Francis Galton the English scientist and writer and a cousin of Darwin was one of the first to focus attention within a Darwinian context on the significant differences among men in relation to their psychological capacities. He offered his opinion in no uncertain terms:

> I have no patience with the hypothesis occasionally expressed, and often implied, especially in tales written to teach children to be good, that babies are born pretty much alike, and that the sole agencies in creating differences between boy and boy, and man and man, are steady application and moral effort. (Galton, p. 14)

In his statistical studies of "hereditary genius," Galton found such reliable levels of achievement within families that he unhesitatingly accepted the hereditary basis of intellectual capacity. In the century since his pioneering efforts, psychologists and geneticists have conducted numerous studies designed to determine the role of genetic factors in a host of psychological attributes. Before we look at their methods and findings, it is necessary first to discuss several basic principles of genetics.

GENETIC PRINCIPLES

All biological growth is based on the continuous multiplication of cells by division. The process of cell division is called *mitosis* and is illustrated in Figure 9-1. Note in Figure 9-1 that from the two cells, four will be formed,

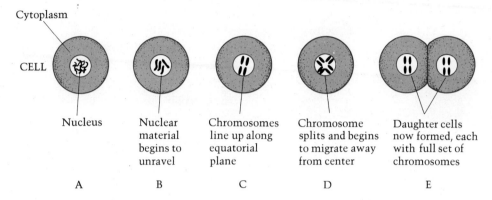

Cytoplasm

CELL

Nucleus

Nuclear material begins to unravel

Chromosomes line up along equatorial plane

Chromosome splits and begins to migrate away from center

Daughter cells now formed, each with full set of chromosomes

A   B   C   D   E

Figure 9-1. *Meiotic division* (the formation of sex cells from parent cells).

then eight, sixteen, and so on. In each instance, the *chromosomes*, the genetic material in the nucleus, will become lined up, each chromosome will split (forming two *chromatids),* and the two daughter cells formed from this division will contain identical choromosomes. In normal tissue, there is only one exception to this manner of cellular division, and that occurs in the formation of the male (sperm) and female (ovum) reproductive cells. These sexual cells are called *gametes,* and they are produced by a form of cell division called *meiosis.*

Meiosis: Reduction-Division

In man and in most animal species, reproduction is achieved by the union of male and female gametes. This process is called fertilization, and the first product of the union is called the *zygote.*

Except for the gametes, all human cells contain 23 pairs of chromosomes in the nucleus. Thus, each nonsexual cell contains 46 chromosomes. During *mitosis,* the chromosomes split so that each daughter cell retains the total of 46. However, fertilization occurs when two cells unite, which is quite different from a single cell dividing. If the sexual cells were formed by mitosis, then the union of the male gamete (23 pairs of chromosomes) with the female gamete (23 pairs of chromosomes) would produce a zygote

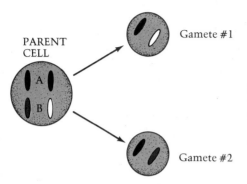

PARENT CELL

Gamete #1

Gamete #2

Figure 9-2. In *meiosis*, the parent cell transmits only *one* member of each chromosomal pair to each gamete. In the illustration above, gamete 1 receives one chromosome from pair A and one from pair B. Gamete 2 receives the other member of each pair.

with 46 pairs of chromosomes. These would participate in fertilization with gametes from another member of the species, and the zygote resulting from this fertilization would contain 92 pairs of chromosomes. Within a few generations, the number of chromosomes would become enormous. However, because of *meiosis*, this does not occur. Instead, as the gametes are formed, each receives only *one* member from each of the 23 pairs. In other words, each sperm or ovum contains only half the number of chromosomes present in all other cells. This half-number is called the *haploid* number. The full complement of 46 chromosomes is the *diploid* number. *Meiosis* is illustrated in Figure 9-2 in which, for the sake of simplicity, only two pairs of chromosomes are shown.

Note in Figure 9-2 that both of the A-chromosomes are identical, while the B-chromosomes are different. This will serve to illustrate how the sex of human offspring is determined. It is known that one and only one chromosome is responsible for the sex of offspring. This chromosome is called the Y-chromosome, and it is carried only by the male of the species. In Figure 9-2, we use the symbol ✒ to represent this X-chromosome, and the symbol 𝒪 to represent the Y-chromosome. In this figure, the parent cell contains both an X- and a Y-chromosome and is, therefore, a male parent cell; females of the species have two X-chromosomes. We now can examine the manner in which the sex of the offspring is determined.

When sperm cells are produced, the male parent cell will pass on either an X-chromosome or a Y-chromosome. About half the population of sperm cells will possess each of these. However, all the ova produced by the female will possess X-chromosomes only. Thus, as noted in Figure 9-3, at fertilization, there are two possible outcomes.

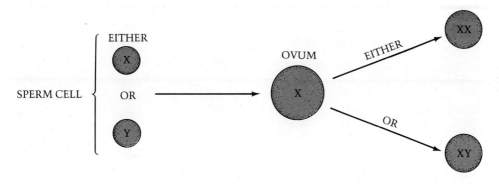

Figure 9-3. If sperm X unites with the ovum, the zygote will possess XX as a chromosome-pair and will develop as a female member of the species. If sperm Y fertilizes the ovum, the resulting pair will be XY and the zygote will develop as a male member of the species.

We can observe in Figure 9-2 that meiosis leads to two different types of sperm cells (X-carrying or Y-carrying), but only one type of ovum (X-carrying) in regard to sexual determination. But a given chromosome (of which X or Y is only one) carries far more genetic information than a single characteristic such as sex. The same Y-chromosome that determines sex also is responsible for baldness, for example; it also participates in those physiological events involved in color-vision. As a result, baldness and color blindness are referred to as *sex-linked* in that their occurrence is linked to the Y-chromosome.

Mendelian Inheritance

While animal breeders had labored successfully for thousands of years and while common sense had long observed the similarities among closely related individuals, the science of genetics actually began with Gregor Mendel (1822-1884), an Austrian monk and botanist.

Mendel studied various strains of pea plants and carefully recorded their most prominent characteristics (color, shape, height) and how these characteristics varied among the offspring of different "crosses" (fertilizations). One of the first facts he noted was that all the offspring of a cross involving yellow-seed plants possessed yellow seeds, even when the other

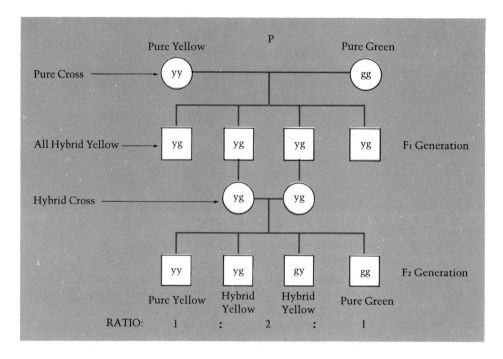

Figure 9-4. F₁ and F₂ phenotypes resulting from a cross of two pure strains. See the text for a full discussion.

member in the cross had green seeds. He referred to yellow in this instance as the *dominant* trait. Interestingly, when two green-seed plants were crossed, all the offspring had green seeds.

We refer to the first plants used in such studies as the parents (P) and their offspring as the *first filial generation* (F_1). When the F_1 plants are mated, their offspring are the *second filial generation*, or F_2. What Mendel observed was this: while all F_1 plants had yellow seeds when *either* parent was yellow seed, some F_2 plants produced by the inbreeding of F_1 had green seeds. The conclusion was obvious. When yellow is present, it is the *dominant* color, and green becomes the *recessive* color. Thus, green occurs *only* when yellow is absent. Thus, yellowness and greenness must be determined by separate and distinct agents! We now refer to these agents as *genes*. We can review Mendel's findings by examining the data in Figure 9-4.

The parents (P), we shall assume, contain the chromosome pair YY (yellow) and GG (green). All F₁ offspring must possess the pair YG, and since Y is a *dominant* agent, all F₁ plants will *appear* yellow. The appearance is called the *phenotype*, and the actual hereditary composition is called the *genotype*. In this example, both parents are said to have *pure* genotypes (YY and GG) whereas the F₁ are said to be *hybrid* (YG).

It is important to note in Figure 9-4 that while all of the F₁ are yellow, only 75 percent of the F₂ are yellow. Mendel found this 3 to 1 ratio reliably in the F₂ products of all crosses in which parent-genotypes were pure-dominant and recessive: YY-GG. Because he was able to recover green seeds in F₂, he knew they had not been lost or destroyed in F₁, even though green seeds did not appear in F₁. He therefore concluded that the traits of yellow and green were passed on independently. This conclusion, sometimes called *Mendel's First Law*, asserts that what we now term as genes are independently segregated. This *Law of Independent Segregation* proved the unitary structure of the genetic material long before microscopes were able to identify the chromosomes.

Mendel next performed crosses involving two characteristics: color, yellow and green seeds (Y, g), and shape, round and wrinkled seeds (R,w). Selecting pure-dominant round, yellow seeds (YR) and pure-recessive green, wrinkled seeds (gw) as parents, he obtained the expected F₁. All offspring were round (R) and yellow (Y), since these are the dominant traits. The basic question, of course, pertained to the appearance of the F₂ plants resulting from the crossing of two of these hybrid F₁ plants. Mendel proceeded to obtain thousands of F₂ offspring by crossing what he knew to be RwYg with RwYg. The summary of his findings is shown in Figure 9-5. In the figure, note that the Rwgg (round and green) and the wwYg (wrinkled and yellow) F₂ forms were not present either in F₁ or in the parent stock. These new forms are *recombinants*, which means they are produced by the recombination of genes that were independently "sorted out" in F₂. The original P's (RRYY and wwgg) yielded F₁ hybrids (all RwYg). Because of meiosis, the gametes produced by these hybrids contained RY, Rg, wY, and wg in equal proportions. It is from these four genotypes that all the entries in Figure 9-5 appeared. The very occurrence of a *recombinant* such as wwYY (wrinkled-yellow) proves that the separate genes (R,w,Y, and g) are sorted out independently during fertilization. That is, we know that meiosis prevents a combination such as Rw in any single gamete, since each—R and w—is delivered to a separate gamete. However, in F₂ we again discover Rw to-

	RY	Rg	wY	wg
RY	RRYY	RRYg	RwYY	RwYg
Rg	RRYg	RRgg	RwYg	Rwgg
wY	RwYY	RwYg	wwYY	wwYg
wg	RwYg	Rwgg	wwYg	wwgg

PHENOTYPES

9 round and yellow

3 round and green

3 wrinkled and yellow

1 wrinkled and green

Figure 9-5. The F₂'s resulting from an F₁ hybrid cross of RwYg x RwYg.

gether, as well as other genotypes not found in any given F₁ gamete. We can conclude, therefore, that the genes are *independently sorted* in hybrid and in dihybrid (RwYg) crosses. This is known as *Mendel's Second Law*, and its principal effect is to allow an even distribution of genes throughout successive generations. All other things being equal, over the long run, the various combinations of genes will appear with predictable frequencies in a given species. If parents are each "pure," or *homozygous*, for a given trait— one parent homozygous for the dominant gene (RR) and the other for the recessive (ww)—then all F₁ offsprings will be *heterozygous* (Rw). The gametes of F₁ will contain either R or w, and F₂ will again display the ww not evidenced in F₁. As the number of genes increases, the number of possible combinations becomes very great. As just an indication, consider the fact that the number of ways 23 pairs of chromosomes from each parent can be drawn upon in fertilization is 2^{23}. That is, if there were only two chromosomes per parent cell, one containing gene-A and one containing gene-A^1 in the male and one with gene-B and its twin with gene-B^1 in the female, the possible genotypes in F₁ would be AB, A^1B, AB^1, and A^1B^1. In this example, two chromosomes per parent allows 2^2, or 4 genotypes. With three per parent, the possible combinations reach 2^3. With n chromosomes per parent, the number of possible combinations becomes 2^n. So even under the most highly simplified conditions, there is great opportunity for variability in successive generations.

Departures from Simple Mendelian Predictions

The fact is that the simplified settings described above are relatively rare in animal and human genetics. The first departure from the simple scheme is that of blended inheritance. This refers to gene-pairs in which neither form (*allele*) of the gene is dominant. Crossing red and white snapdragons, for example, produces *pink* offspring. Next, most complex physiological processes are affected by many genes, not just one. Thus, any human phenotype—such as height, weight, skin color, and so on—is more likely to be under *polygenic* rather than single-gene influence. Exceptions to this are found mainly in certain disease conditions. Then there is the phenomenon of *crossing over* (Figure 9-6) in which a portion of two chromosomes break and each segment re-fuses with a complementary segment of its neighbor.

How the genes are ultimately expressed in the varied aspects of the adult organism is only now being unraveled. The mechanisms of gene action are complex, and even the highlights of current knowledge may confuse the beginning student. However, some very general features will suffice for our present purposes.

It appears to be the function of DNA (deoxyribose nucleic acid) to issue various "instructions" to cells, in response to which certain proteins

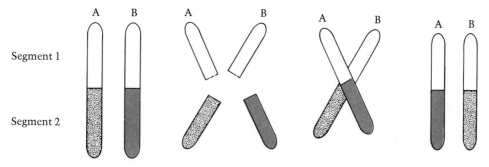

Figure 9-6. Chromosomes A and B, each with two segments, break apart at corresponding locations. The upper segment of A *crosses over* toward the lower segment of B. Finally, two new forms of A and B result.

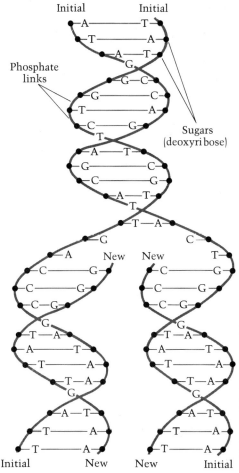

Phosphate links

Sugars (deoxyribose)

Figure 9-7. DNA strand undergoing replication. The initial chain consists of alternating sugar-phosphate links; the latter, joining the sugars together. The two strands in the chain are connected by pairs of bases —adenine-quanine and thymine-cytosine. The sequence of base pairs can alter. The helix splits with each of the initial strands and is now ready to join with a newly formed strand. Thus two copies of the original molecule are yielded.

are made, enzymes manufactured, growth and death processes initiated. The present model of DNA (see Figure 9-7) assumes a large, spirally coiled, double-stranded molecule with the strands linked by four bases: two purines (adenine and guanine) and two pyrimidines (thymine and cytosine). Alternating along the lengths of the two strands are molecules of sugars (deoxyribose) and phosphates. The arrangement of these molecules never changes; only the sequences of purines and pyrimidines are free to alter.

Thus, it is in the arrangements of these bases that geneticists look for the "language" of cellular processes. Different configurations of purines and pyrimidines can lead to the production of different proteins, hormones, and enzymes and, therefore, can determine the physiological events that are controlled by these substances.

GENETIC PSYCHOLOGY

Research concerned with genetic aspects of psychological functions has followed three rather distinct lines. The first consists of studies of instinctive behavior in lower organisms. The rationale for this research is based on the common observation that members of the same species often display rather stereotyped, or species-specific, behavior: dogs tend to be loyal, cats independent, lions ferocious, and so on. Darwinian biology and these age-old observations have inspired a search for those instinctual mechanisms in animals that may also govern human behavior. What tendencies in his behavior are "natural"—that is, genetically predetermined—in man? Thus, theories of instinct and studies of instinctive behavior in animals have been central to issues in human genetic psychology.

A second approach in genetic psychology has utilized inbred strains of animals and through such selective-breeding studies, has investigated traditional psychological variables such as learning, memory, and emotion. The rationale underlying this method of investigation is that successive generations of inbred strains contain members with increasingly similar genotypes. Thus, since genetic differences have been reduced to a minimum, environmental factors become more and more important as determinants of any observed differences in behavior.

The third principal method used in genetic psychology focuses on human attributes (especially intelligence and personality) and their similarity in individuals of varying degrees of genetic relatedness. These experiments are called *familial concordance studies.*

Instincts

The psychologist and philosopher William James (1890) defined an instinct as "the faculty of acting in such a way as to produce certain ends, without foresight of the ends, and without previous education in the performance." More modern definitions preserve the basic flavor of this older view. Instincts are considered to be genetically determined, irrepressible impulses to act shared by all members of a species. The behavior awaits only certain cues from the environment. In their presence, instinctive mechanisms "release" a chain of highly organized (ritualistic) responses. Instincts have been treated as distinct from simpler reflexes and tropisms. The word *tropism* is usually applied to very great, total-body orientations toward or away from specific stimuli; for example, the plant's *phototropism* causes it to turn toward light. Reflexes are generally viewed as fractional responses of the organism, responses of a single limb or gland to stimulation of another specific structure. For example, the "patellar reflex" is elicited by striking the tendon just below the kneecap. Such stimulation results in the contraction of extensor muscles in the thigh causing the leg to kick.

By convention, the term *instinct* has been reserved for more complex behaviors which, unlike tropisms and reflexes, appear to be *intentional*. The robin seems to be preparing for her offspring as she busily constructs a nest. The digger wasp carefully chews out the salty flats around San Francisco Bay until she has created a vertical tunnel. She camouflages the hole and flies away and returns repeatedly with worms she has paralyzed until she has placed five in the shaft. One of the worms has the egg of this wasp fastened to its body. With egg and worms in place, mother flies away, never to return. Later, when the egg has grown to be an adult wasp, this young creature, without benefit of rearing, will perform the same complex series of acts to care for her own eggs. It is sometimes hard to accept such clever and complex behavior as unintentional at first. But on further examination, it becomes apparent that the digger wasp is ritualistically emitting a chain of uncontrollable behavior that will disintegrate to meaninglessness if interrupted at any point in the chain. Removal of one of the worms by an experimenter will lead to chaotic fluttering and eventual resignation. She will not replace the missing worm, even when it is placed very near the burrow. In short, unless the chain of events is permitted to unfold in its prescribed manner, the mother wasp is at a total behavioral loss (Kellogg, 1923). She is, in James's sense, "acting . . . to produce certain ends, without foresight of the ends" and clearly, given the "orphaned" rearing of wasps, "without previous education in the performance."

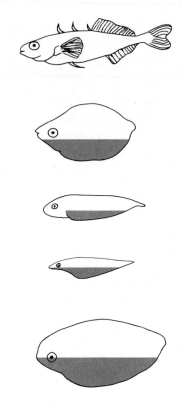

Figure 9-8. Models used by Tinbergen to test the cues effective in releasing mating behavior of the male stickleback. The top model—which otherwise resembles the stickleback closely but which contains no red markings—was ineffective in mating. All of the other models were effective even though they do not resemble sticklebacks. (After Tinbergen, 1948.)

Innate Releasers

Konrad Lorenz, Niko Tinbergen (1969), and other leading ethologists have provided a number of examples of *innate releasing mechanisms* (IRM). The model for such patterns of instinctive behavior is as follows. On the basis of selection pressures throughout the evolutionary history of a species, certain highly integrated chains of behavior are "wired into" the response capacities of the organism. In nature, there are certain crucial cues called *sign stimuli*, which, when presented to the organism, will elicit the behavioral chain. Male stickleback fish fight furiously with each other. They recognize other males quite easily since the male has a vivid red throat and belly. "Dummy" sticklebacks, such as those shown in Figure 9-8, have been placed in tanks with male sticklebacks and the ensuing behavior has been observed. The "dummy" figure (no red color) is very much like a male stickleback in appearance. The other four models, none of which looks at all like a male stickleback but all of which have red markings, were all successful in triggering fighting behavior in a male stickleback. The "dummy" model had no such effect. Quite clearly, the coloration of the decoy is the sign-stimulus that excites the IRM. Such effects have led Tinbergen to challenge traditional American behaviorism: "The reason why the dependence of innate behavior on sign stimuli has not yet been generally recognized probably lies in the fact that so many laboratory psychologists have been studying conditioned reactions" (Tinbergen, p. 37).

Throughout the animal kingdom, one can find a very high incidence of behavior analogous to that of digger wasps and sticklebacks. Ants will follow in the path used previously by other ants who were successful in finding food. Here, the cues are chemical; the original search party exudes a chemical in its wake, and followers will proceed along these chemical paths. Such chemical communicators are called *pheromones*. Robins hatched in an incubator and reared alone in a simulated forest will build nests at appropriate times. Porpoises will "aid" a drowning man to shore. Many animals will signal vocally the approach of a predator. The list is a long one.

What Is Instinctive Behavior?

Because instincts seem common to all animals, it became fashionable in post-Darwinian psychology to apply the concept to a broad range of human behavior. Thus, man was "instinctively" aggressive, "instinctively" social, "instinctively" greedy, "instinctively" protective, "instinctively" lustful. In the first few decades of the twentieth century, this strongly nativistic attitude had a great impact on psychology's theoretical language. Darwin had provided the reason for instincts, Mendel had offered a mechanism, and the behavior of men and nations seemed to justify explanations based upon instinct. In time, however, resistance to the fad mounted. As we mentioned in Chapter 6, Hitler made the concept of race objectionable, and race was based upon the same genetic principles as instinct theories. Moreover, the behaviorist "revolution" launched in the 1920s enjoyed a growing following with Skinner's influential *Behavior of Orga-*

nisms (1938) and Hull's *Principles of Behavior* (1943). As "isms," behaviorism and nativism have always been treated as irreconcilable adversaries, and the emergence of behavioristic psychology necessarily threatened instinct theories. Finally, the instinct theories themselves had much to do with furthering their own unpopularity. They created an explanatory system in which complex human enterprises were reduced to mere names, and the names, after all, explained nothing. Psychology grew wary of statements like "Man does X because man is instinctively Y." This skepticism led to reasearch that seemed to weaken consistently the doctrines of the instinct theorists.

An early and influential research program was undertaken by Zin Yang Kuo (1921) and was concerned with the cat's "instinctive" hostility toward rats. Kuo found that cats reared with rats would kill and eat infant rat litters or even adult rats whose fur had been shaved. However, cats reared with rats from an early but postinfant age did *not* kill the rats, but actually befriended them. And cats reared by mothers who killed but did not eat rats would kill also, but generally did not eat rats. In other words, the cats learned to treat rat littermates as *mates*. This learning involved many cues including furriness. Infant rats (which are born without hair) and shaved rats were, from the cats' perspective, not part of the rat family.

Kuo's research strongly suggests that the cat's "instinct to kill" is, in fact, behavior that is very much influenced by environmental conditions. Similarly, the "suicidal instinct" of the lemming (a form of rodent), the "instinctual" return of the swallows to Capistrano, and the "instinctual ferocity" of the lion are discredited by careful investigations (Pronko, 1969). A child who has seen the motion picture *Born Free* will reject any suggestion of the "natural" visciousness of lions. By the same token, a hunter who owns a Labrador retriever will reject the suggestion that his dog was *taught* to retrieve the prey. Prudence and experimental findings both force us to accept the existence of unlearned patterns of behavior throughout the animal kingdom. For many species, survival depends on elaborate behavioral capacities in organisms that are too young to have learned much of anything, organisms that spend their earliest days in solitary existence. For many species, survival depends on *group*-behavior that, given the capacities of the individual members, could not be developed rapidly enough through the procedures of operant conditioning. Rather, such species have been endowed genetically with complex physiological mechanisms that release appropriate chains of behavior in the presence of certain specific environmental conditions. However, it is quite another matter to hypothesize about *human* instincts. If one views instincts as nature's concession to the ignorant, then it is likely that instincts will flourish least where the capacity to learn exists in the greatest degree. Robins, wasps, and human mothers "feather their nests," but it would be ridiculous to suggest that the three are prompted by identical mechanisms and considerations. The instinct hypothesis requires that observed behavior cannot be explained on the basis of learning alone. It is always difficult to guarantee that learning has *not* occurred. Generally the instinct theorist has been satisfied to view any behavior as innate if (a) it is invariant in form, (b) it is found throughout a species, (c) it appears in organisms isolated since birth, and (d) it appears, fully developed, in the absence of practice (Lehrman, 1953). One must wonder if *any* instance of human behavior satisfies these four criteria. But by the same token, one wonders if such criteria are not too rigid. Clearly, for the environment to be influential, there must be *something* to be influenced. Even the principles of operant conditioning depend, in the first instance, upon the emission of behavior.

The anti-instinct movement launched by classical behaviorism was in response to an unwarranted declaration of countless human instincts. But recently, as the luster of behaviorism has begun to fade, there has occurred a resurgence of interest in nativistic explanations of human conduct. In 1966, there appeared the English-language edition of Konrad Lorenz's *On Aggression.* The same year, Robert Ardrey's *The Territorial Imperative* enjoyed a large general readership, and in 1968, Desmond Morris' *The Naked Ape* reached the list of nationwide best sellers. Each in its own fashion solidly adopts the nativistic view of human behavior. Each accepts the idea of evolutionary continuity according to which the complex psychological equipment of the higher (and highest) primate is judged to be an elaboration of those forms found among lower animals.

In his numerous and suggestive ethological studies, Konrad Lorenz has found aggression among members of the same species to be universal. Its function, he contends, is to enhance the adaptive potential of the species. A hungry animal attacks outside its species to kill and eat, but aggression is *intraspecific,* because "what directly threatens the existence of an animal species is never the 'eating enemy' but the competitor" (Lorenz, p. 22). Thus, "the most important function of intraspecific aggression is the even distribution of the animals of a particular species over a habitable area . . ." (Lorenz, p. 35). In addition, fighting enhances the adaptive potential of a species by eliminating the weak, and it thereby not only improves the "stock," but creates successive generations more impelled by instinctual aggression. "Why has aggression not simply been eliminated in those animal species in which close social aggregation is of advantage to survival? The reason is that [its] functions . . . are indispensable" (Lorenz, p. 105). A committed Darwinist, Lorenz sees no reason to assume that *homo sapiens* has been spared the instinct to aggress against his own kind. Man, as other animals, has evolved ritualized, or symbolic, forms of aggression so that the instinct may be exercised while its consequences are avoided:

> A good example of how a rite originates phylogenetically, how it acquires a meaning, and how this becomes altered in the course of further development, can be found by studying a certain ceremony of females of the duck species. This ceremony is called "inciting." As with birds with a similar family life, the females of this species are smaller but no less aggressive than the males. Thus, in quarrels between two couples it often happens that the duck, impelled by anger, advances too near the enemy couple, then gets "frightened by her own courage," turns around, and hurries back to her own strong, protective drake. Beside him, she gathers new courage and begins to threaten the neighbors again, without however leaving the safe proximity of her mate. (Lorenz, p. 55)

Thus, competing impulses allow both the expression of aggression and successful avoidance of a suicidal encounter. Although symbolic, it is intraspecific aggression nonetheless and is as "natural" as life itself. Warfare, an example of what Lorenz calls *militant enthusiasm,* is but the culturally ritualized display of the aggressive instinct. It is avoidable but not unnatural.

The works of Morris and Ardrey, while interesting in their own right, add little to those basic nativistic premises advanced by Lorenz. Man is but one more animal protecting his own and killing his competitors by whatever means nature has allowed. The driving forces are those biological processes that are instinctual. But the biological processes are not known; they are inferred. And even if known, they surely would be modified by the environment. To explain both the inciting behavior of a duck and World War II in terms of ritualized aggression raises many questions but answers none. As Daniel Lehrman (1953) has written:

Now, what exactly is meant by the statement that a behavior pattern is "inherited" or "genetically controlled"? Lorenz undoubtedly does not think that the zygote contains the instinctive act in miniature, or that the gene is the equivalent of an entelechy which purposefully and continuously tries to push the organism's development in a particular direction. Yet one or both of these preformistic assumptions, or their equivalents, must underlie the notion that some behavior patterns are "inherited" as such. . . . The use of "explanatory" categories such as "innate" and "genetically fixed" obscures the necessity of investigating developmental processes in order to gain insight into the actual mechanisms of behavior and their interrelations. . . . The interaction out of which the organism develops is not one, as is so often said, between heredity and environment. It is between *organism* and environment!" (Lehrman, 1953)

Selective Breeding Studies

Because of the difficulty of specifying or controlling human genetic composition, contemporary research in genetic psychology uses selectively bred lower organisms. This method owes much of its inspiration to Tolman (1924) and Tryon (1929), whose pioneering studies pointed to genetic factors in the learning ability of rats. Current findings, based upon improved methods and instruments, tend to support their early results: learning, memory, "emotionality," and the like can be altered in successive generations by selectively breeding for a desired trait.

Typically, a large number of animals (usually mice or rats) are tested on some task—for example, the ability to solve a maze. The best-performing opposite-sexed animals are mated, as are the poorest. The respective offspring are tested on the same task, and extreme performers are again segregated and mated. One representative study is that of Bovet et al. (1969), who selectively bred animals for avoidance conditionability. The apparatus consisted of a shuttle-box (see Figure 9-9) that required the animal to move from one chamber to another in order to avoid an electrical shock. The discriminative stimulus was an overhead light. Five seconds after the onset of the light, shock was delivered. Animals were scored in terms of percent successful avoidances in blocks of 100 trials.

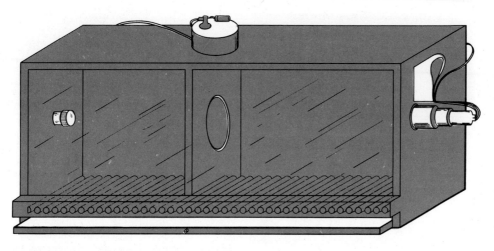

Figure 9-9. A shuttle-box consisting of two compartments separated by a partition. The floor of one compartment is electrified; the other floor is wooden. The animal can escape the shock by running through the door of the partition into the compartment with the wood floor. Visual stimuli are used to signal the onset of shock. (After Bovet et al., 1969.)

Initially the experimenters used a mixed strain of Swiss Webster mice whose performance showed great intersubject variability. Several of the mice were very quick to learn the response; others, agonizingly slow. By successively mating generations of only the "quick learners," group performance improved steadily, as is shown in Figure 9-10. Of course, before concluding that learning was "inherited," other possibilities would have to be ruled out or controlled to a greater degree—sensitivity to shock, sensitivity to light, level of "motivation," and so forth.

The same researchers provide a demonstration of strain-differences in patterns of learning. A variable of traditional concern in the psychology of learning is distribution of practice: Is it better to cram material into one long session or to distribute practice sessions over many short periods? Studies of distributed versus massed practice have led to conflicting findings with results depending strongly upon the specific task chosen for study. Using a maze-learning task, Bovet et al. compared two different strains of mice under conditions in which blocks of 50 trials were massed (uninterrupted) or distributed and separated from 5 minutes to 24 hours.

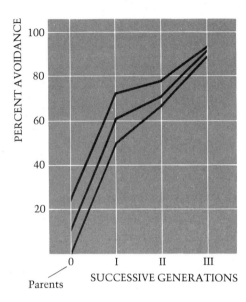

Figure 9-10. Inbreeding for avoidance behavior. Successive generations reveal systematic increases in the percentage of avoidance responses. (After the data of Bovet et al., 1969.)

The effects of these different practice regimens were completely opposite for the two strains! The results are shown in Figure 9-11.

In the research of Bovet, et al., it has been observed that if an animal learns a response—for example, an avoidance response—and is quickly administered a shock to the brain, postshock amnesia for the response occurs. Furthermore, the interval between the response and the shock is crucial. Also certain drugs may be substituted for shock in order to produce the amnesia. Without examining the details, it is sufficient to point out that there are considerable strain differences in degree of amnesia, in the effective response-shock intervals, and in the consequences of different drugs.

Familial Concordance Studies

Studies of familial concordance are based on the assumption that if certain characteristics are strongly influenced by genetic factors, then genetically related individuals will display more similarity (*concordance*) in these characteristics than will unrelated individuals. It is further assumed that the degree of similarity will increase as the degree of genetic relatedness increases. In light of these assumptions, it is easy to appreciate the great interest that has been given to studies of identical and fraternal twins. Identical twins, having identical genetic composition, have been considered ideal "control" subjects for research. Any differences between such twins are not attributable to heredity since they are genetically identical. While genetically dissimilar, fraternal twins do share a gene pool

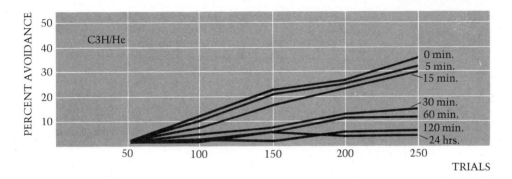

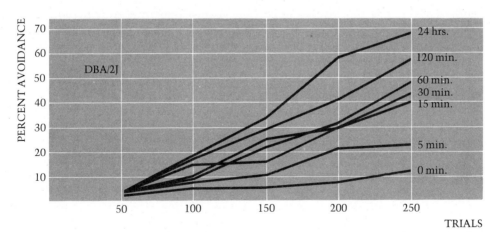

Figure 9-11. Strain differences in the effects of distributed and massed practice. One strain (C3H/He) shows systematic improvement as training trials are spaced closer and closer together. The other strain (DBA/2J) displays the opposite effect. More distributed practice leads to improved performance. (After the data of Bovet et al., 1969.)

much more common to each than it is to any unrelated pair of individuals. Siblings, as much alike genetically as fraternal twins, are born at different times and are exposed to an environment presumably more different than that of fraternal twins, born at the same time. Concordance studies have sought to compare:

1. Identical twins, or MZ's (monozygotic), reared together with MZ's reared apart.
2. MZ's reared together with DZ's (dizygotic or fraternal twins) reared together.
3. DZ's reared together with DZ's reared apart.
4. DZ's reared together with SIB's reared apart.
5. MZ's reared apart with DZ's reared together.
6. MZ's reared apart with SIB's reared together.
7. All of these twins and SIB's with individuals drawn randomly from the unrelated population.

Studies along these lines have been limited by a number of considerations. First, it has not always been easy to distinguish identical twins and fraternal twins, since birth records frequently utilize insufficient criteria for that determination. For example, the sharing of the same amniotic sac is not a guarantee of monozygosity. Similarly, apparently identical appearance is not sufficiently objective or reliable. Determination of monozygosity requires—minimally—a matching of blood types and a matching of footprints and fingerprints. While current hospital practices will allow less uncertainty in future twin studies, many twin experiments in the past involved subjects of questionable zygosity.

A second and more difficult problem in twin research is that of defining the equality of difference of environments. Since psychology has not yet been able to isolate those features of the environment that are essential to normal development, any specification of psychologically different environments is difficult. Given the fact of genetic individuality, every individual lives in a different environment. The unanswered question concerns the nature of those differences that are of *psychological* relevance.

Even when on reasonably firm genetic and environmental footing, concordance studies have difficulty in unambiguously specifying the dependent variables. It is relatively straightforward to administer tests of "personality," "intelligence," and "ability" to twins, siblings, and strangers. It is quite another matter, however, to know just *what* has been measured. To understand this problem, it is necessary for us to examine several basic assumptions of psychological testing.

INTELLIGENCE TESTS

One assumption in intelligence testing is that, as with all psychological and physical attributes, the distribution of intelligence is normal (see Figure 3-3). According to this assumption, most individuals (68 percent) are expected to fall within ± 1.0 S.D. of the average (mean) score. Every test of intelligence must satisfy this assumption, that, if given to a large and randomly selected sample of the population, resulting scores will be normally distributed. The assumption precedes the construction of intelligence tests; the latter are designed in such a way as to satisfy the assumption of normality. Any test that yields abnormal distributions of measured intelligence is revised until it conforms to expectation. If intelligence is similar to other phenotypic characters, it should be distributed normally. But this is merely hypothetical, not factual. Thus, a certain circularity becomes evident in the testing of intelligence: "What is intelligence?" "It is a score on an I.Q. test." "What is an I.Q. test?" "It is a measure of intelligence."

Another basic assumption is that intelligence is a *capacity* and as such is virtually unchanged over the lifetime of an individual. Therefore, every test of intelligence, according to this view, must yield very similar I.Q. scores for the same individual tested repeatedly at different ages. The degree to which a test yields similar results on repeated administration is a measure of the test's *reliability*. Last, and most importantly, since they are assessing capacity, tests of intelligence are expected to be essentially uninfluenced by culture, education, special training, practice, and even motivation. They are designed and revised to confirm this expectation. Since no test is close to perfect in these respects, violations of the assumption are treated either as statistical errors (due to random or uncontrolled influences) or systematic biases due to environmental factors. What this assertion means is this: since intelligence is a capacity, analogous to the volume of a container, a measure of it should not be unduly influenced by experiences (by what is poured into the container). Of course, a more reasonable view considers intelligence to the *ability* rather than capacity. However, this view has been the exception rather than the rule.

Additionally, we still must ask ourselves whether a test measures that which it was designed to measure. This involves the criterion of *validity*. For example, the foregoing assumptions would be satisfied by measures of pulse, shoe size, or height, at least in any individual older than fifteen or sixteen years of age. These measures, however, are not assessments of intelligence. Why not? Principally, because a knowledge of them does not enable a prediction of success in those endeavors presumed to require intelligence. The degree to which a test measures what it has been designed to measure defines the test's validity, but the determination of validity is always arbitrary. For example, if one defines intelligence as the capacity to lift weights, then weight-lifting performance is a valid measure of intelligence. Traditionally, the validity of I.Q. tests has usually rested on their ability to predict academic performance, that is, the capacity to learn in school. It must be noted, however, that there is nothing necessarily valid about this particular criterion of validity. One could just as well use the criterion of financial success or personal satisfaction or desire to improve oneself or number of friends or love of learning. If these were chosen as evidence of intelligence, then conventional I.Q. tests would be less valid.

A graphic example of one type of test validity is shown in Figure 9-12. The ordinate is the grade-point average obtained by students in four years

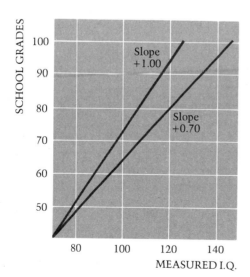

Figure 9-12. Hypothetical data relating performance in school with I.Q. scores. A slope of +1.00 implies a perfect correlation. The slope of +0.70 reflects a high positive correlation.

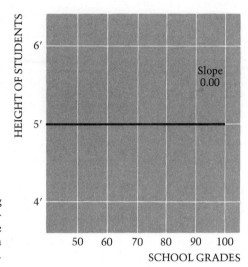

Figure 9-13. Hypothetical data indicating the absence of a correlation between a student's height and his grades in school. The "best fit" line through the above data has a slope of zero; that is, there is no correlation.

of college. The abscissa (baseline) contains a range of I.Q. scores for these students. A best-fit line has been drawn through the points. Clearly the higher the I.Q., the higher the average. The slope of this best-fit line is a measure of the correlation between grades and I.Q. If every unit increase in I.Q. were matched by an exactly equivalent increase in grade-point average, the slope would be +1.0 and the correlation would be (positively) perfect. If the scores produced functions such as those in Figures 9-13 and 9-14, the correlations would be 0 and −1.0, respectively. In the case of a correlation of 0, one would conclude that no relationship existed between I.Q. and academic achievement. A perfectly negative correlation (−1.0) indicates that every increase in one measure is matched by an exactly equivalent decrease in the other.

Most of the frequently used intelligence tests correlate with academic performance to the degree of about +0.4 to +0.6—moderately well. While such correlations are not as high as educators would wish, they are higher than what is obtained using alternatives to I.Q. tests—teacher evaluations, writing samples, and the like. No one can state whether or not these tests are measuring intelligence, but they do appear to be sampling those intellectual characteristics of the individual that are necessary for academic success, assuming that grades are a measure of success.

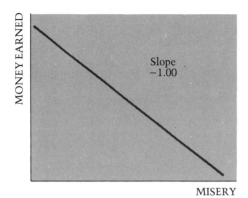

Figure 9-14. Hypothetical data suggesting that the degree of misery decreases exactly as the amount of money earned increases. In this doubtful illustration, each increment in earnings is matched by a corresponding decrease in misery; that is, there is a perfect negative correlation.

Computation of the I.Q. (intelligence quotient) is straightforward. Each test assigns a certain score to successfully completed items. Based on the performance of a very large number of individuals covering a broad range of ages, these scores are converted to age equivalents. That is, based upon normative data, it is known that most people of n years of age are able to answer so many items. The individual is then awarded so many years of mental age on the basis of how many items he has correctly answered. The ratio of his earned mental age (MA) to his true chronological age (CA) is multiplied by 100, and the product is his I.Q. For example, suppose a boy of 10.5 years of age successfully completes all of the items that in the entire population 11 year olds complete, but he completes none of the items that 12 year olds complete. The earned MA is, therefore, 11 and his CA is 10.5. His I.Q. is:

$$\text{I.Q.} = \frac{\text{MA}}{\text{CA}} \times 100 = \frac{11.0}{10.5} \times 100 = 1.048 \times 100 = 104.8,$$

which, rounded to the nearest whole number equals 105.

While I.Q. scores have remained relatively stable over the years, there is some variability. Thus, if an individual is tested every other year for ten years, his scores will vary around some mean. For most I.Q. tests, the standard deviations are obtained from the distribution of scores taken from a large number of different individuals. Taking the value of 10 for the standard deviation (S.D.), this implies that, if John Smith's I.Q. is found to be 100, then repeated measures of his I.Q. will fall between 90 and 110 on 68 percent (±1 S.D. from the mean) of all retests. Similarly, for a large and representative sample, 68 percent of all I.Q. scores will fall within ±1 S.D. from the (sample) mean.

The I.Q. tests that are widely used yield national means of about 100 and standard deviations of approximately 15. An individual with a measured I.Q. of 60, therefore, is considered significantly lower than the general population. A score of 65 is 2.0 S.D.'s below the mean, and random chance would produce a departure this great with less than 5 percent frequency.

Heredity and I.Q.

Numerous studies have examined hereditary factors with respect to measured I.Q. Estimates of the contribution of heredity in the observed variability of I.Q.'s have ranged from 50 to 90 percent. In a summary of fifty-two reported studies, conducted at different times by different investigators using different tests, Erlenmeyer-Kimling and Jarvik (1963) argue convincingly that I.Q.'s become progressively more similar as the degree of genetic similarity increases. Table 3 provides the obtained correlations among related and unrelated subjects' I.Q.'s and the correlations one would expect on the basis of simple Mendelian inheritance.

Applying simplistic arithmetic to these correlations, it would appear that about 20 to 25 percent of the obtained concordance is attributable to "environmental" influences and the balance to "genetic" influences. There are several good reasons, however, why we should avoid conclusions of this sort. First, it is obvious that intelligence, whatever it is, is not passed on by a single gene. Evidence suggests that genes at seventy or more loci are involved in those processes that come to influence mental deficiencies (Morton, 1963). Thus, intelligence must be considered as being influenced *polygenically*, and this fact argues against reliance on narrow Mendelian expectancies. Second, it is still very much debated whether there is "intelligence," or whether there are "intelligences." Theoreticians increasingly tend to treat intelligence as a constellation of different abilities rather than some single, general attribute. Vandenburg (1962) has reported measures of "heritability" of different mental abilities, and the results are summarized in Table 4. Two of the abilities—reasoning and memory—were found to be insignificantly heritable. If only intuitively, it would appear that these two nonheritable abilities converge more on our usual ideas about intelligence than some of the other four shown in Table 4.

TABLE 3.   Correlations for Intellectual Ability Observed and Expected Among Relatives on the Basis of Mendelian Inheritance

Comparison Groups	Observed Correlation	Expected Correlation
Unrelated persons reared separately	−.01	0.00
Unrelated persons reared in same home	+.23	0.00
Parents and children	+.50	+0.50
Siblings reared separately	+.42	+0.50
Siblings reared in same home	+.49	+0.50
Fraternal twins (same sex)	+.53	+0.50
Fraternal twins (opposite sex)	+.53	+0.50
Identical twins reared separately	+.75	+1.00
Identical twins reared in same home	+.87	+1.00

Adapted from Erlenmeyer-Kimling and Jarvik (1963).

Despite these limitations, there is little doubt that genetically identical individuals perform more similarly on I.Q. tests than do unrelated individuals. How this fact is to be interpreted is still open to debate. I.Q. tests tend to sample rather superficial aspects of our overall mental life. Performance is influenced by emotionality, attention, perseverance, and expectations. Of the great number of personal attributes that produce the final I.Q., it remains to be seen which of them are especially influenced by genetic factors. One could whimsically offer an hypothesis to account for the results given in Tables 3 and 4. It may be called the "malleability hypothesis." Assume that genetic factors govern those physiological processes that determine the degree to which an individual is affected by his environment. Assume further, that intelligence is *exclusively* a function of malleable individuals (MZ's) who would be equally sensitive to environ-

TABLE 4. Heritability (h$_r^2$) of Thurstone's Primary Mental Abilities Test Scores in Michigan Twins

Abilities	Computed Value of Heritability	
Numerical	+0.61	(statistically significant)
Verbal	+0.62	(statistically significant)
Spatial relations	+0.59	(statistically significant)
Language fluency	+0.61	(statistically significant)
Reasoning	+0.28	(insignificant correlation)
Memory	+0.20	(insignificant correlation)

Adapted from Vandenberg (1962).

mental pressures and, thus, attain equal I.Q.'s. Unrelated individuals, being differentially malleable, would incorporate aspects of their environments differently, and their I.Q.'s would differ accordingly. Finally, if we assume that the prenatal environment of the womb is uniquely important, then we can predict the sorts of results as given in these two tables.

This hypothesis is intended to illustrate the problem of identifying causal dependencies in an area as complex as that of intelligence. Genes do not transmit traits; they produce variability in the expression of traits. Intelligence, which is a phenotype, is not a "thing" created by genes. Of the many processes on which intellectual behavior depends, genetic composition will result in differences among individuals in regard to these processes. For example, gene action may limit the amount of a particular enzyme produced by an individual. This enzyme may be vital to the formation of photopigment in the rods and cones of the retina of the eye. In the absence of some dietary supplement, this enzyme deficiency may impair color vision. In this case, the departure (variation) from normal color vision may be attributed to variations in enzyme physiology. The gene has not *transmitted* a color deficiency; it has caused a *variation* in enzyme physiology. The latter, a phenotypic phenomenon, might be corrected or aggravated by environmental events such as nutrition. The genotype, therefore, is not precisely or directly obvious from the phenotype; the former does not cause the latter in any fixed sense of the word. Any phenotypic expression is the outcome of an interaction between environmental and genetic factors. Genetic influences affect the intensity and quality of the interaction itself (as in the malleability hypothesis). A leader in this field (Hirsch, 1967) has cautioned:

> Since each genotype has its unique norm of reaction, there is no a priori reason to expect any environmental condition to be universally beneficial or harmful. Some average measure of an environmental influence, therefore, is applicable only to those genotypes affected by it in the same way or, at least, in the same general direction. This means that the characterization of a genotype-environment interaction can only be ad hoc. (Hirsch, p. 422)

It may be informative at this point to consider the frequently reported differences in I.Q. scores obtained from different races, particularly, comparisons between American blacks and whites. The findings presented in Figure 9-15 (Charles, 1936) are not uncommon.

A comparison of mean I.Q.'s reveals a difference of a little more than nine points. About 25 percent of the black children scored higher than

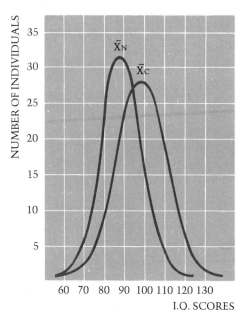

Figure 9-15. Comparison of two samples (Caucasians—X_c, and non-Caucasians—X_n) in terms of measured I.Q. Mean I.Q.'s differ by approximately ten points. (After the data of Charles, 1936.)

the mean for whites, while over 75 percent of the white children exceeded the black mean. For reasons that should be obvious by now, any simplistic interpretation of these differences according to race is without foundation. Two genetically different populations reared in environments that could not be equal display an average difference in phenotype. But the fact that a trait is highly heritable does not necessarily mean that it will not respond to environmental manipulations, that the value of heritability will not change, or that individual members of the group providing the average should be dealt with as if they were the average (or mean).

Heritability is a technical term meaning the fraction of the variance displayed by a given phenotype in a population. Thus, if we know that the heritability of height is 1.0 (that is, the maximum), we can be sure that the total *variance* displayed by a distribution of heights is entirely attributable to the genetic differences present in the population. In other words, what is heritable is not the average value but the variance. The average height of human beings has increased over the centuries, but the heritability of height has not changed. The average height has increased principally because of improved nutrition and general health. Accordingly, the high heritability of height has kept the *variance* of the distribution relatively constant, but the *mean* has increased significantly.

Only those who fail to understand the concept of heritability would argue that because a characteristic is highly heritable the environment is unlikely to affect it. And it takes even more than a lack of understanding to suggest that opportunities be made available to individuals on the basis of the average performance of some group with which they have been arbitrarily identified.

SUMMARY

What we have learned in this chapter is that a psychological event has not been explained once it has been called "inherited." Genes are not diminutive characteristics; they are not little ions of aggression or cheerfulness. It has also been noted that it makes little sense to ask how much of a given trait is under genetic control and how much is under environmental control. These questions are not merely naïve but dangerous as well. They tempt us into believing in a kind of human perfectability, if we could only discover the right combination of genes and settings.

The definable features of living systems, at every level of biological organization, are the result of a constant interplay between those metabolic processes regulated by cellular DNA and those environmental events that would otherwise disturb that biological equilibrium on which continued survival depends. A species survives to the extent that its genetic composition is sufficiently diverse to permit survival over a range of environmental changes. The individual member of the species survives to the extent that its genetic limitations are not exceeded by the demands of the environment and/or to the extent that its behavior can eliminate or reduce the environmental threats. One means of eliminating the threat is simple migration. A more successful means is that form of environmental manipulation we call *invention*. This involves the most complex of human characteristics; it is more than behavior or perception. We can come close to naming it by using the term *personality*. In the next chapter, we will examine this elusive psychological concept.

SUGGESTED READINGS

BIRNEY, R. C. and TEEVAN, R. C., eds. *Instinct*. New York: D. Van Nostrand Co., 1961.

This anthology consists of fourteen excellent papers written for, against, and about the concept of instinct, which will serve as an excellent supplement to Chapter 9.

LORENZ, K. *On Aggression*. New York: Bantam Books, 1969.

Dr. Lorenz writes science as a novel. His plot is evolutionary. His characters are chosen from various reaches of the animal kingdom. His message is classical nativism.

ROBINSON, D. N., ed. *Heredity and Achievement*. New York: Oxford University Press, 1970.

The anthology contains seventeen papers intended to convey the methods and perspectives of behavior genetics. There are prefaces to each major section (Heredity and Learning, Heredity and Personality, Intelligence, Ability, and Race) with a critical discussion of theoretical and experimental issues.

CHAPTER

10

Personality

DEFINITIONS AND ORIENTATIONS

Languages contain words that are *denotative* and others that are *connotative*. We can point to a round, red, sweet-smelling object and say, "apple," and nearly all English-speaking people will agree with our designation and will know what we are referring to. A *denotation*, then, is the more objective term we use to refer to a class of particulars, for example, apples. Terms that are *connotative* must be understood in relation to other terms and they vary more in subjective interpretation. Connotations involve meanings and associations. We think of a warm fire in the middle of winter as *connoting* friendliness and cordiality.

In attempting to define *personality*, we discover that the term as used by psychologists is a rich mixture of denotative and connotative elements: it *denotes* a set of particular behaviors, perceptions, and feelings; it also *connotes* a certain "approach to life," a certain "attitude" about one's self and others. On the purely denotative account, the person with a "disordered personality" is someone who cannot do specific things, who fails to perceive connections of a definable sort, who reliably reports specific, negative feelings. On the connotative account, one has a "disordered personality" when the emotional and rational bases of his life fail to satisfy those conditions that a particular *theory of personality* offers as appropriate.

Contemporary approaches to the subject of personality can be divided along the lines of *denotative* and *connotative* definitions of the subject. This difference in the language used to discuss personality reveals an even more basic difference—that between the *behavioristic* and the *psychoanalytic* schools of psychology. In behavioristic terms, personality can mean no more than a set of particular behaviors frequently emitted by the individual in environments sharing known or knowable features. Once the significant connections between the social environment and the person's behavior have been catalogued, the person's "personality" has been completely defined. That is, there is no personality above and beyond these connections. The "healthy personality," then, is simply environmental-behavioral relationships judged to be appropriate by the person himself and by his society.

Psychoanalytic approaches to personality are fundamentally different from this. The psychoanalyst uses the term *personality* connotatively. Personality is a set of essentially fixed attitudes, beliefs, feelings, and perceptions that the person brings to bear on all environments. As likely as not, this set of characteristics can be found in behavior. Usually, overt behavior conveys some aspects of the personality, but not enough of them for the total personality to be understood. However, the relevant connection is that between personality and behavior, not environment and behavior. A personality of a given "type" will remain relatively constant in a staggering diversity of environments, just as the mechanisms of digestion will remain the same no matter how the diet varies.

Until very recently, these two approaches remained unreconciled and seemingly never to be reconciled. The behavioristic approach had its roots firmly in a radically empiricistic philosophical tradition. Personality, like every other psychological dimension of life, was to be understood in environmental terms, in terms of rewards and punishments, practice, socialization. As we will see shortly, the psychoanalytic movement was conceived by Sigmund Freud, whose pioneering theories were rich in nativistic concepts. Personality in this view must be understood as the stage by stage unfolding of *native* dispositions, essentially genetic forces doing battle with society and never attaining more than an unsteady truce. From these beginnings, psychoanalytic theories of personality drew attention to "types," to inheritance, to physiological differences stamped in at the moment of conception. Personality was just another problem in "individual psychology."

Over the past twenty or thirty years, the barriers separating these competing perspectives, the behavioristic and the psychoanalytic, have been attacked or increasingly ignored. As we noted in Chapter 6, the language and the methods of behavioristic psychology have been adopted more and more even by those who would not call themselves behavioristic psychologists. Nevertheless, psychoanalytic concepts continue to occupy a significant, if more quiet, place in the field of personality study. These concepts still animate theories of personality and still guide therapeutic endeavors. What we find is not so much a declaring of new allegiances as a borrowing of ideas and terms across "party lines." The orthodox Freudian therapist now has less compunction when taking advantage of some conditioning technique developed by those working as "behavior-modification" specialists, and the behaviorist, if the situation calls for it, will comfortably talk of "repression" or a "phobia."

SIGMUND FREUD: A PSYCHOANALYTIC THEORY OF PERSONALITY

A theory, as any creative work, is the product not only of imagination, but of historic conditions. It both rests upon and challenges what has come before. It rearranges the facts in an attempt to secure the truth. The rearrangements are governed by the psychological processes of the theorist— his learning, his perception, his passion. The character of psychoanalytic theory becomes more meaningful when the context of its creation is examined.

Freud was born in Moravia in 1856 and received his doctorate in neurology in 1881. He grew up and lived nearly all of his eighty-three years in Vienna. But Vienna was German and Freud was a Jew. It became clear to him that his ambition to hold a professorial chair in the medical school would never be satisfied because of this. Thus, bigotry was a vital factor in his decision to enter private practice. The scientific climate surrounding his development was exciting, committed, and productive. Darwin's theory of evolution appeared in 1859. Johannes Müller's great laboratory had hosted the incomparable Hermann von Helmholtz, biologist, psychologist, physicist, and leading spokesman for the "new science." German biology and psychology, he asserted, must follow the model of physics. Nothing occurs without a cause. All causes fundamentally are physical; all physical events are measurable. It was von Helmholtz who in 1847 at the age of twenty-six fostered that principle that came to be the Law of the Conservation of Energy: All physical phenomena require energy for their occurrence, and in any closed physical system, the net exchange of energy is zero. In essence, all natural events could be viewed as shifting distributions of energy. The implication for biology was clear: "No other forces than common physical-chemical ones are active within the organism" (Boring, p. 708). So pledged von Helmholtz's colleagues, Emil du Bois-Raymond and Ernst Brücke. It was under Brücke that Freud studied neurophysiology.

The sciences in Freud's formative years were physically oriented and deterministic, but German philosophy retained the Kantian emphasis on nativism. The philosopher's psychology was still fixed upon the mind in all of its dynamic, creative, and mysterious splendor: the mind, which organizes, re-creates, transforms; the mind, with a life of its own, rich with native tendencies. Darwin had established the essential continuity of animal evolution—man included—and had demonstrated the unrivaled importance of instinct in the battle for survival. Von Helmholtz and his following forced biology into the orderliness of physics. Kant had given the mind of man *a priori* knowledge. It remained for Freud to integrate the biological, the physical, and the philosophical and to offer a theory of human psychology that was evolutionary, mechanistic, and instinctual.

In his days as a graduate student, Freud became commited to neurophysiological research and, under Brücke's guidance, made several important contributions. Denied a professorial chair in Vienna and with the responsibilities of marriage imminent, Freud entered private practice. His patient load was heavily weighted with cases of *hysteria*, a diagnostic category designed to embrace a wide range of sensory and motor incapacities of unknown neurological origin. Nearly coinciding with his entry into medical practice was the revival of interest in hypnotism as a therapeutic approach to psychoneurotic disorders. Franz Anton Mesmer (1734-1815) had discovered procedures for inducing hypnotic states, but had used his discovery in such a flamboyant manner that the phenomenon was scorned in professional medical circles. It was not until the respected Jean Martin Charcot summarized his own research in hypnotherapy (1882) that the method began to enjoy some measure of confidence. Freud attended Charcot's lectures at the University of Paris (1885–1886) and returned to his practice armed with the hypnotist's skills. He began to collaborate with Joseph Breuer, a doctor who had also studied under Brücke and who was already treating hysterics with hypnosis. Of the early relationship between Breuer and Freud, Edwin Boring writes:

> Breuer held that a certain amount of the organism's energy goes into intracerebral excitation and that there is a tendency in the organism to hold this excitation at a constant level. Psychic activity increases the excitation, discharging the energy. . . . What Breuer and Freud had from it, however, was the conception of psychic events depending upon energy which is provided by the organism and which requires discharge when the level is too high. Because Brücke had trained them into being uncompromising physicalists, they slipped easily over from the brain to the mind. . . . (p. 709)

Under hypnosis, the patient's hysterical symptoms could be transferred from one part of his anatomy to another. The hysterically paralyzed hand could be made to move while a leg was rendered immobile. Sight could be restored with deafness in its wake. The patient showed no understanding of the cause of his problems and had no explanation for the capriciousness of his symptoms. Breuer had observed that excessive and emotionally charged talking by the patient would often result in partial relief of the symptoms. This process of *catharsis* apparently allowed the dissipation of psychic energies. Catharsis under hypnosis would allow the patient to recall traumatic events that immediately preceded the onset of symptoms. Reliving the episode hypnotically seemed to effect temporary remissions of symptoms.

In 1895, Freud and Breuer summarized their findings in a monograph, *Studies of Hysteria*. They discussed the methods of hypnosis and catharsis and recognized the mechanism of hysteria as being essentially *unconscious:* the patient's behavior was motivated by forces unknown to him. It was not, as many believed, an intentional attempt to gain pity or attention. Moreover, contrary to traditional opinion, Freud and Breuer declared that hysteria was not a uniquely female neurosis. (The word *hysteria* itself derives from the Greek word for *uterus*.)

From this point on, the thought of the two men increasingly diverged. Freud's theorizing led to dramatic departures from tradition, which did not help further his own or Breuer's career. They remained friends, but by 1900 their professional association was on little more than a conversational plane. In 1900, Freud published his *Interpretation of Dreams* and became a figure of great visibility. This was enhanced the following year with the appearance of *The Psychopathology of Everyday Life*. By 1910 he had a following, by 1920 a movement, and by 1930 he was—and has since remained—the preeminent figure in the history of theoretical psychology. Over the period, Freud's position on psychic matters shifted often, and in this respect there is no single "Freudian" psychology. Year by year, he modified earlier ideas, added new concepts, and rejected those that failed to accommodate his transformed conceptualizations. If one is to present a Freudian psychology, he must pass through those decades of theoretical evolution, bringing to each more recent one only those signposts that make the voyage possible.

Unconscious Motivation

The cornerstone of Freud's psychology is the concept of *unconscious motivation*. Behavior is determined by psychic forces whose presence is not accessible to awareness. The idea of unconscious states was not original with Freud. Johann Herbart, the mathematician-philosopher, and Gustav Fechner both postulated the presence of subthreshold sensory events. In Herbart's terms, thoughts journeyed from states of complete excitation (consciousness) to states of complete inhibition (unconsciousness). Fechner, in purely psychophysical terms, spoke of "negative sensations" as those that were correlated with inadequate stimuli. Moreover, great literature from the Bible to Goethe, and especially that created by Shakespeare, was full of allusions to the unconscious. Even the demonology of the Middle Ages, for all of its superstition, reflected a primitive awareness of forces that so gripped the soul of man as to place his actions beyond control.

Freud's direct appeal to unconscious processes was instigated by the peculiar neurotic symptoms of the hysteric. He had to discover a force that was able to control behavior even though the patient was oblivious to the actions of this force. When Breuer's patient was relieved of her hysterical symptoms through hypnosis and catharsis, it was clear to Freud that the power of certain memories to control behavior was reduced once those past events "surfaced." In one respect, the temporary cure was analogous to an exorcizing of evil spirits. Breuer's patient, as it happened, had gone through a terrible ordeal in caring for her father, whose illness ended in death. Her symptoms included paralysis of the right hand and leg, poor vision, irregular eye movements, difficulty in ingesting food and drink, nausea, aphasia, and states of "absence" or delirium. All of these symptoms can occur as a result of *neuro*pathology. But hers were found to be the result of *psycho*pathology. She had been traumatized by her father's illness and death. She had converted the psychic trauma into physical form; hence, the designation of hysteria as a *conversion reaction.* Only when she relived the emotionally agonizing memories of the past was there any remission of symptoms. As long as the supercharged psychic energy remained in the unconscious, the trauma continued to devastate her health.

From this and many similar cases, Freud offered the generalization that, *"hysterical patients suffer from reminiscences. Their symptoms are the remnants and the memory symbols of certain* [traumatic] *experiences."* But only part of the reminiscences live in the patient's conscious recollections. The most influential features, those that carry the full emotional consequences of the trauma, are driven to the depths of the unconscious. The driving force, the mechanism by which the horrors of the past are kept from awareness was called by Freud *repression.* Here, then, was the application, thirdhand (von Helmholtz to Brücke to Freud), of the "conservation of energy" to psychic life. A trauma enters the system, is forced by repression to the otherwise unreachable recesses of the unconscious, and is "conserved" in producing the symptoms of hysteria. Hypnotherapy is only partially successful in allowing a temporary leakage of the repressed energies.

Freud soon became skeptical of hypnosis. As a physicalist, he found it, to use his own words, "a fanciful and, so to speak, mystical aid." As a pragmatist, he was frustrated by its unreliability: "[W]hen I discovered that, in spite of all my efforts, I could not hypnotize by any means all of my patients, I resolved to give up hypnotism and to make the cathartic method independent of it." Freud realized that a remission of symptoms was not a cure and that the patient had to come to grips consciously with those conditions that triggered the mechanisms of repression. The cathartic method (the "talking cure") was augmented by the practice of *free association.* Freud reasoned that neurotic symptoms were the outcome, in part, of the failure of the patient to repress completely memories of the traumatic episode. Events in day-to-day life would often include circumstances and conditions that served to remind the patient of some aspect of the repressed material. Forces—what Freud called *resistances*—were constantly operative in keeping these memories within the unconscious. But the resistances would fail or, by free association, could be "tricked." In encouraging the patient to verbalize freely that stream of conscious thought, in prodding him constantly to react to certain words and ideas, in teasing him into a search for guarded secrets, Freud found that repressed ideas could win over the counterefforts of the patient's resistances. Often, however, when resistance was especially strong, the repressed ideas would emerge in disguised form. On the one hand, the patient wishes to unravel the threads of his unconsciousness; on the other, there is resistance to confronting these repressed events. A compromise is struck. The unconscious surfaced ambiguously, often deceptively, and revealed itself in symbolism. In a manner similar to the formation of conversion reactions, the ideation of the patient became a new symptom in its own right. Freud's treatment of this symbolic appearance of repressed events was extensive. For the present, it is sufficient to consider only the *parapraxes* and *dreams*.

The Unconscious in Disguise

The "Freudian slip" has enjoyed a very wide audience. Freud himself, in adhering to a strict deterministic natural philosophy, was unwilling to treat "slips of the tongue" (*parapraxes*) as simple mistakes or the outcome of random processes. Certainly, some word-chains and sequences of syllables cause frequent mistakes in pronunciation. But there are numerous instances of mistaken speech and writing that appear to be rooted in the communicator's attitudes toward the subject matter: a student, feeling guilty that he has raised an irrelevant topic in class, refers later to the professor's reaction as "brisk" when he meant to say "brusque." Unconsciously, there is an awareness that he took too much of the class time, even an unconscious wish that someone would have cut him short. Consciously, his self-image demands that others are seen as impatient and rude. Thus, "why does he respond so brisk . . . I mean brusquely?" Another example, this one from the writer's own experience, is rather amusing. In the spring of 1970, a degree of campus restlessness was met by a series of liberal proposals by a number of faculty members. One professor, fearing that his motion would be strongly opposed by more conservative colleagues, arose and stated, "I would like to propose the following *revolution* . . . (laughter) . . . I think I meant to say *resolution*. . . ."

The parapraxis to Freud was important not only as a means of identifying crucial contents of the unconscious, but also as *prima facie* evidence of the unconscious control of conscious behavior. In addition to the verbal "slip," Freud wrote extensively on the significance of *wit, errors*, and *forgetting* as symbolic of repressed conflicts. He appreciated the aggressive content of many "harmless" jokes and pranks. He reasoned that they were motivated often by repressed hostility. Similarly, forgetting the name of an enemy, misplacing car keys just before leaving on a trip one does not wish to take, appearing late for a meeting, losing a dental appointment card, all may be symbolic manifestations of negative or hostile emotions.

Far more important than the foregoing, however, in attempting to assess the structure and function of the unconscious is the analysis of dreams. Freud considered *The Interpretation of Dreams* his finest work, and the process of dream interpretation "the *via regia* to the interpretation of the unconscious, the surest ground of psychoanalysis and a field in which every worker must win his convictions and gain his education. If I were asked how one could become a psychoanalyst, I should answer, through the study of his own dreams" (Freud, 1910). The dream, for Freud, is a symbolic fulfillment of the patient's repressed desires. It is the unconscious and distorted working through of a conflict, which if addressed consciously, would be too upsetting to allow sleep. The distortion, again through symbolism, is necessary lest the reality of the conflict invade peaceful slumber and defeat the very purpose of the dream. Thus, dream content is governed by a censor, a psychic mechanism that beclouds the dreamy images, writes false speeches for the dreamy cast, and renders the plot nearly insoluble. On the surface, of course, characters and events may unfold in simple, even transparent fashion. This is what Freud termed the dream's *manifest* content. But the dream is a plot within a plot, and beneath the surface of otherwise harmless happenings there can be found a *latent* content, which embodies the full and true record of repression.

Several means are available by which the content of dreams obscures the underlying content. First, there is *condensation*. The separate features of two or more people, places, or things may be condensed into a single entity. For example, the deceptive *manifest* content may include a brief episode in which a cartoon-like policeman steals an apple and is caught as he trips over several small dogs. Should such a dream recur in the life of a man who resented an authoritarian father for the affection he lavished upon his other children ("little pets"), the latent content clearly would relate to repressed hostility toward the father coupled with the wish for the father's undoing at the hands of his favorites. The manifest content has condensed the father's authority, his unfairness, the other children's smallness and innocence, and the dreamer's complex desires regarding father and siblings into a tidy vignette, almost sparse with respect to detail.

The second means of obscuring the dream's latent content is that of *displacement.* The dreamer assigns his most intense emotional response to an aspect of the dream that in all manifest respects is trivial. Conversely, the dreamer may treat a most grave occurrence with neutral affect or even with joking; for example, he finds himself in the dream attending a funeral and dressed as a clown.

A third feature of dreams that divulges the relationship between manifest and latent contents is that of *dramatization.* Dreams invariably unfold as stories or at least as events running in one direction in time. As a wish fulfillment, the dream takes place in a present time, which in the conscious state is a desired future. The theme of the drama and its style reveal those brooding wishes whose repression caused the dream itself. Is the drama a mystery? Is it a farce? Is there a large cast? An audience? What, indeed, were the themes that motivated this creative exercise of the unconscious?

Finally, there is what Freud labeled *secondary elaboration,* or the patient's conscious re-creation of the dream. Seated in the presence of his analyst, the patient reaches back to the obscure and fragmented images of hallucinated sleep and reconstructs a tale with rhyme and reason. The unique ordering imposed upon the dream by the conscious patient reveals his general view of life and the dominant impressions he entertains of his own condition. Thus, the secondary elaboration uses the dream content as something of a projective test. Presumably, the organization imposed upon it would be quite different for different people even if the content were the same.

Psychic Structure and Development

As Freud's patient-population expanded and became more diverse, he came to realize that neurosis need not be the residual of unitary traumatic episodes. Instead, each individual was engaged in a struggle within himself, and, therefore, to one or another degree, neurosis was the constant companion of every man. Freud was an evolutionist and as such, was committed to the belief that human behavior is predisposed by instinctual drives found elsewhere in the animal kingdom. He accepted Darwin's thesis, which assigned to instincts the principal responsibilty for the survival of the species. However, when applied to man, the hypothesis had to be modified considerably. Man, as Freud viewed him, was conscious, creative, more complex, and potentially infinitely more capable of destruction than any other species. Thus, survival—both of the individual and of the species—required the successful "socialization" of the human animal. Freud termed that constellation of biases, which if unrestrained would loose upon others man's homicidal, incestuous, and sexual instincts, the *id*. Driven by the psychic energy of the *libido*, the passions of the id were constantly threatening to break out and to show man for what instinctually he is—a rapacious, destructive animal mindlessly impelled toward a gratification of his appetites, most important of which was the sexual.

To protect itself from its members, society had evolved customs, taboos, training procedures, laws, and attitudes, which when embraced by the individual forged a morality, a conscience. Freud called these anti-*id* dispositions the *superego*, that which resides "above the self" and is antagonistic to those lusty instincts of self-gratification. The product of these opposing forces, the reconciliation of their competing tendencies was psychological man, himself—the *ego*.

Governed from birth by the *pleasure principle*, the human organism begins his career of sexual gratification early. One of the most shocking concepts Freud was to spring on proper Viennese society was that of *infant sexuality*. In a search that never ends, the infant seeks his first pleasures through a stimulation of *erogenous* (sexually exciting) zones. The first stage of psychosexual development is called the *oral* stage because of the gratification obtained through the act of sucking. Soon after, the *anal* stage ensues during which maximum sexual pleasure is achieved through acts of an anal nature. The child discovers that he can stimulate himself (*autoeroticism*) by thumb-sucking and, later, by genital manipulation. The *phallic* stage leads to the *genital* stage, and psychosexual development concludes when the individual has progressed from autoeroticism to sexual gratification produced by others and when the function of sexual gratification is tied to the motive for reproducing. However, in the process of identifying others as sources of sexual pleasure, the child comes naturally to select his parents: the girl choosing (and being chosen by) her father; the boy, his mother. "But his *libido* must not remain fixed on these first-chosen objects, but must . . . transfer from these to other persons. . . . You may regard the psychoanalytic treatment only as a continued education for the overcoming of childhood remnants." (Freud, 1910) The male's childhood passion for mother and resulting competition with, fear of, and guilt in the face of father creates a collection of psychic disturbances that Freud called the *Oedipus complex.* Socialization forces the oedipal impulses to be repressed, and the damage they do depends upon whether or not the person, in adulthood, can find a suitable (nonparental) substitute for their channeling.

Each stage of psychosexual development is met by the stern mandates of civilized society. Toilet training works in opposition to anality. Thumb-sucking soon is scorned. Masturbation is treated as wicked and sinful. Presumably, society is attemping to hasten the child's commitment to a sexual partner for purposes of procreation. Trauma or failure at any stage causes the child to regress to a previous (successful) stage. Should social or familial restrictions deny access to an open exercise of an earlier form of gratification or should a particular stage be allowed to succeed too long and too effectively, symbolic habits and even "perversions" may result. Moreover, the adult personality will be marked by its dominant period of psychosexual development. The "anal-retentive" personality is guarded, stingy, and acquisitive. The "oral" personality may be verbal, sarcastic, and outspoken. Kissing, smoking, spitting, and gum-chewing have clear oral implications. The "lady's man" who must enjoy intimacy with every woman he meets may well be searching for the mother he was forced to abandon. And so the litany unfolds, laying bare man's basic nature and the goals and motives impelling his multifarious behavior.

Freud escaped from Nazi Germany in 1938 and died in England in 1939. He created an age and contributed a perspective that has changed man's view of himself. He was a giant in the field of psychology.

ADLER AND JUNG

Alfred Adler (1870-1937) and Carl Gustav Jung (1875-1961) were among the earliest and most devoted followers of Freud, although both of them gradually created theories of their own that departed from orthodox

Freudianism. Their departures, however, did not constitute a rejection of Freud's ideas as much as a shift in emphasis.

The Freudian theory of psychosexual development, as incorporated and revised by Adler, became a theory of socialization. Adler interpreted childhood experiences as disposing the individual not merely to patterns of sexual activity, but more generally, to an entire "style of life." The central element in this is the *ego*, and it is in the defense of it that the person's personality reveals the effects of childhood traumas. Of these, feelings of *inferiority* are, by far, the most significant. This is especially the case among first-born children whose younger siblings "dethrone" them from the position of central importance to the parents. However, the pampered child fares no better in that his selfish motives prevent him from enjoying the reality of a well-adjusted, social life.

Among the early members of the psychoanalytic school, it was Adler who most rejected the "medical model" and sought to place psychoanalytic theory in a social as opposed to a purely individual context. We can trace to Adler contemporary practices such as treating the family or treating the community held responsible for the difficulty of the individual in adjusting. It was Adler, too, who drew attention to the compensatory nature of the *superiority complex* and its twin, the *inferiority complex*. The Adlerian system addresses itself to the success and failure experienced by individuals who must cope with society. Their failures are—as Freud would agree—the result of childhood residuals. Most often, these residuals afflict the adult with a sense of inferiority including, but not solely, sexual inferiority. The intensity of the affliction is determined by a constellation of factors and especially those created by parents and the immediate social context; the school, the church, near relatives. For the sickly child, the matter is, of course, much more severe.

As Adler "socialized" the Freudian theory of psychosexual development, Jung extended the Freudian concept of *libido*. It was Jung who argued that, notwithstanding subtle differences and numerous exceptional characteristics among people, all of us tend to fit into one of two classes: *introverts* and *extroverts*. These "types" of personality, according to Jung, do not reflect merely a social style. Rather, they are produced by fundamentally antagonistic processes of the libido. The introvert tends not merely to be shy, but also to be self-punishing, reflective, intuitive, creative, pessimistic, sensitive. The extrovert is extrapunitive, is motivated from without, is controlled more by social realities than by inner feelings. Indeed, so pervasive are the consequences of the libido's direction of flow that it ultimately determines basic attitudes and values.

Freud's evolutionary hypotheses were directed principally at the psychosexual evolution of the individual. The *id* was understood as deriving from our primitive animal heritage, but Freud did not go much further than this in his Darwinian thinking. Jung, however, carried the idea to its logical end: if the *id* is a residual of evolutionary processes, then each individual contains within his unconscious those unconscious processes of all earlier forms of life. That is, the individual possesses a *collective unconscious* through which he is psychologically united with the balance of nature. The combination of a personal, individual unconscious and a collective unconscious forms the psychological identity of the individual. This is what he brings to the world. The social world, however, places demands upon the individual. It requires him to repress certain aspects of his true self and to accentuate aspects that are at variance with the true self. To achieve peace with the world, the individual puts on a mask, a *persona*, and plays that role that stands the best chance of success. The more durable the *persona*, the more difficult it is for the individual to make contact with his collective unconscious where the wisdom of the ages is found: all the knowledge, experiences, and primitive instincts and insights of his ancestry. These ancestral elements occupy the mind in the form of *archetypes*. Thus, the individual is said to be possessed by (or in possession of) such archetypical characters as appear in dreams, fits, or intoxicated states. Our fascination with mythology is but the most superficial sign of deep-rooted, inherited, archetypical ideas and images. One line of evidence presented by Jung to support this theory was drawn from studies of the symbols used by late-Medieval and Renaissance alchemists. These very same symbols frequently occurred in the dreams of his patients despite the fact that they did not recall ever seeing alchemical symbols, or even knowing what an alchemist was.

The central aim in Jungian therapy is the integration and reconciliation of otherwise competing and contradicting tendencies: the integration of life in the "now" with the older and pervasive life of the collective unconscious; the integration of repressed femininity in the male with his maleness and of repressed masculine archetypes in the female with her femaleness; the integration of active, socially prompted strivings with the more basic needs of peace and self-possession. In Jung's terms, these integrations require the process of *individuation*, or to use the current expression, *self-actualization*.

Together, Freud, Adler, and Jung provided the foundations of all contemporary personality theories within what we have called the psychoanalytic tradition. While the so-called *neo-Freudian* theories in contemporary psychology often avoid Freudian terms or Adlerian ideas or Jungian "types," their claims are invariably either reformulations of the older views or downright repetitions. The contemporary "humanistic" theorist, who insists that we have an "undiscovered self" to be liberated by our awareness of our true feelings, by love shared with the community of man, and so on, can be saying nothing more than what Jung said one half century ago. The theorist who draws our attention to the tendency of children to mimic adult models, who warns us of the affects of pampering or overpowering the young, who tells us that delinquency is a compensatory pattern of behavior is, in the last analysis, rediscovering Adlerian psychology.

If there has been a genuinely new contribution to our understanding of these matters, it must be credited to the behavioristic school, which we will now examine.

CLARK HULL: BEHAVIORISM AND PERSONALITY

The school of behaviorism most closely identified with B. F. Skinner has had less influence on the psychology of personality than it has had on the other many areas of psychology. Part of the reason for this is that the "Skinnerian" approach has always been opposed to theorizing, and this opposition has, until recently, preserved a certain distance between the Skinnerian psychologist and the very concept of personality. Perhaps a more significant reason is that the methods and the language of Skinnerian behaviorism do not seem to be applicable, at first glance, to a study as complex as personality. That is, the bridge from one to the other appears to be too long.

It is not surprising that the earliest attempts to place personality within a behavioristic context were made not by Skinnerian behaviorists, but by those coming from a more theoretical and biological background in behaviorism. The most important exponent of this school of behaviorism was the Yale psychologist Clark Hull (1884-1952), whose theory we discussed briefly in Chapter 6. While not concerned directly with personality, Hull advanced a theory of learning that proved to be surprisingly applicable to personality and, even more surprisingly, at one with psychoanalytic theories.

Hull's Theory of Learning

In 1943, Clark Hull's *Principles of Behavior* was published with none of the clamor, excitement, and consternation that greeted *The Psychopathology of Everyday Life*. With respect to dreams, personality, neurosis, mind, sexuality, child development, perception, Hull's index was deadly silent. He announced his intentions as the setting down of those "behavioral laws underlying the 'social' sciences," but nowhere in his 422 pages can one find even a reference to most of what the social sciences take as their own. Instead, the book is filled with graphs and equations, with discussions of hunger and reflexes, with measures of salivation, and with scores of rats in harnesses pulling weights down runways. And yet, no less than Freud, Hull offered psychology a perceptive, integrated, and, in its own special way, compelling theory of the causes of behavior. His literary style was heavy, and he allowed himself none of the rich metaphorical devices that enlivened the works of Freud. Hull was methodical, almost plodding. He had little patience for opinion and none whatever for unverifiable intuition.

> In the view of the scientifically sophisticated, to make an incorrect guess whose error is easily detected should be no disgrace; scientific discovery is in part a trial-and-error process, and such a process cannot occur without erroneous as well as successful trials. On the other hand, to employ a methodology by which it is impossible readily to detect a mistake once made, or deliberately to hide a possible mistake behind weasel words, philosophical fog, and anthropomorphic prejudice, slows the trial-and-error process, and so retards scientific progress (Hull, pp. 398-399)

Notwithstanding these differences, Hull did share certain similarities with Freud. Hull, too, was a Darwinist, but he focused on the adaptive features of *observable behavior* rather than the instinctual basis of mental life. Hull also entertained a mechanistic conception of psychology. (His hobby was making robots!) Like Freud, he assumed the presence of those biological mechanisms necessary to account for his observations. However, he was far more conservative in his selection of such hypothetical biological mechanisms. Unlike Freud, he was unwaveringly committed to the experimental approach—to what is called the *hypothetico-deductive method.* In Hull's theory, this method involved a three-stage process. First, given available information based upon rather general observations, an hypothesis is advanced to account for a relationship. The hypothesis, as a general principle, predicts certain particulars. In the second stage, these particulars (deductions) are tested experimentally. Finally, the experimental findings are used to support, modify, or abandon the initial hypothesis. His labored devotion to the method yielded sixteen major principles (postulates) and an even greater number of corollaries. His book contains seven pages of symbols and hundreds of equations. Only the highlights of the Hullian system can be offered here, but these should be enough to convey the kind of psychological theory that springs from an empiricistic orientation.

    Hull's theory is associationistic and hedonistic. It is a "learning theory" in the tradition of Thorndike and Pavlov. In his first two postulates, he acknowledges that stimulation must register in the nervous system to be effective and that within the system constant sensory interactions occur. Appreciating that nervous tissue is never completely silent, he recognizes that a certain instability of behavior is inevitable. He calls his *oscillation* and thus sets the stage for what is really a *probabilistic* behavior theory. While cautious in assigning "endowed traits," to the organism, Hull recognizes the essentiality of certain unlearned stimulus-response connections. Conditions that threaten survival create needs that instinctively impel behavior. The needs are therefore considered as primary animal drives (*D*). He illustrates the relationship between drives and behavior with data like those shown in Figure 10-1. Using hunger pangs as a measure of need, this figure indicates that restless movements increase during sleep as hunger becomes more intense. Numerous findings support such a relationship. This leads to Hull's third postulate, one of the few that falls back on nativistic determinants. It states that from birth, organisms under condiions of primary drive are more likely to emit certain behaviors than others. Any stimulus that reduces the intensity of a primary drive is a primary reinforcer, and under conditions of primary drive, responses that have led to drive reduction in the past are most likely to be emitted. This fourth postulate is Hull's restatement of the Law of Effect. However, he derives a number of specific relationships from it that were not uncovered by earlier theorists. He argues, first, that each reinforcement increases some undefined quantity of learning, which he calls "habit." Thus, the strength of a habit is proportional to the number of reinforcements. Hull chose the term

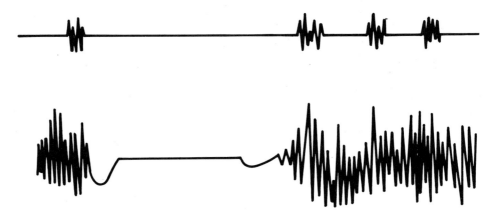

Figure 10-1. Restless sleep and stomach contractions. The top trace indicates the restless movements of a subject who is asleep. The lower trace shows the pattern of gastric contractions correlated with these movements. (After the data of Wada, 1922.)

habit to represent those processes by which certain stimuli and certain responses become connected. In his notation, $sH_R = f(N)$, *habit strength* is a function of the number *(N)* of reinforcements. Among other measures, Hull used speed of response as a measure of habit strength. In addition to the frequency of reinforcement, habit strength is affected by the quality, quantity, and delay of reinforcement as well. Illustrative of the dependency of habit strength upon the delay of reward are shown in the data plotted in Figure 10-2. The greater the delay, the weaker the strength of the habit.

In strict associationistic fashion, secondary drives and secondary reinforcers are created by occurring in the same time and space with primary drives and reinforcers. Moreover, these secondary, or acquired, drives and reinforcers obey the same laws as those of primary drives and reinforcers. Principal among these laws is that of *stimulus generalization*. Hull realized that strictly speaking, drives and reinforcers never repeat themselves identically. The animal learns, however, because habit strength, which is increased by specific conditions, generalizes to stimuli in the vicinity of conditioned stimuli. He invented the concept of *effective habit strength* $(s\overline{H}_R)$, which is maximum (equal to sH_R) when no difference exists between separate reinforcing conditions, but which becomes weaker and weaker than sH_R when new conditions become physically more dissimilar to those prevailing at the time sH_R *was first established*. (Refer to Chapter 6 for data and a further discussion of generalization).

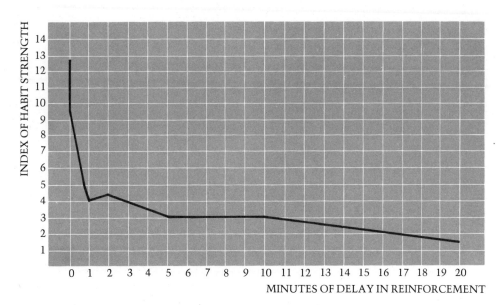

INDEX OF HABIT STRENGTH

MINUTES OF DELAY IN REINFORCEMENT

Figure 10-2. Response strength diminishes as the interval between the response and the application of reward increases. Note that the greatest decrement occurs in the first minute. (After the data of Wolfe, 1934.)

Neither habit strength (sH_R) nor effective habit strength ($s\overline{H}_R$) is sufficient, however, to predict when behavior will occur. For example, if an individual knows how to drive a car, this habit is with him always, although it is not always expressed. In the Hullian system, sH_R and $s\overline{H}_R$ represent learned abilities to perform, but do not determine that performance will occur. Two other variables interact with $s\overline{H}_R$ in determining when a given response will occur. These variables are drive (D) and inhibition (I). Drives have, according to Hull, a multiplicative effect on the likelihood of a response. In Hullian terms, $sH_R \times D = sE_R$, where sE_R is an "excitatory potential." To use the earlier example, the learned driving habit is more likely to be expressed when the need to get home is great. This effect of drive-level upon response probability is shown in Figure 10-3. Using responses-to-extinction as a measure of learning, the difference between low (3 hours) and high (22 hours) food-deprivation condition is seen. The "hungrier" animals are far more resistant to extinction.

However, even when drives (motivations) are high and habits strong, responses may not occur. Again using the automobile example, the driver

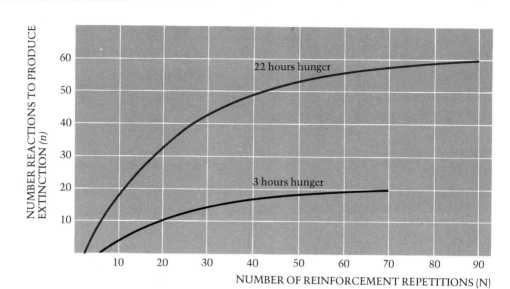

Figure 10-3. The effects of drive on extinction. The two curves above denote the responses of the organism during extinction (nonreinforcement) as a function of the number of reinforcements delivered during original learning. Under the conditions of strong hunger (22 hours without food), there is much more responding during extinction than under the conditions of weak hunger (3 hours without food). (After the data of Perin, 1942.)

may have been driving for many hours and still be quite a distance from home. Fatigue sets in, and despite a great desire to get home (high D) and all of the skill (sII_R) necessary, he is forced to stop. Hull hypothesized that each response-occurrence produces the build-up of a fatigue substance, an inhibitory process. By conditioning, certain stimuli would reliably come to elicit this inhibitory "potential" (I_R). Both the response-produced inhibition (I_R) and the conditioned inhibition (sI_R) combine to reduce the likelihood of a response. This combined and total inhibition ($\dot{I}_R$) works in opposition to the excitatory potential. The residual of this interaction was termed, by Hull, the *effectve reaction potential* ($s\bar{E}_R$):

$$s\bar{E}_R = sE_R - \dot{I}_R$$

Finally, to predict the moment-to-moment probability of a response, a correction for "oscillatory," or random, fluctuations is necessary. Thus, the *momentary effective reaction potential* $(s\dot{\bar{E}}_R)$ is expressed in the equation:

$$s\dot{\bar{E}}_R = {}_s\bar{E}_R \text{ modified by } sO_R$$

Since response-produced inhibition (I_R) is fatigue, it will lessen with time. Thus, if learned behavior does not occur when D and sH_R are both high, it will occur once sufficient time has elapsed for the weakening of (I_R).

"Hullian" Theories of Personality

The foregoing sketch has probably given you an indication of the way a "Hullian" might approach the concept of personality. Suppose, for example, the starved rat who has received rewards by running down a runway, in the past, now meets an obstacle. The rat will initiate those behaviors that, in the past, have successfully removed obstacles; that is, the rat will emit *aggressive* behavior toward the obstacle. If under these circumstances, a toy rat is dropped next to the animal, the aggressive behavior will now be directed at the toy. This is a model of what is called *displacement* in psychoanalytic literature. The person frustrated by his supervisor but unable to behave aggressively toward him will *displace* the aggression onto a nonthreatening object or person. For example, he might kick a wastebasket or insult a friend.

In the above example, we see an instance of the reliable connection between frustration and aggression. Frustration creates high levels of drive (in the Hullian system), and aggression is a form of behavior that reduces drive. That is, in the animal's (or person's) history of reinforcements, there has been a reliable association between aggression directed against an obstacle and the removal of that obstacle. Thus, aggression becomes a means of coping. In its more complex form, it is "compensatory." Here, then, we can see the behavioristic version of a concept that Adler in particular advanced in the psychoanalytic tradition.

It is also possible to create intense conflict in experimental animals. For example, the hungry rat may have to cross a charged grid in order to obtain food. That is, the competing drives for food and shock-avoidance may be made equal, so that the animal's tendency to approach the food is counteracted by the tendency to avoid shock. In such circumstances, the animal will display a behavioral paralysis: first lunging, then retreating; then lunging, then retreating. The animal may also display physiological signs of conflict: quivering, defecation, urination, even ulcerations in the digestive system. Is this not akin to the Freudian idea of a "conversion reaction" in which the hysterical symptom is the physical sign of a psychological conflict?

Some psychologists believe that attempts to reduce personality to these behavioristic concepts and operations are, at best, naïve and simplistic. Others, however, find in the behavioristic approach not only a useful means of describing and organizing the factors responsible for the disordered personality, but even a means of treating that disordered personality. It is this latter group that provides "behavior-therapy" and "behavior-modification" treatments.

While the success of such efforts has been limited, their very presence indicates the surprising degree of elasticity in Hull's theory. It is a general theory of psychology despite its ponderous equations and well-documented arguments. Hull himself viewed it as a modest beginning, the most one could do with the limited data available. He reviewed his labors, proclaimed his hopes, and admitted his fears as such:

> If one may judge by the history of the older sciences, it will be a long time before the "social" sciences attain a status closely approximating that contemplated here. . . . The task of systematically developing the behavior sciences will be both arduous and exacting. . . . Progress in this new era will consist in the laborious writing, one by one, of hundreds of equations: in the experimental determination, one by one, of hundreds of the empirical constants contained in the equations; . . . in the meticulous performance of thousands of critical quantitative experiments and field investigations. . . . There will be encountered vituperative opposition from those who cannot or will not think in terms of mathematics; from those who are apprehensive of the ultimate exposure of certain personally cherished superstitions and magical practices. . . . (Hull, pp. 400-401)

BEHAVIORAL MODIFICATION

The principles of reinforcement already discussed in Chapter 6 and the theory of learning advanced by Clark Hull have both been adopted by many psychologists engaged in the treatment of psychological disturb-ances. Their efforts, although varied and altered to meet the unique re-quirements of each situation, are generally listed under the heading of *behavior-therapy* or *behavior-modification*. This terminology is appropriate not because the psychologists who identify their procedures with it all conform to the same methods and theories, but because all these psy-chologists consider psychological disturbances to be rooted in *behavioral* problems.

Psychoanalytic theories such as those advanced by Freud, Adler, and Jung turn to the underlying causes of conflict, to childhood traumas, to interferences with otherwise fixed and natural stages of development in an attempt to explain the abnormal personality. Behavioristic psychology confines itself to the observable features of psychological life, to behavior and those variables in the environment that have a controlling influence on behavior. With this view, psychological adjustment becomes *behavioral* adjustment, and a disordered personality is no more than a collection of behaviors failing to support the motives of the individual. The motives themselves are no more than the sorts of things the person claims to want. A very simplified illustration might make it clearer how the psycho-analytic and the behavioristic psychologists differ in their perspectives and, therefore, in their methods.

The disorder we will use in our illustration is that of *school phobia*. It is not uncommon for the young child, just beginning to attend primary school on a full-time basis, to display a monumental fear of the school. He screams and cries when told that he must get ready for his classes. He runs away from the schoolroom at the first opportunity. He hides from teachers and friends. He may also develop symptoms of illness and claim that he is too sick to leave home.

Psychoanalytic theory offers many explanations in a case such as this. The child may, for example, not really fear the school, but rejection by his mother. That is, as he approaches the earliest stages of an Oedipal relationship with her, he develops the earliest signs of fear of rejection. He may also view the teacher as one who will vie for his affections with his mother or who may discover inadequacies of his and proceed to make them known to his mother. Then, too, his leaving for school may give a younger sister or brother his mother's full attention, so that the real source of fear is the prospect of being replaced by baby brother or baby sister. Having decided on the most likely source of fear, the therapist will counsel parents and teachers accordingly. To discover the source of the fear, however, it is necessary to have lengthy interviews with both parents, to probe the child's mind with questions, tests, or mock games, to examine the child's drawings, and so forth.

The behavioristic psychologist will tend to reduce this problem to one of getting the child to go to school willingly. He will be largely indifferent to so-called deep and underlying causes and principally concerned with the *obvious* causes. There is something about the school that the child finds not to his liking; something about the home that the child finds positive. Thus, if the pleasure-producing stimuli of the home are moved closer and closer to the school, and, finally, can only be secured by entering the school, the child will behave in a way that will make him want to go to the school. It might even be appropriate for the child to awaken and find that his mother is not at home and to be told that she is at school waiting for him. Usually, far less drastic methods will succeed. Essentially, the child is confronted by "reinforcement contingencies" that work to increase the probability of his moving in the direction of the classroom. Unwanted behavior is extinguished through nonreinforcement; desired behavior is strengthened through positive reinforcement. Hidden variables such as an Oedipal complex are completely ignored or translated into meaningful terms that are behavioral and environmental.

If we look only at what the psychoanalyst and the behavior therapist are doing, we might be tempted to conclude that there really is very little difference between them. Both, for example, might attempt to change the mother's behavior in an attempt to affect the child's behavior. Both may instruct the teacher to do or say this or that to encourage the child. But despite the superficial similarity in their instructions and procedures, the psychoanalyst and the behaviorist offer radically different concepts for what might be responsible for the child's fear and conduct.

The difference between psychoanalytic and behavioristic conceptions is further illustrated in the matter of the *heritability of personality*. Recall in Chapter 9, the discussion of the interest psychology has in the genetic foundations of such psychological characteristics as intelligence. Psychology is equally interested in the genetic foundations of personality, although from a behavioristic perspective, this interest often seems misplaced. Since we do not inherit our behavior and since environmental manipulations are often dramatically successful in altering our behavior, why would anyone be interested in something as doubtful as "the inheritance of personality"? Even to raise this question is to raise all sorts of subsidiary issues about measurement and meaning: What is personality? How is personality to be measured? What is a "unit" of personality?

THE "MEDICAL MODEL"

A number of influential writers, particularly Professor Thomas Szasz, have argued convincingly for the abandonment of the "medical model" in dealing with problems of personality and adjustment. Unlike diabetes or cancer, diseases in which pathological changes occur in tissue, so-called psychological diseases are often no more than perceptual or behavioral characteristics different from those usually confronted in the "normal" population. Specialists in the mental health field may elect to call such individual differences instances of disease, but the customary signs of disease are simply not present. Indeed, Dr. Szasz has defined psychiatry as that medical specialty which treats patients *without* diseases. In this connection, it is worth noting that at a recent annual convention of the American Psychiatric Association, it was decided *on the basis of a vote* that homosexuality is not a disease. It would be inconceivable that specialists in, for example, neurosurgery, would vote that brain tumors are no longer diseases or, for that matter, that they are.

Once the medical model is surrendered, psychological problems take on the character of specific behavioral problems or of mere idiosyncracies. The "patient" becomes a "client"; therapy becomes "management"; the goal moves from "cure" to "change."

PERSONALITY AND GENETICS

The limitations and qualifications discussed in connection with intelligence and genetics also apply to the relationship between personality and genetics—even more so. There is far greater agreement among both professionals and laymen about what intelligence is than there is about personality. Numerous descriptive terms have been used to classify personality "types": aggressive-submissive, optimistic-pessimistic, euphoric-depressive, hostile-congenial, radical-temperate, volatile-stable, honest-devious, trusting-suspicious. Each implies some sort of continuum with those individuals who fall in the extremes considered abnormal, if only statistically. The measurement of personality varies according to definitional assumptions, cultural norms, and the theoretical context within which the personality test was developed.

As noted at the beginning of this chapter, personality types are defined either in terms of observable behavior, in terms of inferred or reported feelings, or in terms of both. Thus, an individual who is opinionated, loud, and unrestrained is said to have an aggressive or hostile personality. Yet within a different context, a mild-mannered individual may be labeled aggressive if he reports the presence of aggressive feelings or hostile dispositions. Finally, some personality theorists contend that a personality may be aggressive in the absence of aggressive behavior *and* in the absence of any conscious awareness of aggressive thoughts or motives. Thus, definitions of personality differ in terms of the criteria of classification. Definitions also differ in relation to presumed causes. In some schemes, personality is a constitutional (genetic) constellation of behavioral dispositions; in others, a learned (empirical) set of tendencies. Finally, definitions vary in their relative emphasis upon either the persistence or the mutability of personality. The former emphasis treats personality as a relatively static and enduring aspect of the organism, which allows predictions of behavior under widely differing circumstances. The latter emphasizes the dynamic and adaptive aspects of personality by which predictability requires a knowledge of the specific situation in which the personality is called on to function. As with intelligence, personality is usually viewed in part as the consequence of constitutional forces and in part as the product of situational pressures.

Social and Cultural Biases

Contemporary views of personality have developed within the context of Western traditions, and they bear the indelible signs of that influence. In attempting to respect other perspectives, scientists studying cultural differences in personality have begun to use "culture-free" projective tests, such as the Rorschach inkblot test. However, there is often a failure to appreciate cultural differences in attitudes about testing, attitudes about strangers, motivations to succeed, reactions to instruction, and so on. Even within a culture, there are often subcultures whose expectancies, attitudes, and orientations depart substantially from the norms of the larger social organization. For example, within the American culture, different groups may have widely different attitudes about privacy, attitudes that might affect their responses to questions on a personality test. All of this is to say that one major obstacle in the study of personality is the relativistic nature of the phenomenon itself.

Theoretical Biases

Personality tests—as all instruments of measurement—are products of a set of theoretical assumptions; for example, that a variable is normally distributed, that an attribute is "good" or "bad," that a condition is universal or unique. To this extent, assessments of personality are of questionable validity, since the theoretical context from which they arose is itself not valid. For example, if Theory A considers aggression a basic fact of human life and Personality Test A includes items designed to "measure" (detect) aggressiveness, then individual A who fails to display aggression is assumed to have repressed it. That is, the theory insists it *must* be there. Thus, when A doesn't show it, he must be hiding it. It is this type of theoretical circularity that has held back advances in the field of personality.

A great diversity of tests exists. These tests are designed to "measure" personality. Their validity, for reasons just noted, is an open question. Their reliability is not as great as that of I.Q. tests, nor have they enjoyed the same extensive correlational analyses that characterize the history of intelligence testing.

Two major types of personality tests are in use. Each includes many subtypes. One, the *objective test*, is a questionnaire, completed by the subject and scored by hand or machine. The test may be limited to 20 to 30 items or, as in the case of the Minnesota Multiphasic Personality Inventory (MMPI), may contain as many as 500 or 600 items. The items chosen depend on the definitional, cultural, and theoretical influences at work. Personality, considered as a self-image, will be assessed by statements pertaining to self: for example, "I often feel inadequate"—"I seldom feel inadequate." Personality, considered as an approach to the world, will lead to items such as, "I would/would not strike someone who offended my mate." The scoring of objective personality tests (inventories) is based on cultural norms, and the final assessment is always relative to these specified norms: for example, individual *A* is aggressive relative to white, middle-class American males between seventeen and twenty-one years of age. It should be noted that the *objectivity* of such tests relates to the methods of scoring and not to the test items themselves.

The second type of personality test is the *projective test*. It is unstructured in that the individual's responses are essentially unlimited by the test. The assumption underlying projective tests is that in an ambiguous setting, the individual will impose order and meaning of a kind dictated by the dominant features of his personality. Three popular projective tests are the Rorschach test, the Thematic Apperception Test (TAT), and the Draw-a-Person (DAP) test. In Figures 10-4, 10-5, and 10-6, an example of each of these tests is given, with an explanation of what is expected of the subject in each case.

By combining objective and projective tests with personal interviews, family histories, and evaluations by peers, the clinical psychologist is able to classify certain personalities as "abnormal" and to assess the relative

Figure 10-4. An inkblot similar to a Rorschach inkblot. An observer is instructed to describe the images he perceives in the card.

Figure 10-5. A picture similar to a TAT card. The observer's task is to describe, in story form, what is taking place in the scene, what might have led to it, and how it will end.

degree of abnormality—borderline psychotic, moderately depressive, and so forth (nominal scaling). The question naturally arises as to whether or not equivalent assessments are reached in testing genetically related individuals. That is, is personality as categorized by these techniques a highly *heritable* aspect of the individual?

Rosenthal (1962) summarized the results of four different studies of the incidence of schizophrenia among male and female twins, both identical, or monozygous (MZ), and fraternal, or dizygous (DZ). Table 5 is adapted from this summary. Research findings generally implicate hereditary predispositions to abnormal personality development, and they also reveal higher same-sexed concordance than that found among different-sexed pairs of relatives.

In an exhaustive study, Gottesman (1963) reported high familial concordance on a broad range of personality attributes. Significantly, many personality traits showed greater dependence on environmental factors; others, upon genetic factors. Thus, it would appear that hereditary influences are sufficient to account for some of the differences (variability) in personality observed across groups of individuals segregated on the basis of genetic relatedness.

Figure 10-6. The Draw-a-Person test. A young child, seeking to escape from a loud and punishing father who never listens to the child's side of an issue, may draw an adult lacking ears (as above).

WHAT IS A DISORDERED PERSONALITY?

So far, we have examined psychoanalytic and behavioristic approaches to the issue of personality and have noted that personality disorders have been treated either by conditioning techniques or by therapeutic measures resulting from psychoanalytic theories. Moreover, we have observed that certain personality disorders display high heritability. However, although competent psychologists all agree on the data, there is growing suspicion that the very concept of a "diseased" personality is invalid.

Traditionally, the conditions of mental health appearing in a society have been categorized as *normal, neurotic,* and *psychotic.* These traditional categories are further divided according to characteristic symptoms observed in a population of patients:

NEUROSES	*PSYCHOSES*
Phobia	Schizophrenia:
Mania	Hebephrenia
Multiple Personality	Catatonia
Obsession	Paranoid
Compulsion	"Simplex"
Hysteria	Paranoia
	Manic-Depressive
	Involutional Melancholia

TABLE 5. Correlations Between Identical and Fraternal Twins Obtained from Responses to Measures of Personality Characteristics

MMPI Scale	(MZ Female Twins)	(DZ Female Twins)	(MZ Male Twins)	(DZ Male Twins)	TOTAL MZ	TOTAL DZ
Hypochondriasis	n.s.	n.s.	n.s.	n.s.	++	n.s.
Depression	+	n.s.	+	n.s.	++	n.s.
Hysteria	+	++	++	n.s.	++	++
Psychopathic Deviate	+	n.s.	++	n.s.	+++	n.s.
Psychasthenia	+	n.s.	n.s.	n.s.	++	n.s.
Schizophrenia	++	n.s.	++	n.s.	+++	n.s.
Social Introversion	+	n.s.	++	n.s.	+++	n.s.
Ego Strength	n.s.	++	n.s.	n.s.	n.s.	++
Anxiety	+	n.s.	+	n.s.	++	n.s.
Repression	n.s.	n.s.	n.s.	n.s.	n.s.	n.s.
Dominance	n.s.	n.s.	++	n.s.	++	n.s.
Dependency	++	++	n.s.	n.s.	+++	n.s.
Social Status	n.s.	+++	++	n.s.	++	+++

n.s. = statistically insignificant.
+   = statistically significant.
++   = highly significant.
+++ = very highly significant.

The neurotic patient, according to the traditional classification, is intensely anxious and troubled. The symptoms may take the form of unreasonable, crippling fear (phobia) or uncontrollable excitability (mania), or psychosomatic illnessess (hysteria), or multiple, rational identities (multiple-personality), or ideas and thoughts that cannot be driven from the mind (obsession), or uncontrollable, repeated actions of a ritualistic nature (compulsion). These neurotic symptoms, although disabling and punishing to the individual, do not involve a complete dissolution of the personality. That is, the individual remains aware of himself and his surroundings. He can think and behave rationally; he can converse and be treated. In fact, it is precisely because he is aware that his fears or obsessions are not natural that he seeks help.

The psychotic patient is quite different. Typically, there is neither fear nor anxiety. Rather, there is a fundamental break between the historical individual and the present reality. The *schizophrenic* "break" may take the simple form of physical isolation (for example, the hermit), or it may take the form of a speechless and motionless suspension of action (*catatonia*), or it may involve a regression to infantile conduct and perception (*hebephrenia*), or it may involve the creation of an entirely new "reality," one filled with delusions of persecution or grandeur (*paranoid*). The *manic-depressive* psychosis, as the term suggests, means that the patient suffers uncontrollable swings in mood from a nearly frantic optimism to a suicidal depression. In neither case is the mood rationally connected to the realities of the situation.

The same is true of *paranoia.* Unlike the paranoid schizophrenic, the *paranoiac* seems reasonable. His explanation of why he has been hospitalized is often convincing; for example, he has written an exposé of a political leader and to keep the truth suppressed, powerful men have had him put away. However, although the story is convincing and delivered in a sincere and almost documentary fashion, it is totally false.

In *involutional melancholia,* we have what has been traditionally described as a "benign" psychosis; one that clears itself up in time; one related to menopausal changes in the individual's hormonal chemistry. Still, the melancholia can be severe enough while it lasts to cause suicide and is always severe enough to prevent rational, social relationships.

For more than a century, these classifications have filled the textbooks and journals devoted to psychiatry, psychotherapy, and the disordered personality. Increasingly, however, there is a tendency to move away from the labels and away from the very idea that psychological problems are diseases. Even the specialty of psychiatry finds the "medical model" too confining. In place of the older classification, we now find the introduction of behavioristic language or the language of the pharmacologist. Yesterday's manic-depressive is today's lithium-deficient patient. Yesterday's involutional melancholiac is today's "client," obtaining a new behavioral repertoire with which to adapt to the environmental demands of a new life-circumstance.

SUMMARY

It is too early to determine how much of the traditional psychoanalytic movement will survive the contemporary trend toward behavioristic sociological, and biochemical explanations. On a strictly materialistic account, we have to assume that *personality* can only be a word invented to represent certain brain states and that, accordingly, alterations of the chemistry and physiology of the brain will alter the personality. To show, then, that personality is heritable is only to show that certain biochemical substances and processes "run in families." Theoretically, personality should be as manageable as diseases such as diabetes or anemia.

On a strictly environmentalistic or radical-empiricistic account, personality can mean no more than the sum total of the historic influences on the individual, and it should be alterable by the same procedures that were responsible for the form it now takes. Thus, the issue is not one of disease or health, but one of *adaptation*. Mr. Smith's behavior or personality might seem "sick" at this time, in this culture, under these circumstances, but it would be most appropriate at some other time and place. All we have to do, if society is unwilling to modify its expectations, is to modify Mr. Smith's behavior so that it is more closely adjusted to the prevailing expectations.

The proponents of the several schools we discussed tend—as proponents will—to speak with a certain assurance and finality on these matters. However, a prudent audience will recognize that psychology has yet to settle the matter of personality and has not even settled the matter of how one would go about settling the matter.

SUGGESTED READINGS

FREUD, S. An Outline of Psychoanalysis. New York: W. W. Norton, 1969.

There is so much that is *implicit* in Freudian theory that, when possible, it is best to read Freud, himself. This selection contains the essentials of Freudian thought.

FREUD, S. *The Interpretation of Dreams.* London: Hogarth, 1953.

This work was considered by Freud to be his best. Dreams, to use Freud's expression, are the *via regia*—the royal road—to the unconscious. It is in this book that this notion is fully developed.

TEEVAN, R.C. and BIRNEY, R. C., eds. *Theories of Motivation and Learning.* New York: D. Van Nostrand Co., 1964.

Selections from Hull, Miller and Dollard, Tolman, and Estes are included. They comprise an excellent supplement to the discussion of Hull given in this chapter. The critical review of drive concepts by J. S. Brown is also highly recommended.

CHAPTER

11

Motives, Feelings, and States

This is another of three chapters that we will devote to vexed issues in psychology. Unlike learning and memory (Chapter 6) or perception (Chapter 5), these issues have yet to be studied with a consistent set of measurements and procedures. Indeed, what sets them apart from the issues treated earlier in this book is that they probably cannot be treated effectively until these other issues have been even more fully explored. We cannot begin to discuss *motivation* constructively, for example, until we have already examined reinforcement, maturation, heredity, social influences, and neurophysiology.

In addition to being difficult to analyze, complex processes such as *personality, motivation, emotion,* and *language* are key to the entire discipline of psychology, because the positions we arrive at with respect to these issues will determine the essential character of our system of psychology. For example, we might accept a theory of learning that is purely associationistic.

369

We may finally agree that all conduct is the result of rewarded practice. And we may even accept an extreme empiricistic view that all knowledge is merely the result of sensory experience. But even in accepting without a doubt all these premises, we could still retain a mentalistic view of man simply by insisting that human *feelings* do not fit into the model. In other words, there are two realms of concern for those interested in a science of psychology. One is the *public* realm, in which we can compare our responses to stimuli and the effects that reinforcers have on our behavior. The other is the *private* realm, the realm of pleasures, dissapointments, fears, and longings. These feelings may not be publicly expressed (or even expressable), but they are real nevertheless to those having them.

Given what has been discussed in the earlier chapters, it should be clear that psychologists of different philosophical persuasions will not agree on the nature and causes of private experiences. The psychologist who adopts the behavioristic point of view will investigate emotional *behavior*, but will insist that there is no way to study emotional *feelings* in an objective way. Those in the idealist tradition are quite at home with private experience and are willing to treat what people say about their feelings as— if not valid—at least able to be validated. Moreover, they will insist that any psychology that avoids the study of private experience can never be complete, can never offer the kinds of facts and theories that the world at large would expect a science of psychology to provide. Psychology in the materialistic tradition expects to find the lawful determinants of feelings in the actions of the nervous system. Accordingly, the physiological psychologist dismisses the possibility that private experience is private. Ultimately, it will be shown to be but one more "output-characteristic" of neuronal physiology.

In this chapter, we will provide a brief outline of the psychology of motives, feelings, and states. We will review the major theoretical orientations that dominate the psychological study of these processes. We will see that one of these has been influenced particularly by the brand of psychology associated with Clark Hull, another by physiological psychology, still another, by psychoanalytic perspectives.

When we have completed this review, it will be unsettling to recognize how tangled our thinking and methods are. We might get a bit ahead of ourselves by acknowledging in advance that there is no *psychology of motivation* as such. Instead, there are groups of studies organized around a set of yet-to-be validated assumptions: one group addressed to the effects of food or shock or training on "emotional" behavior (for example, defecation, vocalization, and so forth); another group focusing on the effects of brain-stimulation or hormonal imbalances; a third group examining early child-hood experience or performance on personality tests or behavior in social situations. What these studies have in common is the belief that behavior is caused, that we can know the causes, and that the methods of science will reveal the causal connections. This is merely a restatement of the positivist position. But more than just this conviction will be necessary to unravel the phenomena of motivation, emotion, and levels of awareness. At the least, we must learn to avoid elementary logical blunders, such as the assumption that two behaviors that have the same form must be caused by the same events. We must also establish greater uniformity in our laboratory pro-cedures; for example, bar-pressing and defecating are both instances of behavior, but there is no similarity beyond that. We must also resist the reassuring but incorrect assumption of the untrained animal as a *tabula rasa*, or blank slate. Species differ, individuals within species differ, and these differences are *guaranteed* by genetic diversity. Studies that fail to reveal the differences—studies that use methods specifically designed to be insensitive to the differences—cannot be very informative. A psychology that searches for the psychological form of the Periodic Table searches in vain. Iron is iron no matter what its shape or weight may be. But there is no category called "rat" or "human" that will permit us in advance to make statements about how all members *must* behave. Individual members of a species are structurally and functionally distinct, and notions of some "type" can only lead to muddled explanations.

With these dangers clearly stated here, we can begin to explore some of the principles and practices that characterize the contemporary study of motives, feelings, and states.

THEORIES OF MOTIVATION

Most men describe the causes of their own behavior in terms of goals toward which they are striving: They work *because* they want nice things. They marry *because* they are in love. They save *because* they want security. They fight *because* they are threatened. Common speech is riddled with such assertions, which at their base are philosophically deterministic. The cyberneticist may demonstrate that purposive behavior is inevitable in a mindless system, but people will not readily accept the suggestion that their own behavior is the inevitable output of a machine designed to avoid blunders. Rather, in attempting to understand and to explain human behavior, philosophers, scientists, artists, and politicians have invoked and used the idea of *motivation*. Often the explanations have been mere tautologies, which utterly confuse causes with effects and attempt to salvage logic with language. Thus, *motives* are said to be *needs* that create *drives*, and learned behavior is *drive-reducing*.

Lewin's Physicalism

In addition to determinism, many workers have adopted *physicalism* as a means of explaining motives. If behavior is motivated, there must be some mechanism that translates the motive to action. The motivation theory offered by Lewin (1936), for example, postulated the presence of "forces" and "valences," which arise in the face of needs. The forces may be viewed as analogous to Hull's sE_R (Chapter 10) in that they are tendencies to act. The valances, on the other hand, constitute the desirability of a given action or object. Thus, confronting alternative and conflicting opportunities for response, the individual will choose that one with the most positive valence and greatest underlying (need-produced) forces.

Lewin's theory of motivation was typical of psychological explanations offered in the 1920s and 1930s. As Watsonian behaviorism was an overreaction to psychology's lack of rigor, Gestalt theories such as Lewin's were overreactions to "reflex" psychologies. Their language was a bit gaudy, their reliance on instincts a bit innocent, and their satisfaction with untestable hypotheses a bit alarming. Lewin really believed he was providing a physical model of brain function, a complex assembly of competing "field" forces, each with a dynamic (time-varying) valence, changing as a function of need-producing tensions. The task of behavior was to reduce tension. In his excellent review of motivation theories, Bolles (1967) indicates the limitations of Lewin's approach:

> There is little indication of how one could possibly validate the constructs of the theory. How do we know what the needs of an organism are? How can we tell whether these needs have created tension? How do we know that the tension is reciprocated in a force or

in a valence perceived by the individual? How can we know how the individual perceives his behavioral possibilities? The constructs of the theory are not even provisionally tied to empirical observations. . . . (Bolles, p. 77)

Murray's Need Theory

As psychology became more temperate in its acceptance of nativistic explanations, theories such as Freud's and Lewin's were modified to allow a greater role for social forces in the determination of human motives. That is, motivation theories were made more compatible with the life of "normal" man and with the goals and tendencies of which he was conscious. Henry Murray's "need" theory (1938), for example, begins with the realization that behavior is often called forth by the "presses" of society, that the feelings, hopes, and purposes of the individual are fashioned by his interaction with the world about him. Murray stays close to Lewin in his use of the need concept:

> A need is a construct (a convenient fiction or hypothetical concept) which stands for force . . . in the brain region, a force which organizes perception . . . and action in such a way as to transform in a certain direction an existing, unsatisfying situation (Murray, pp. 123-124)

Moreover, in his list of over two dozen needs he adheres to the nativistic doctrine that many are characteristic of a certain personality "type": for example, a "creative" person has innate needs not present—or at least not present in the same degree—in one who is less creative. Borrowing from Freud's concept of dreams, Murray also distinguishes between manifest and latent needs, the latter repressed but effective in motivating behavior. Some of the more comprehensible "needs" in his system, with their attending characteristics in parentheses are: *affiliation* (friendliness, dependence, respect, kindness), *deference* (compliance, devotion, suggestibility), *harm-avoidance* (timidity, fears), *abasement* (subservience, blame-acceptance), *seclusion* (isolation, reticence, shyness), *aggression* (temper, sadism, combativeness, destruction), *construction* (mechanical, aesthetic), *sex* (masturbation, homosexuality, bisexuality, precocious heterosexuality), *cognizance* (curiosity, experimentation, sexual) and *achievement* (general, physical, intellectual, rivalry). These and other needs grow and recede in intensity, interact with each other, and lead to behavior whose consequences feed back to the need structure and modify it. An essential function of behavior is the maintenance of some sort of psychic equilibrium, or *homeostasis,* as it was for Freud and Lewin. Murray, however, extends the functions of behavior to include *disequilibrium* as well. Curiosity, for example, serves the "cognizance need" and is an example of man's desire for stimulation and excitement.

A central element in Murray's theory of motivation is that of the *perceptual press.* It is a transformation of Lewin's idea of "valences" in that it attempts to describe the perceived incentive value or significance of a stimulus. How the individual comes to perceive a given feature of the environment depends on his need structure. Therefore, press and needs are intimately associated. A person with high need-achievement, for example, will be more affected by the press of poverty than will one with low need-achievement. When a given set of needs dominates the *internal proceedings* of an individual (memories, fantasies, aspirations, fears, and the physiological correlates of all of these), there will be a certain uniformity of perceptual press. That is, even under widely diverging environmental conditions, there will be a pronounced tendency to relate these conditions to the dominant need structure. The illusion of an oasis that appears repeatedly to the thirst-driven desert wanderer is an extreme example of the relationship among needs, internal proceedings, and perceptual press. Murray reasoned that because of this relationship, it should be possible to test a person's perceptual press by encouraging him to report the happenings in a number of ambiguous situations. He devised the Thematic Apperception Test (TAT) for this purpose. It is a *projective* device (Chapter 10) consisting of relatively "neutral" photographs. The subject's task is to examine each picture and then make up a story: What is going on in the picture, how did things get that way, and how will it all end? Should the perceptual press *affiliation* be dominant, then affiliative themes will be a consistent feature of all of the stories composed by the individual in response to a variety of highly ambiguous pictures. According to the theory, the themes will permit a specification of the press, the press will permit a delineation of the need structure, and the need structure will characterize the basic motivational complex responsible for the individual's behavior.

McClelland's Affective Arousal

Murray's work has been very influential in psychiatry and clinical psychology. The TAT is a widely used diagnostic instrument, and the lists of "needs" and "press" have helped to codify the semantics of practitioners. On the theoretical side, the system has been reduced in scope by McClelland (1961), Atkinson (1958), and their students, who have focused upon the *achievement motive* and who view all purposive behavior within the context of an *affective arousal* model. Their revision of Murray's theory is extensive in that they postulate the learned basis of motives and place the very concept of motivation within the broader domain of *affect*, or emotion. They still subscribe to the practice of measuring motivational states with projective tests (often the TAT), which is based on the Freudian conviction that fantasies reveal underlying aspirations and come to exist through repression, frustration, and fear. However, for McClelland at least, the behavior of Western man is motivated by an acquired need to achieve, and his total personality may be understood in these terms.

The threads that tie together these otherwise unconnected views of Freud, Lewin, Murray, and McClelland are those of *determinism* and *homeostasis*. They all agree that behavior, in its variety of complexities, is caused by isolatable mechanisms and that the root cause is the maintenance of some necessary level of equilibrium. Each of them, in one way or another, invokes a hedonistic construct: for Freud, the pleasure principle; for Lewin, tension reduction; for Murray, need reduction; for McClelland, achievement (in the broader sense). Each of these theorists is unique in his selection of mechanisms of motivation, although all take recourse, finally, to biological substrates. Freud's mechanism is unconscious motivation established during the course of psychosexual development but based on instinctual energies. Lewin's mechanism is "field forces," energy systems in tension. Murray's "needs" are homeostatically produced; McClelland's, autonomic, at least in the sense that emotion and arousal can be traced to autonomic function.

Hull's Drive Concept

Hull's formal theory (see Chapter 10) incorporates many elements of these theories of motivation. His *drive* concept grows out of homeostatic considerations. Drives originate in the biological (physiochemical) needs of the organism. Reinforcement involves drive reduction. Reinforced behavior is more likely to reoccur. In these very general terms, there is not much to distinguish the Hullian drives from Freud's id-superego conflicts, Lewin's forces, Murray's needs, and McClelland's affective arousal. Moreover, in his 1952 theoretical revision, Hull adds the variable K to represent the incentive value of a stimulus as made known by the vigor of the organism's response to it. What was once $sE_R = sH_R \times D$ was expanded:

$$sE_R = sH_R \times D \times K$$

He was prompted to this addition in part by the "elation" and "depression" effects discussed in Chapter 6. The reduction in running speed produced by decreasing the amount of reward and the increase in running speed following a shift to greater amounts of reward suggested to Hull that response tendencies could be "motivated" by reinforcement quality and quantity. The Hullian K would appear analogous both to Lewin's *vectors* and to aspects of Murray's and McClelland's *perceptual press*. Because of these close conceptual parallels and because of the ease with which Hullian principles lend themselves to experimental assessment, the issue of motivation has become central to the psychology of animal learning. In fact, in some systems the incentive value of stimuli, through its effects upon the emotional life of the organism, is considered the very foundation of learning. (Sheffield, Wulf, and Backer, 1951). As research and theory progress, the distinctions between motivation and emotion seem to dissipate. Whether one returns to Freud or to a more empirically oriented theorist (such as Hull), the causes of behavior are treated in terms of internal states that produce tensions (disequilibria, needs, drives) only relieved by action. Behavior, according to such views, is a means of controlling feelings that themselves are only products of physiological events.

Festinger's Cognitive Dissonance Theory

An interesting extension of the Hull-type model to complex social settings has been offered by Festinger (1957), under the heading *cognitive dissonance*. In a representative study, subjects were paced through a boring task and then were asked to encourage others to participate. Their encouragement was to take the form of enthusiastic "salesmanship" by which the recruits would conclude that the task, in fact, was exciting and enjoyable. In one instance, those selected to do the deceiving were paid one dollar for their efforts. A matched group was paid twenty dollars. At the end of their own experience with the task, members of both groups were tested for their attitudes about the task, and they were uniform in their boredom and disdain. They were tested once more *after* they had engaged in selling recruits on the idea of participation, and then it was found that the one-dollar group had significantly modified its attitude about the task. The twenty-dollar group, however, remained quite consistent in its attitude. The theory of cognitive dissonance describes such effects in terms of a need for consistency. No one wants to deceive another and certainly not for a dollar. Yet for twenty dollars, the decision becomes easier. Somehow, the one-dollar group must reconcile its cognitions and its guilts. It does so, that is, it reduces *dissonance,* by altering its attitudes. The twenty-dollar group, enduring far less conflict, simply does a poor job of prosyletizing. Dissonance is minimal because the extent of their deception is kept at a minimum. At the very base of it, the theory of cognitive dissonance is really a homeostatic theory; it emphasizes the need to maintain a cognitive or self-impressional equilibrium.

THE VALIDITY OF MOTIVATION THEORIES

Notwithstanding the common-sense appeal of these deterministic, hedonistic, homeostatic views of motivation, there are both logical and empirical bases on which to challenge their validity. The first question raised by such theoretical formulations is whether, in fact, they explain the phenomenon of interest. To suggest that behavior occurs *because* it is moti-vated only raises the question of what a motive is. To answer this by de-fining motives as those processes that cause behavior is simply to complete a circle—with understanding left on the outside. Furthermore, while be-havior may restore some condition of equilibrium or reduce "tension," it does not follow that that is *why* the behavior occurred. Much of human behavior is not adaptive. Large numbers of people smoke cigarettes, drive recklessly, consume too much food and alcohol, get too little exercise, and generally "live dangerously." Certainly in no usual or biological sense does behavior of this kind appear answerable to self-preservative, equilibrium-establishing, drive-reducing motives. To account for such discrepancies, theorists have drawn attention to *acquired* drives, which, even if counterproductive in their present form, came to exist by virtue of being reliably associated with *primary* drives. In Chapter 6, these features were discussed briefly. One need only add to that this caution: if the role of primary-drive reduction is insufficient to account for behavior, the addition of acquired drives will add little to an understanding of motivation.

Data from studies of latent learning and sensory preconditioning have already been summarized (Chapter 6). They pose a considerable challenge to the hypothesized essentiality of drive reduction. Sheffield and his collaborators have added to the challenge by demonstrating that groups of sexually naïve rats allowed to copulate but not to ejaculate (Sheffield, Roby, and Campbell, 1954) and hungry rats fed nutritionally irrelevant saccharin (Sheffield and Campbell, 1954a) both showed learning, as it is usually measured, although in neither case were "drives" reduced, at least if by drive reduction, a return to some condition of physiological equilibrium is implied. Even the milder role proposed for drives, that of simply "energizing" behavior, does not enjoy unequivocal experimental support. The casual observation that hungry animals increase their activity—an observation often explained in Darwinian terms—has not proved to be of general validity. Sheffield and Campbell (1954b), for example, measured the activity of an experimental group of rats whose daily feeding was preceded by a five-minute interval of auditory and visual stimulation. A control group was used that did not have this prefeeding regimen. Figure 11-1 compares the groups in terms of their activity levels. These data do not support the view that drives are internal states that energize and goad behavior. Rather, the experimenters noted that, left to their own devices, very hungry rats actually sleep most of the time!

The normally observed energization of behavior appears to be elicited more by external signs of reinforcement than by internal motivating states. As in the law's "rules of evidence," the rat apparently requires both opportunity and motive. That is, whatever the internal states may be, resulting behavior is shaped by the possibilities inherent in the environment. Hungry rats in a cage may sleep; in an open field, run; in an ocean, swim. Whether one is observing Freud's hysterics, Lewin's tensions, Murray's needs, or Sheffield's activity, the data are behaviors, and these are always circumstantial. The psychologist always must ask at least two questions: *What behavior follows a particular experimental condition? What behavior*

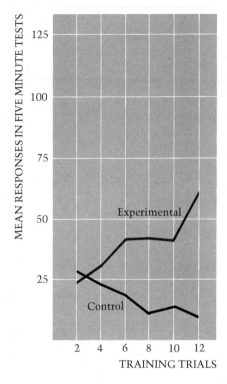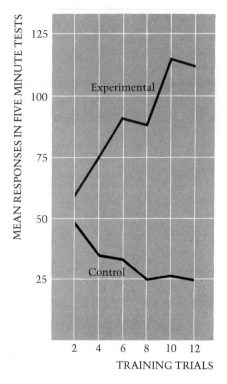

Figure 11-1. The behavior of hungry animals under different environmental conditions. For the experimental groups, a regular five-minute change in the environment occurs before feeding. On the left, the change involved a shift from darkness to light and the termination of an otherwise constant hissing sound. On the right, the change involved one from light to darkness and also the termination of the sound. For the control groups on both the left and right, the changes did not occur before feeding. The control groups rapidly adapted to these changes in stimuli while both experimental groups showed progressive increases in activity during the periods of environmental change. Thus, increased activity in hungry animals is not due simply to the "energizing" effects of a hunger drive. (After the data of Sheffield and Campbell, 1954.)

can *follow a particular experimental condition?* These questions logically precede any attempt to explain why a particular response occurs. In a severely limited environment, a given response may occur because it is just about the only one possible. As researchers increase the complexity of experimental settings, animals are found to engage in many behaviors never

witnessed in the early-Quaker austerity of the "Skinner box." Studies indicate, for example, that animals will learn one response in order to gain
acccess to a complex maze containing no reward of any kind other than
"complexity" itself (Berlyne and Slater, 1957). Berlyne's research (1950)
and theory have led him to postulate a "curiosity" or "exploratory" drive,
which can be added to the list including hunger, thirst, sex, and pain
avoidance. It is somewhat disconcerting, however, to find that as animal
research becomes more realistic, the number of basic animal motives begins
to approximate the number of basic human needs.

MOTIVATION AND EMOTION

It is not simply fortuitous that theories of motivation and theories of
emotion have had parallel development. McClelland's affective-arousal
model of motivation simply acknowledges the fact that if motives are at
work in forging the behavior of organisms, then those organisms must
sense (have feelings deriving from) these internal motivating conditions.
Simply stated, what is motivating about a condition is its ability to excite
affective (emotional) states. Moreover, when people reveal what they view
as the causes (underlying motivation) of their behavior, their language is
rich in emotional content. "I did X because of _____." The "_____"
can be filled in with *love, hate, anger, fear, hope, frustration, boredom,
excitement, compassion, depression, elation, tension,* and ten times as
many words, all designed to reflect a certain feeling. The feeling, according
to the individual, gives rise to his behavior; the emotion motivates the
action. As with the concept of motivation, emotion has been viewed as the
outcome of needs, tensions, states of disequilibrium, alterations in "adaptation level," and so forth. It, too, has been discussed in terms of both survival value and, therefore, instinct. The validity of the concept, of course,
is total: every man *knows* he has feelings; he knows, too, that he has goals.
Finally, he senses some relationship between his feelings and his attain-
ments. But how this relationship is established continues to elude the
layman's understanding as well as the scientist's. Since motives and feelings
are invariably explained in terms of mechanisms (internal states), it is not
surprising that much of physiological psychology has been devoted to the
specification of some of these mechanisms. The primary drives of hunger
and thirst have already been discussed and "pleasure" centers have been

described (Chapter 6). It is worthwhile at this point to examine a broader range of emotional states in terms of those physiological events that are assumed to create them.

EMOTIONAL STATES AND PHYSIOLOGICAL EVENTS

Emotion and the Autonomic Nervous System

William James helped to kindle interest in the biology of affect by declaring that emotions were only the consequence of visceral (autonomic) events. His view was that environmental conditions are perceived and related to past experience, thereby triggering autonomic activity, and the sensation of this visceral action was the emotion. As he put it, we see a bear, run, and *then* become afraid. By 1929, Cannon had collected enough information in opposition to James's theory to discredit it completely. Cannon studied pain, hunger, fear, and rage in experimental animals subjected to a variety of surgical and pharmacological treatments. His general observations were the following:

1. In producing autonomic effects biochemically, the behavior of the animal did not match that resulting from normally induced emotional states.
2. Gross measures of autonomic activity (heart rate, respiration, gross blood-chemistry) show little difference from emotion to emotion.
3. Emotional responses can be elicited from an animal whose sympathetic nervous system has been severed (*sympathectomy*).

The significance of the third observation derives from the fact that sympathetic stimulation is known to recruit the defensive reactions of the organism's general physiology. Figure 11-2 shows the relationship of the *sympathetic* branch of the autonomic nervous system (ANS) to the spinal cord and shows the anatomical paths of the *parasympathetic* branch of the ANS. The sympathetic branch sends fibers to, and carries fibers from, the thoracicolumbar (middle) regions of the spinal cord. The parasympathetic fibers come from and return to the craniosacral (top and bottom) regions of the spinal cord. The sympathetic ganglia run as a chain right along the vertebral column. The parasympathetic ganglia are distributed out in the

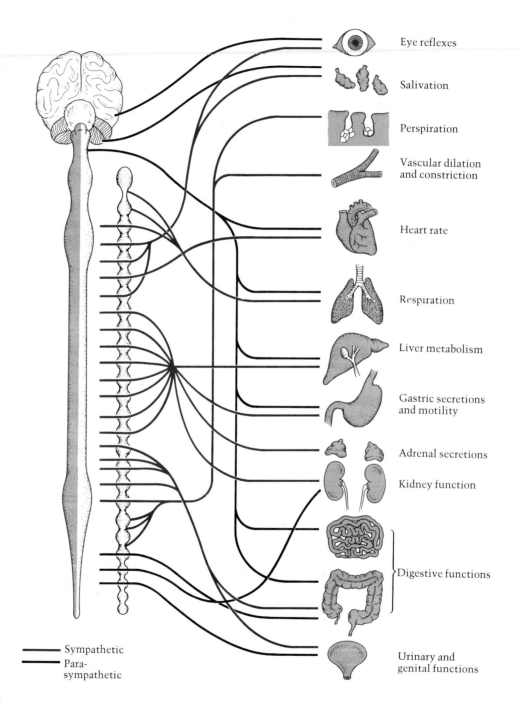

Eye reflexes

Salivation

Perspiration

Vascular dilation
and constriction

Heart rate

Respiration

Liver metabolism

Gastric secretions
and motility

Adrenal secretions

Kidney function

Digestive functions

Urinary and
genital functions

Sympathetic
Para-
sympathetic

body near the muscles and glands that they serve. The two branches of the ANS tend to function in opposition. Sympathetic excitation, largely through its activation of the adrenal glands, leads to a diffuse mobilization of the biological processes involved in "fight" and "flight." Heart rate is increased, gastric activity is reduced, pupils are dilated, arteries constricted. Parasympathetic action results in exactly opposite effects. The latter is sometimes described as mediating the vegetative and excitement-reducing states of the organism, while the former is seen as mediating the stress systems. Given this neurological organization, it was surprising to find, as Cannon did, that sympathectomized animals were quite capable of emitting emotional responses. Furthermore, because of the diffuseness of sympathetic action, it is unlikely that James's theory, rooted as it is in "visceral" phenomena, could account for the differences in both the range and subtlety of human emotional states.

Emotion and the Limbic System

Cannon's efforts pushed theories of emotion away from the viscera and toward the head. Recall in (Chapter 6) how peripheralist theories of hunger and thirst gradually migrated to the hypothalamus. After Cannon, physiological theories of emotion migrated toward the limbic system, outlined in Figure 11-3. Concern with the structures that form this system was raised by a number of studies conducted in the 1930s and 1940s and by the influential theory of Papez advanced in 1937. As early as 1928, Bard had shown that intense and highly organized rage reactions were present in cats whose entire cerebral cortex had been removed. Interestingly, the rage was directed at any location toward which the animal faced; that is, not at the aversive stimulus (pinching the skin), but at something "out there." Papez himself noted that patients suffering from rabies were highly volatile, and autopsies indicated subcortical damage in these cases. In short, numerous research and clinical findings all pointed to the phylo-

Figure 11-2. Sympathetic and parasympathetic branches of the autonomic nervous system. Note the long, direct connections between parasympathetic fibers and their organs of destination. The sympathetic fibers terminate in synapses soon after leaving the sympathetic ganglia. During stages of stress, anxiety, and excitement, all of the functions indicated above are affected by autonomic influences.

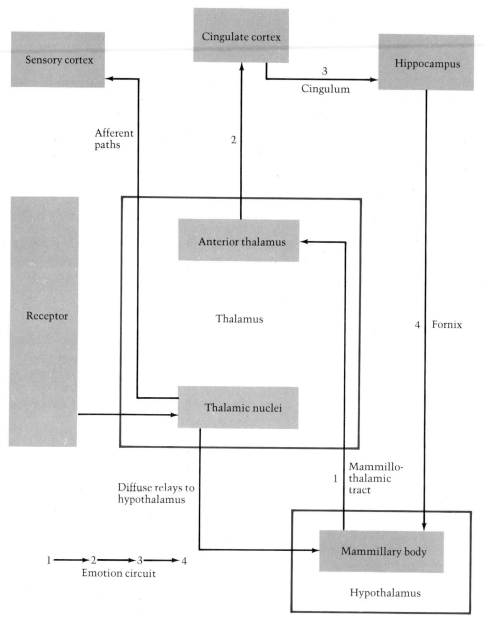

Figure 11-3. The limbic system and neighboring structures. The arrows indicate the presumed course of excitation within the system. These structures are directly involved in the expression of "emotional" behavior in higher organisms. (After Isaacson et al., 1971.)

genetically older portions of the brain as the loci of emotional expression. The structures shown in Figure 11-3 were assumed by Papez to form a "circuit" underlying the emotions. Stimulation and ablation studies tend to confirm the functional organization of the *Papez circuit.* Aggression, rage, placidity, sexuality, listlessness—the whole ensemble of behaviors of emotional origin—have been created in rats, cats, and monkeys by stimulating or removing the various structures of the limbic system. When stimulated, the anterior portion of the hypothalamus leads to "flight"; the posterior, to "fight" (Hess, 1954). Some investigators report that amygdaloid stimulation makes their animals friendly; others report ferocity. Human neurosurgical patients have also been called on to report the consequences of limbic stimulation. Here, conflicting findings are more the rule than the exception. For some there is general discomfort, perhaps because of the visceral consequences of brain stimulation. Others report only mild, emotionless sensations. In animals, injury to the amygdala (as opposed to stimulation) generally leads to tameness. In human patients, chronic anxiety has been relieved by removal of portions of the cingulate gyrus. The list of effects is truly long and does little to aid the beginner in getting a general impression of the neuropsychology of emotion. Most of the research along these lines supports the following generalizations:

1. The emotional effects of stimulation or removal of brain areas varies with different species, with different brain regions, with different stimulational and surgical procedures, and with organisms having different individual histories. This last feature is extremely important. It has been shown, for example, that amygdala lesions reduce flight from aversive stimuli in wild cats but have no effect upon tame cats (Ursin, 1965).

2. As with aggression as an instinct, the presence of emotions in animals is demonstrated only at a behavioral level. Judgments of "states" are speculative and anthropomorphic. This does not deny the presence of emotions in lower organisms. However, the feelings that may attend the cat's clawing, salivating, hissing, and biting can never be known through current procedures. When the consequences of behavior include destruction, it is not necessarily the case that this effect was intended. The amoeba engulfs and digests food particles. Can one argue that this unicellular organism "feels hungry"? Leaves blow in the wind. Is this "flight"? Are moths "happier" near light? Are they "afraid" of the dark?

3. If, given the above, behavior is an insufficient basis upon which to judge the presence of emotional states, then only the verbal report of conscious human beings is left in support of the concept of emotion. This being the case, animal studies may offer presumptive evidence regarding the conditions under which emotional *behavior* occurs, but no evidence regarding emotional *states*.

THE DESCRIPTION OF EMOTIONAL STATES

It appears as if the proper study of mankind is man, at least with respect to feelings. In looking to man, however, one must accept all of the limitations characteristic of research with lower organisms with the exception of the generalizability of the findings. That is, generalizations about *homo sapiens* are on firmer ground when man is the experimental subject. But there is still the problem of describing internal states on the basis of overt behavior, even though (or especially since) the latter is verbal; there is still the difficulty of distinguishing different degrees, durations, and qualities of emotion; and there is still the equivocality implicit in identifying the determinants of the emotional responses. These problems are worthy of further discussion.

Are Feelings Reportable?

Do two people see the same red scarf? Can one person know how another feels, perceives, and thinks? Can words communicate the variety of experience? Such questions have created difficult problems for psychology and philosophy and have engendered a skepticism toward all "introspective" data. Mandler (1962) has expressed a rather general attitude:

> It is unreasonable to expect that private experience can ever be anything but that. It becomes public, that is, comprehensible to others, only after it has been put into some sort of communicable symbolism, namely language. . . . I cannot possibly use the rather crude instrument of language to express the myriad impressions, feelings, ideas, notions, and emotions that flood my private screen. . . . If private experience can only be communicated through lan-

> guage, then the events that . . . a psychologist investigates [are] the verbal behavior of subjects, patients and friends. (Mandler, p. 303)

This being the case, any study of emotional states in man must either hope for a certain uniformity in language usage or arbitrarily impose such uniformity by restricting the semantic domain available to experimental subjects. Even in limiting the number and nature of words the subject may use to describe his internal states, seemingly insurmountable obstacles arise. What if no word matches the feeling? How has the subject come to understand the given word? How do the words themselves alter the very nature of the feeling? The most an investigator can do is to be aware of these problems and try to design experiments in a way that will allow some control over the more obvious variables. When the basic datum in a study of emotion is verbal report, it is certainly essential to establish effects due to the age and education of the subject, cultural nuances in his verbal behavior, other languages he may use, and his overall linguistic proficiency.

The foregoing by no means invalidates studies of human emotion based on introspective reports. After all, people do seem to be able to understand each other when describing their feelings. When one says, "I'm depressed today," his friend is not able to "feel" those conditions responsible for the statement, but in his own experience, he does know what "depressed" implies. No two feelings may ever be alike, and no feeling in one individual may ever be reproduced exactly in another. By the same token, no two electrons may ever behave in exactly the same manner, although the laws governing their behavior are the same for both. The psychologist's task is to specify the determinants of psychological events. Verbal reports of feelings are psychological events. Thus, the task is one of ascertaining the necessary and sufficient conditions for the report of a given feeling by a particular subject. History and personal experience lend some credence to the idea that a very large number of individuals will tend to feel good, bad, or indifferent under various, specifiable circumstances. In fact, if it were not for the considerable uniformity of emotional responses to a range of experiences, the very concept of psychopathology would lose all meaning.

Of course, verbal behavior is not the only way in which people express their feelings. Posture, facial expression, overt gestures of friendship and aversion, muscle tension, heart rate, skin resistance, EEG activity, dryness of the mouth, constipation, diarrhea, rashes, laughter, blushing, wincing—these are only a sampling of the nonverbal signs of emotionality. Methods of so-called lie detection are based on the reliability with which inner feelings manifest themselves in the form of certain gross physiological changes. Actors, salesmen, and public figures learn and can simulate with considerable fidelity the postural and facial manifestations of genuine emotional states. In fact, and consistent with James's otherwise untenable position, these muscular components can be so effective that the actor reports actually feeling the emotion he is attempting to communicate. There is, then, a large assortment of measures available for the study of human emotion. Yes, feelings *are* reportable. They are expressed by everyone in a multitude of ways. It is their expressability that allows shared experiences among men. At the present time, it is still unclear which of man's methods of report is most reliable. There is no single measure that clearly differentiates among states. The future, no doubt, will see odd combinations of measures used to identify emotional conditions. For now, this area must be viewed as in its early stage of development.

How Are Feelings Differentiable?

Any complete discussion of human emotions, whether based on physiological, verbal, or behavioral data, must specify qualitative differences among emotions, quantitative differences among emotions, the relative duration of the emotional states, and the conditions unique to their occurrence. Affection and satisfaction are different feelings. Anger and rage are different feelings. The momentary worry over being late and a lifelong worry over one's future are two very different feelings. The sorrow produced by the death of a friend and that produced by the death of a loved one differ as well. Existing methods of scaling emotions often fail to consider these factors. It is one thing to measure heart rate variations under mildly unpleasant and highly aversive conditions of electrical shock. It is quite another matter to ascertain the physiological consequences of persisting fears or hopes or sorrows.

An extraordinarily imaginative series of studies conducted by Schachter and Singer (1962) sheds light on the conditions necessary to produce specific emotions and also suggests the kind of research strategies that will further illuminate the area. They were concerned, among other things, with situational determinants of emotion. One group of subjects was invited to participate in a study of drug effects upon vision. They were told that the drug to be injected by a physician was harmless but would produce a slight tremor, an increase in heart rate and blood pressure, and, perhaps, some light-headedness. The drug was, in fact, adrenalin, and these were indeed the symptoms that would follow administration. A second group, also told that the experiment was in visual perception, was misinformed about the effects of the drug. They were cautioned, instead, that a mild headache, some numbness in the feet, and a bit of itchiness would follow administration of the drug. Individually, each member of the two groups was asked to stay in a waiting room where a "stooge" was stationed. Shortly after the subject entered, the stooge began to engage in a series of childish behaviors: tossing paper planes, running about, playing basketball with rolled paper. During this display, the stooge invited the participation of the subject. Those subjects who had been correctly informed about the consequences of the injection politely refused to join in; they were relatively unaffected by the behavior of the stooge. However, the misinformed subjects tended to get caught up in the spirit of the occasion. Physiologically, adrenalin is a euphoriant. The subject who is prepared for those autonomic events correlated with euphoria is resistant to environmental conditions designed to capitalize on his feelings. The subject who is not aware of the effects of adrenalin and who cannot, therefore, comprehend the source of his feelings can be made a slave to them. One is reminded of Aristotle's assertion, "Everything that is done by reason of ignorance is involuntary" (*Nichomachean Ethics*).

What Determines Feelings?

It should be clear that all of the processes discussed in Chapters 4 to 9 participate in determining the emotional life of man—and of any other organism having even the fundamentals of emotions. Rats and men are subject to conditioned avoidance. Man reports that his behavior in such settings is in anticipation of punishment. He knows that if he is late for the opera, he will be kept out in the lobby during the first act. Discriminative stimuli (his ticking watch) elicit visceral responses of an aversive nature. He calls these *anxiety*. These states can be terminated only by punctuality. He must drive quickly. He's caught in traffic. His watch ticks loudly. His heart races. He perspires. Traffic grinds to a halt. His fantasies find him driving *over* the cars in front of him. Frustration mounts. Momentary relief comes as he leans on his horn and shouts obscenities. He finds himself taking deep breaths. He doesn't know why. He turns on the radio but, of course, is oblivious to its message. Traffic picks up. His heart slows down. His watch slows down. Somehow, he gets to the theater on time. Slouching in his seat, he is for a time oblivious to the music and the surroundings. For a time, he is functionally *sympathectomized*, his emotional energies are spent.

Meanwhile, the rat's "curtain time" is signaled by an amber bulb. If he fails to reach the end of the runway before it lights, shock is his fate. He runs rapidly. Then, an obstruction! He scratches at it, bites it, and becomes fitful. A small rubber doll is dropped next to him. He attacks it. The obstruction is removed and the race is on again. Somehow, he gets to the goal. He is panting. Food, for the moment, has little appeal. His energies, too, are spent.

Other rats and men are less fortunate. One man under the same conditions left a little later for the opera (he *always* seems to be a bit behind). He missed the opera. He also failed to get a raise, a raise he had already spent. His childhood dream to be a writer has been, in his view, perverted by the press of modern life. Oh, if he could just "take off," leave all the middle-class trappings—the two-car garage, fire insurance, Dacron suits. But with a son in private school and a daughter in college, leaving for Walden Pond is tantamount to desertion. Weekends, he writes three to five pages. Who can concentrate? At work he dreams of writing. At home he worries about his career. A lifelong history of secondary reinforcements dispensed in variable-ratio fashion precludes all hope of extinction. A year later—maybe two or three—he faints walking up the steps of his house. He is diagnosed as having a case of ulcerative colitis. Surgeons find his intestines engorged with blood, swollen with edema, perforated in spots, and spilling the products of digestion into the abdominal cavity.

A hungry rat confronts a wired bridge to food. He places one front paw forward and is shocked. He jumps back. He tries again. This time, there is no shock. He moved quickly, but before reaching the center of the bridge, shock is reapplied. He hastens back, crouching in a corner, defecating and quivering. Hunger mounts. He approaches the bridge. He oscillates forward and back, abortive lunges. His weight is maintained by feedings every other day. But, on alternate days, the conflict between approach and avoidance is raised again. Weeks go by. Then, the animal is observed to avoid food even in the secure environment of his home cage. In a day or two, he is dead. The autopsy reveals ulcerative colitis.

There are men and rats who show remarkable resistance to the physiological ravages of pain and conflict. Rats, in fact, can be *bred* for such resistance. Certain human personalities, too, seem to be characterized by a kind of psychological immunity. Thus, in part, the genetic constitution of the individual organism provides one route to an understanding of the determinants of feelings—or their equivalent in lower organisms. Learning, needless to say, is a surpassing factor. Man's reinforcement history designates certain stimuli as affective, others as neutral. Those with affective properties elicit measurable changes in his autonomic physiology. Presently, only the grossest of these effects are discernible. The consequences of these visceral events are communicated through neurons and circulating blood to the "business end" of consciousness, the brain. Here, current stimuli are compared with older memories, filtered and screened for meaning, and used ultimately to excite behavior. The behavior in turn alters the world outside the organism. It brings it closer or removes it. It makes it more vivid or drives it to the innermost recesses of the unconscious. This altered world now alters perception, and this somehow transforms the viscera and these cycles repeat and repeat in the lifelong episode of experience, feeling, and action.

Feelings During Sleep

Among South American Indians, African, Asian and South Sea tribesmen, and numerous European peasants, there is a belief that the soul leaves the body during sleep. It wanders, visits places, sees people, and performs the actions contained in dreams. The great danger is that the soul may not be able to get back into the body (Murray, p. 302).

Since recorded time, man has had a compelling interest in the meaning of his dreams. With the exception of Freud, this phenomenon has remained principally in the hands of poets and mystics until quite recently. Now, one of the most active areas of psychological and neurological research is concerned with dreaming and with sleep.

From a purely psychobiological perspective, sleep would be a significant phenomenon if only because it is a form of behavior that represents one-third of a human's life. Given its frequency and its universality, one would expect it to be relatively simple to understand. However, this is not the case. For example, it is not at all clear that sleep states are initiated by fatigue, that they are directly related to physiological restoration, or that they are a means of "relaxation." Cause-and-effect sequences have proved difficult to establish. One thing its clear, and that is that the effects of sleep deprivation are severe. A summary of the effects of sleep deprivation on personality is shown in Table 6 (Murray, 1965). The contexts in which deprivation occurred varied widely, and as a result, the effects also show variability. But one generalization is apparent: sleep deprivation induces either felt or overtly expressed aggression. With animal subjects, viciousness leading to death is a consequence of such procedures. Disc jockeys and contestants for prizes awarded for remaining awake also exist in sufficient number to allow study. The general findings are consistent. As sleeplessness progresses, behavior becomes more disorganized; delusions and hallucinations are common. In the extreme, psychotic episodes requiring hospitalization may ensue. Clearly, sleep is a state of basic biological significance to the organism.

TABLE 6.   Degree of Frustration and Aggression During Sleep-Deprivation Studies

Representative Study	Deprivation	General Effects
A	112 hours	1. Unprovoked fights 2. Paranoid tendencies 3. High drop-out rate
B	98 hours	1. Zero drop-out rate 2. No overt hostility 3. Provokable irritability
C	37 hours	1. Feelings of hostility but no overt signs
D	24 hours (smoking forbidden)	1. Verbal aggression directed at experimenters 2. Drawing of mangled psychologists

Dreams, too, appear to be essential to the psychological integrity of the individual. Scientific studies of dream states awaited a technical means of determining when sleeping subjects were dreaming. In a pioneering study, Aserinsky and Kleitman (1955) measured eye movements during sleep and in a number of subsequent investigations found a high correlation between the presence of *rapid eye movements* (REM) and dreaming. That is, when electrical recordings from the ocular muscles revealed REM, the sleeping subjects were awakened and, in most cases, reported that they had been dreaming. In far fewer instances were dreams reported during non-REM sleep. The relationship between REM-sleep and dreaming has been challenged by other investigators, but the bulk of available data does suggest that dreaming is reliably (but not perfectly) correlated with REM. Moreover, when sleep is interrupted at the first sign of REM, the subject becomes anxious, often hostile, and increasingly fatigued. It is as if the psychologically restorative functions of sleep depend on dreaming. Freud, of course, would have expected this.

THE CONTINUUM OF CONSCIOUSNESS

Consciousness, that condition which has prompted philosophic discourse and psychological debate for centuries—whatever its basis may be —exists in varying degrees. Subjective reports, behavior measures, and physiological indices all indicate this. Gross measures, such as the electro-encephalogram (EEG) are sufficient to discriminate a number of "states" of consciousness as is shown in Figure 11-4. The full continuum of consciousness, from intense emotion to clinical death, has been suggested by Lindsley (1957) and is summarized in Table 7. In each of these states, with the possible exception of the last, consciousness moves to a new level, to some mysterious domain beyond will and hope. It is only in a narrow region of the continuum that man can function and cope, reason and wonder. For tens of centuries, the authors of mysticism and metaphysics have suggested that the "real truths" are to be found at just those levels at which consciousness abandons its home. Practitioners of meditation and yoga have contended that somewhere on the continuum between alertness and sleep there is another point, an uncharted sea of possibilities filled with islets of creativity and insight. Science has just begun to travel upon this sea, and the preliminary findings are worthy of mention.

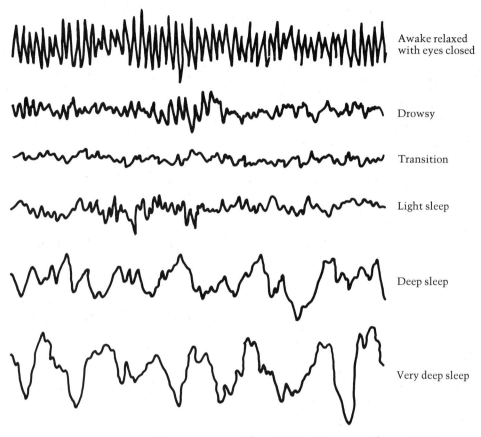

Awake relaxed
with eyes closed

Drowsy

Transition

Light sleep

Deep sleep

Very deep sleep

Figure 11-4. Responses from the human brain during various stages of activity. (After the data of Lindsley, 1957.)

Research conducted with accomplished yogis or experts in transcendental meditation has been frustrated by the reluctance of the scientific community to probe the alleged virtues of transcendental states and by the relative scarcity of appropriate subjects in the neighborhood of necessary research facilities. These obstacles have been overcome on several occasions and Wallace (1970) has both summarized and contributed to the recent investigations. The various studies, although conflicting in details, do agree on the following:

1. Meditation states are not to be confused either with light or deep sleep. Behavioral and physiological measures, as well as subjective reports, are different in the two states. For example, in deep sleep the alpha rhythm (8 to 13 cps) is absent while it dominates the EEG of the meditator. Total oxygen consumption may fall as much in the first 30 minutes of meditation as it does in an entire night of sleep.

2. Meditation states seem to enhance cognitive efficency while at the same time allowing rest; they are described as states of "restful alertness."

3. Because of the pattern of autonomic, biochemical, and subjective indices obtained from the postmeditation subject, the transcendental state appears to be unique.

TABLE 7. Psychological States and Their EEG, Conscious, and Behavioral Correlates

Behavior	EEG Characteristics	Awareness Level	Performance
Highly emotional and agitated	Desynchronized with a variety of frequency components	Confused	Disorganized
Controlled attention	Mostly high-frequency components; some synchrony	Episodes of inattentiveness	Good and rapid
Relaxation	Maximum *alpha* rhythm	Frequent inattentiveness	Good
Drowsiness	Some *alpha* and some slow waves	Reverie	Poor
Light sleep	*Alpha* absent; sleep spindles present	Unconscious with dreams	Absent
Deep sleep	Synchronous slow waves of high amplitude	Unconscious; dreams not recalled	Absent
Coma	Irregular; periods of no EEG signal	Unconscious and unarousable	Absent
Death	No EEG signal	None	Absent

A further discussion of yoga and mind control will be taken up in Chapter 12.

The Status of States

One finds, in classical philosophy, a recurrent warning to remain mindful of the distinction between the attributes of a thing and the thing itself; for example, between beauty as an ideal and that which is beautiful. Psychological states—arousal, attention, consciousness, sleep, dreaming—have been examined in terms of certain attributes, such as EEG frequencies, behavioral (muscular) activity, and introspective reports. At present, it is by no means clear that these attributes (correlates) are valid reflections of the conditions or processes they are presumed to describe. Consciousness is not the EEG. It is man's sense of himself. Science's inability to accommodate the phenomenon in these terms does not in any way dissolve the phenomenon. Moreover, the abiding question is whether anything is left of the phenomenon once it has been transformed to accommodate the methods of science. This question still remains unanswered.

SUMMARY

In this Chapter, we have explored the traditional problem of "private experience." We have seen that experimental methods, particularly those borrowed from physiology, have shed some light on the causal sequences involved in motivation and emotion. Although the findings are useful and interesting, it is nevertheless the case that modern psychology does not have theories adequate enough to account for the facts of private experience and states of consciousness.

SUGGESTED READINGS

BERLYNE, D. E. *Conflict, Arousal and Curiosity*. New York: McGraw-Hill Book Company, 1960.

Professor Berlyne reviews older theories of motivation and advances his own in this text. He draws material from neurophysiology, ethology, and clinical psychology.

GLICKMAN, S. E. and MILNER, P. M., eds. *The Neurological Basis of Motivation.* New York: D. Van Nostrand Co., 1969.

Fourteen research papers are presented in this anthology. Most are concerned with hunger, thirst, and sex in relation to neurological structures.

PLUTCHIK, R. *The Emotions: Facts, Theories and a New Model.* New York: Random House, 1962.

Professor Plutchik provides a very readable and critical summary of traditional views of human feelings. His own theory is interesting and a rather welcome departure.

Challenges for Psychology

CHAPTER
12

Exceptions to the Rules

At each point in our history, we become somewhat confident and complacent in the face of contemporary knowledge. To the ancient Greeks, all earlier times were barbarous. To Renaissance man, the ages between antiquity and his own, "Dark" and "Middle." Each era enjoys the privilege of naming itself and its predecessors—for example,, the "Age of Reason," the "Enlightenment," the "Atomic Age."

Science, as an extension of culture and society, shares the same complacency. It labors diligently with tools provided by older times and guards its every discovery against the inevitable revisions of the future. Science and society, both developing from a transformation of the old, seem to bridle in the face of the new. In the case of science, the delicate balance between adventurous speculation and loyal adherence has always been elusive. Adventurousness sometimes can lead to a Darwin; at other times, to alchemy. Adherence preserves what is good but also perpetuates what is wrong.

As a branch of natural science, psychology, has become progressively conservative in defining its subject matter and developing its methods. It began as a study of the soul. It soon moved on to the mind, then to consciousness, and then to behavior. It abandoned philosophic discourse in favor of introspection. From these subjective reflections, data of awesome complexity emerged and forced psychology toward greater and greater objectivity. Much has been gained as a result of the narrowing of issues and the objectification of methods. But in science, as in life, everything has a price, and the cost of precision is often very high.

In this chapter, we will examine some peculiar psychological phenomena that do not fit easily into the niche of psychology's current orthodoxy. Some of the phenomena we will explore are paradoxical in that they seem to be precisely the reverse of what well-established principles would predict. Others are exceptional in that, if valid, they violate one or another of the discipline's more cherished tenets.

ESP

There is no doubt that "sensationists" and "Gestaltists" disagree on fundamental grounds. The former view the latter's explanations as mentalistic and generous. Perception theorists consider the reductionism of sensationists simplistic and overly mechanical. Both schools, however, do agree that experience is some function of the interaction between physical parameters of stimulation and physiological characteristics of neural systems. Gestalt psychology leaves ample room for the nervous system to impose order and structure on sensory events, but at the same time, it accepts these events as purely physical outcomes. Thus, one phenomenon that traditionalists in sensory and perceptual research have been unable to explain (and therefore unwilling to accept) is telepathy, a special case of which is extrasensory perception (ESP).

Reports of ESP appear to be coexistent with educated human beings. The ancients recorded it as did the authors of the Bible. Medieval lore is filled with it, and certain religious sects accept it as a given. Unable to suggest a mechanism to explain it, science has treated ESP with indifference, doubt, or even scorn. In the face of considerable hostility and ridicule, Dr. J. B. Rhine launched and has sustained an institute for parapsychological research at Duke University. The field has its own thirty-five-year-old journal, and some of the studies reported in it are worthy of examination.

ESP Experiments

A number of compelling studies have been conducted by the British mathematician S. G. Soal. In one study, he worked for more than two years with a very good ESP subject, Basil Shackleton. Over this two-year period, Shackleton's "hit rate" on standard ESP cards was far greater than what probability theory predicted. Indeed, the likelihood of chance resulting in Shackleton's performance was computed to be 10^{-35}.

At Duke, too, in Professor Rhine's laboratory, many subjects performed at far better than chance levels. One of Rhine's colleagues, J. G. Pratt, was careful to keep his experimental subjects and the ESP cards in separate buildings in order to avoid inadvertent sensory cues. Under these circumstances, one subject (Pearce) completed 1,825 trials over which he averaged 7.5 "hits" per run. The chance probability of this rate of success is about 10^{-20}.

A typical ESP experiment involves an experimenter, a "sender," and a "receiver." The experimenter may present the sender with a number, for example, 1, 2, 3, 4, 5. Each number is associated with a certain photograph, such as one of five different animals. On seeing the number, the sender stares at it and thinks about the appropriate animal. In another room, the receiver is called on to name the animal that the sender is viewing. In one such study (Soal, 1949), the sender made 17,000 observations of this kind in runs of 25 trials. The receiver was correct on better than 25 percent of the trials. Since chance would predict the probability of a "hit" 1 in 5 times (20 percent), this success rate proved to be significantly better than chance.

To test whether the strength of ESP diminishes with distance, McMahan and Rhine (1947) required a Yugoslavian physician to judge the order of cards in 354 different decks. The experimenters were in North Carolina and the receiver was in Zagreb, Yugoslavia, nearly 7,000 miles away. The doctor proved to be far superior in his performance than would be predicted by chance expectations, and the Duke workers concluded that telepathy is not limited by distance.

The apparatus for ESP studies is quite simple, often consisting only of ESP cards. These are plain, white cardboard sheets, each of which contains a symbol, for example, *, †, △, ○, □. A sender examines one of the five cards, and a receiver in another room or building (or country) specifies which symbol is "in the sender's mind." Over a very large run of trials, the predicted score is 20 percent due to random chance alone. Significantly higher scores are interpreted as supportive of the ESP hypothesis.

For reasons that should be obvious, ESP researchers have been extraordinarily careful in their creation of experimental settings. Senders and receivers cannot see each other and usually cannot hear each other. Often the entire transaction is written, and results are tallied by judges who have access to neither of the subjects. Great variability has been found to exist among senders and receivers. Some have high ESP in transmitting information but low ESP in receiving it. For others, the reverse is true. Some are good at both; others, poor at both. Some subjects are good over short runs but poor over long runs. A somewhat reliable finding is that good subjects are best during the middle range of a large number of runs, as if a warm-up was necessary and fatigue inevitable.

The number of "successful" ESP experiments is now in the thousands, and fairness requires one to conclude that at least some of these were conducted with rigorous controls. In fact, some ESP studies utilize methods of control that are without precedent in established fields of experimental psychology. Surprisingly, the likelihood of positive findings does not seem to depend very much on the experimenter's methodological compulsions. Under widely divergent conditions, senders and receivers take their respective seats and appear to communicate in nonsensory fashion. A close examination of some reported successes does reveal errors in statistical analyses, for example, using a large number of trials but averaging only over the middle range, and then predicting chance success based on that total number. But most of the recent publications on ESP are free of any hint of statistical naïveté. It may be argued that with the thousands of experiments that have been conducted, it is likely that some would be successful on a chance basis and that only these have been reported. A similar assertion may be made about research findings in any research area, since journals do not tend to publish experiments that fail to obtain positive results. It may also be conjectured that the phenomenon is valid but that the interpretation is incorrect, that is, subjects do perform better than chance would allow, but ESP is a fiction. In this case, the burden of proof falls on those who believe some other variable is responsible. That variable must be found, controlled, and shown to alter the outcome once it has been controlled. For now, the wary scientist must leave room for the possibility that the routes of communication may extend beyond the classical five senses of Aristotle and the seven of modern psychology.

As ESP constitutes an exception to traditional conceptions of sensory processes, *tactile color vision* is a paradox. For several years, between 1964 and 1967, a number of reports appeared that described the incredible ability of experimental subjects to "feel" colors with their fingers. One that came from Russia (Nyuberg, 1964) told the amazing story of Roza Kuleshova, who could read newspaper print with her fingertips—even when a glass plate covered the print! While Roza's performance seems to be one of a kind, a number of subjects were also found in the United States who could reliably reach into a box, feel cloth or tiles, and report their colors (Youtz, 1966). Although many animals, especially some fish and reptiles, do have color-sensitive skin, it appeared paradoxical that some *homo sapiens* shared this capacity. After much controversy, W. L. Makous (1966) finally offered a rather basic explanation for this newfound sense. Reporting other findings that show the thermal sensitivity of the fingertips capable of detecting changes as small as 0.001°C., Makous argued convincingly that cutaneous color vision was readily understood in terms of cutaneous temperature sensitivity.

The short history of tactile color vision is something of an object lesson in science. Paradoxes abound in studies of man, but their paradoxical status usually vanishes as careful measurements and critical thinking are applied. Perhaps the future holds a similar destiny for ESP.

GENIUS

That system of psychology whose roots extend to British associationism and to Bentham's pleasure principle places the major responsibility for molding the individual in the hands of the "reinforcement history." At the common-sense level of wisdom, it is a view of behavior captured by the maxim "As the twig is bent, so grows the tree." In

Chapter 6 the considerable efficacy of reinforcement operations was described, and a current version of the Law of Effect was offered. In the same chapter, cognitive arguments were reviewed and cognitive data presented in an attempt to reveal the lines of controversy between empirical and nativistic theories of learning. Both systems, the behavioral and the cognitive, do agree that human action is the outcome of lawful dependencies. While the empiricist's focus is somewhere outside of the organism and the nativist's is somewhere "in the head," both confidently assert that the same basic principles are applicable to all members of a species. Piaget discusses cognitive development in the child the way Skinner speaks of the acquisition of operants in the rat. Neither system confronts directly the facts of individual differences that were reviewed in Chapter 9. What reinforcement history produced a Newton, a Beethoven, a Leonardo da Vinci, and a Tolstoi? What characterized the preoperational thought of a Copernicus or a Darwin? What model of syntactic structure or what regimen of verbal operant conditioning will produce a Shakespeare? In short, what has traditional psychology to say about *genius?*

Since Galton's time, psychologists have studied the characteristics of exceptional people. Since the time of Alfred Binet, psychologists have tried to devise tests to predict exceptional mental ability. In some quarters of the profession, a sort of game is played in which, *ex post facto*, one attempts to determine the I.Q. of a John Stuart Mill or an Aristotle. Others have used the writings of a Poe or a Melville in order to discover the personality of the artist. As one reviews the various findings, a picture results that is very vague. The geniuses of history come in assorted temperaments, from heterogeneous backgrounds, with parents of varying abili ties, and with needs and ambitions of every imaginable variety and intensity.

Given the chief tenets of what may be called radical behaviorism, the creative and intellectual character of a population should become progressively improved through systematic improvements of the environment. Today, more than 7 million Americans between the ages of sixteen and twenty-five are enrolled in colleges and universities. Since 1900, more people have been exposed to higher education than in the preceding two centuries. Every year more families become affluent. Nutritional requirements are now better met. Television, books, motion pictures, and high-speed travel shrink the world and compress experience so much that today's ten-year-old knows more about more things than his ancestors did at fifty. But

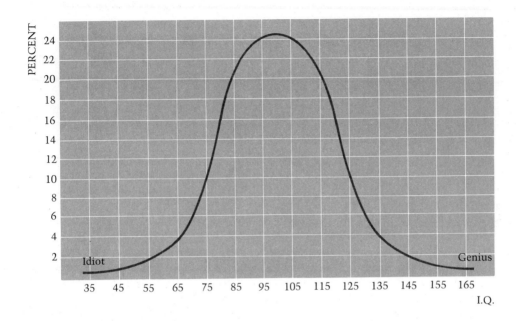

Figure 12-1.   I.Q. distribution involving a
large sample of children.

where are the geniuses? Is it not unsettling that the degree to which a
generation is informed seems to bear little relationship to the degree to
which it creates? Each year, for the past three or four decades, thousands
of Ph.D. degrees have been awarded in English, biology, physics, music,
psychology, education, art. Every Ph.D. physicist knows more about his
discipline than did Galileo or Newton. Biologists are so much more knowl-
edgeable than were Darwin or Mendel. What professor of English has not
read more drama than Shakespeare or more poety than Keats?

In response to these facts, it has been suggested that intellectual capacities are normally distributed in the population and that only a very small
number of people enjoy the "amount" necessary for creative achievements.
On the Stanford-Binet, scores above 140 were once taken to imply genius-
level intellectual potential (see Figure 12-1). The word now used is *gifted*,
because it has become obvious that if everyone with an I.Q. above 140
were a genius, the problems of the world would have been solved ages ago.

Studies of the gifted do support the prediction that high I.Q. and intellectual achievement go hand-in-hand. But *gifted* and *genius* are not the same. Nor are *achievement* and *creation*. To know that a child of seven with an I.Q. of 165 is more likely to write a book thirty years later than a peer whose I.Q. is 93 is to know very little. Since the I.Q. test is based on the same skills as those involved in writing a book, the correlation is almost inescapable. Far more helpful and revealing would be a test that predicted the quality of the achievement, its durability and originality. No simple combination of tests offers any hope of doing this.

Newton left school in his teens to work on his mother's farm. Nine years later he invented the calculus of differentiation and formulated the theory of universal gravitation. Faraday left school at seventeen. Mendelssohn composed his first symphony at eight years of age. Thomas Aquinas was ostensibly a dolt; Leonardo da Vinci, a charmer. Einstein's early difficulties with mathematics are legendary, and Goethe died still unable to comprehend Newton's theory of light. Kant was a quiet, isolated figure; Voltaire, a gadfly; Beethoven, a nuisance; Eugene O'Neill, a brute. There is no evidence that Michelangelo "saw" things differently until one examines the ceiling of the Sistine Chapel. Thus, the key to genius is not to be found in the senses or in early behavior or in measured I.Q. or in personality or in ancestry. The genius stands apart from his contemporaries, often not understood by them, living as posterity's hero. This makes it difficult for us to study him; typically, the person is no longer alive when it dawns on people that he was exceptional after all.

At present, psychology does not have a method or a plan for investigating truly exceptional people. To dismiss them as "mutants" does nothing to elucidate those processes underlying creative expression. Furthermore, the validity of any theory of human learning or cognition depends, in part, on its ability to include the exceptional cases as well as the typical. New methods must be found if newer theories are to be effective in this way. It would appear that a continued reliance on biography and mental tests will do little to reduce the relative ignorance that now prevails.

Geniuses are by no means the only organisms that haunt the halls of behaviorism. In 1961, Breland and Breland published a delightful paper entitled "The Misbehavior of Organisms." As good and practical behaviorists, the Brelands began to train various animals for zoos, circuses, television shows, trade conventions, and so on. They worked with thirty-eight different species, ranging from cockatoos to whales—about 6,000 animals in all. In the process, they observed a rather persistent tendency for animals not only to resist the tempting promise of reward, but also to engage in highly entertaining behaviors that bore no relationship whatever to the reinforcement operations used by the experimenters. They found chickens who insisted on "dancing," pigs who refused to work for a living, whales who swallowed the apparatus, rabbits who wouldn't eat at the feeder, cows who wouldn't kick. In desperation, the Brelands offered this observation:

> In our attempt to extend a behavioristically oriented approach to the engineering control of animal behavior by operant conditioning techniques, we have fought a running battle with the seditious notion of instinct. (Breland and Breland, p. 681)

The Brelands' experiences cannot be dismissed as slipshod workmanship. They simply amplify the facts that were presented in Chapter 9 and draw further attention to the numerous exceptions to basic behavioristic rules. As with the human genius, the renegade animal will also have to be analyzed as theories in behavioral psychology ripen.

MINDS AND BRAINS

There is a difference between a paradox and an enigma. Many aspects of brain function are enigmatic, a description that will encompass less as research and theory develop. The doctrine of equipotentiality advanced by Lashley (Chapter 5) is clearly at crossed purposes with the idea of localization of function. Part of this enigma is due to the expectation of parsimony, the a priori faith that brain function behaves in either localized or equipotential fashion. As findings emerge, it becomes increasingly evident that certain functions are mediated by highly circumscribed regions of the brain, whereas other functions are either directed or can be directed by almost any region of cortex left intact. The principle of localization of function is not invalidated when postoperative deficits are removed by retraining. The CNS (Central Nervous System) is a new system with each experience. It is functionally workable within rather broadly defined limits. Certain capacities are controlled by specific centers whose removal results in a shifting focus of command. Precisely how these foci are established is an enigma, but there is nothing paradoxical about it. That is, one would expect such behavior in any system designed to record and be modified by stimulation. Equipotentiality is compatible with a purely mechanical model of mental processes. It complicates the machinery that must be proposed to account for the facts, but a machine will still do.

The genuine paradoxes in the field of neuropsychology involve phenomena that have enjoyed relatively little experimental attention and even less theoretical exposition. One of these is found in the demonstration of yoga. The experienced practitioner of yoga is able to control a host of basic physiological functions to a truly remarkable degree using meditative procedures. Numerous instances have been witnessed in which the yogi suspends his own cardiac activity for periods of minutes. He enters states in which normal reflexes to aversive stimulation cannot be elicited. He maintains postural rigidity over periods of time that would appear to defy the known physiology of fatigue.

The phenomena of yoga are usually treated as special examples of "mind over matter." Included in this category are the thousands of documented cases of miraculous cures, the great diversity of psychosomatic illnesses, and the extraordinary feats alleged to occur during hypnotic trances. But alluding to the mind's ability to control the body does not answer the question; it dismisses it. The classical materialist argument contends that those processes usually described as mental are nothing more than the consequence of basic, physical events in the CNS. What is paradoxical about the foregoing phenomena is that they appear to suggest the reverse of the mechanist's script. They seem to imply that the basic, physical events occurring in the CNS are nothing more than a consequence of mental processes. It is interesting, in this connection, to report a story that was told to Konrad Lorenz by Liddell, one of Pavlov's most famous students. Liddell, it seems, was observing a dog locked in a Pavlov frame during an experiment in conditioned salivation. The CS (Conditioned Stimulus) was a ticking metronome. Liddell wondered what the dog's salivary response would be like in the absence of the restraining harness. Removed from the frame, the dog ran immediately to the metronome and attempted to operate it. He salivated profusely, according to Liddell, in order to activate the metronome. This behavior is inappropriate for a Pavlovian machine!

Freud, of course, was no stranger to the paradoxical nature of mind-

body interactions. The successful use of hypnotherapy in treating everything from skin disease to blindness was sufficient evidence for him to
postulate a "psychical" system of energies. But these are just words, not
explanations. The techniques and perspectives of physiological psychology
must be expanded to include such phenomena. If successful in this task,
the discipline will return attention to the issue that was responsible
for its creation—that of consciousness itself. It has been more than three
centuries since Descartes attempted to describe a psychology partly along
the mechanistic lines of Kepler's astronomy. Even then, Descartes realized
that consciousness could not fit into the machine except as a spiritual
force, an entity that was insubstantial, but that nevertheless exerted its
influence. The growth of science, which has fostered an almost religious
zeal for physicalism, leaves no room for Cartesian spirits, and this might
seem all to the good. Yet it is one thing to reject a metaphysical explanation, but quite another to ignore the phenomena for which it was invented.

In regard to the paradoxical nature of the relationship between neural
and mental processes, it is also helpful to examine recent studies involving
brain stimulation in human beings. Contemporary theory holds that, somehow, memories are coded neurochemically, stored somewhere, and re-
trieved in some way. The details of these processes presumably will be
elucidated through continued research. Penfield and Rasmussen (1950)
have summarized findings obtained from hundreds of patients whose brains
have been stimulated in numerous loci under local anaesthetic (the patients were conscious throughout the operative procedure). Sure enough,
temporal lobe stimuli elicited reports of past experiences. But there are
two unexpected aspects of the research. First, there is the surprisingly
high percentage of patients from whom such reports cannot be gotten.
Second, the reports themselves seldom contain the vividness and detail of
normal recollections. Sounds are distant and sights faded. Voices are often
unidentifiable. The experiences have a dreamy quality and also a *sensory*
quality that everyday memories usually do not possess. For example, recalling a conversation with a friend, one does not actually hear his voice
or see his face. Penfield's patients do. Moreover, with electrode placements
in nearly every major structure of the limbic system, it is also unexpected
that the range of elicited feelings and emotions should be so narrow and
their intensity so shallow. Failures of this kind may, of course, be the
result of methodological limitations imposed by the current "state of the
art." Perhaps with multiple simultaneous stimulations, the application of

visual and auditory "lifelike" stimuli, and recourse to longer-lasting sessions, more realistic experiences could be aroused. Since the patient's health is the first objective, research in this area is limited to an extent that may be responsible for the less than dramatic results. But other causes may be involved: causes unique to the fact of consciousness; causes of a *mental* nature.

T. X. Barber (1956) has successfully undermined some of the tenets of modern mentalism with his empirical studies of hypnotic states. Among other findings, Barber has shown that many of the acts engaged in under hypnosis are rather easy to perform while fully conscious: rendering one's body so rigid as to be supportable by one stool under the head and another under the feet; not responding to pin pricks or even flames; lying on a bed of blunted nails. Barber argues persuasively that many of the startling facts of hypnosis are understandable in simple operant terms and can be produced merely by asking a subject to cooperate. Trances may often be no more than complete relaxation, deep and even breathing, and at times, light sleep.

Hypnosis, yoga, miracles, ESP—all of these at one time or another have carried the taint of charlatanism. Even when the participants are above ethical reproach, there is a natural tendency to treat these phenomena as part of some other, better understood process. This is a respectable and properly conservative position for anyone put on guard by the early mysticism of every science. But a strong challenge does exist to confirm the doctrines of physicalism and to demonstrate how these ageless effects can be better explained by the methods of science.

THE MNEMONIST

It is important for science to concern itself with exceptional cases, because throughout its entire history, its perspective has been altered by observations of rare events or small effects. The barely visible retrograde motion of certain heavenly bodies were the only observable flaws in Ptolemy's system. Copernican astronomy better accounted for the epicycles, even though the Copernican universe was no more predictable than the Ptolemaic. Similarly, Einstein's formulations lead to greater accuracy in their specification of certain events than do those of Newton. The actual calculations in these two systems of physics yield almost but not quite identical results, despite the fact that, conceptually, the relativistic and the mechanical offer entirely different views of "truth." We stated in Chapter 1 that a theory in science must be more than correct; it must also provide a more satisfying account of the facts than its competitors do. Because of this, rare events have played a particularly significant role in the evolution of scientific thories. Typically, any one of several theoretical systems is adequate in handling average or typical cases. Thus, Thorndike's Law of Effect and Tolman's hypothesis-formation in rats are not challenged by what nearly every hungry rat does in a Skinner box. With respect to memory, trace theories, interference theories, and neurochemical theories can all be patched up in one way or another to conform to the results from the typical experiments in memory research. But how do these expositions fare in the presence of a rare case?

A. R. Luria (1968), a renowned Soviet neuropsychologist, has summarized his observations of subject S, then a Russian newspaperman reported to have an extraordinary memory. Ultimately, S became a professional *mnemonist*, entertaining throngs with his remarkable mental feats. Luria followed S over a period of years. He contrived numerous tests to get a general picture of S's total memory capacity. For example, S devoted a total of three minutes to an examination of a matrix of 52 symbols. Then, in 40 seconds he recited it perfectly. To determine whether S was just exceptionally good in serial learning, Luria required him to recite the numbers diagonally as well. No problem. In 50 seconds he rattled off the horizontal rows sequentially. In fact, S was not recalling the table, but *reading* it! That is, after examining it once, he formed an image in his mind and he was able to read the contents of the table as if he were holding a piece of paper on which they were written.

The fact is that S retained nearly permanent pictures of any material he was asked to memorize. Somehow, as with normal memory, he could file these scenes for future reference and then recall them in nearly their original visual detail. In addition to this peculiarity, S also experienced what Luria referred to as a *synesthesia*, an altered or disrupted sensitivity if sounds were uttered while material was being recorded in memory. For example, if while memorizing a table of numbers, S was spoken to, he reported that a blur was imposed on the visual image. S would mentally have to move the numbers away from the visually blurred region. Sounds to S created visual sensations. Low tones were seen as colored strips, high tones as "fireworks." Voices of different people were seen as changing spectral patterns. In reading prose, S was struck with a series of images, not just words. Each new phrase would touch off a new sequence of vivid visual experiences. Metaphorical and idiomatic speech proved to be especially taxing on his comprehension. Phrases such as "weighing one's words" or "wind-driven clouds" would immediately elicit the expected visual experience and thereby confuse him.

Luria's skepticism was modified not only by the staggering capacity of S's memory, but by equally startling demonstrations of a physiological nature. Simply by "seeing" himself place one hand in an oven and the other around an ice cube, S could alter the temperature of each hand simultaneously. By "picturing" himself chasing a train or lying in bed, he could drive his heart rate up and down at will. By imagining that he was hearing an intense and high frequency sound, S manifested a cochlear-pupil reflex.

One of S's severest problems was the inability to forget. Only through diligent practice was he able to restrict his attention sufficiently to allow just a few necessary elements of a scene to be stored for recall. In a very literal sense, S's memory was a collection of photographic traces whose persistence and detail would be modified by practice and by their implicit meaningfulness. In serial learning, the effects of primacy and recency (Chapter 6) were unknown to him. Years, even decades, after original learning, recall was perfect. Only by intentionally laboring to forget could S enjoy what many of us dread—forgetfulness. Even after committing thousands of items to memory over extended periods of time, S was virtually exempt from the effects of proactive or retroactive interference. His traces neither disappeared with time nor were they erased by subsequent images. As for his family, Luria has this to say:

> There is some evidence that S's parents demonstrated peculiarities of memory similar to those described here. According to S, when his father owned a bookstore, he could easily recall where any book was located; and his mother, a devout Jewish woman, could quote long paragraphs from the Torah . . . a nephew also had a remarkable memory. However, we do not have enough reliable information to conclude that S's memory was by nature genotypic. (Luria)

The unusual case of S is matched in small measure by a rare but reliably occurring phenomenon known as *eidetic imagery*. Almost never found in Western adults, it is reported with some regularity among very young children. The eidetic image is an almost photographically clear persistence of scenes recently witnessed. Days and even weeks later, the child can draw the scene as if he were copying it from a book. Moreover, he reports "seeing" it just as if it were still present.

Interestingly, there are reports of adult eidetic imagery among certain primitive tribes (Segall, Campbell, Herskovits, 1966). However, members of the tribe who migrate to urban or at least relatively developed locales or those who become literate quickly lose the capacity. A hypothesis advanced to account for this suggests that in the absence of verbally mediated memory, children and certain primitives possess their peculiar visual substitute. Accordingly, once verbal learning provides a richer and more direct means of memory storage and retrieval, the older system is abandoned and becomes extinct. This, of course, is not a full explanation, but it does offer an interesting point of departure for research.

Finally, under memory paradoxes, there is the phenomenon of *phantom limb*. It has been observed often that following the amputation of an extremity, the patient not only continues to sense the presence of the removed part, but often experiences intense pain in it. Moreover, the sensations in the phantom limb will respond to the same palliatives in the same way that a real injured limb would. The human phenomenon of phantom limb is analagous, in its challenge to neuropsychological theories, to those findings of Lashley and of Klüver (Chapter 6) in their ablation studies. Any theory of memory based on effector-receptor connections will have difficulty accounting for the persistence of experience in the absence of those very pathways by which the experience is communicated. Somehow the phantom limb is represented in the patient's brain, as are those initial signals of pain that are no longer emanating from the extremity. But the phantom pain comes and goes and varies in intensity and duration. It has these normal properties despite the fact that those peripheral cues that are otherwise necessary for the appearance of such properties are totally absent. Moreover, one of the fascinating features of post-traumatic shock is that pain often is not experienced at all. For example, the soldier hose limb is shot off very often reports no pain whatever until hours later when he finally receives attention. Thus, even in the instance of limited real pain, subsequent phantom pain may be quite severe. Current theories of memory do not fully account for these rare phenomena.

Luria's mnemonist, the eidetic imagery of children, and the loss of these capacities with the development of language are events that confound contemporary theories of memory. They constitute exceptions to stated laws and violations of assumed processes. On the positive side, they hold out a possible key to psychology's future understanding of this vital capacity.

SUMMARY

In selecting for discussion a few of the more confusing paradoxes and exceptions to contemporary psychological thought, there has been a not-too-hidden plea for the liberalization of perspective. But the extent of this needed liberalization is difficult to specify. Science cannot run off half-cocked, as it were, each time some peculiarity in nature is reported. In science, the handmaid of wisdom is knowledge. While wisdom may bloom with little notice, knowledge grows in small, deliberate, halting steps. Each principle is based on many reliable facts and each law on numerous and varied tests. The constant conflict between patience and boldness, perseverance and impetuosity, care and abandon characterizes all scholarly pursuits and certainly that of science. This process was aptly described by the great nineteenth-century historian Thomas Macaulay:

> Every where there is a class of men who cling with fondness to whatever is ancient, and who, even when convinced by overpowering reasons that innovation would be beneficial, consent to it with many misgivings and forebodings. We find also everywhere another class of men sanguine in hope, bold in speculation, always pressing forward, quick to discern the imperfections of whatever exists, disposed to think lightly of the risks and inconveniences which attend improvements, and disposed to give every change credit for being an improvement. In the sentiments of both classes there is something to approve, but of both the best specimens will be found not far from a common frontier. (Macaulay)

Indeed, psychology must strike out boldly, but with one step at a time. As an experimental discipline, it is barely a century old, and this alone urges a certain restraint. As an ensemble of questions and puzzles, it is thousands of years old, but in the long history of this part of psychology, boldness and progress have not been highly correlated.

SUGGESTED READINGS

LURIA, A. R. *The Mind of a Mnemonist: A Little Book About a Vast Memory.* New York: Basic Books, 1968.

This is a most enjoyable and fascinating study which can be read in one evening.

MAUROIS, A. *Illusions.* New York: Columbia University Press, 1968.

This work, published soon after Maurois' death, is the view a man of letters has of the nature of illusion. It is Platonic; Kantian. A careful reading leads inexorably to a liberalization of the perspective.

CHAPTER

13

From Principles to Proposals

A society and its institutions reflect the philosophic premises of its members. They may not, and usually do not, have an academic familiarity with the philosophies they embrace, nor can they, at an intellectual level, describe their actions in formal philosophic terms. Instead, each citizen is raised to believe that certain acts are right and others wrong, certain traits good and others evil, certain attitudes virtuous and others not.

Traditionally, the *zeitgeist* that pervades a society or subculture has its immediate determinants in religious precepts. It is easier to teach children the lessons of religion than it is to tutor them in the ways of philosophy. Moreover, religious tenets are usually absolute, while philosophy offers only alternatives. Thus, the process of socialization is facilitated by adherence to the strictures of theology but may be seriously retarded by the indecisiveness implicit in the arguments of philosophy.

Even in societies apparently devoid of formal religion, it is safe to conclude that a religious tone characterizes the socialization process. That is, the dictates of the society are not validated through logical proofs and philosophic analyses. Rather, they are taken on faith, either the faith that what has worked in the past will continue to be successful or faith in the wisdom of the society's founding fathers.

While the instruments of socialization often incorporate religious principles, the more distant ancestry of these very principles is philosophical. The world's religions teach similar lessons, but the lessons are based on different conceptions of the nature and destiny of man. At some point in their evolution, existing systems of thought were called on to defend their precepts against those ideas they came to replace. The philosophical elements of any religion can usually be found during its earliest history, during the period when debate is still spirited. As it gains adherents and as conflicting views lose support, dialogue gives way to conviction and philosophy to faith. Each age fashions its own candles to light the way along the endless tunnels of the human experience. Often, it mistakes its own flame for a light at the end. It is this confusion that leads to movements and "isms," to crusades and persecutions.

The conditions under which reliable psychological data have been obtained are far too constricted and controlled to allow them to be brought to bear on the complex relationship between man and society. At present, research findings can provide no more than challenges to certain traditional views. That is, while psychological science cannot define the relevant dimensions of man (his needs, possibilities, unfailing tendencies, and so on) or the best form of social order, it can raise objections to and suggest the limitations of certain traditional social conceptions. It is worthwhile to consider here several of the more prominent of these conceptions in light of contemporary psychological principles.

PHILOSOPHICAL ORIENTATION AND SOCIAL ORGANIZATION

When translated into political theory, nativistic philosophy provides the justification for caste and class systems of social organization. The kings and pharaohs of ancient times derived their authority from the popular belief that they were *inherently* different from the great bulk of humankind. Earlier, elite status was no doubt based simply on differences in physical strength. But with the evolution of complex social organizations, more subtle factors participated in the emergence of class hierarchies. At the root, all of these factors finally reduce to the conviction that some men are better than others and that the differences between them cannot be changed. This conviction is most obviously manifested in *eugenics* movements, one of the first of which was proposed by Plato in his *Republic*. Using the success achieved in breeding hunting dogs as a justification, Plato argued that Greek leadership would have to be created by arranged marriages in which partners were selected for desirable phenotypic combinations. Infants born with deformities or born to parents of undesirable "stock" were to be taken away to some unspecified place—and fate.

Plato was a deeply troubled man, overcome by the senseless repetition of wars, the corruption and dwindling moral commitment of Athenians, and the demise of a civilization that had been unequaled in history. He saw in the military successes of Sparta a justification for civil and legal reform. Sparta was the model for his proposals on government, marriage, education, and civil rights and responsibilities. The philosopher-king of the *Republic* appeared to be the only alternative to a democracy in which vice had replaced valor.

Since that time, the ideas of Plato have been raised often and in many contexts. In modern times, the threats and realities of overpopulation have rekindled enthusiasm for the principles of eugenics. Moreover, since Darwin, many political theorists have based their propositions on concepts drawn from evolutionary biology. A vivid example is *social Darwinism*, which sees a means of improving the human stock in its completely laissez faire approach to social organization. The argument goes something like this: People are innately different. Some are weak and always will be. Others are strong and contain the greatest capacities for adaptation and species success. By allowing unimpeded competition, the strongest will endure and the weakest will ultimately perish. Since the laws of Darwinian biology sustain these principles, human interference is both unwarranted and, over the long run, futile.

Some eugenicists see no reason to wait for the agonizingly slow processes of natural selection to create the hardiest of humankind. They see in modern science the potential for "genetic engineering," which would produce specific genotypes for specific functions on the basis of social requirements.

Significantly less radical forms of eugenic planning have been part of state marriage laws for decades. In many places, it is illegal for feeble-minded couples to bear children. Moreover, parents carrying certain heritable diseases are urged strenuously not to have offspring. Thus, the nativistic perspective can be found in varying degrees in social and political theory. In the extreme, it may be racist and genocidal, such as that of Nazi Germany. In its most moderate form, it leads to special grouping arrangements, such as "track" systems of education, placing the brightest students in one curriculum, average students in another, and the least gifted students in yet another. Between psychopathic racism and common-sense conveniences, each point on the spectrum of possibilities is touched. Given the perspective, any number of institutions and attitudes can be generated: some hopelessly banal, some ritualistic, some nearly cosmic in implication. The selection of kings by familial succession, the "Four Hundred," the "chosen people," the "natural rhythm" of the black man—these are just a small sample of practices, stereotypes, and rituals springing from nativism or, in its social manifestation, *elitism*. It has served as the intellectual justification for tyranny, for discrimination, for greed, for war.

If the nativistic perspective were ridiculous, it would not appear with such frequency nor would it enjoy such successful application as it has. A mere scanning of the data presented in Chapter 9 is enough to establish the role of hereditary factors in physical and psychological development. There is no doubt that on the average, tall children have tall parents and short children have short parents. Mice can be inbred to solve maze problems quickly or poorly. Certain mental deficiencies are, indeed, highly heritable. Psychological attributes do tend to run in families, even when environmental variations are substantial. To the extent that discrimination and generalization are unavoidable correlates of all learning, it is not surprising that man has come to stereotype others on familial, ethnic, and national bases. In a restaurant named "Mario's," is it not more likely to find veal Marsala on the menu than it is to find Peking duck? The same thing holds true for Chinese laundries or Italian opera singers. And so the list unfolds, and the speaker using these stereotypes is certain that he has uncovered a principle of unfailing utility. In his ceaseless attempts to understand the world around him, he has successfully located the "them" in the "us-and-them" tension.

There can be no challenge to the assertion that basic differences exist among individuals. It is in this very diversity that the success of *homo sapiens* is rooted. That is, given the challenges likely to confront the species during its existence, it is only through a broad diversification of genotypic constitution that man can survive to perpetuate his kind. The history of royal families and the history of civilizations both point to the detrimental consequences of biological and social inbreeding. For the sake of argument, one may assume that intelligence and even genius can be increased in the population by selective breeding. Even granting this symplistic assertion, there is still the question "For what?" Is there any evidence in the long history of ideas that the genius has answers to the abiding questions? Was Plato the model genius and, if so, is the wisdom of his *Republic* sufficient for a solution to the many human dilemmas? If it is, then no further geniuses are necessary. If not, is it reasonable to assume that more satisfactory alternatives will come from the pens of future giants? If destruction by war is our most imminent threat, is there a guarantee that intelligence and pacifism are highly correlated? Are pacifism and long-term survival compatible? Add to these questions the inescapable folly of homogenizing genotypes for an environment that may change precipitously, and the conceptual limitations of radical eugenics become conspicuous.

Practically, of course, the issue is not less complex. Presently, not enough is known about either genetics or psychology for a social experiment to be launched with enthusiasm. In the Dark Ages, intelligence was the vehicle by which man came to appreciate the unavoidable hopelessness of life and came to understand his duty to submit to otherworldly forces. In the epoch of the cave, intelligence was no more than an understanding of the jungle, the cunning and strength of the warrior, the courage to fight and the prudence to run. From the nineteenth century until recently, intelligence was the capacity to rob the environment of her riches and to turn the beautiful pastoral reaches of the earth into mechanized, man-serving instruments. Thus, even if the mental and behavioral dispositions of man prove to be genetically manipulable, it is by no means clear what the phenotypes should be. And then, who is to decide? What body ascertains the feasibility of allowing a particular type to survive? Is the same wisdom that has done so much to rid the world of so many precious animal species to be brought to bear upon the task of selectively improving mankind?

Elitist (nativistic) conceptions of man and society derive support ultimately from naïve interpretations of heredity and evolutionary biology. They rest upon typological inferences and generally fail to acknowledge the broad "reaction range" (Chapter 9) permitted by genetic mechanisms. They leap from the facts of additive genetic influences (as a result of which phenotypic characters come to be normally distributed) to the assumption of qualitative hierarchies. They ignore gene-environment interactions and thus assume fixity where, in fact, plasticity is the rule. Quite easily, they then come to treat individuals according to some "average" feature of the group to which these individuals belong.

The philosophical tension between nativism and empiricism forms the basis of the tension in social theory between *elitism* and *egalitarianism*. The latter views the potentials and limitations of man as the product of the circumstances of his life, that is, of environmental conditions. The former locates these potentials and limitations within man himself. While elitism forces distinctions to be made among men, egalitarianism either ignores or denies the differences in proposing its social structures and practices. By and large, the elitist emphasis is on growth and improvement of the race or culture, while the egalitarian emphasis is on individual happiness. Thus, it is the latter perspective that has proposed utopias and the means of obtaining them. Two such models are worthy of examination, one from the fifteenth century and a recent one proposed by B. F. Skinner.

THE UTOPIAN IDEAL

Thomas More (1478-1535) in his *Utopia* fashioned fifty-four little villages, physically identical, in which everyone worked only six hours a day and each family changed houses periodically so as not to feel that they owned any of them. Presumably, this was More's answer to territoriality (Chapter 9). Farms were governed by the old because they were wise. Popular election was used to determine who would live a life of scholarship, and government was to be run only by the educated. A prince was elected for life, but he could be impeached if he attempted to be tyrannical. In families, the father ruled. While any religion was tolerated, citizenship required belief in the immortality of the soul and in one true God. All ownership was public, and most living was communal. War was fought only in defense of Utopia or of neighbors threatened by hostile forces. In either case, fighting was voluntary and usually done by foreign mercenaries. Lawlessness was punished by labor, not by death. Church and state were separated, and priests enjoyed respect without temporal authority.

There is little reason to expect that Thomas More's *Utopia* is either possible or desirable. The prince who can be impeached is no prince at all, but only a functionary for the popular will. An army of mercenaries can just as well turn its weapons on the paymaster. If fighting is voluntary and private ownership impossible, what inducements are there for a citizen to risk his life? What competence have the uneducated in the task of choosing those who will be scholars? What ensures the continuing support of a minority whose candidates never win?

More's social system was a naïve communism contrived with more wit but less perspective than Marx's. But even Marx, for all his brilliance, fails to acknowledge the motivational determinants of behavior and the facts of biological individuality. It is not conceivable that a human organism can be raised in the absence of secondary reinforcement and, once so raised, that he will cease to work for reward. The application of piecemeal reinforcement, by which reward is proportional to fixed quantities of work, produces predictable outcomes. Since individuals differ in ability, proportional reinforcement either discourages excellence or creates a class system in which the best soon become the richest. To avoid an economic class system by keeping financial gains constant but moving the best workers into increasingly more critical occupations is simply to substitute occupational elitism for economic elitism.

Of course, a temporary way around the Law of Effect and the ubiquity of secondary reinforcements is to substitute a grand abstraction for material compensation. That is, by making reward contingent upon the citizen's commitment to some encompassing system of thought, the latter will come to control behavior even after the former is removed. Moreover, if the citizen is reared in a social community already so committed, then social pressures, through their reinforcement strength, will be successful in homogenizing attitudes and behaviors. The durable effects of religious training can be accounted for in part by the fact that ultimate rewards are scheduled to arrive after life. Marxian principles, which promised an end to strife in *this* life, have already undergone considerable modification in Russia. The success of Marxian orthodoxy in China must be considered in light of the fact that life under the regime of Mao *is* better than it was in pre-Marxian times or so we are told.

The difficulty every leader has in attempting to create a utopia is at least threefold. First, he must convince the people that things are not as good as they should be. Second, he must convince them that things are bad because they have subscribed to a system of thought that is deficient. Finally, he must hold out some opportunity for secondary reinforcements for those who pledge loyalty to his view. Of course, if the leader controls an army, he now can control behavior through the mechanism of primary (negative) reinforcement. But, historically, control of armies is more a consequence than a cause of political success. To follow through on promises, the leader must begin to redistribute available resources (reinforcers). Usually this requires taking from the rich and giving to the poor. Unfortunately, the latter are much more numerous than the former, and there isn't really as much to go around as the leader (or leaders) originally believed. Moreover, progress requires skills and excellence, and both usually are costly. Soon a class structure reappears, which may be military, religious, technological, or intellectual, depending on the laws of supply and demand.

Skinner is perhaps the most recent utopian and the only psychologist who has tried his hand practically at a utopian model society. In his novel *Walden Two*, a society is structured around the principles of reinforcement as mastered by Dr. Frazier and applied to all members. Enough has been said of these principles, but nothing of a defense of their social applications. Skinner's book elicited predictable condemnation from "humanistic" circles, the most ardent response being Joseph Wood Krutch's *The Measure of Man*. Apparently in answer to these criticisms, Skinner summarized the ethics of *Walden Two* in an article entitled, "Freedom and the Control of Men." Regarding the idea of behavioral control, he says:

> If we are not to rely solely upon accident for the innovations which give rise to cultural evolution, we must accept the fact that some kind of control of human behavior is inevitable.

In other words, what men have done throughout history is not the result of some random process. Their conditioning histories have caused their behavior. Walden Two is a place where child-rearing proceeds as it always has except it is conducted effectively. Skinner observes that energy is expended in both work and play. Men do not avoid the former because it is tiring, but because it has been given aversive properties. Similarly, with proper conditioning, man need not constantly strain to be good or moral. There is no reason why the tendencies to morality and selflessness should not come as naturally as those of malice and greed.

> It is reasonable to look forward to a time when man will seldom "have" to do anything, although he may show interest, energy, imagination, and productivity far beyond the level seen under the present system. (B. F. Skinner)

In the context of Skinner's proposals, Hitler is a most revealing subject. He ascended to power in a Christian country dedicated to the same moral precepts expounded by Western societies since Athens. Yet through careful manipulation of real and implied reinforcements, he created patterns of behavior that were totally at variance with these stated principles. Freud was not surprised by World War I because he never believed that man was basically good. Skinner is not surprised by Nazi Germany because he does not believe that man, behaviorally, is "basically" anything.

Skinner sees the emergence of behavioral engineering, a true science of human behavior, as an inevitable developmnt that will finally permit the creation of people and conditions suited to each other and suited to the survival of *homo sapiens*. Moreover, the arrival of that day promises to deny man nothing of what he cherishes most:

> The achievements of man in science, art, literature, music, and morals will survive any interpretation we place on them. . . . Man, in short, will remain man. . . . Possibly the noblest achievement to which man can aspire, even according to present standards, is to accept himself for what he is, as this is revealed to him by the methods which he devised and tested. . . . (B. F. Skinner)

While it is certainly true that human creations remain a matter of record independent of how science interprets their causes, it is also true that an understanding of the creative process is totally dependent on the validity of interpretations. *Hamlet* remains *Hamlet* whether viewed as the outcome of Shakespeare's reinforcement history or as the result of human genius, whether considered an empirical inevitability or a nativistic imperative. But as Skinner or anyone truly concerned with a science of human behavior must admit, each of these opposing alternative explanations carries with it a unique conception of humankind and, therefore, unique proposals for human society.

Walden Two and Skinner's whole system of psychology have met with disfavor among those who insist that there is more to man than the pleasure principle. They state that the essence of man is to be found in precisely those behaviors that are not amenable to manipulation by reinforcement. In this respect, modern romantics and humanists are re-creating, in their anti-Skinnerianism, the arguments that greeted LaMettrie's radical physicalism (discussed in Chapter 4). Descartes' mechanistic psychology was tolerable because the essentiality of the soul was preserved, but when LaMettrie extended the model to include the soul as an "enlightened machine," there was a strong and stern reaction. Today Skinner enjoys the favor even of humanists for his considerable contributions to an understanding of the basic processes of learning. But when he attempts to extend these principles to the broadest sweep of human experience, he immediately invites opposition. He is denounced as a prophet of robotism, a messenger of sameness, an enemy of the human spirit. Aware of this, he recognizes that *Walden Two* is distant:

> It will be a long time before the world can dispense with heroes and hence with the cultural practice of admiring heroism, but we move in that direction whenever we act to prevent war, famine, pestilence, and disaster. It will be a long time before man will never need to submit to punishing environments or engage in exhausting labor, but we move in that direction whenever we make food, shelter, clothing, and labor-saving devices more readily available. We may mourn the passing of heroes but not the conditions which make for heroism. We can spare the laundress on the river's bank struggling against fearful odds to achieve cleanliness. (B. F. Skinner)

Thomas More's utopia was made necessary by the tyranny and corruption of leaders. Marx's was in response to the savagery instilled in man by capitalistic systems of economy. Skinner's ideas rest on the technological successes enjoyed by the laboratory manipulation of animal behavior. Each of these theorists is optimistic and, at the root, humanistic. Each subscribes to the view that the human potential for peace and happiness is vast and that its failure to materialize is the consequence of error, evil, or both. All of them view happiness (defined differently by each) as the ultimate objective of human life. Thomas More emphasized freedom from tyranny; Marx, freedom from exploitation; Skinner, freedom from choice. All can be reduced to a kind of contentment. Each would feel at home with the utilitarianism of Jeremy Bentham or of

John Stuart Mill. In his essay "On Liberty," Mill declares, "I regard utility as the ultimate appeal on all ethical questions," and by utility, Mill means the pleasure principle. For Mill, personal liberty is limited only to the extent that it harms others. Government's essenial function is to ensure a maximum of personal, individual freedom while guaranteeing that no action of one individual will cause injury or a denial of liberty to another. Mill created his theory of government, as did More and Marx, without benefit of modern psychology. One might suppost that had Mill or Marx known of the principles of Freudian psychology or of the data that support nativistic conceptions of man, each would have had second thoughts—although it seems that Skinner has not. Mill's ideas would be more challenged than Marx's by nativistic implications of modern psychological thought, for Mill was so decidedly empiricistic. The utopias imaginable to the mind of an empiricist are but fantasies to traditional nativists such as Kant, Freud, and Lorenz.

For the radical environmentalist, all things are possible. Since human action derives automatically from human experience, the ideal man is an inevitable product of the idealized environment. The proper application of rewards and punishments, administered judiciously from birth to young adulthood, will eventuate in a socialized, moral, and competent man of character. Good and evil, by such a view, are only the creations of a society, products of custom and culture, which are themselves only inventions. As Bentham put it, "The business of government is to promote the happiness of the society, by punishing and rewarding," and it does these in response to behavior, not intention. With pre-Skinnerian rigor, Bentham relegated conceptions of will, motive, intention, and disposition to the category of shameless conjecture. These conceptions are, of course, the central themes of nativistic psychology. The nativist, in assuming that the basic nature of man includes a constellation of behavioral propensities, contends that societies must establish institutions and methods for dealing with certain inevitabilities. With respect to lawlessness, however, a certain theoretical bind is encountered. For whether one embraces a Skinnerian model of behavioral causation or a nativistic conception, personal responsibility vanishes. If all behavior is the consequence of the individual's reinforcement history, then the responsibility for antisocial behavior rests with those who controlled and dispensed the reinforcements. Similarly, if hostile actions are innately determined, the law is put in the position of punishing a man for his genotype. In either case, justice cannot be served by retaliation. Moreover, if one embraces a nativistic conception of malevolent behavior, he is forced to wonder if the law can ever hope to be effective; that is, can retribution alter what is innate? Presumably, through the process of ritualization (Chapter 9), the "baser" instincts can be forced to express themselves in symbolic and even constructive ways. Freud referred to this as *sublimation*. But from a nativistic perspective, social institutions would appear to be fighting a losing battle with inborn dispositions to violence, malice, greed, and corruption. There are, of course, humanistic versions of nativism that accentuate the positive: man is predisposed to kindness, benevolence, charity, and virtue. A third version, that of eugenics, argues that the human population contains both sets of dispositions and that selective breeding will allow the most virtuous to prevail.

EGALITARIANISM VERSUS EUGENICS

Even Aristotle, the empiricist, was persuaded to believe that great and unchangeable differences exist among people. He argued that while all people were capable of understanding reason, all did not possess reason. Those who did not he called "natural slaves." Locke, Hume, and Mill also acknowledged inborn differences among men, but, as with later behaviorists, considered these differences small relative to those created by experience. Similarly, traditional nativists, from Plato to Leibnitz and Kant, appreciated the role of experience in shaping many aspects of individual psychology, but in the most important features of mental life, they emphasized innate forces.

While the philosophers of each persuasion were temperate in their dealings with contrary points of view, political engineers have tended to be more absolutist. Social egalitarianism begins with the aphorism "All men are created equal," and then attempts to prove it. The assumption is that if no artificial barriers to achievement are constructed, all people will reach the social niche to which they aspire. Accordingly, the egalitarian doctrine requires an equalization of opportunity, the establishment of equal intensities of motivation, and the periodic redistribution of resources in order to fulfill its prophesies.

On the other side, some political eugenicists misapply the Darwinian hypothesis of "survival of the fittest" and then attempt to prove it. Their assumption is that no force on earth will eliminate the innate differences among men and that in a freely competitive society the best will win out. War, competition, and strife will purge the community of those least fit to succeed, and successive generations will become hardier and more resilient. They view socialism and welfare as doomed practices, last efforts to preclude the inevitable.

Nations have been moved to action by both of these attitudes. Lacking wisdom, people are persuaded by rhetoric, which, historically, has been the cornerstone of political success. Of late, many citizens, especially the young, have grown tempestuous in their devotion to rhetoric and anguished by the perpetuation of the human dilemma. They see vast sums of money expended for research in science, but what follows is just a greater capacity for annihilation. They read of research in the social sciences, but discover no answer to the eternal questions. They demand relevance and action. Looking to scholars, they get neither. They conclude, therefore, that the "ivory tower" is filled with indifference and ineptitude. In fact, their target is often reason itself. Even contemporary scholars are heard with increasing frequency to voice objections to the so-called rationalist tradition. The past decade has witnessed a revival of humanistic attitudes made famous by Jean Jacques Rousseau. The central thesis in all of Rousseau's important works is that man is born good and that his evil is the product of civilization. In Rousseau one finds the virtues of the "noble savage," who has achieved rapport with nature, who kills only to eat, who occupies himself with the simple pleasures of life, and who surrounds his senses with an atmosphere of peace and innocence, sharing nature's gifts communally with his fellow human beings. All this natural bounty is sacrificed on the altar of reason. Goodness is perverted by competition and extravagance. Harmony with the life of the world is upset by the cultivated need to control. Love is stilled in the breast by the excessive demands of the brain.

The history of ideas offers many instances of the humanist-rationalist tension. One finds it in Saint Augustine's *City of God,* the only true and eternal city, which unlike Rome, is never to be beset by the imperfections and vices of pride. One finds it later in the "pre-established harmony" of Leibnitz; a predetermination of history leading inescapably to love and selflessness. Often, but not always, the humanist ideal presents itself as reason's adversary. The implication is that man's rational and emotional faculties are in opposition; that faith, hope, and empirical knowledge somehow cannot co-exist; that science and poetry are mutually exclusive;

that tenderness withers in the intellect. Those so inclined will look down on an "Age of Reason" and will lay at the doorstep of science complete responsibility for the problems of the world.

It is not always clear what "rationalism" means in these debates. In the most academic sense, it is the contention that the laws of nature are accessible to the human mind and that valid and general principles can be deduced through a critical exercise of the intellectual faculty. That men of such persuasion have cut themselves off from the human condition and have found more interest in theory than in practice is no proof against the validity of the proposition. The inept physician is not an argument for the elimination of scalpels. Nor is it at all clear that reason is any less "natural" to man than is goodness nor that the activity of the former retards attainment of the latter. In the extreme, the antirationalist spokesman would have reasoned skepticism give way to passionate commitment. He would have everyone drop whatever it is they are doing and unite in solidarity against the enemy he has discovered. He would suspend the sterile searches for truth and begin the harder and more honest work of healing, helping, and loving. Even further into the extreme, he would censor what can do man harm. His scholarship would be the scholarship of reassurance and his lesson the lesson of love. Debate would center on means, not ends. Instruction would be not in facts, but in values.

Not only is there something to recommend this perspective, but there is even an object-lesson of its consequences to be found. There was indeed a time when love and faith did not complement reason, but replaced it. There was an entire age devoted to goodness; an age whose debates were limited to means and not ends, whose goal was salvation and not knowledge. Since that age, the scientific disciplines have avoided unrelenting concern with what is "good." Since that age, scholarship in general has been ill-disposed toward "feeling" as a basis for wisdom and "love" as the only end.

The age to be discussed is what has come to be called the Middle Ages. It is a much-maligned period historically as shall be seen. Too often, reviews of the medieval era focus to such a degree on the pillage of the Crusades and the barbarism of the Inquisition that the underlying humanism of that period is totally obscured. The Middle Ages did not invent bigotry. They did not discover exploitation and greed in high office. They did not vote on the value of ignorance. Every age, indeed every year, finds man steeped in injustice and pulled along by fear, obedience, ignorance, and hope. As for inquisitions, they too were not patented by the medievalist. Socrates had been victimized by them long before and Galileo, long after. What distinguishes the Middle Ages from both ancient Greece and the Age of Reason is not what was bad about them, but what was *good*. It was a period of self-induced innocence. It was the only post-Socratic period in the history of the Western world that proclaimed the inferiority of the intellect. The human experience is, among other things, an expanding list of crusades and inquisitions. But the unique distinction of the Middle Ages is found in the role of her outstanding scholars. Uniformly, they were apologists rather than critics. They too joined communally in the single-minded commitment to rid the world of sin.

MEDIEVAL PSYCHOLOGY: A PERSPECTIVE

The fifteenth century launched the tradition of treating that period between 500 and 1500 A.D. as "the night of a thousand years." In their courtship with ancient times scholars of the fifteenth and, especially, the sixteenth centuries displayed a contempt—a visible envy—for those who had separated them in time from what they wished to be their direct ancestry (De Wulf, 1926). Perhaps to exaggerate the intellectual accomplishments of the emerging Renaissance, it proved fashionable to view their present enlightenment against a background of homogeneous darkness. That their prejudices and historical gaps were preserved and intensified by posterity is due in part to the power of persuasion and to what, in psychological terms, may be called either the "halo effect" or stimulus generalization. After all, scholarship from 1500 A.D. to the present was right about so many things, why should it err in the matter of the Middle Ages?

According to these received doctrines, the age separating the death of Saint Augustine (430) from the birth of Saint Thomas Aquinas (1225) was "Dark" and that between the latter's death (1274) and the fall of Constantinople (1453) was "Middle."

Expositions of the history of psychology have supported the foregoing rendition with little equivocation. Boring's classic work, *A History of Experimental Psychology*, for example, contributes one paragraph to the millennium beginning with 500 A.D. The Herrnstein-Boring "Source Book" contains no reference between the ancient philosophers and Kepler

(1604). Sahakian's excellent anthology, *History of Psychology*, respects the "void" presumed to separate Augustine and the thirteenth century. One finds in a modern text (Chaplin and Krawiec, 1968):

> The atmosphere was dominated by authoritarianism, both political and theological; and consequently scientific progress came to a virtual halt. . . . (p. 17)

Robert Holt, writing in Wolman's anthology, offers this:

> Around 400 A.D., Saint Augustine brought a good deal of Plato into Christianity, and about 850 dark years later Saint Thomas Aquinas. . . . (p. 198)

Not limited to psychology, the mathematician, Eric Temple Bell (1934) takes an even stronger position:

> The Middle Ages (300-1500 A.D.) in Europe provided the world with its first official theory of truth. Either you believed what you were told or you were consigned to hell. (p. 141)

In other words, there is a surprising uniformity of agreement on the insignificance of the Middle Ages in the history of psychology. A natural question in light of this is, *Can a period that gave the world its first universities, its first mental institutions, and a litany of thinkers, which included Boethius, Duns Scotus, Abelard, Anselm and Thomas, not warrant inclusion in the history of psychology?* An affirmative reply seems warranted. It is important for us to examine why.

Psychology is founded on those traditions that flowered in Greece and reappeared only after the sixteenth century. Given these traditions and a belief in the permanence of the issues they spawned, it is not unfair that historians of psychology accord significance only to Thomas Aquinas and perhaps Roger Bacon in treatments of the pre-Renaissance period. Even in the instance of these two, however, there is little sense of indebtedness, for Thomas did not present his assertions in a form directly amenable to experimental assay, and Bacon, while promoting the virtues of experimentation, did not specify the questions to which his methods should be applied. Those philosophers who came before the school of experimental psychology were much more deliberate in their statement of variables and much more direct in their emphasis upon the mental. What, then, happened to the Middle Ages?

To begin with, from Thales to Lord Russell, philosophers—as humans kind—have speculated on those issues raised by their times and not accommodated by older solutions. Some scholars of the Middle Ages were well aware of ancient philosophical wisdom, but they were also aware of the fate of that enlightened antiquity. Clearly, philosophic wisdom was not enough, and yet it was the most that reason could attain. Christianity was embraced by some of the best Western minds, not because they failed to understand the lessons of Greece, but because they had learned the *lesson* of Greece. It is often overlooked that the Church's hold on the people was gained by conversion, a new technique by ancient standards. Churchmen were able to convince large masses of struggling humanity that the gnomic wisdom contained in scripture would provide them with the practical wisdom necessary for everyday life. Thus, both the best minds —conditioned first by the collapse of Hellenism and then by the demise of the "eternal" city—and the average minds—anxious to survive the challenges of life—found the substance of Christian dogma intuitively appealing.

It is true that a genuine scholarship obtained at least from 900 A.D. It must be praised for its genuineness because it continued to teach and to translate the very philosophies to which the medieval scholar did not completely subscribe. The monastic curriculum, as early as the sixth century, included classical Greek and Roman works under Grammar, Rhetoric, and Dialectic. But, since Greek philosophy ignored the medievalist's greatest problem (saving one's soul) and was never intended to be of help with the smaller ones, the study of philosophy was considered to be merely a means of exercising the mind.

The Middle Ages bred an intensely practical man. Law and medical schools flourished. Hospitals were founded in many major cities. The administration of civic justice, the construction of churches and monasteries, the maintenance of large armies—all of these vital functions required the cultivation of a laboring class committed to certain social and spiritual tenets. The Church not only preserved scholarship, but kept civilization together as well. Astrology was ridiculed, sorcery outlawed, and money lending contained. Rewards and punishments were skillfully meted out over a wide range of practical matters. All that concerned the medievalist in these situations was simply whether a practice worked. The vagaries of coincidence combined with the absence of theory to lead the pragmatist to absurdity: a 1474 court in Bâle "condemned a cock to be burned alive for having laid an egg, in derogation of its proper sex." But even in the equally burlesque sentencing of a hog to death by hanging, the court justified its decision, "in order to keep exemplary justice" (Coulton, 1935). Contrary to the image of the medievalists as a band of terrified soul-savers, the first great institutions—after church and state—were devoted to law and medicine, the practical arts through which earthly life was enriched. Salerno's famous medical school dates not later than 1050 A.D., and its part in the "medical renaissance" predates the earliest infusion of Arab scholarship into Western culture. The humoral mechanics, which modern times have attributed to Descartes, was an established physiological concept by 1260 A.D. In summarizing the principal biological tenets of his day, the thirteenth-century Franciscan, Bartholomew asserts:

> The vital spirit is spread into all the body and worketh in the artery veins the pulses of life . . . this animal spirit is gendered in the foremost den of the brain, and is somewhat spread into the limbs of feeling. But yet nevertheless some part thereof abideth in the aforesaid dens, the common sense, the common wit, and the virtue imaginative may be made perfect.

After discussing the intellect and memory, Bartholomew argues that the diverse effects should be considered as deriving from a common mechanism:

> One and the same spirit is named by divers names. For by working in the liver it is called the natural spirit, in the heart the vital spirit, and in the head, the animal spirit. We may not believe that this spirit is man's reasonable soul, but more soothly, as saith Austin, the care thereof and proper instrument . . . with the service of such a spirit, no act the soul may perfectly exercise in the body.

It is important to realize that Bartholomew was not a statistician, a lone genius buried under the principles of medieval spiritualism. His treatise is not a summary of personal insights, but an outline of what was generally held. Why, then, does psychology's history of philosophic materialism so typically jump from the Greek atomists to Descartes? One reason is that Descartes is careful to acknowledge the influence of Kepler on his thinking; Locke acknowledges Descartes; Condillac, Cabanis, La Mettrie—all the way to Gall, Broca, Flourens—the entire French "school" also pays homage to Descartes as the English empiricists did to Locke. In other words, historical procession is more orderly with the medievalists omitted. But most important is the medievalists' disinclination to theorize on psychological matters. Bartholomew apparently saw no need to argue the merits of psychophysical monism, psychological materialism, or behavioral reflexology. Rather, intuition, medical practice, and the known symptomatology of common disorders all pointed to a humoral mechanism for sensation, feeling, and behavior—period! In such matters, church authority was essentially unfelt. Surely, had materialism been expanded to include the soul, orthodoxy would have intervened, *as it did throughout the Renaissance.* But perhaps because of the unwavering acceptance of his spiritual origins and destiny, the medievalist had less difficulty in accepting simple, mechanistic explanations of psychobiological processes than did later scholars. By the time science became self-consciously positivistic, too little patience for "practitioners" was left to rescue medieval scholarship from the forgotten abode in which it has since resided.

To assail the absence of experimentation of Bartholomew's part is to offer a criticism that can embrace all of the thinkers from whom psychology has derived its problems and most of those who provided its methods. Locke contended that it could "be granted easily that if a child were kept in a place where he never saw other but black and white till he were a man, he would have no . . . ideas of scarlet or green." Locke used no method but deduction in fashioning this view. Nor did Bentham search for hungry rats in order to determine the role of pleasure and pain in human behavior. Nor did Kant require a "visual cliff" to ascertain the inborn quality of depth and space perception. What occurred from the seventeenth to the nineteenth centuries was the emergence of experimentalism in the context of a philosophic spirit, which had never really ended, and a new technology, which granted this experimentalism some access to philosophy. As Alfred North Whitehead once said, the nineteenth century "invented the method of invention." The history of psychology since has been largely a matter of determining the degree of this access. As such, historians of psychology have been understandably indifferent to pre-experimentalist periods, or, at least, to periods lacking controlled experimental methods.

It is too early to tell whether Gustav Fechner's dream—reflecting the optimism of the nineteenth century—will find ultimate expression in modern psychology, which already can boast of a large volume of facts and basic principles. One thing, however, is certain. Experimentalism has permitted very old philosophic questions to be addressed at new and exciting levels, and to this extent, psychology's debt to the eighteenth and nineteenth centuries is great. Medieval scholars did inspire their successors and provided much of the practical wisdom on which subsequent discovery was based. But in their commitment to relevance, the medievalists denied their age the privilege of fathering a scientific psychology. All they could produce was a helpful *applied* psychology. Perhaps history has been too harsh in emphasizing this limitation; but then history is harsh.

SUMMARY

Behind most social tragedies we will find the corruption of a philosophic tenet. In 1969, three men journeyed from earth to the moon, and two of them actually trod its ancient dust. It was a remarkable technological triumph. To some it seemed cruelly paradoxical that we could journey to the moon but could not solve our problems on earth. Such critics failed to realize that the Apollo capsule was driven by Newtonian principles incalculably simpler than any now available for a sophisticated understanding of human psychology. The evolution of such principles cannot occur until psychology acknowledges that they do not now exist.

SUGGESTED READINGS

BENTHAM, J. and J. S. MILL. *The Utilitarians.* Garden City, N.Y. Doubleday & Co., 1961.

This is a paperback edition of Bentham's *Principles and Morals and Legislation* and Mill's *On Liberty* and *Utilitarianism.* It is instructive to read these nineteenth-century works in light of B. F. Skinner's *Walden Two.*

HOLTON, G. (ed.) *Science and Culture: A Study of Cohesive and Disjunctive Forces.* Boston: Beacon Press, 1967.

Scientists, artists, philosophers, and sociologists are represented in this collection of sixteen essays. The papers by D. K. Price and Herbert Marcuse are particularly relevant to Chapter 13.

HUIZINGA, J. *The Waning of the Middle Ages.* Garden City, N.Y.: Doubleday & Co., 1954.

This classic, nearly fifty years old, is an exciting path to those days of knights and saints and unshakable conviction. An understanding of this "Age of Belief" is preliminary to any appreciation of the need for detachment in scholarly pursuits.

Glossary

ablation. The surgical removal of tissue.

absolute refractory period. The period following stimulation during which the neuron is totally unresponsive to further stimulation of any strength.

absolute threshold. The smallest or weakest stimulus that can be detected with better than chance frequency.

acalculia. The loss of calculational skills.

acetylcholine. A neuromuscular-junction transmitter.

affect. Mood, feeling, or emotion.

agnosia. Literally, "not knowing." Agnosia may be visual, auditory, olfactory, or tactile. The person recognizes that a stimulus is present but can derive no meaning from it and cannot name it.

agraphia. The inability to write, usually as a result of neurological disease.

alexia. The inability to read, usually due to neurological disease.

allele. Either of a pair of Mendelian characters (genes). Alleles may be the same (homozygous) or different (heterozygous).

All-Or-None Law. The law that states that a neuron either responds completely to stimulation (in the form of a nondiminishing neural impulse) or not at all.

alpha rhythm. The dominant electrical rhythm of the relaxed, awake, human subject (normally from 8-13 Hz and from 50-100 microvolts in amplitude).

animal spirits. Descartes' hypothetical mechanism for activating muscles and glands.

aphasia. The inability to speak with any coherence and/or the inability to comprehend the spoken word.

apperception. An awareness that we are aware or, loosely used, "consciousness." According to Kant, it refers to the mind examining its own contents.

archetype. In Jung's psychoanalytic theory, the human mind houses beliefs, fears, superstitions, and primitive awarenesses in the form of symbols. Various cultures and tribes, separated by time and distance, display in their rites and their art symbols of fertility, death, resurrection, birth, and so on. The similarity of symbols across time and cultures suggested to Jung a universal archetype in the unconscious for each of these characteristics and events.

association. This term has a logical status akin to that of *motive* or *gravity*. No one has ever *seen* an association between stimuli and responses or between two stimuli. However, it is known that repeated presentations of stimuli to a subject will result in the substitution of one for the other when only one is presented. It is assumed that some type of association has been formed physically to account for the temporal association.

associationism. The belief that all complex psychological processes—such as learning, memory, cognition, and emotion—result from associations among simpler, more elemental processes.

autonomous. In Piaget's theory of moral development, that moral disposition according to which the rightness and wrongness of acts is determined by personal, individual standards (cf. **heteronomous**).

axon. The portion of the neuron along which the neural impulse is conducted.

axoplasm. The fluids and salts comprising the space enclosed by the membrane of axons.

behavior. The term used by psychologists to refer to the observable, gross movements of animals and people as they manipulate features of the environment. As currently used, however, it can also refer to any observable movement of any organism, even the microscopically observed action of muscle fibers or neurons.

behaviorism. A school of psychology that restricts the subject matter of psychology to the observable behavior of organisms.

Bell-Magendie Law. The law that sensory and motor functions are mediated by anatomically distinct (spinal) pathways.

catatonia. The variety of schizophrenia characterized by sensory and motor withdrawal or inactivity.

catharsis. (1) The "talking cure," or verbalization of conflicts, traumatic experiences, hopes and fears. (2) In psychoanalytic theory, the process by which psychic energies can be released through the public expression of painful thoughts and feelings.

centration. (1) In Piaget's theory, the perceptual tendency of the child to limit attention to only the center of visual space. (2) The tendency to ignore or be insensitive to peripheral sources of stimulation. (3) The tendency to be limited to the processing of only restricted portions of the field of stimulation.

cephalic. Used to refer to the head or head-end of animals.

chromatids. During cell division, the split strands of chromosomes that line up along the equatorial plane of the cell.

chromosomes. Protein chains in the nuclei of cells containing the genetic information of the cells.

cognitive processes. Presumed states or events in the nervous system (or the mind) that lead to the organization, coding, and retrieval of information and to the formation of ideas.

concordance. A degree of agreement or form of correlation.

condensation. In Freud's theory of dreams, the property of dreams that results in the combining of many different elements into a single or small set of significant themes.

conditioned reflex. The reflex-response of an organism to a stimulus as the result of repeated associations of this stimulus with one that elicits such responses naturally.

connotative. Connotative terms, or connotations, are terms that refer to general meanings, not to particular instances alone. Thus, "justice" connotes a higher principle according to which particular acts become right or wrong. Justice, itself, is not found in the mere summation of all right acts but is, instead, the concept according to which actions can be classified (cf. **denotative**).

consciousness. An awareness of self, including an awareness of one's sensations.

continuous variable. Some outcomes are discrete in that they can take on only one of a limited number of values; e.g., coins can fall only as either "heads" or "tails." This is referred to as a discontinuous variable. Other outcomes can take on any one of an infinite number of possible outcomes; e.g., a tree, in principle, can attain a height of 2 ft. or 2.0006 ft. Height, then, is a continuous variable.

conversion reaction. That property of hysteria that leads to the translation of psychic disturbances into physical symptoms.

correlation. As used in statistics, the degree to which one variable can be predicted from the values taken on by another variable.

corticalization. The later stages of embryological development of the higher species in which the cerebral cortex takes shape and becomes defined.

cosmology. Any philosophical or metaphysical system concerning the origin, nature, and destiny of the universe.

covering law. A truth held to apply universally. The Law of the Conservation of Energy, for example, is such a universal or covering law because it is assumed to "cover" all physical processes.

critical flicker-fusion threshold (c.f.f.). (1) The flicker rate of a visual stimulus at which flicker is no longer perceived. (2) The upper limit on temporal discrimination of pulses within trains of flashes.

decremental conduction. Graded conduction in which the strength of the conducted signal diminishes as a function of its distance from the stimulating source.

deduction. The process of reasoning by which conclusions are drawn from premises.

deductive logic. A system of argument in which premises and conclusions are connected according to the rules of logic. These rules are what make certain deductions valid and others invalid. Deductive logic should be viewed as a truth-preserving and not a truth-creating system;

that is, deduction presents proofs whereas scientific demonstration, for example, seeks for new explanations of facts. The rules of deduction preserve whatever is contained in the premises.

dendrites. Projections of the neuron especially suited to make contact with the axon-terminals of other neurons. In neural conduction, stimulation of the dendrites is generally the first event in the chain.

denotative. Denotative terms, or denotations, refer to particular instances or things. The term "tasty," for example, denotes those objects that many choose to eat. According to this system, the term "justice" would mean only those actions that most people would describe as proper, right, or desirable (cf. **connotative**).

dependent variable. In experimental work, the variable whose value depends on the independent variable (cf. **independent variable**).

depolarization. The elimination of electrical polarization (cf. **polarization**).

determinism. The doctrine that nothing occurs without a cause. There are "hard" and "soft" versions of determinism in psychology. Hard determinists argue that psychological events are no more than interactions among the material components of the body; soft determinists assert that the gross, observable behavior of organisms can be predicted from the history of reinforcement and controlled by the proper application of reinforcing stimuli.

difference threshold. The smallest change in the value of a stimulus that can be detected with better than chance reliability.

diploid number. The full complement of chromosomes. In homo sapiens, the number is 46 (23 pairs).

discontinuous variable. Cf. **continuous variable**.

discriminative stimulus. In conditioning, the stimulus whose presence signals the availability of reinforcement (cf. **reinforcement**).

displacement. (1) In Freud's theory of dreams, the dreamer's adoption of behavior or invention of themes at variance with his true feelings or entirely inconsistent with the realities of the situation; e.g., attending a funeral dressed as a clown. (2) Also refers to the acting out of aggressive feelings against innocent objects or people.

dorsal root ganglia. The population of cell bodies (ganglia) producing a bulge in the dorsal segments of spinal nerves.

dramatization. In Freud's theory of dreams, the tendency of dreams to be cast in dramatic and even theatrical form, rich in plots and characters, and with an atmosphere of simulated reality.

egalitarianism. The social philosophy derived from empiricism: the belief that people are equal in their fundamental humanity and therefore should share equally in the decisions, resources, and opportunities of the state.

ego. Freud's term for that psychological self resulting from the antagonistic interactions between id and superego (cf. **id, superego**).

eidetic imagery. The nearly photographic images retained by individuals after removal of the stimulus; found among very young children and among tribal members lacking developed languages.

electrical potential. Cf. **polarization.**

elitism. The social philosophy deriving from nativism: the belief that society is best served and best led by a small group of highly (and often genetically) endowed individuals who, because of their talents, should be given the ruling voice in the affairs of state or community.

empirical. Describes events or issues that can be known or settled on the basis of observation.

empirical law. It is customary to distinguish between the perfectly reliable and fundamental *physical laws* (for example, Newton's laws of motion) and those *statistical laws* that are true only on the average (as in psychology and sociology). Some philosophers and scientists have proposed that statistical laws will ultimately be reduced to fundamental or physical laws, but at present that statistical laws are only generalizations based on a number of observations. They are, then, *empirical laws.*

empiricism. The equivalent of psychological environmentalism: the belief that the psychological features of the individual are established by experience.

encephalization. The rapid development of the head-end—especially the brain—of advanced species during maturation.

epistemology. (1) The study of knowledge and of the methods developed to provide knowledge. (2) The critical examination of the assumptions that guide scholarly and scientific study.

equipotentiality. Lashley's term for the apparent ability of various regions of the brain to take over the control of functions normally controlled by other regions.

erogenous. Stimuli effective in exciting sexual sensations.

ethology. The science of animal behavior in natural settings; that is, the study of the natural habits of animals.

eugenics. (1) The study of genetics in relation to social phenomena. (2) The movement for a genetic approach to the solution of social problems.

excitatory post-synaptic potential (EPSP). An electrical potential set up in dendrites by depolarization that makes them more responsive than normal to stimulation (cf. **depolarization**).

extinction. The process of reducing conditioned behavior to its preconditioned level by nonreinforcement.

extrovert. A personality type characterized by outgoing behavior, sociability, and socially acceptable exhibitionism.

fovea. The central region of the retina containing only cone-receptors and responsible for maximum visual acuity (cf. **visual acuity**).

funtionalism. In the history of psychology, the system developed by William James, John Dewey, and others, stating that the mind is properly understood in terms of the (Darwinian) functions it serves. Functionalism, in its more pragmatic form, was a forerunner of behaviorism.

gamete. A sex cell (either sperm or egg) that participates in fertilization.

ganglia. In the peripheral nervous system, a population of neural cell bodies.

genotype. The genetic makeup of the organism.

Gestalt psychology. A school of psychology emphasizing the patterning and organizing inclinations of perceptual and cognitive systems; in opposition to reductionism and most forms of behaviorism.

graded conduction. Electrical conduction in which the strength of the conducted signal is proportional to the strength of the applied stimulus; the contrary of all-or-none conduction (cf. **All-Or-None Law**).

gustation. The sense of taste.

haploid number. Half the number of chromosomes possessed by cells other than gametes. In homo sapiens, the haploid number is 23.

hebephrenia. The variety of schizophrenia characterized by regressive and infantile forms of behavior.

heritability. The technical term for the fraction of total variance attributable to genetic variations in the sample.

heteronomous. In Piaget's theory of moral development, the moral disposition to seek justification from others and define moral standards in terms of the standards of others (cf. **autonomous**).

heterozygous. (1) A hybrid combination of genes. (2) Allele pairs in which the characters (genes) are different (cf. **allele**).

homeostasis. The process by which physiological processes are maintained in a state of equilibrium.

homozygous. A "pure" genetic combination in which the two genes associated with a given phenotype are the same (cf. **phenotype**).

hybrid. A genetic composition containing two different genes for a given phenotype. Where the two genes are the same, the condition is referred to as "pure" (cf. **phenotype**).

hyperphagia. Excessive and apparently uncontrollable eating.

hyperpolarization. A condition of increased or unnatural polarization induced by increasing the charge difference across a membrane or barrier (cf. **polarization**).

hypophagia. Pathologically diminished consumption of food.

hypothesis. In scientific contexts, an assumed but unproven connection between two events or variables. Scientific hypotheses generally take the form of assumed causal connections.

hypothetical construct. (1) A construct that is not visible or tangible. (2) A hypothesized state or condition by which cause-effect sequences are to be understood; e.g., homeostasis or gravity.

hypothetico-deductive method. Science, as conceived by Francis Bacon, was to be an essentially inductive enterprise leading to orderly generalizations based on careful observation of particular events. The hypothetico-deductive method of Galileo and Newton expanded Bacon's model to include theory (or hypothesis)as the proper starting point of scientific work. The hypothesis takes the form of a presumed law that, if true, makes certain predictions logically necessary. Experiments are then undertaken to test these predictions. If confirmed, the hypothesis gains the (temporary) status of law. If disconfirmed, the hypothesis is modified to agree with the observed facts.

hysteria. A condition of agitation, anxiety, and fear, often accompanied by physiological disturbances thought not to be of organic origin.

id. Freud's term for the instinctual and primitive psychic apparatus inherited by human beings from their animal origins.

idealism. The Platonic theory that the ultimate truths of nature exist as ideas rather than in the form of sensations or phenomena.

identity. The concept of "x is y" as an identity is based on Leibnitz's Law of Universal Substitutivity. Thus, x and y are identities when one can be substituted for the other universally without altering the truth value of the proposition x = y. Statements of the sort "He is Smith" can satisfy this criterion, whereas "Man is a machine" does not.

independent variable. In experimental work, the factor, quantity, or event over which the experimenter has control and that can be manipulated to produce changes in the dependent variable. The relationship between independent and dependent variables is similar to that between cause and effect (cf. **dependent variable**).

induction. The process by which we make generalizations to unmeasured or unobserved instances on the basis of known observations or measurements; i.e., reasoning from known particulars to general principles.

inhibitory post-synaptic potential (IPSP). A form of hyperpolarization rendering post-synaptic dendrites less responsive to subsequent stimulation.

insight. The sudden solution of a problem without apparent trial-and-error practice.

intelligence. The presumed condition of the brain or mind by which learning, memory, and creative industry become possible. A number of psychologists believe that there are tests that can measure the degree or amount of intelligence, but many people have serious doubts about the tests now available and their methods of construction.

internuncial neurons. Neurons entirely within the central nervous system (brain and spinal cord) and serving to mediate activity in sensory and motor neurons; also called **interneurons.**

interval scaling. Scales that provide not only rank among items but measures of the quantitative distance between adjacent ranks. A common interval scale is the ruler.

introvert. A personality type that is withdrawn, inhibited, shy, socially distant, and private.

intuition. A private sense or personal awareness of a truth where knowledge of it is neither based on experience nor publicly observable.

involutional melancholia. A benign psychosis, tending to disappear in time and generally associated with those endocrinological upsets of menopause. Sometimes called the menopausal psychosis, it is characterized by deep depression and suicidal tendencies.

ions. Elements and compounds bearing an electrical charge.

kinesthesia. The movement sense by which we are able to guide such actions as walking, reaching, and so on.

Law of Specific Nerve Energies. Müller's law, according to which the quality of sensory experiences is determined by the specific nerves conducting the information and not by the environmental event producing these neural responses.

learning. Under conditions in which genetic factors can be plausibly ruled out, systematic and reversible changes in behavior are said to be the result of learning.

libido. In Freud's theory, the psychic energy system.

lobectomy. The surgical removal of one of the lobes of the cerebral cortex.

localization of function. The principle that specific psychological and behavioral functions are housed in specific locations within the brain.

luminance. The intensity of visible radiation.

Malthusian. Refers to Thomas Malthus' theory that population increases at a faster rate than the potential for food production. Malthus concluded that population must, in light of these two facts, be limited by war, pestilence, and starvation.

manic-depressive. The variety of psychosis characterized by wide swings of mood and behavior, from the suicidal depths of depression to uncontrollable levels of excitability and activity.

Manichaeanism. An early Christian belief in the presence of a godly force for good and a satanic force for evil—God and Satan each vying for man's soul.

masking. The diminished ability of a stimulus to elicit a response as a result of influences from other stimuli that are close to the first in space and time.

mass action. Lashley's term for the hypothesis that the brain functions as a whole rather than as a set of distinct subsystems.

materialism. The theory that the contents of the universe—including man—are matter and only matter and that the subject of psychology, therefore, will finally be reduced to the observation of matter in motion. According to the materialist position, there are not psychological *and* material events; there are only material events. What appears to be psychological appears so only because we have not yet discovered its material foundations (syn. *mechanistic philosophy*).

mean. The sum of an array of scores divided by the number of scores yields the average or mean of the array.

mechanistic philosophy. Cf. **materialism.**

median. When scores are arranged according to rank, from highest to lowest, the median divides the scores in half, leaving as many scores above the median as there are below.

meiosis. Reduction division; a form of cell division producing gametes containing the haploid number of chromosomes.

mentalism. The theory or belief that mental states are real, not merely physical, and must be included as an integral part of psychological inquiry.

mitosis. Cellular reproduction by division.

mnemonist. A person (often a professional entertainer) gifted with extraordinary powers of rote memory.

mode. The modal value of an array of scores is that score which occurs most frequently.

morphemes. Strings of phonemes combined to form meaningful linguistic units, or words (cf. **phonemes**).

motivation. Cf. **motive.**

motive. An assumed condition or state of the organism that impels it to action.

myelin sheath. The insulating sheath covering many axons.

nativism. The theory or belief that the psychological characteristics of organisms (or the sources of these characteristics) are laid down in the genetic endowment, such that, through the process of maturation alone, these characteristics will appear (syn. *psychological hereditarianism*).

natural selection. The process whereby environmental conditions favor certain natural variants as more fitted for survival.

natural variation. As used by Darwin, the "natural" differences between members of a species that confer or might confer advantages on some members. Since the advantages make survival more likely, these differences are preserved in successive generations.

neural impulse. The nondiminishing wave of depolarization that passes down the length of axons following adequate stimulation.

neuron. The structural unit of the nervous system.

neuropsychology. Cf. **physiological psychology.**

node of Ranvier. The break in the myelin sheath occurring at approximately every millimeter along myelinated axons.

nominal scaling. A scheme of classification based on the assignment of names; as in anatomy.

normal distribution. (1) The normal (bell-shaped) curve of distribution, as generated by the equation for normal distribution. (2) The distribution of values formed by natural events, such as rainfall or the height of trees. Events acted upon by numerous factors tend to achieve average values most of the time and extreme values only rarely. Accordingly, the likelihood of a given value increases in the vicinity of the average and decreases with distance from the average.

nuclei. In the central nervous system, a population of neural cell bodies.

numerology. The ancient science according to which the laws of nature were to be understood as particular numerical combinations and relations similar to those found in the harmonic structure of music.

olfaction. The sense of smell.

ordinal scaling. The arrangement of items according to measured properties—for example, rank in class.

oscillation. The hypothetical process in Hull's theory of learning that explains the moment-to-moment fluctuations in behavior.

ovum. The egg cell or female gamete.

Papez circuit. The anatomical "circuit" proposed by Papez as the biological foundation of emotion. The circuit involves the major structures of the limbic system and includes the amygdala, hippocampus, hypothalamus, fornix, and septum.

parameter. A separate set of independent variables (for example, a, b, c) employed in studies of the relationship between x and y. Thus, in a study of the effects of diet on growth, amount of exercise may be a parameter.

paranoia. The form of psychosis in which the patient presents an apparently rational and coherent system of beliefs, perceptions, and actions, all of which are, nevertheless, based on delusion and deceit.

paranoid. The variety of psychosis characterized by delusions of persecution and/or grandeur.

parapraxes. Mispronunciations assumed by Freud to be evidence of repression. Also commonly called "Freudian slips," or psychological slips-of-the-tongue.

perception. Used to describe the consequences of stimulation. Currently, the trend is to treat perception and sensation as synonyms. Historically, however, some philosophers have made careful distinctions between the two; that is, between an internal sensation and the perception of external objects or qualities. For example, in the expression, "I see a rose," the object (rose) has an existence outside the subject. However, in the expression, "I have a toothache," the object (toothache) does not have an existence independent of the individual's sensation of pain. The former expression is evidence of perception and the latter of sensation.

perceptual constancy. The constancy of an effect even under dramatically altered conditions of stimulation. For example, an object seems to be of normal height even when seen at a great distance and even though it forms a very small image on the retina. This is an instance of perceptual *size-constancy*.

permeability. The property of membranes that allows particles to pass through them.

The "mask," or public face, worn by the individual concealing the truer, private self.

personality. As used by some psychologists, the perceptual and behavioral *dispositions* of individuals under a wide variety of circumstances. Personality, in this light, is a social and emotional fingerprint. Other psychologists, however, are persuaded that the term can have no meaning beyond those ensembles of *learned behavior* available to the individual.

phenotype. Any physical characteristic of the organism.

pheromones. Chemical secretions left behind by animals (especially insects) allowing other members of the species to follow their path.

phi phenomenon. The phenomenon of apparent movement produced by alternating flashes of spatially displaced light in an otherwise dark room.

phonemes. Sound elements that, when combined, produce morphemes (cf. **morphemes**).

photochemistry. The study of the chemical responses produced by light; particularly the study of those chemical changes in the retinal receptors elicited by photic stimulation.

photopic vision. Vision mediated by receptors responsive to moderate and high levels of illumination (cone vision).

phrenology. The science according to which the psychological and moral features of human life were to be understood in terms of the conformations of the skull.

physiological psychology. The study of the biological foundations of consciousness and, more specifically, of the neural mechanisms of sensation and emotion. Today, this field is often indistinguishable from neuropsychology.

polarization. When unequal electrical charges occur across a barrier, a condition of polarization is said to exist.

polygenic. A mode of hereditary influence produced by two or more genes.

positivism. The theory that scientific knowledge constitutes the ultimate truths of the world and that all that exists can—in principle—be known scientifically.

primary drives. Those biological events that subserve life and that are thought to impel the quest for food, drink, and sex.

primary reinforcer. A stimulus that satisfies or eliminates primary drives; e.g., food for the food-deprived organism (cf. **primary drives**).

psychophysics. The study of quantitative relations between physical stimuli and perceptual-sensory responses.

rationalism. The philosophical conviction that truths regarding the world can be uncovered by essentially deductive means (cf. **deduction**).

ratio scaling. Ratio scales provide all the information given by interval scales—rank among items and measures of the distance between adjacent ranks—with the addition that they have true zero values; e.g., on a ruler "zero" corresponds to "no length."

recombinants. The recovery of segregated gene combinations in subsequent generations.

reductionism. The philosophical conviction that all events, including complex psychological ones, can be reduced to elemental components.

reinforcement. The application of stimuli (rewards and punishments) following specific responses in such a way as to make these responses more likely.

relative refractory period. The period following stimulation during which additional neural responses can be elicited only by particularly strong stimuli.

reliability. A statistical term that assigns to observations or experimental outcomes a measure of reproducibility. Findings and observations are said to be reliable when they reoccur under the same experimental conditions.

REM. Rapid eye-movements; a feature of eye movements in sleeping persons who are dreaming.

resemblance. A similarity or point of likeness. In Hume's theory of causation, resemblance between two or more events or things is one of the determinants of their being associated or treated as the same.

response latency. The interval between the application of an adequate stimulus and the system's response to it.

resting membrane potential. The state of electrical polarization existing across the membrane of the axon prior to stimulation.

salatory conduction. Neural impulses conducted from node to node rather than continuously down the length of axons (cf. **node of Ranvier**).

schedules of reinforcement. The various schedules according to which responses are rewarded in the experimental situation; e.g., by a fixed ratio, fixed interval, variable ratio, and so on.

scotopic vision. Vision mediated by receptors responsive to the lowest levels of illumination (rod vision).

secondary drives. The drives created through association with a primary drive. Thus, if food is the object of a primary drive and if money is necessary for food, then there is said to be a secondary drive for money (cf. **primary drive**).

secondary elaboration. Freud's term for the dreamer's expanded version of the dream; the dream as "filled in" by the dreamer after relating the skeletal features that are clearly recalled.

secondary reinforcer. A stimulus that has reinforcing properties by virtue of being associated with a primary reinforcer (cf. **primary reinforcer**).

self-actualization. The process, according to psychoanalytic and neoanalytic theories, by which the true or unrepressed self breaks through the clouds of fear, denial, and inhibition.

sensation. The consequences of stimulation applied to a sensible creature.

social psychology. Whereas sociology examines social transactions on a large scale, social psychology generally restricts itself to the study of interpersonal influence—especially the influences on perception, belief, and behavior. The line between sociology and social psychology, however, is often a thin one.

sociology. The field of inquiry devoted to exploring the laws of social conduct and social organization.

somaesthesis. Sensory processes associated with sensitivity to temperature, touch, pressure, and pain.

sophists. Among the ancient Greeks, those philosophers who specialized in rhetoric and debate and who emphasized the dependence of philosophical understanding on the meaning of the terms used in debate.

spectrum. The distribution of all wavelengths (cf. **wavelength**).

sperm. A male gamete (cf. **gamete**).

standard deviation. (1) The square root of the variance (cf. **variance**). (2) The measure that marks off departures from the average value of a distribution in unit-area; i.e., a measure of dispersion about the mean.

stereoscope. A device for creating three-dimensional scenes from photographs or drawings by presenting the scenes to disparate retinal loci.

structuralism. In the history of psychology, the system developed by Titchener that emphasizes the structural features of the mind, such as sensations, images, and feelings.

subjectivity. Any enterprise involving human perception and judgment must contain subjective elements; that is, elements not directly caused or conditioned by external stimuli. The term is best restricted to those situations in which *only* the private perceptions and judgments of a person are available—where there is not, in addition, an object, or public event.

superego. Freud's term for the conscience instilled in people through the process of socialization; that which keeps the id in check (cf. **id**).

surrogate. A substitute, as for example the surrogate (usually cloth-doll) mother used in Harlow's research on mother-infant interaction.

sympathectomy. A surgical procedure resulting in the disconnection of the sympathetic ganglia from the spinal cord.

synapse. The space between the axon terminals of one neuron and the dendrites of the next.

synesthesia. The neurological disturbance or irregularity that results in the formation of visual sensations in response to sounds or in the general confusion of sensory effects.

tau phenomenon. The tactile equivalent of the phi phenomenon—apparently continuous movement produced by spatially separated tactile stimuli (cf. **phi phenomenon**).

tract. In the central nervous system, a band of axons.

transducer. A device or biological process by which energy impinging on one form produces a response of energy in a different form, e.g., photic energy impinges on rods and cones, which respond chemically and then electrically.

transit time. The amount of time it takes to travel from one location to another.

transmitters. Chemicals that serve to depolarize or hyperpolarize dendrites and cell bodies, thereby initiating neural responses in them.

tropism. Generally, a total-body response by the organism to stimuli of a specific sort; e.g., phototropic withdrawal.

true forms. In Platonic theory, ultimate truths; that is, the essential nature of that which is only ambiguously revealed in perception.

utilitarianism. The Philosophy based on the principle of "greatest good," according to which the value of an undertaking is established by its usefulness in securing the greatest good or happiness of the greatest number of people.

variance. The sum of the squared deviations around the mean of a distribution. The total variance of a distribution is the total area under the curve formed by plotting the scores.

vestibular sense. The sense of the body's position in space, or the balancing sense; mediated by receptors in the inner ear.

visual acuity. (1) The resolving power of the human visual system. (2) The angular size of one object and the angular separation between objects allowing for visual discrimination between objects.

wavelength. The distance covered by a wave in completing one full cycle.

Weber's Law. The psychophysical law that discriminability is a linear function of the base level of the stimulus. According to this law, the amount a stimulus must be changed for the change to be discriminated depends on the initial level of the stimulus. Thus, if one inch must be added to three feet in order for the subject to detect that the new stimulus is longer, then two inches would have to be added to a length of six feet, three inches to a length of nine feet, and so on.

zeitgeist. Literally, the "ghost" or "spirit" of the time; the attitudes, perceptions, beliefs, and general intellectual dispositions of a culture or community.

zygote. A cell formed by the sperm's fertilization of the ovum.

References

ADAMS, J. *Human Memory*. New York: Mc-Graw-Hill, 1967.

ADLER, A. "Individual Psychology." In *Psychologies of 1930*, ed. by C. Murchison, pp. 395–405. Worcester: Clark University Press, 1930.

AMOORE, J. E. "Current Status of the Steric Theory of Odor." *Annals of the New York Academy of Sciences* 116 (1964): 457–476.

AMOORE, J. E., JOHNSTON, J. W., and RUBIN, M. "The Stereo-Chemical Theory of Odor." *Scientific American* 210 (1964): 42–49.

AMSEL, A. "Frustrative Nonreward in Partial Reinforcement and Discrimination Learning: Some Recent History and a Theoretical Extension." *Psychological Review* 69 (1962): 306–328.

AQUINAS, SAINT THOMAS. *Summa Theologica*. In *Basic Writings of Thomas Aquinas*, trans. by Anton Pegis. New York: Random House, 1945.

ARISTOTLE. *De Anima*. In *Aristotle: Selections*, ed. by W. D. Ross. New York: Charles Scribner's Sons, 1955.

———. *De Memoria et Reminiscentia*. In *Basic Works*, trans. by Richard McKeon. New York: Random House, 1941.

———. *Nicomachean Ethics*. In *Introduction to Aristotle*, ed. by Richard McKeon. New York: Random House, 1947.

————. *Posterior Analytics*. In *Introduction to Aristotle*, ed. by Richard McKeon. New York: Random House, 1947.

————. *Rhetoric*. In *Aristotle: Selections*, ed. by W. D. Ross. New York: Charles Scribner's Sons, 1955.

ASHBY, W. ROSS. *Design for a Brain: The Origin of Adaptive Behavior*. London: John Wiley & Sons, 1960.

ATKINSON, JOHN W., ed. *Motives in Fantasy, Action, and Society*. Princeton, N.J.: D. Van Nostrand Co., 1958.

AUGUSTINE, SAINT. *The Enchiridion*. In *Basic Writings of Saint Augustine*, ed. by Whitney J. Oates, trans. by J. F. Shaw. New York: Random House, 1948.

AZRIN, N., HUTCHINSON, R. R., and HAKE, D. F. "Pain-Induced Fighting in the Squirrel Monkey." *Journal of the Experimental Analysis of Behavior* 6 (1963): 620.

BACON, F. *Novum Organum*. In *The Works of Francis Bacon*, Vol. I. Cambridge, Mass.: Hurd & Houghton, 1878.

————. *Of the Proficience and Advancement of Learning Divine and Human*. In *The Works of Francis Bacon*, Vol. I. Cambridge, Mass.: Hurd & Houghton, 1878.

BADDELEY, A. D. "Short-Term Memory for Word Sequences as a Function of Acoustic, Semantic and Formal Similarity." *Quarterly Journal of Experimental Psychology* 18 (1966): 362–365.

BANDURA, A., ROSS, D., and ROSS, S. "Transmission of Aggression Through Imitation of Aggressive Models." *The Journal of Abnormal and Social Psychology* 63 (1961).

BARBER, T. X. "Comparison of Suggestibility During 'Light Sleep' and Hypnosis." *Science* 124 (1956): 405.

BARD, P. "A Diencephalic Mechanism for the Expression of Rage with Special Reference to the Sympathetic Nervous System." *American Journal of Physiology* 84 (1928): 490–515.

BARNES, J. M., and UNDERWOOD, B. J. "'Fate' of First-List Associations in Transfer Theory." *Journal of Experimental Psychology* 58 (1959): 97–105.

BARTHOLOMEW, A. *Mediaeval Lore*. Ed. by Robert Steele. London: Alexander Moring, 1905.

BARTLEY, S. H. *Principles of Perception*. New York: Harper & Row, 1958.

BECK, E. C., and DOTY, R. W. "Conditioned Flexion Reflexes Acquired During Combined Catalepsy and De-efferentation." *Journal of Comparative Physiological Psychology* 50 (1957): 211–216.

BEKESY, G. Von. "Über Akustische Reizung des Vestibularapparates." *Pflüger Arch. Ges. Physiol.* 236 (1935): 59–76.

BELL, ERIC TEMPLE. *The Search for Truth*. New York: Reynal & Hitchcock, 1934.

BENTHAM, JEREMY. "An Introduction to the Principles of Morals and Legislation." In *The Utilitarians*. Garden City, N.J.: Doubleday & Co., 1961.

BERKELEY, G. *Three Dialogues Between Hylas and Philonous*. Ed. by Colin M. Turbayne. Indianapolis: Bobbs-Merrill, 1954.

BERKOWITZ, L. *Aggression: A Social Psychological Analysis*. New York: McGraw-Hill, 1962.

BERKOWITZ, L., and LePAGE, A. "Weapons as Aggression-Eliciting Stimuli." *Journal of Personality and Social Psychology* 7 (1967): 202–207.

BERLYNE, D. E. "Novelty and Curiosity as Determinants of Exploratory Behaviour." *British Journal of Psychology* 41 (1950): 68–80.

BERLYNE, D. E., and SLATER, J. "Perceptual Curiosity, Exploratory Behaviour and Maze Learning." *Journal of Comparative Physiology* 50 (1957): 228–232.

BERRY, R. "Quantitative Relations Among Vernier, Real Depth, and Stereoscopic Depth Acuities." *Journal of Experimental Psychology* 38 (1948): 708–721.

BEVERIDGE, W. B. *The Art of Scientific Investigation.* New York: Random House, 1957.

BIJOU, S. W., and BAER, D. M. "Some Methodological Contributions from a Functional Analysis of Child Development." In *Advances in Child Development and Behavior,* Vol. 1, ed. by L. P. Lipsitt and C. C. Spiker. New York: Academic Press, 1963.

BIRREN, JAMES E. *The Psychology of Aging.* Englewood Cliffs, N.J.: Prentice-Hall, 1964.

BIRREN, JAMES E., BICK, M. W., and FOX, C. "Age Changes in Light Threshold of the Dark Adapted Eye." *Journal of Gerontology* 3 (1948): 267–271.

BLODGETT, H. C. "The Effect of the Introduction of Reward upon the Maze Performance of Rats." *University of California Publications in Psychology* 4 (1929): 113–134.

BOLLES, ROBERT C. *Theory of Motivation.* New York: Harper & Row, 1967.

BORING, EDWIN G., ed. *A History of Experimental Psychology.* 2nd ed. New York: Appleton-Century-Crofts, 1950.

BORST, C. V., ed. *The Mind/Brain Identity Theory.* New York: St. Martin's, 1970.

BOVET, D., BOVET-NITTI, F., and OLIVERIO, A. "Genetic Aspects of Learning and Memory in Mice." *Science* 163 (1969): 139–149.

BRACKBILL, YVONNE. "Extinction of the Smiling Response in Infants as a Function of Reinforcement Schedule." *Child Development* 29 (1958): 115–124.

BRAUN, H. W., and GEISELHART, R. "Age Differences in the Acquisition and Extinction of the Conditioned Eyelid Response." *Journal of Experimental Psychology* 57 (1959): 386–388.

BRELAND, KELLER, and BRELAND, MARIAN. "The Misbehavior of Organisms." *American Psychologist* 16 (1961): 681–684.

BREUER, J., and FREUD, S. *Studies on Hysteria.* London: Hogarth, 1955.

BROWN, ROGER. *Social Psychology.* New York: The Free Press, 1965.

BRUNER, J. S., GOODNOW, J., and AUSTIN, G. *A Study of Thinking.* New York: John Wiley & Sons, 1962.

CALKINS, MARY W. *Association: An Essay Analytic and Experimental.* Psychological Review, Monograph Supplement 1, No. 2. New York: The American Psychological Association, 1896.

CANNON, W. B. *Bodily Changes in Pain, Hunger, Fear and Rage.* New York: Appleton-Century-Crofts, 1929.

CANNON, W. B., and WASHBURN, A. L. "An Explanation of Hunger." *American Journal of Physiology* 29 (1912): 441–454.

CARMICHAEL, L. "The Development of Behavior in Vertebrates Experimentally Removed from the Influence of External Stimulation." *Psychological Review* 33 (1926): 51–58.

CARROLL, JOHN B. *Language and Thought.* Englewood Cliffs, N.J.: Prentice-Hall, 1964.

CATANIA, A. C., ed. *Contemporary Research in Operant Behavior.* Glenview, Ill.: Scott, Foresman & Co., 1968.

CHAPLIN, J. P., and KRAWIEC, T. S. *Systems and Theories of Psychology.* New York: Holt, Rinehart & Winston, 1968.

CHARLES, C. M. "A Comparison of the Intelligence Quotients of Incarcerated Delinquent White and American Negro Boys and a Group of St. Louis Public

School Boys." *Journal of Applied Psychology* 20 (1936): 499–510.

CHERRY, C. "Some Experiments on the Recognition of Speech, with One and with Two Ears." *Journal of the Acoustical Society of America* 25 (1953): 975–979.

CHESTERTON, G. K. *Saint Thomas Aquinas —"The Dumb Ox."* Garden City, N.Y.: Doubleday & Co., Image Books, 1956.

CHOMSKY, NOAM. "Review of *Verbal Behavior*, by B. F. Skinner." *Language* 35 (1959): 26–58.

———. *Current Issues in Linguistic Theory.* The Hague: Mouton, 1964.

———. *Syntactic Structures.* The Hague: Mouton, 1965.

COHEN, M. J., HAGIWARA, S., and ZOTTERMAN, Y. "The Response Spectrum of Taste Fibres in the Cat: A Single Fibre Analysis." *Acta Physiologica Scandinavica* 33 (1955): 316–332.

COMTE, AUGUSTE. *The Positive Philosophy of Auguste Comte.* Trans. by Harriet Martineau. New York: Peter Eckler, 1853.

CONRAD, R. "An Association Between Memory Errors and Errors Due to Acoustic Masking of Speech." *Nature* 193 (1962): 1314–1315.

COPERNICUS, NICOLAUS. *De Orbium Caelestium Revolutionibus.* In *Classics of Modern Science (Copernicus to Pasteur)*, ed. by William S. Knickerbocker. Boston: Beacon Press, 1962.

COULTON, G. G. *The Medieval Scene: An Informal Introduction to the Middle Ages.* Cambridge: Macmillan & Co., 1931.

———, ed. *Life in the Middle Ages*, Vol. 3. Trans. and annotated by G. G. Coulton. New York: Macmillan, 1935.

D'AMATO, M. R. "Instrumental Conditioning." In *Learning Processes*, ed. by H. H. Marx. New York: Macmillan, 1969.

DAMPIER, SIR WILLIAM C. *A History of Science and Its Relations with Philosophy and Religion.* 4th ed. Cambridge: Cambridge University Press, 1966.

DARWIN, C. *Origin of Species.* New York: Collier, 1909.

DAVIS, H., et al. "Acoustic Trauma in Guinea Pig." *Journal of the Acoustical Society of America* 25 (1953): 1180–1189.

DEESE, J. *Psycholinguistics.* Boston: Allyn & Bacon, 1970.

DE VALOIS, R. L., SMITH, C. J., KITAI, S. T., and KAROLY, A. J. "Response of Single Cells in Monkey Lateral Geniculate Nucleus to Monochromatic Light." *Science* 127 (1958): 238–239.

DE WULF, M. *History of Medieval Philosophy*, Vol. 1. Trans. by Ernest C. Messenger. London: Longmans, Green, 1926.

DINGMAN, W., and SPORN, M. B. "The Incorporation of 8-Azaguanine into Rat Brain RNA and Its Effects on Maze Learning by the Rat." *Journal of Psychiatric Research* 1 (1961): 1–11.

DUNCAN, C. P. "The Retroactive Effect of Electro-Shock on Learning." *Journal of Comparative Physiology* 42 (1949): 32–44.

EBBINGHAUS, H. *Über das Gedächtnis (Leipzig)* [Memory]. Trans. by H. A. Ruger and Clara Bussenius. Educational Reprint, No. 3. New York: Teachers College, Columbia University Press, 1913.

EKDAHL, A. G., and STEVENS, S. S. "The Relation of Pitch to the Duration of a Tone." *Journal of the Acoustical Society of America* 10 (1939): 255.

ELKIND, D. *Children and Adolescents: Interpretive Essays on Jean Piaget.* New York: Oxford University Press, 1970.

ENGEL, E. "The Role of Content in Binocular Resolution." *American Journal of Psychology* 69 (1956): 87–91.

————. "Binocular Fusion of Dissimilar Figures." *Journal of Psychology* 46 (1958): 53–57.

ERLENMEYER-KIMLING, L., and JARVIK, L. F. "Genetics and Intelligence; A Review." *Science* 142 (1963): 1477–1479.

ESSMAN, W. B. "Effects of Tricyanoaminopropene on the Amnesic Effect of Electroconvulsive Shock." *Psychopharmacologia* 9 (1966): 426–433.

FANTZ, R. L. "Pattern Vision in Young Infants." *Psychological Record* 8 (1958): 43–48.

FECHNER, GUSTAV. *Elements of Psychophysics*, Vol. 1. Ed. by Davis H. Howes and Edwin G. Boring, trans. by Helmut E. Adler. New York: Holt, Rinehart & Winston, 1966.

FESTINGER, LEON. *A Theory of Cognitive Dissonance*. Evanston, Ill.: Row, Peterson & Co., 1957.

FLAVELL, J. H. *The Developmental Psychology of Jean Piaget*. Princeton, N.J.: D. Van Nostrand Co., 1963.

FOWLER, H., and TRAPOLD, M. A. "Escape Performance as a Function of Delay of Reinforcement." *Journal of Experimental Psychology* 63 (1962): 464–467.

FOX, J. C., and GERMAN, W. J. "Macular Vision Following Cerebral Resection." *Archives of Neurology and Psychiatry* 35 (1936): 808–826.

FREUD, S. *The Interpretation of Dreams*. London: Hogarth, 1953.

————. *The Psychopathology of Everyday Life*. In *The Basic Writings of Sigmund Freud*, ed. by A. A. Brill. New York: Random House, 1938.

FRIEND, CELIA M., and ZUBEK, J. P. "The Effects of Age on Critical Thinking Ability." *Journal of Gerontology* 13 (1958): 407–413.

FRITSCH, G., and HITZIG, E. "Über die Electrische Erregbarkeit des Grosshirns." *Archives des Anatomie und Physiologie* (1870): 300–322.

GALAMBOS, R., SHEATZ, G., and VERNIER, V. G. "Electrophysiological Correlates of a Conditioned Response in Cats." *Science* 123 (1956): 376–377.

GALL, FRANZ JOSEPH. "On the Functions of the Brain and Each of Its Parts . . ." In *A Source Book in the History of Psychology*, ed. by Richard J. Herrnstein and Edwin G. Boring. Cambridge, Mass.: Harvard University Press, 1966.

GALTON, SIR FRANCIS. *Hereditary Genius: An Inquiry into Its Laws and Consequences*. 2nd ed., reprint. New York: Horizon Press, 1952.

GARDNER, E. *Fundamentals of Neurology*. 5th ed. Philadelphia: W. B. Saunders Co., 1968.

GARDNER, R. A., and GARDNER, B. T. "Teaching Sign Language to a Chimpanzee. Part 1. Methodology and Preliminary Results." Report presented at meeting of Psychonomic Society, 1967, in Chicago.

GAZZANIGA, MICHAEL S. *The Bissected Brain*. New York: Appleton-Century-Crofts, 1970.

GAZZANIGA, MICHAEL S., BOGEN, J. E., and SPERRY, R. W. "Observations on Visual Perception After Disconnection of the Cerebral Hemisphere in Man." *Brain* 888 (1965): 221.

GELDARD, F. A. "Adventures in Tactile Literacy." *American Psychologist* 12 (1957): 115–124.

————. *The Human Senses*. New York: John Wiley & Sons, 1953.

GERARD, R. W. "Material Basis of Memory."

Journal of Verbal Learning and Verbal Behavior 2 (1963): 22–33.

GIBSON, E. J. *Principles of Perceptual Learning and Development.* New York: Appleton-Century-Crofts, 1969.

GIBSON, E. J., and WALK, R. D. "The Effect of Prolonged Exposure to Visually Presented Patterns on Learning to Discriminate Them." *Journal of Comparative and Physiological Psychology* 49 (1956): 239–242.

GIBSON, E. J., and WALK, R. D. "The 'Visual Cliff.'" *Scientific American* 202 (1960): 64–71.

GLICKMAN, S., and MILNER, P., eds. *The Neurological Basis of Motivation.* New York: D. Van Nostrand Co., 1969.

GOTTESMAN, I. I. "Heritability of Personality: A Demonstration." *Psychological Monographs* 277, No. 9 (1963).

GOULDNER, A. W. *Enter Plato.* New York: Basic Books, 1965.

GRAF, DE LA ROSÉE. "Untersuchungen Über Das Normale Hörvermögen In Den Uerschiedenen Lebensaltern Unter Besonderer Berücksichtigung Der Prüfung Mit Dem Audiometer." *Ztschr. Laryng. Rhin. Otol.* 32 (1953): 414–420.

GRAHAM, C. H., ed. *Vision and Visual Perception.* New York: John Wiley & Sons, 1965.

GRAHAM, C. H., and KEMP, E. H. "Brightness Discrimination as a Function of the Duration of the Increment in Intensity." *Journal of General Physiology* 21 (1938): 635.

GREGORY, R. L. *Eye and Brain.* New York: McGraw-Hill, 1966.

GROSSMAN, S. P. "Eating or Drinking Elicited by Direct Adrenergic or Cholinergic Stimulation of Hypothalamus." *Science* 132 (1960): 301–302.

GUILFORD, J. P. *Fundamental Statistics in Psychology and Education.* New York: McGraw-Hill, 1956.

GUROWITZ, E. M. *The Molecular Basis of Memory.* Englewood Cliffs, N.J.: Prentice-Hall, 1969.

GUTTMAN, N., and KALISH, H. I. "Discriminability and Stimulus Generalization." *Journal of Experimental Psychology* 51 (1956): 79–88.

HAGBARTH, K. E., and KERR, D. I. B. "Central Influences on Spinal Afferent Conduction." *Journal of Neurophysiology* 17 (1954): 295–307.

HALAS, E. S., JAMES, R. L., and KNUTSON, C. S. "An Attempt at Classical Conditioning in the Planarian." *Journal of Comparative and Physiological Psychology* 55 (1962): 969–971.

HALL, MARSHALL. *Synopsis of the Diastaltic Nervous System.* In *A Source Book in the History of Psychology*, ed. by Richard J. Herrnstein and Edwin G. Boring. Cambridge, Mass.: Harvard Unisity Press, 1966.

HARLOW, H. F. "The Formation of Learning Sets." *Psychological Review* 56 (1949): 51–65.

HARLOW, H. F., and HARLOW, M. K. "Learning to Love." *American Scientist* 54 (1966): 244–272.

HARTLINE, H. K., and GRAHAM, C. H. "Nerve Impulses from Single Receptors in the Eye of *Limulus.*" *Proceedings of the Society of Experimental Biology* 29 (1932): 613–615.

HEBB, D. O. *The Organization of Behavior: A Neuropsychological Theory.* New York: John Wiley & Sons, 1949.

HECHT, S., and MINTZ, E. V. "The Visibility of Single Lines at Various Illuminations and the Retinal Basis of Visual Resolution." *Journal of General Physiology* 22 (1939): 593–612.

HECHT, S., and SHLAER, S. "Intermittent Stimulation by Light. V. The Relation

Between Intensity and Critical Frequency for Different Parts of the Spectrum." *Journal of General Physiology* 19 (1936): 965–979.

HECHT, S., SHLAER, S., and PIRENNE, M. H. "Energy, Quanta, and Vision." *Journal of General Physiology* 25 (1942): 819.

HECHT, S., and SMITH, E. L. "Intermittent Stimulation by Light. VI. Area and the Relationship Between Critical Frequency and Intensity." *Journal of General Physiology* 19 (1936): 979–989.

HELD, R., and HEIN, A. "Movement Produced Stimulation in the Development of Visually Guided Behavior." *Journal of Comparative and Physiological Psychology* 56 (1963): 872–876.

HEMPEL, C. *Aspects of Scientific Explanation and Other Essays in the Philosophy of Science.* New York: Macmillan, Free Press, 1965.

HERNANDEZ-PEON, R., SCHERRER, H., and JOUVET, M. "Modification of Electrical Activity in Cochlear Nucleus during 'Attention' in Unanesthetized Cats." *Science* 123 (1956): 331–332.

HERRNSTEIN, RICHARD J., and BORING, EDWIN G., eds. *A Source Book in the History of Psychology.* Cambridge, Mass.: Harvard University Press, 1966.

HERSHENSON, M., and HABER, R. N. "The Role of Meaning in the Perception of Briefly Exposed Words." *Canadian Journal of Psychology* 19 (1956): 42–46.

HESS, E. H. "Imprinting in Birds." *Science* 146 (1964): 1128–1139.

HIRSCH, I., and SHERRICK, C. "Perceived Order in Different Sense Modalities." *Journal of Experimental Psychology* 62 (1961): 423–432.

HIRSCH, JERRY, ed. *Behavior-Genetic Analysis.* New York: McGraw-Hill, 1967.

HOBBES, T. *Leviathan.* Baltimore: Penguin Classics, 1974.

HOLMES, G. "The Organization of the Visual Cortex in Man." *Proceedings of the Royal Society* (London) 132b (1945): 348–361.

HOLT, ROBERT R. "Beyond Vitalism and Mechanism: Freud's Concept of Psychic Energy." In *Historical Roots of Contemporary Psychology,* ed. by Benjamin B. Wolman. New York: Harper & Row, 1968.

HUBEL, D. H., and WIESEL, T. N. "Receptive Fields of Single Neurons in the Cat's Striate Cortex." *Journal of Physiology* 148 (1959): 574–591.

HUIZINGA, J. *The Waning of the Middle Ages.* New York: Doubleday & Co., 1954.

HULL, CLARK L. *Principles of Behavior: An Introduction to Behavior Theory.* New York: Appleton-Century-Crofts, 1943.

HUME, DAVID. *An Enquiry Concerning Human Understanding.* In *Essential Works of David Hume,* ed. by Ralph Cohen. New York: Bantam Books, 1965.

INHELDER, BÄRBEL, and PIAGET, JEAN. *The Growth of Logical Thinking: From Childhood to Adolescence; An Essay on the Construction of Formal Operational Structures.* Trans. by Anne Parsons and Stanley Milgram. New York: Basic Books, 1958.

ISAACSON, R. L., DOUGLAS, R. J., LUBAR, J. F., and SCHMALTZ, L. W. *A Primer of Physiological Psychology.* New York: Harper & Row, 1971.

JAMES, WILLIAM. *The Principles of Psychology.* New York: Holt, Rinehart & Winston, 1890.

JENKINS, J. G., and DALLENBACH, K. M. "Obliviscence During Sleep and Waking." *American Journal of Psychology* 35 (1924): 605–612.

JOHN, E. ROY. *Mechanisms of Memory.* New York: Academic Press, 1967.

JUNG, C. G. "Psychological Types." In *Contributions to Analytical Psychology.* London: Kegan Paul, 1928.

KAGAN, J. "A Conception of Early Adolescence." *Daedalus,* Fall 1971.

KALISH, H. I. "Stimulus Generalization." In *Learning: Processes,* ed. by M. Marx. New York: Macmillan, 1969.

KANT, IMMANUEL. *Critique of Pure Reason.* Trans. by F. Max Müller. Garden City, N.Y.: Doubleday & Co., 1966.

————. *Critique of Pure Reason.* In *The Philosophy of Kant as Contained in Extracts of His Own Writings,* trans. by John Watson. 2nd ed. Glasgow: Jackson, Wylie & Co., 1934.

KELLER, F. S. *The Definition of Psychology.* New York: Appleton-Century-Crofts, 1937.

KELLOGG, VERNON L. *Mind and Heredity.* Princeton, N.J.: Princeton University Press, 1923.

KEMENY, JOHN G. *A Philosopher Looks at Science.* Princeton, N.J.: D. Van Nostrand Co., 1959.

KEPLER, JOHANN. *Classics of Modern Science: Copernicus to Pasteur.* Ed. by William S. Knickerbocker. Boston: Beacon Press, 1962.

KIMBLE, G. A. "Behavior Strength as a Function of the Intensity of the Hunger Drive." *Journal of Experimental Psychology* 41 (1951): 341–348.

KLOPFER, PETER H. *Habitats and Territories: A Study of the Use of Space by Animals.* New York: Basic Books, 1969.

KLÜVER, H. "Functional Significance of the Geniculostriate System." *Biological Symposium* 7 (1942): 263–264.

KOHLBERG, L. "The Development of Children's Orientations Toward a Moral Order. Part 1: Sequence in the Development of Moral Thought." *Vita Humana* 6 (1963): 11–33.

KÖHLER, WOLFGANG. *The Mentality of Apes.* New York: Harcourt Brace & World, 1925.

KRECH, D., ROSENZWEIG, M. R., and BENNETT, E. L. "Effects of Environmental Complexity and Training on Brain Chemistry." *Journal of Comparative Physiology* 53 (1960): 509–519.

KRUTCH, JOSEPH WOOD. *The Measure of Man: On Freedom, Human Values, Survival and the Modern Temper.* Indianapolis: Bobbs-Merrill Co., 1954.

KUO, ZIN YANG. "Giving Up Instincts in Psychology." *Journal of Philosophy* 18 (1921): 645–664.

LASHLEY, K. S. "Studies of Cerebral Function in Learning." *Psychological Review* 31 (1924): 369–375.

————. "In Search of the Engram." *Symposium of the Society of Experimental Biology* 4 (1950): 454–482.

————. "The Problem of Serial Order in Behavior." In *Cerebral Mechanisms in Behavior,* ed. by L. A. Jeffers. New York: John Wiley & Sons, 1951.

LASHLEY, K. S., and WADE, M. "The Pavlovian Theory of Generalization." *Psychological Review* 53 (1946): 72–87.

LATANÉ, B., and DARLEY, J. "Group Inhibition of Bystander Intervention in Emergencies." *Journal of Personality and Social Psychology* 10 (1968): 215–221.

LAURENS, H., and HAMILTON, W. F. "The Sensibility of the Eye to Differences in Wavelength." *American Journal of Physiology* 65 (1923): 547–568.

LEHMAN, H. C. *Age and Achievement.* Princeton, N.J.: Princeton University Press, 1953.

LEHRMAN, DANIEL S. "Problems Raised by

Instinct Theories." *Quarterly Review of Biology* 28 (1953): 337–365.

LEIBNITZ, GOTTFRIED WILHELM. *New Essays Concerning the Understanding.* Trans. by Alfred G. Langley. New York: Macmillan, 1896.

LENNEBERG, ERIC H. *Biological Foundations of Language.* New York: John Wiley & Sons, 1967.

LETTVIN, J. Y., MATURNA, H. R., Mc-CULLOCH, W. S., and PITTS, W. H. "What the Frog's Eye Tells the Frog's Brain." *Proceedings of the Institute of Radio Engineers* 47 (1959): 1940–1951.

LEWIN, KURT. *Principles of Topological Psychology.* New York: McGraw-Hill, 1936.

LEWIS, MICHAEL M. *How Children Learn to Speak.* New York: Basic Books, 1959.

LILLY, JOHN. *Man and Dolphin.* Garden City, N.Y.: Doubleday & Co., 1961.

LINDSLEY, D. B. "Psychological Phenomena and the Electroencephalogram." *Electroencephalography and Clinical Neurophysiology* 4 (1952): 443–456.

LINDSLEY, OGDEN. "Operant Behavior During Sleep: A Measure of Depth of Sleep." *Science* 126 (1957): 1290–1291.

LIPSITT, L. P. "Learning in the First Years of Life." In *Advances in Child Development and Behavior,* ed. by L. P. Lipsitt and C. C. Spiker, Vol. 1. New York: Academic Press, 1963.

LOCKE, JOHN. *An Essay Concerning Human Understanding.* Ed. by Alexander C. Fraser. Oxford: The Clarendon Press, 1894.

LOGAN, F. A., and WAGNER, A. R. *Reward and Punishment.* Boston: Allyn & Bacon, 1965.

LORENZ, KONRAD. *On Aggression.* Trans. by Marjorie K. Wilson. New York: Harcourt Brace Jovanovich, 1966.

LOW, M. D., BORDA, R. P., FROST, J. D., and KELLAWAY, P. "Surface-Negative, Slow-Potential Shift Associated with Conditioning in Man." *Neurology* 16 (1966): 771–782.

LURIA, A. R. *The Mind of a Mnemonist.* Trans. by Lynn Solotaroff. New York: Basic Books, 1968.

MACAULAY, THOMAS B. *The History of England from the Accession of James II,* Vol. 1. London: George C. Harrap & Co., 1949.

McCLEARY, R. A., and MOORE, R. Y. *Subcortical Mechanisms of Behavior: The Psychological Functions of Primitive Parts of the Brain.* New York: Basic Books, 1965.

McCLELLAND, DAVID C. *The Achieving Society.* Princeton, N.J.: D. Van Nostrand Co., 1961.

McCLURE, M. T. *The Early Philosophers of Greece.* New York: Appleton-Century-Crofts, 1935.

McCONNELL, J. V. "Memory Transfer Through Cannibalism in Planarians." *Journal of Neuropsychiatry,* Supplement 1, Vol. 3 (1962): 542–548.

———. "On the Turning of Worms: A Reply to James and Halas." *Psychological Record* 14 (1964): 13–20.

McGEOCH, J. A. "Forgetting and the Law of Disuse." *Psychological Review* 39 (1932): 352–370.

McKINLEY, R. W., ed. *IES Lighting Handbook.* New York: Illuminating Engineering Society, 1947.

MACLEAN, P. D. "Psychosomatic Disease and the 'Visceral Brain.' Recent Developments Bearing on the Papez Theory of Emotion." *Psychosomatic Medicine* 11 (1949): 338–353.

McMAHAN, ELIZABETH A., and RHINE, J. B. "A Second Zagreb-Durham ESP Experiment." *Journal of Parapsychology* 11 (1947): 244–253.

McNEILL, WILLIAM H. *The Rise of the West: A History of the Human Community.* Chicago: The University of Chicago Press, 1963.

MacNICHOL, E. F. "Three-Pigment Color Vision." *Scientific American* 211 (1964): 48–56.

MacNICHOL, E. F., and SVAETICHIN, G. "Electric Responses from Isolated Retinas of Fishes." *American Journal of Ophthalmology* 46 (1958): 26–40.

MAKOUS, W. L. "Cutaneous Color Sensitivity: Explanation and Demonstration." *Psychological Review* 73 (1966): 280–294.

MANDLER, GEORGE. "Emotion." In *New Directions in Psychology,* ed. by R. Brown, E. Galanter, E. H. Hess, and G. Mandler. New York: Holt, Rinehart & Winston, 1962.

MILGRAM, S. "Behavioral Study of Obedience." *Journal of Abnormal and Social Psychology* 67 (1963): 371–378.

MILL, J. S. *A System of Logic.* London: Longmans, Green, 1900.

———. "On Liberty." In *The Utilitarians.* Garden City, N.Y.: Doubleday & Co., Dolphin Books, 1961.

MILLER, N. E., and DOLLARD, J. C. *Social Learning and Imitation.* New Haven, Conn.: Yale University Press, 1941.

MILNER, PETER. *Physiological Psychology.* New York: Holt, Rinehart & Winston, 1970.

MORTON, N. E. "The Components of Genetic Variability." In *The Genetics of Migrant and Isolate Populations,* ed. by E. Goldschmidt. Baltimore: Williams & Wilkins Co., 1963.

MURRAY, EDWARD J. *Sleep, Dreams, and Arousal.* New York: Appleton-Century-Crofts, 1965.

MURRAY, HENRY A. *Explorations in Personality.* New York: Oxford University Press, 1938.

NAFE, J. P., and WAGONER, K. S. "The Nature of Pressure Adaptation." *Journal of General Psychology* 25 (1941): 323–351.

NAGATY, M. O. "The Effect of Reinforcement on Closely Following S-R Connections, II." *Journal of Experimental Psychology* 42 (1951): 333–340.

NEWMAN, E. B. "Hearing." In *Foundations of Psychology,* ed. by E. G. Boring, H. Langfeld, and H. P. Weld. New York: John Wiley & Sons, 1948.

NORMAN, D., ed. *Models of Human Memory.* New York: Academic Press, 1970.

NYUBERG, N. D. " 'Finger Sight'—the Phenomenon of Roza Kulcshova." *Proceedings of the Federation of American Societies for Experimental Biology* 22 (1964): T701–T705 (Translation Supplement).

OLDS, J., and MILNER, P. "Positive Reinforcement Produced by Electrical Stimulation of Septal Area and Other Regions of Rat Brain." *Journal of Comparative and Physiological Psychology* 47 (1954): 419–427.

OLDS, M. E., and OLDS, J. "Approach-Avoidance Analysis of Rat Diencephalon." *Journal of Comparative Neurology* 120 (1963): 259–315.

OSGOOD, C. E. "The Similarity Paradox in Human Learning: A Resolution." *Psychological Review* 56 (1949): 132–143.

PAPEZ, J. W. "A Proposed Mechanism of Emotion." *Archives of Neurology and Psychiatry* 38 (1937): 725–743.

PAVLOV, I. P. *Conditioned Reflexes.* Trans. by G. V. Anrep. Oxford: Oxford University Press, 1927.

PENFIELD, W., and RASMUSSEN, T. *The Cerebral Cortex of Man.* New York: Macmillan, 1950.

PERIN, C. T. "Behavioral Potentiality as a Joint Function of the Amount of Training and the Degree of Hunger at the Time of Extinction." *Journal of Experimental Psychology* 30 (1942): 93–113.

PETERSON, L. R., and PETERSON, M. J. "Short-Term Retention of Individual Verbal Items." *Journal of Experimental Psychology* 58 (1959): 193–198.

PIAGET, J. *Logic and Psychology.* New York: Basic Books, 1957.

————. *The Moral Development of the Child.* Glencoe, Ill.: Free Press, 1965.

PLATO. *Phaedo.* In *Plato's Phaedo,* ed. by R. Hackforth. Cambridge: Cambridge University Press, 1955.

POLYAK, S. L. *The Retina.* Chicago: University of Chicago Press, 1941.

POSTMAN, L., and RAU, L. "Retention as a Function of the Method of Measurement." *University of California Publication of Psychology* 8 (1957): 217–270.

POSTMAN, L., and RILEY, D. A. "Degree of Learning and Interserial Interference in Retention." *University of California Publication of Psychology* 8 (1959): 271–396.

PRONKO, N. H. *Panorama of Psychology.* Belmont, Calif.: Brooks/Cole, 1969.

RABB, D. "Backward Masking." *Psychological Bulletin* 60 (1963): 118.

RATLIFF, F., HARTLINE, H. K., and MILLER, W. H. "Spatial and Temporal Aspects of Retinal Inhibitory Interaction." *Journal of the Optical Society of America* 53 (1963): 110–121.

REYNOLDS, G. S. *A Primer of Operant Conditioning.* Glenview, Ill.: Scott, Foresman & Co., 1968.

RHEINGOLD, HARRIET L., GEWIRTZ, J. L., and ROSS, HELEN W. "Social Conditioning of Vocalization in the Infant." *Journal of Comparative and Physiological Psychology* 52 (1959): 68–73.

RIESEN, A. H. "The Development of Visual Perception in Man and Chimpanzee." *Science* 106 (1947): 107–108.

RIGGS, LORRIN A. "Visual Acuity." In *Vision and Visual Perception,* ed. by C. H. Graham. New York: John Wiley & Sons, 1965.

ROBINSON, D. N. *An Intellectual History of Psychology.* New York: Macmillan, 1976.

————, ed. *Heredity and Achievement.* New York: Oxford University Press, 1970.

————. *The Enlightened Machine: An Analytical Introduction to Neuropsychology.* Encino, Calif.: Dickenson, 1973.

ROBINSON, D. N., and SABAT, S. R. "Elimination of Auditory Evoked Responses During Auditory Shadowing." *Physiological Psychology* 3 (1975m): 26–28.

ROSENTHAL, DAVID. "Familial Concordance by Sex with Respect to Schizophrenia." *Psychological Bulletin* 59 (1962): 401–421.

RUSSELL, BERTRAND. *A History of Western Philosophy.* New York: Simon & Schuster, 1945.

SAHAKIAN, WILLIAM S., ed. *History of Psychology: A Source Book in Systematic Psychology.* Itasca, Ill.: F. E. Peacock, 1968.

SCHACHTER, S., and SINGER, J. "Cognitive, Social, and Physiological Determinants of Emotional State." *Psychological Review* 69 (1962): 379–399.

SEGALL, M. H., CAMPBELL, D. T., and HERSKOVITS, M. J. "Cultural Differences in the Perception of Geometric Illusions." *Science* 139 (1963): 769–771.

————, et al. *The Influence of Culture on Visual Perception.* Indianapolis: Bobbs-Merrill Co., 1966.

SENDEN, M. Von. *Raum-und Gestalt-Auffassungun bei Operierten Blindgeborenen*

Vor und Nach der Operation. Leipzig: Barth, 1932.

SHANNON, C. E., and WEAVER, W. *The Mathematical Theory of Communication*. Urbana: University of Illinois Press, 1949.

SHEFFIELD, F. A., and CAMPBELL, B. A. "The Role of Experience in the 'Spontaneous' Activity of Hungry Rats." *Journal of Comparative and Physiological Psychology* 47 (1954): 97–100.

SHEFFIELD, F. A., ROBY, T. B., and CAMPBELL, B. A. "Drive Reduction versus Consummatory Behavior as Determinants of Reinforcement." *Journal of Comparative and Physiological Psychology* 47 (1954): 349–354.

SHEFFIELD, F. D., WULFF, J. J., and BACKER, R. "Reward Value of Copulation Without Sex Drive Reduction." *Journal of Comparative and Physiological Psychology* 44 (1951): 3–8.

SIDMAN, M. "Two Temporal Parameters of the Maintenance of Avoidance Behavior by the White Rat." *Journal of Comparative and Physiological Psychology* 46 (1953): 253–261.

SIMMONS, M. W. "Operant Discrimination in Infants." Ph.D. dissertation, Brown University, 1962.

SKINNER, B. F. *Beyond Freedom and Dignity*. New York: Knopf, 1971.

———. *Science and Human Behavior*. New York: Macmillan, 1956.

SLAMECKA, N. J. "Proactive Inhibition of Connected Discourse." *Journal of Experimental Psychology* 62 (1961): 295–301.

SMITH, G. H. "Size-Distance Judgements of Human Faces (Projected Images)." *Journal of General Psychology* 49 (1953): 45–64.

SOAL, S. G. "The Experimental Situation in Psychical Research." *Journal of Parapsychology* 13 (1949): 79–100.

SOLOMON, R. L., and WYNNE, L. C. "Traumatic Avoidance Learning: The Principles of Anxiety Conservation and Partial Irreversibility." *Psychological Review* 61 (1954): 353–385.

SPERRY, R. W. "Effect of 180-Degree Rotation of the Retinal Field on Visuomotor Coordination." *Journal of Experimental Zoology* 92 (1943): 263–279.

———. "Physiological Plasticity and Brain Circuit Theory." In *Biological and Biochemical Bases of Behavior*, ed. by Harry F. Harlow and Clinton N. Woolsey. Madison: The University of Wisconsin Press, 1958.

———. "Preservation of High-Order Function in Isolated Somatic Cortex in Callosum-Sectioned Cat." *Journal of Neurophysiology* 22 (1959): 78–87.

———. "The Great Cerebral Commissure." *Scientific American* 210 (1964): 42–52.

STEVENS, S. S. "Mathematics, Measurement, and Psychophysics." In *Handbook of Experimental Psychology*, ed. by S. S. Stevens. New York: John Wiley & Sons, 1951.

STRATTON, G. M. "Vision Without Inversion of the Retinal Image." *Psychological Review* 4 (1897): 341–360, 463–481.

SUTTON, H. E. *Genes, Enzymes and Inherited Diseases*. New York: Holt, Rinehart & Winston, 1961.

TEES, R. C. "Effects of Early Auditory Restriction in the Rat on Adult Pattern Discrimination." *Journal of Comparative and Physiological Psychology* 63 (1967): 389–393.

TEITELBAUM, P. "Sensory Control of Hypothalamic Hyperphagia." *Journal of Comparative and Physiological Psychology* 48 (1955): 156–163.

———. "Disturbances of Feeding and Drinking Behavior after Hypothalamic Lesions." In *Nebraska Symposium on Motivation*, ed. by M. R. Jones. Lincoln: University of Nebraska Press, 1961.

TERMAN, L. M., and MERRILL, M. A. *Measuring Intelligence*. Boston: Houghton Mifflin Co., 1937.

TERWILLIGER, ROBERT F. *Meaning and Mind: A Study in the Psychology of Language*. New York: Oxford University Press, 1968.

THORNDIKE, E. L. "Animal Intelligence: An Experimental Study of the Associative Processes in Animals." *Psychological Monograph* 2, No. 8 (1898).

TINBERGEN, N. "Social Releasers and the Experimental Method Required for Their Study." *Wilson Bulletin* 60 (1948): 6–52.

———. *The Study of Instinct*. New York: Oxford University Press, 1969.

TOCH, H., and SMITH, C., eds. *Social Perception*. New York: D. Van Nostrand Co., 1968.

TOLMAN, E. C. "The Inheritance of Maze-Learning Ability in Rats." *Journal of Comparative Psychology* 4 (1924): 1–18.

TRYON, R. C. "The Genetics of Learning Ability in Rats." *University of California Publication of Psychology* 4 (1929): 71–89.

URSIN, H. "The Effect of Amygdaloid Lesions on Flight and Defense Behavior in Cats." *Experimental Neurology* 11 (1965): 64–79.

VAN BERGEIJK, W. A., PIERCE, J. R., and DAVIE, E. E. *Waves and the Ear*. Garden City, N.Y.: Doubleday & Co., 1960.

VANDENBERG, S. G. "The Hereditary Abilities Study: Hereditary Components in a Psychological Test Battery." *American Journal of Human Genetics* 14 (1962): 220–237.

VOLTAIRE. *Ignorant Philosopher*. In *A History of Science and Its Relations with Philosophy and Religion*, ed. by Sir William C. Dampier. 4th ed. Cambridge: Cambridge University Press, 1966.

WADA, T. "An Experimental Study of Hunger in Its Relation to Activity." *Archives of Psychology* 8, No. 57.

WALLACE, ROBERT K. *The Physiological Effects of Transcendental Meditation: A Proposed Fourth Major State of Consciousness*. Los Angeles: Student's International Meditation Society, 1970.

WALTER, W. G., COOPER, R., ALDRIDGE, V. J., McCALLUM, W. C., and WINTER, A. L. "Contingent Negative Variation: An Electric Sign of Sensorimotor Association and Expectancy in the Human Brain." *Nature* 203 (1964): 380–384.

WEINTRAUB, D., and WALKER, E. *Perception*. Belmont, Calif.: Brooks/Cole, 1966.

WEISBERG, P. "Social and Nonsocial Conditioning of Infant Vocalizations." *Child Development* 34 (1963): 377–388.

WERTHEIMER, M. "Experimentelle Studien über das Sehen von Bewegung." *Z. Psychol.* 61 (1912): 161–265.

WHORF, BENJAMIN L. *Language, Thought, and Reality*. Cambridge: The Massachusetts Institute of Technology Press; New York: John Wiley & Sons, 1956.

WIENER, NORBERT. *Cybernetics: Or Control and Communication in the Animal and the Machine*. Cambridge, Mass.: The Massachusetts Intitute of Technology Press, 1948.

———. *The Human Use of Human Beings: Cybernetics and Society*. Boston: Houghton Mifflin Co., 1954.

WILCOXON, HARDY C. *Reinforcement and Behavior*. New York: Academic Press, 1969.

WITRYOL, S. L., and KAESS, W. A. "Sex Differences in Social Memory Tasks." *Journal of Abnormal and Social Psychology* 54 (1957): 343–346

WOLFE, J. B. "The Effect of Delayed Reward upon Learning in the White Rat." *Journal of Comparative Psychology* 17 (1934): 1–21.

WOOLSEY, C. N. "Organization of Cortical Auditory System: A Review and a Synthesis." In *Neural Mechanisms of the Auditory and Vestibular Systems*, ed. by G. L. Rasmussen and W. F. Windle. Springfield, Ill.: Charles C. Thomas, 1960.

YOUTZ, R. P. "Tactile Color Sensing under Three Intensities of Illumination." Paper read at Eastern Psychological Association, April 1966, in New York City.

ZEAMAN, D. "Response Latency as a Function of the Amount of Reinforcement." *Journal of Experimental Psychology* 39 (1949): 466–483.

ZIMBARDO, P. "The Psychological Power and Pathology of Imprisonment." A statement prepared for the U. S. House of Representatives, Committee on the Judiciary, Subcommittee No. 3, 25 October 1971, in San Francisco, California.

ZIPF, G. K. "The Repetition of Words, Time-Perspective, and Semantic Balance." *Journal of General Psychology* 32 (1945): 127–148.

———. "The Meaning-Frequency Relationship of Words." *Journal of General Psychology* 33 (1945): 251–256.

———. *Human Behavior and the Principle of Least Effort.* Cambridge, Mass.: Addison-Wesley Press, 1949.

Name Index

Abelard, 433
Adams, J. A., 240
Adler, A., 346–349, 355, 357
Albertus Magnus, 36, 37
Alexander the Great, 33, 34, 35
Amoore, J. E., 152, 154
Amsel, A., 195
Anselm, 433
Aquinas, Saint Thomas, 36–38, 48, 167, 408, 432, 433
Archimides, 68
Ardrey, R., 318, 319
Aristotle, 19, 24, 26, 31–33, 36, 48, 68, 77, 167, 176, 197, 210, 248, 280, 405, 406, 429
Aserinsky, E., 393
Atkinson, J. W., 375
Augustine, Saint, 35, 37, 48, 288, 430, 432, 433
Austin, G. A., 240
Azrin, N., 194

Backer, R., 376
Bacon, F., 68, 69, 70
Bacon, R., 433
Baddeley, A. D., 215
Baer, D. M., 274, 275
Bandura, A., 292, 293
Barber, T. X., 412
Bard, P., 383
Barnes, J. M., 211
Bartholomew Anglicus, 435, 436

Subject Index